LIVIN' THE BLUES

Wisconsin Studies in American Autobiography

WILLIAM L. ANDREWS
General Editor

Frank Marshall Davis

Livin' the Blues

MEMOIRS OF A BLACK JOURNALIST AND POET

Edited, with an Introduction,

by John Edgar Tidwell

The University of Wisconsin Press

The University of Wisconsin Press
114 North Murray Street
Madison, Wisconsin 53715

3 Henrietta Street
London WC2E 8LU, England

Library of Congress Cataloging-in-Publication Data
Davis, Frank Marshall, 1905–1987.
    Livin' the blues: memoirs of a Black journalist and poet
  Frank Marshall Davis; edited by John Edgar Tidwell.
    408 pp.   cm.—(Wisconsin studies in American autobiography)
    Includes bibliographical references and index.
    ISBN 0-299-13500-4
    1. Davis, Frank Marshall, 1905–1987—Biography.   2. Afro-American
journalists—United States—Biography.   3. Afro-American
journalists—United States—20th century—Social conditions.
    4. United States—Race relations—History—20th century.
I. Tidwell, John Edgar.   II. Title.   III. Series.
PN4874.D372A3   1992
811'.52—dc20
[B]   92-50248

Contents

Illustrations

Acknowledgments

Publishing one's memoirs can be either an extremely arrogant gesture or an incredible risk that the self will be exposed for what it actually is. Before his death in 1987, Davis proceeded, undaunted by the challenges, to bring his life story before the reading audience. For him, *Livin' the Blues* would serve not just as a memorial constructed to provide additional tangible evidence that he had lived in this world. It would also provide new insight and fresh perspectives on the meaning of being an African American poet and journalist in these United States. These twin purposes had a special appeal to a number of people Davis reached out to for assistance. Davis's importance as a writer and his numerous achievements in life generated a loyal following, who shared a common obligation—that his story must be told. Fulfilling Davis's vision, in his absence, has therefore necessitated an inspired collaborative effort. I wish to thank publicly some of the persons whose cheerful assistance made the publishing of this life story possible.

I am extremely grateful for the discerning perception of William L. Andrews in recognizing the importance of *Livin' the Blues,* when he had barely seen a hint of its potential in a poorly xeroxed copy of the manuscript generously provided by his colleague Elizabeth Schultz. Although he is general editor for the series in which this autobiography appears, I am very pleased he never chose to remain aloof from the process. He has been intimately involved as a "hands on" editor, reading and offering candid assessments of the manuscript, the Introduction, and the Note on the Text. Where he was unable to answer questions, he made available to me Daniel Murtaugh and Amy Southerland, two very capable and conscientious research assistants, whose yeoman library work uncovered most of the annotations for the text.

I am indeed a better scholar for having worked with the superb editorial staff at the University of Wisconsin Press. Ms. Barbara Hanrahan, senior editor, was quite rigorous in her editorial demands, but her wonderful sense of humor made the task much easier. At the next stage,

Raphael Kadushin continued the congenial working relationship and facilitated ushering the manuscript through the various stages of production. One of his most significant accomplishments was securing the services of Ms. Lydia Howarth as copy editor. She demonstrated an exceptional knowledge of her craft by superbly improving my prose and also by suggesting judicious emendations that Davis, had he lived, would most certainly have given his highest approval to.

To Ms. Beth Charlton, Frank Marshall Davis's daughter, and to Mrs. Helen Canfield Davis, his former wife, I cannot express enough appreciation. Editing this manuscript required me to know more than words on a page; more crucially I needed to understand Frank Marshall Davis *the man*—a formidable task since I never met him personally. Their fond memories and anecdotes not only humanized Davis but offered perfect complements to the text of his life story. Equally important were their cheerful responses to my many urgent requests for more research materials, which resulted in a steady stream of manuscripts, photographs, interviews, newspaper clippings, and photocopies of Davis's hard-to-locate newspaper work.

After I began the editing process, other people, who either knew Frank Marshall Davis personally or had done research on him, came forward with assistance at critical moments. I wish to thank Dr. Margaret Burroughs, now emeritus executive director of Chicago's DuSable Museum, for providing me with this version of *Livin' the Blues,* which I used for an earlier Davis project; E. Ethelbert Miller, director of Howard University's Afro-American Resource Center, for sending me copies of his taped interviews with Davis; Fred Whitehead, editor of *People's Culture,* for sharing in the commitment to ensure Davis's wish of seeing *Livin' the Blues* published; Michael Weaver, for providing copies of Davis's poetry contribution to *Blind Alleys*; poet-publisher Peter J. Harris, for giving me his insights into Davis's poetics; Gerald Early, of Washington University, for rendering indispensable assistance in the research on Davis's journalism; and Jerry M. Ward and Anne M. Emmerth for carefully reading and suggesting improvements in the manuscript.

Of course, the whole project benefitted from the generous collegial support offered by Miami University. The Department of English, under the chairmanship of C. Barry Chabot, assisted me at very crucial moments. Hugh Morgan, for instance, rendered important advice on early drafts of the introduction. The technical preparation of the manuscript fell largely to the very capable hands of Mrs. Jackie Kearns, our Department administrative assistant, and to her staff of student workers. William Wortman, reference librarian at Miami University's King Library, was invaluable in locating difficult to find source materials. The College of Arts and Science and the Graduate School both provided timely funding for proofreading the final copy of the text. But when problems seemed to proliferate and solutions were not to be found, Drs. Augustus J. Jones, Jr., and Michael E. Dantley, wonderful friends, reminded me to seek spiritual guidance through prayer—advice that most assuredly produced ways when there seemed to be none.

Last, in my mother, Mrs. Verlean Tidwell, I found an example of hard work, persistence, and, above all, the belief that good things will happen if you have faith. My wife, Mandie Barnes Tidwell, offered what might be the ultimate sacrifice. When a simple editing job turned into a major research undertaking and the computer threatened to consume all my time, she very generously encouraged me to complete the book. I am most appreciative, then, for her unfailing support and understanding.

Introduction

Reliving the Blues:
Frank Marshall Davis
and the Crafting of a Self

The publication of four collections of poetry during the Depression and World War II brought Frank Marshall Davis high visibility and name recognition at a time when publishing poetry was especially difficult for African Americans. Alain Locke, publicist of the New Negro Renaissance of the 1920s and self-proclaimed "mid-wife of the younger generation of Negro writers," effusively greeted Davis in 1936 as a "Newer Negro" whose poetry demonstrated a talent for realistic portraiture, irony, and knowledge of black life. To Locke, Davis seemed destined to fulfill the unfinished promise of the New Negro Renaissance poets. Others less motivated by Locke's need to enlist cultural warriors for service in a renaissance found much that was innovative in Davis's work. For instance, Sterling A. Brown celebrated Davis in 1937 as "at times a mystic escapist, but at his best . . . bitterly realistic." Harriet Monroe would notice from her editorship of *Poetry: A Magazine of Verse* that Davis's *Black Man's Verse* (1935) " . . . is enough to show that we have here a poet of authentic inspiration, who belongs not only among the best of his race, but who need not lean upon his race for recognition as an impassioned singer with something to say."[1] As if in agreement with this high praise, the Julius Rosenwald Foundation awarded its first prize for poetry to Davis in 1937. Despite this auspicious beginning, though, Davis turned his back on his best chance for a sustained American literary career by leaving the mainland for Hawaii in 1948.

Interest in Davis's work and life was rekindled, however, when the cultural phenomenon begun in the 1960s announced as the Black Arts Movement issued the call to reclaim black literary history. Black American poets and scholars rediscovered Davis in their efforts to establish a canon of *black* poetry. By the early 1970s, he found himself being hailed as a *black* poet who had written before being *black* was politically correct.

Such accolades, though, had an unfortunate effect. His reputation was increased, but only marginally so, and it came to rest on the repeated anthologizing of the same five or six poems and biographical facts routinely reprinted in over seventy-five anthologies. With the publication for the first time of *Livin' the Blues,* however, we now have the opportunity to rediscover this poet, this writer, and above all, this man behind the masks that for too long have screened him from a much-deserved readership.

Davis virtually disappeared from American literary history after 1948, and, when he reemerged in 1973, he seemed little more than a shadowy figure, one enshrouded in mystery. What had set him on the path toward near-anonymity were dramatic changes that occurred in his life in 1948.

On 7 December 1948, Frank Marshall Davis packed up his belongings and, with his wife Helen, followed Horace Greeley's advice with a vengeance. From Chicago, they journeyed West. The West they settled in, though, was not Nevada or California, but Hawaii, then a remote tropical U.S. territory. Helen, made curious by an article in a popular magazine describing Hawaiian life, had suggested a lengthy vacation there. Paul Robeson also provided an incentive. Fresh from a concert tour in Hawaii to aid striking longshoremen in their union effort, Robeson could hardly contain his exuberance over the comparative racial harmony there. For him Hawaii contained a veritable "lesson in racial matters to be learned," one that "could speed democracy in the United States," if Hawaii were to be admitted to the Union as a state.[2] Davis not only consented to the vacation but offered to make the visit a permanent resettlement, if conditions were agreeable. The Davises left in their wake Chicago's notorious winters, frustration with, for them, a stagnant civil rights program, and an at times acerbic social intolerance for their interracial marriage.

For the next twenty-five years, little news about Davis drifted back to the mainland. Except for contributions to a special issue of *Voices* (Winter 1950), guest-edited by Langston Hughes, almost nothing poetic was heard from Davis until the round of reprints began in the late 1960s, when a few Davis poems started appearing in such works as Robert Hayden's *Kaleidoscope: Poems by American Negro Poets* (1967) and Langston Hughes and Arna Bontemps's *The Poetry of the Negro* (1970). This attention from anthologists encouraged Stephen Henderson, then director of Howard University's Institute for the Arts and Humanities, and poet-publisher Dudley Randall to undertake the "rediscovery" of Davis in 1973 via a lecture tour that visited Howard University, Atlanta University, Chicago's DuSable Museum, and several West Coast schools. Preceding the tour on 11 August 1973, Randall conducted what appears to be the first interview of Davis by a mainlander since the poet's departure in 1948. "'Mystery Poet': An Interview with Frank Marshall Davis," published in the January 1974 issue of *Black World,* attempted to probe the silences in Davis's life and poetry. From the "mystery poet," Randall elicited an unprecedented amount of biographical information, especially about his move to Hawaii and his reasons for staying there:

> I came over and liked the place so well that I have stayed here and not paid a visit to the mainland since coming here in 1948. I am not too fond of what I read about the current mainland scene, so I prefer staying here, and the locale in which I live has so much of interest that I find it extremely exciting. *Since we do not have the confrontations that exist between white and Black in so many parts of the mainland, living here has been a relief . . .*" (my emphasis)

Did Davis leave Chicago because he was tired of the civil rights struggle? His reply to Randall suggests that Hawaii was a haven, a shelter from the storms of the civil rights struggle and of personal indignation. Yet even a cursory glance at Davis's record of activism in Hawaii proves that the move was never an abrogation of responsibility, only a change in the site of conflict. For example, as a columnist for the progressive newspaper the Honolulu *Record* from 1949 to 1958, Davis wrote "Frank-ly Speaking," which vigorously asserted the rights of union workers and spoke out for other political causes.[3] Unfortunately for Davis's reputation, little of his activism came to the attention of mainlanders, and the same was true of the new poetry he wrote while living in Hawaii. It was during the lecture tour of 1973 that Davis announced the completion of a project he hoped would help dispel the mystery surrounding him. In a 24 October 1973 interview with E. Ethelbert Miller, at Howard University, the poet disclosed the completion of his autobiography, *Livin' the Blues: Memoirs of a Black Journalist and Poet.* The expressed intention of this life story was to describe in considerable detail the events that had shaped and defined the man and the writer. In notable ways the book accomplishes this goal by revealing many previously unknown details about the life and times of Frank Marshall Davis. Yet it does not take long for a reader to see that *Livin' the Blues* is much more than a recounting of a life.

2

Livin' the Blues is a virtual collage, pulling together, among other things, the recollections of a jazz reporter and music historian, a photographer, an editorial writer, a fictionist, a sports historian, a political activist, and, of course, a poet. The richness of the book derives from the constant ebb and flow of these various selves within a historical context. Ultimately, then, any effort to know Frank Marshall Davis through *Livin' the Blues* is dependent upon the insights and limitations imposed by the form in which this life story is cast. The subtitle—*Memoirs of a Black Journalist and Poet*—is both a succinct and subtle guide to resolving this problem.

Read as memoirs, *Livin' the Blues* sets up expectations different from the ones in autobiography proper. Unlike autobiography's creative and imaginative engagement with the past, memoir points to the past as history and fact. A controlling idea or thematic unity in memoir is less important than the assembly of facts, names, dates, and places. What this means, as James M. Cox admirably says, is that memoir ". . . will relate itself to the external world of the author in history, not to the inner world of self-reflection."[4]

Livin' the Blues bears out Cox by showing us a man *remembering* the events of his life, *not discovering* their importance by seeing for the first time the complex relationships that gave his life shape and meaning. Davis's is a self-conscious attempt to place his life in a historical milieu, while, at the same time, divulging little of his innermost feelings and fears. Nevertheless, *Livin' the Blues* moves unconsciously toward a careful ordering and shaping that at once reveals the inner side of the autobiographer and also demonstrates the life in the context of other people.

From one of the classic studies in autobiography, Roy Pascal's *Design and Truth in Autobiography* (1960), we learn that an enduring feature of "true" autobiography is a sense of discovery, which "represents a new stage in self-knowledge and a new formulation of responsibility toward the self; it involves mental exploration and change of attitude."[5] By writing from a vantage point in the present, the autobiographer, looking back over past moments, establishes links and connections among disparate events and lives. From these interconnections emerges a theme, an organizing principle of one's life. In the "best" autobiographies, the theme arises not simply from listing the series of recorded events but from a previously unrealized insight into their interconnection. In other words, the surprise revealed in the juxtaposition of previously unexplored relationships of past events becomes a fundamental ingredient in and an indication of the quality of an autobiography's crafting. Part of the distinctiveness of *Livin' the Blues* is that despite Davis's efforts to contain his life story in memoir, as a pattern of external events, something of the "surprise" of autobiography willfully or spontaneously shines through.

As a result of the way Davis has reconstructed his past, the reader emerges from his life story feeling far more enlightened about a number of significant historical events. For instance, he alters and enlarges our understanding of what constituted the New Negro Renaissance of the 1920s and 1930s. Largely through the efforts of Alain Locke, *The New Negro* (1925), and a network of literary patrons and publishers, the renaissance has been perceived as an exclusively New York or Harlem phenomenon. But, as Davis asserts, the establishment of several writers' groups in Chicago during the 1920s and 1930s was no mere effort to emulate Harlem but, instead, was motivated by these midwestern writers' sense that the East was effete, its literature inadequate. In this view, Chicago and possibly Kansas City function as sites of energy and inspiration—two qualities these Midwesterners found lacking in New York. From this example, then, something of the general approach of *Livin' the Blues* can be discerned. Davis liked to write personal history against the grain of received notions and popular impressions of history, especially African American history in the first half of the twentieth century. Yet even though Davis's purpose does not seem to be the revelation of an inner self absorbed by its own need for self-understanding, *Livin' the Blues* is punctuated by a number of highly personal moments in which the author seems to be struggling to uncover, to name, and perhaps to exorcise something within.

Helen Canfield Davis, who, before their divorce in 1970, was married to Frank for twenty-four years, has spoken of a tension in the man that emerges in the autobiography as well. As she explains it, Frank probably intended the autobiography to act in place of a will. In effect, it would offer the testament "Here I stand!" Where he stood, though, is often described in large, masculine, even macho, terms. For, as she said, one of his worst fears was to be considered effeminate. Public opinion hated anything soft, and her husband acceded uncritically to this notion "by not writing in contrast," that is, by not acknowledging his tender side. As a consequence, Helen Davis concludes, Frank was fragile inside himself. Like everyone, Davis had his inner fragilities; but, in his case, being black made him more vulnerable to damage. Thus he crafted his image to reinforce an impression of strength and thereby testified implicitly to his anxieties about inner weaknesses.

In large measure, Helen Davis's analysis is supported throughout *Livin' the Blues.* For instance, the autobiography crafts the image of a self locked in a tenacious struggle to get rid of an acute sense of racial inferiority. By positioning this struggle at the beginning of the narrative, Davis makes this complex establish the theme, tone, structure, and subtext for the life story.

Livin' the Blues begins on Davis's graduation night in 1923, as he sits poised to emerge from high school. As if documenting the impact of nearly two decades of life in Arkansas City, Kansas, he describes himself as seventeen years old, six feet one inches tall, and one hundred ninety pounds. And yet that night, this rather hulking young man felt as if he were *one foot six inches* tall. What conditioned this response is revealed sardonically, at times, and humorously at others. For instance, part of the way he came to view himself so negatively no doubt owed to an experience he had when he was five years old. A group of white third-graders had heard their parents discussing the nature and practice of lynching. With piqued curiosities, they selected Davis for an experiment. As he recounts:

> I was on my way home alone, crossing a vacant lot, when these white boys, who had been lying in wait, jumped me. They threw me to the ground and held me down while one lad produced a rope and slipped it over my head. I kicked and screamed. Just as one started to snatch the noose tight around my neck, a white man appeared. He took one look, chased the boys away, freed me, and helped brush dirt and trash off my clothes. He walked with me until I was close to home nearly a mile away, then turned around and went on about his business. I never learned who he was, nor could I single out the embryo lynchers at school next day. Naturally, school officials did not push their probe. I was still alive and unharmed, wasn't I? *Besides, I was black.* (my emphasis)

Rudely initiated into an often cruel, pathologically violent world, Davis came to see black life in terms of nothingness. He embraced the specious racial argument that "Being black meant being inferior." And why not!? Many of the examples he saw around him, instead of refuting, actually reinforced a worldview in which blacks were psychologically, socially, and spiritually inferior to whites. In this world, black girls had no need of a high school diploma, if life only promised them opportunities to cook in the kitchens or wash the clothes of whites. The life promised for black boys was just as deprived and poor. Hardly surprising, then, are the two predictable responses Davis makes.

First, a typical situation of oppression generally forces the victim to seek some measure of balance by finding someone else to blame or oppress. Poor whites in the South, for instance, were notorious for accommodating themselves to their poverty with the argument that their whiteness made them better off than blacks. For Davis, the "balance" was achieved through caste superiority. Sadly, he embraced another mistaken notion—that the only people lower in this degrading status quo were southern blacks because, as he said, ". . . I know I am superior to Negroes reared in Dixie for they have not attended school with whites. I view them with contempt; they are my inferiors."

Such prejudice was followed by another rather pitiful response. *Livin' the Blues,* for instance, will remind readers of another tortured self—the fictional character Bigger Thomas from Richard Wright's novel *Native Son* (1940). Bigger imbibed so much personal indignation and felt so manipulated by unseen power that he became consumed with rage. Davis too felt powerless. A sullen, smoldering anger pervaded his being. But instead of erupting in violent crime like Bigger, the anger turned inward, into unexpressed brooding. As a result, as a boy Davis developed a profoundly deep lack of self-esteem. In an effort to break free from the constrictions imposed by a disabling inferiority complex, Davis left Arkansas City to attend college, and it was in order to empower himself that he sought salvation and strength in imaginative and journalistic writing and in the informal study of African American history.

After a brief stop at Friends University in Wichita (1923–24), Davis proceeded up the road to Manhattan, to what was then Kansas State College. There, two passions were nurtured that promised to provide him means for getting out from under the cloud of low self-esteem. First, after considering the merits of several degree choices, he decided on journalism. He had studied toward the journalism degree for nearly two and a half years when a startling reality rudely confronted him. The course of study expressly prepared him for work on a *daily* newspaper. But if white dailies would not employ black reporters and black dailies were virtually nonexistent, what purpose would be served by continuing in school? With no answer to this question, Davis decided to withdraw from classes for a while.

Before Davis left Kansas State in 1927, Miss Ada Rice developed a special interest in the poetry he had written to fulfill an assignment for her English class. This auspicious beginning was actually accidental, since Davis elected to write a poem instead of an essay for her class. But its favorable reception and Miss Rice's encouragement propelled Davis on a path that led to a multifaceted writing career. When he returned to Kansas State in 1929, intending to complete his degree, Davis found himself to be something of a celebrity, since he had already published several of his poems and had worked in the real world as a journalist. The Depression, though, counted him a casualty and prevented his stay in college long enough to earn a degree.

3

The Depression, impervious and implacable, wore the face of deprivation haughtily, with proud disdain. For suffering souls cut off by unemployment, eviction, and hunger from self-sufficiency and self-esteem, it was more than a failed economy. It meant a loss of manhood or womanhood, of humanity. The myth of the era has led readers to expect any representation of a self in the literature of the Depression to engage the horror, despair, and hopelessness of the Depression—or to explain how one escaped its debilitating effects. And curiously, though Davis's title seems to promise just such a despairing catalog, he is rather silent on these issues. Instead of recalling his hardships during the Depression, he focuses our attention on his major achievements—of which there were many.

From 1930 to 1948, Davis worked on a succession of black and labor newspapers, including the Chicago *Evening Bulletin,* the Gary (Indiana) *American,* the Chicago *Whip,* and the Chicago *Star.* Under Davis's editorship, the Atlanta *World* evolved from a twice- to a thrice-weekly paper, before becoming the Atlanta *Daily World.* Here again we find the curious pattern of the public self dwarfing the private one, and evasions substitute for revelation of the man behind the mask. Davis's sojourn in Atlanta, his first trip South, poignantly illustrates the point.

Beginning in childhood, Davis had heard many wild yarns about the de facto rules governing interracial relations in the South, and any mention of life in old Dixie brought sheer terror to his mind. Not surprisingly he converted his fear of Jim Crowism into a series of humorous anecdotes and regional chauvinisms that let him evade revealing what he really felt. (A notable exception to the pattern occurs when Davis shares the humiliation he felt when a white medical doctor in Atlanta forced Davis either to address him as "sir" or risk the injection of a poison into the wound Davis wanted sutured.) These evasions are, however, not the nervous humor of "whistling while walking through a graveyard at night." They are closer to haughtiness or contempt. And instead of detailing how he combatted his crippling fear of being in Dixie, Davis retreats behind caste superiority and projects a bold, public image of himself—one that looms large against a background of the cowering, subjugated Southern blacks of Davis's perception. For instance, there is no denying that the many angry editorials Davis wrote for the *World,* "swinging at the racists" as he describes them, were courageous. And he is justified in the credit he takes for having refused to remain silent about the "use of capital punishment as a racist weapon against my people," and for speaking out about the blatantly biased accounts of the Scottsboro case published by the white press, and about the common practice of blacks being shot by trigger-happy southern white police who went unpunished. However, Davis is all too ready to claim credit for this courage by diminishing the strength of the southern blacks he lived among. He writes: "As a group in 1931, we were black defeatists. When you stuck your neck out, you did it alone. We were grateful for any victories, but if you lost the reaction was 'you shoulda known you couldn't do that in the South.'" Crediting Dr. Martin Luther King, Jr., with "goosing us into mass militant action," Davis makes the civil rights struggle into a post–World War II phenomenon, even though *Livin' the Blues* shows how earlier resistance to racism in the South helped to build the momentum needed to carry the civil rights movement of the sixties to victory.

In recalling his years as an editor for the Associated Negro Press (ANP), Davis treats us to a variety of expressions of a public self, while private moments often cry out for more disclosure. For instance, the process by which he extricated himself from the mire of racial inferiority is not as clearly delineated as one would hope. What we learn is that Davis encountered several persons and texts that, through informal study, made possible the development of a rigorous, positive self-esteem that did not depend on depreciating other African Americans. Monroe Work's series of *Negro Yearbooks* provided him facts about Negro contributions to history, enabling him to develop racial pride. In addition, several individuals helped raise his racial consciousness. Edgar Brown, whom Davis likens to an early Stokely Carmichael, represented a daring spokesman against racism in the 1930s and 1940s. Capt. Harry Foster Dean, a latter-day African American Herman Melville, shared with Davis a knowledge of sea travel and African history that did more than instill racial pride; it gave him an invaluable sense of how historians shape history. Finally, the work of W. E. B. Du Bois, Carter G. Woodson, and J. A. Rogers was of inestimable value.[6]

While Davis was not careful to delineate the precise moment of his liberation from racial inferiority, if there was one, several important events show how an improved self-image enabled him to excel in the world, unencumbered by low self-esteem. One sign of his growing liberation was his involvement in the Abraham Lincoln School in Chicago, a left-of-center, integrated night school for adults, where Davis taught a course on the history of jazz. In 1937, Davis started collecting jazz records and, two years later, he began writing a jazz review column for the ANP. From these inchoate stirrings emerged a very commendable knowledge of jazz. A personal perspective on Davis's improved view of himself at this time is offered by Helen Davis, who was a student in a night course in the history of jazz that Davis taught at the Lincoln School.

Helen Davis confirms what Davis describes in *Livin' the Blues,* that he considered black history as having its roots in "African culture, 'work' songs, spirituals and blues—before jazz" and that he found ". . . fascinating how jazz grew musically from reflections of black history—cultural, sociological, political parallels."[7] For Frank, then, Lincoln School provided a forum to showcase his developing racial pride and strong sense of self. In this forum, both recorded jazz and live sets served higher purposes: Davis made them forays into music history and traced the origins of jazz backward from the experiences of blacks in America to roots in African culture. In his autobiography, the recollection of this teaching experience represents an act of affirmation not only of the "heart and soul of jazz," but also the heart and soul of a black man who found inspiration and consolation in jazz.

Another liberating moment is signaled in Davis's courage to go before the microphone and broadcast his own radio show, "Bronzeville Brevities." In 1945, WJJD in Chicago, owned by department store magnate Marshall Field, hired Davis as a disc jockey to do a series of fifteen-minute jazz shows. Once again he was provided a forum. Within the few allotted minutes, he offered genuine jazz (as opposed to the popular rhythm and blues), gave current news about artists, and used records by interracial groups, as he said, "to propagandize on the democracy of jazz and suggest increased integration in other fields."

Finally, Davis's liberation from a crippling sense of low esteem is readily discerned in his political activism. From 1944 to 1947, he served the Chicago Civil Liberties Committee as vice chairman. An especially gratifying gesture was Davis's nonpartisan appearance before both the Democratic and Republican platform committees in 1944, where, in an unprecedented presentation, he shocked the conferees by urging their inclusion of a plank outlawing anti-Semitism. He was also a member of the national board of the Civil Rights Congress from 1947 to 1948. Along with Helen, Frank participated in the American Youth for Democracy group. Davis's courage and assertiveness at this point in this life, when he was nearing forty, are indications of how far he had come emotionally. The Frank Marshall Davis of Arkansas City was not capable of transforming ignorance and low self-esteem into knowledge, and knowledge into activism. But the Frank Marshall Davis who had traversed the world from Arkansas City to Chicago to Atlanta and back to Chicago again had acquired considerable self-knowledge and knowledge of black history. Acquiring history, then, both personal and racial, empowered Davis; and history began to figure in his writing, especially in the poetry.

Davis's poetry is another indication of his personal liberation. He was motivated by a need to address largely social issues, not to reveal a private self. Indeed, many critics regarded his poetry as too propagandistic, too close to his journalism. In an interview Davis responded: "To me, poetry is a subjective way of looking at the world. All poetry worthy of the name is propaganda. Milton's *Paradise Lost* is Christian propaganda as is Joyce Kilmer's 'Trees.' But such works are not likely to be condemned as propaganda because the beliefs expressed in those and similar poems are shared by a majority of the population."[8]

The view Davis expresses here is articulated in many poems in his several collections: *Black Man's Verse* (1935), *I Am The American Negro* (1937), *Through Sepia Eyes* (1938), and *47th Street: Poems* (1948). Later, a small collection of his jazz poems was culled from these collections and published as *Jazz Interlude* (1985). Before his death, he had worked on a manuscript entitled "Black Moods: New and Collected Poems," a few of which were published in *Blind Alleys: A Journal of Contemporary Literature* (1984). In nearly all of these works, Davis eschews the tender mercies of lyrical verse for the largeness of social issues and poetic confrontations with public concerns. The form he found conducive to his vision was free verse, where Walt Whitman echoes faintly but Carl Sandburg and Edgar Lee Masters more loudly. In fact, two sections in his first collections bear the title "Ebony Under Granite" and appear to be modeled on Masters's

Spoon River Anthology (1915). Although informed by previous poetic practice, Davis's verse is by no means merely derivative. The experiences that engendered his wry, satiric wit and his willingness to engage in jazz experimentation enabled him to place his personal signature on such memorable poems as "Dancing Gal," "Charlie Parker," and "Billie Holiday."

Davis always shunned a common practice—that of having a well-established figure write an introduction to his collections. The poetry had either to stand or fall on its own merits. A famous name would be a crutch, a form of assistance that would detract from the poetry. Nowhere is his fiercely independent nature more fully revealed than in "Frank Marshall Davis: Writer," a poem that arguably best sums up his aesthetic vision:

> I was a weaver of jagged words
> A warbler of garbled tunes
> A singer of savage songs
> I was bitter
> Yes
> Bitter and sorely sad
> For when I wrote
> I dipped my pen
> In the crazy heart
> Of mad America
>
> . . . . . .
>
> But
> I did not die
> Of diabetes. . . .

4

A reading of *Livin' the Blues* goes a long way toward dispelling the mystery surrounding Dudley Randall's "Mystery Poet." By presenting new information, Davis's life story illuminates the achievements and successes of a previously well-known man whose life and work had descended into obscurity. But *Livin' the Blues* does more. In between the facts, where silences and unexplained ideas lie, the autobiography speaks volumes about its author, a man who spent a lifetime of living the blues as well as triumphing over them too. In the formal representation of his life as a blues narrative, *Livin' the Blues* constitutes a major achievement in African American autobiography.

One of Davis's contemporaries, Sterling A. Brown, made selected blues lyrics into touchstones of sheer poetic language and of philosophical expressions indicating a view of the world too. In one poignant example he said, "The blues ain't nothing but a poor man's heart disease."[9] Certainly *Livin' the Blues* contains its fair share of complaints and grief, as one often finds in the blues. But as a figuration of the blues into a narrative, this life story shares with its musical archetype another, more profound quality—transcendence. Self-pity, according to Brown, is not the defining spiritual mode of the blues, and *Livin' the Blues* can hardly be described as morose. But stoicism, again borrowing from Brown's concept of the blues, better represents Davis's persistence and his doggedly determined effort to prevail over life's many obstacles and to proclaim a self.

Davis understood with Brown the significance of the blues as a metaphoric example of confrontation, transcendence, and triumph. The idea is an implicit organizing principle of *Livin' the Blues*. In a 1955 newspaper article, however, Davis made this notion explicit:

> Basically, [the blues] are personal songs of protest and rebellion, growing out of individual needs. They may have any subject matter, ranging through love, politics, current events, race relations, and whatnot. They may poke fun or they may be deadly serious. A true blues is always realistic; it is never maudlin or escapist.[10]

Livin' the Blues persuasively demonstrates this definition of the blues. It plainly states the fact that hardship and deprivation were no strangers to Davis. For instance, as Helen Davis explains, Frank started the Oahu Paper Company shortly after arriving in Hawaii. It burned down in 1952. Later, in the same year, he ventured into another independent business, the Paradise Paper Company, and through it acted principally as a seller of "advertising specialties," such as business cards, personalized calendars, and the like. Even though he carried some active accounts to his death in 1987, this business was never financially successful. Instead of seeking refuge in self-pity or other forms of self-protection, Davis confronted his impoverishment courageously, by attempting to write his way out of the poorhouse.

Early in *Livin' the Blues,* Davis recounts a time in 1927, after arriving in Chicago, when he was forced to hack out fiction "for bread and beans." Writing under different versions of his actual name and also pseudonyms, Davis published popular fiction emphasizing action and crime in a number of sources, including *National Magazine, The Light,* and the Chicago *Evening Bulletin.* [11] He must have felt his life had come full circle when, in Hawaii, severe economic reversals forced him once again to take up the pen for purely monetary reasons. Under the pseudonym Bob Greene, Davis published *Sex Rebel: Black (Memoirs of a Gourmet Gash)* in 1968.[12] A soft-core pornographic novel, it tells the misadventures of its author and main character. By casting the novel in a semi-autobiographical form, Davis raised a number of questions. To what extent is the novel based on his own life experience? Is the "sex rebel" another version of Davis revealed fictively but obscured autobiographically? Is there any particular reason for the pseudonym Bob Greene? Just why did Davis choose to invent an author-character for the novel? Had Davis devoted more of *Livin' the Blues* to the years 1948 to 1973, when he completed the manuscript, perhaps many of these questions would have been addressed. It is quite possible that "That Incredible Waikiki Jungle,"a memoir he left uncompleted, was intended as a sequel and therefore a fuller description of his life in Hawaii. From the fragment that survives, Davis led an extraordinary life in an area many would describe as a ghetto in Waikiki.[13]

Readers of Davis's prose will likely find his vocabulary a reflection of language used by "hip" speakers in the forties and fifties. Women, for instance, are routinely called "broads," "chicks," "babes," and "janes," while men are referred to as "grannydodgers," "spades," and "jellybeans." As a product of an earlier time period, Davis probably gave no thought to the implications of this vocabulary for readers today. This is not to apologize for or to excuse such referents. Instead, it is to call attention to the very important way Davis anchors his expressiveness in the parlance of the "hip" generation of jazz musicians at mid-century. As the title of his memoir suggests, music is the metaphor through which he articulates his life.

The tough-minded, earthy grittiness of *Livin' the Blues* is true to the blues tradition and invigorates the memoir's apparently conventional life-and-times narrative form. Davis's representation of economic hardship, low personal esteem, racial oppression, and his triumph over them recalls the struggles against debilitating color consciousness and the evolving racial, as well as individual, pride that have won *The Autobiography of Malcolm X* such a wide reading. Because *Livin' the Blues* is not an extended moan over lost opportunities and loves, it becomes a statement of its own achievement. It recalls another blues line that goes something like this: "Been down so long, down don't bother me." This line has, on occasion, been misunderstood as a confession of resignation, self-pity, and defeat-ism. But actually, the existential axis turns in a different direction. It is a profound assertion of self: it sets forth the courage to stand one's ground and the power to exercise some control over one's life. In this sense, the line becomes a distilled declamation of transcendence. *Livin' the Blues* bears out the same declaration. It too details a life that has been down, but the story of its triumph, told from within the paradigm of the blues, is especially poignant too. Although it has taken nineteen years for the autobiography to find its way into print, it has not arrived too late to enrich a growing body of excellent life histories. The manuscript has seen its difficulties, but its publication indicates that "trouble don't last always."

JOHN EDGAR TIDWELL

Miami University
Oxford, Ohio

A Note on the Text

This edition of *Livin' the Blues* represents the first published version of the *entire* manuscript. In 1986, *Cottonwood Magazine* published 80 of the 469 manuscript pages in a special issue on African American writers.[1] Except for a few silent emendations to improve readability, the text of the *Cottonwood* manuscript corresponds substantively to the present edition of *Livin' the Blues*. It is worth noting, however, that although the *Cottonwood* text is described as chapter one of Frank Marshall Davis's autobiography, the text on which the present edition of *Livin' the Blues* is based shows no evidence of division by chapters. Both manuscripts follow Davis's practice of numbering each section of his narrative with Arabic numerals. However, when Davis shifts from one topic to another without following his usual practice, some disagreement may arise concerning the most appropriate place to mark a new section. The problem of determining the best possible division of sections is directly related to which copy of the text is used to make such determinations. A brief history of the typing of the manuscript, then, lays out the special editorial problems that have had to be resolved.

Davis's announcement in 1973 of the completion of his memoirs can be taken to mean that a complete, typed version of *Livin' the Blues* was then available.[2] Unfortunately, of that manuscript, only a segment survives, a carbon copy of pages 310–76. This excerpt is divided into sections 51–64. At the bottom of page 376 is found the word "-finis-," suggesting that the entire manuscript ends at this point. Yet we know that Davis authorized a retyping of his memoirs. It is also clear that the *retyped* version, which is the one used for this edition, is longer and differs in significant ways from the first one.

In the *first typed* version, for instance, section 61 begins on page 362 with an observation: "I have often regretted the passing of Edgar Brown before the Supreme Court handed down its long list of historic rulings outlawing discrimination." The second or *retyped* version introduces

Edgar Brown at the beginning of section 67, on page 374: "Edgar Brown would have made a fitting companion for Stokely Carmichael. Unfortunately he died before the Supreme Court handed down its long list of historic rulings outlawing segregation" (section 59 in this book). This revision illustrates Davis's tendency to elaborate in the *retyped* version what he had stated more succinctly in the *first typed* version. In this example, the *revised* version is also more poignant because of Davis's improvements in style and his attempt to situate his and Brown's lives in the context of black activist Stokely Carmichael's life and political influence.

The *retyped* version of the manuscript presents additional editorial problems. The first difficulty is in trying to establish the years in which revisions were made and the entire manuscript retyped. In this edition of *Livin' the Blues,* Davis pensively muses near the end of his life story: "Looking back upon my existence between 1905 and 1980, I have seen radical changes." Without further corroborating evidence, 1980 is taken here to be the last date in which he made any changes in the manuscript.

Another problem with the *retyped* version is that one segment of manuscript is typed twice, and the second copy is inserted in the text with no indication which placement is correct. The portion of the *retyped* draft beginning on page 88 and extending to page 96 of the manuscript is not only out of sequence but is repeated later in the manuscript, from pages 115 to 127. As a consequence, the pagination is not only thrown off, but the section numbers also lose their order.

Finally, the *retyped* version contains passages in which section numbers were omitted altogether, although an unknown proofreader attempted to restore some by inserting them into the margins of the text. When photocopied, however, the insertions were often too faint to be readable or failed to reproduce at all. A corollary problem occurs in section 11 of this book. Either a portion of the original manuscript was omitted when it was first typed, or it was accidentally omitted when the *revised* version was typed. Not only is there a break in the continuity of the manuscript, but the effect created by the omission is that Davis wrote very little about his first college experiences, at Friends University in Wichita. In order to account for this lacuna and to make the text more cohesive, I reorganized several events to ensure a more logical chronological time sequence. I also placed two deleted passages in notes 5 and 6 to the "1923–1926" chapter.

What role Davis played, if any, in overseeing the retyping of his own manuscript is suspect at this point. While Davis remained in Hawaii, his manuscript wound up in Chicago because he needed assistance with its retyping, and he relied upon his old friend Dr. Margaret Burroughs, then executive director of Chicago's DuSable Museum, to make the necessary arrangements. The resulting textual inconsistencies and errors in the *retyped* version suggest Davis lost some measure of editorial control over his own text. In 1982 when I asked him whether he had a copy of the manuscript, Davis replied that because of a "typing mess-up," "I do not have a copy of 'Livin' the Blues,' although I was to be sent a carbon."[3] Clearly implied in Davis's letter is a problem with the quality of the typing, meaning typographical errors and lapses in the text. Davis's was only one perspective on the typing problem, however. Mrs. Marion Taylor Hummons, the typist, explained "mess-up" in quite another way. As she recounted to me in a telephone interview, she was asked to type Davis's manuscript in 1981, in addition to fulfilling her regular responsibilities as a secretary for the DuSable Museum in Chicago.[4] However, when the work load became too great, she was forced to hire an assistant to take on the job of typing Davis's manuscript. The unforeseen problem necessitated a financial arrangement that at first confused Davis, Mrs. Hummons said, when she had to pay the assistant three hundred dollars from her own pocket. Davis originally did not understand these new arrangements, although he ultimately reimbursed her. Notwithstanding the confusion about typing expenses, in the final analysis, Davis had no opportunity to resolve textual inconsistencies and typing errors. Nor did he immediately receive a copy of the *retyped* version of the manuscript.

How I came into possession of the current manuscript is not without its disputed history too. When I conducted research for an essay on Davis for the *Dictionary of Literary Biography* in 1981, I found little new biographical information. Through Dr. Margaret Burroughs, I secured Davis's address and, in a letter, asked him to suggest possible sources of new facts that would enable me to offer a fuller description of his life and work. In our exchange of letters in 1981, he said he would intercede on my behalf with Dr. Burroughs, who had made arrangements for the manuscript to be retyped. His 24 September 1981 letter to me indicated that the manuscript was being retyped, and that Howard University Press wanted to consider it for publication. In November 1981, Dr. Burroughs responded to Davis's request and sent me what I have termed the *retyped* version. The complete manuscript consisted of original typed pages, some photocopied pages, and some carbons. At this point, my records and recollections are at variance with Mrs. Hummons's memory. She recalls sending the *retyped* manuscript, complete with cover letter, directly to Howard. In my files, however, is the original draft, not a copy, of the cover letter addressed to Howard University. What my records indicate is that after I received the manuscript from DuSable, I forwarded to Howard University Press a complete photocopy of the version Dr. Burroughs sent me. In either case, after considering the *retyped* manuscript for nearly two years, Howard decided against its publication and returned it to Davis in 1983.[5]

I have sought through Dr. Burroughs and Mrs. Hummons to locate the original materials that were typed into the present draft. In a series of telephone calls in September and November 1991, both of them have assured me that the materials from which this draft was typed were returned to Davis. These materials have since disappeared. Because they have disappeared, because I never received specific instructions from Davis on what was wrong with the *retyped* version, and because I have no knowledge of extant revisions made in other versions of the manuscript during Davis's lifetime, I consider the *retyped* version used for this edition of *Livin' the Blues* authoritative.

In Davis's absence, I have made every effort to determine and follow his intentions for a final draft, using the *retyped* version of the manuscript as authority for Davis's wishes. The guiding editorial principle I've followed in this text is to step out of the way and allow the voice of Davis to speak unimpeded. Only when necessary to facilitate the readability of the text have I made any changes. I have silently and, I hope, unobtrusively emended spelling and punctuation when needed. I have restored chronological order to the text by renumbering the pages and sections consecutively. Where references may be unfamiliar to readers, I have offered annotations of key words, phrases, and names. I have indicated the two places where Davis offered his own annotations by specifying in notes that these are his glosses. Since Davis provided no table of contents, I have divided his numbered sections into seven chronological parts which function as chapters. Last, I created a suggestive, not comprehensive, index of important names and organizations, using a topical arrangement.

LIVIN' THE BLUES

1905–1923

1

A soft night in late spring, 1923, at Arkansas City, Kansas, a yawn town fifty miles south of Wichita, five miles north of Oklahoma, and east and west of nowhere worth remembering.

I fidget in my hard chair on the mazda bombed stage of the Senior High School Auditorium awaiting completion of the annual commencement exercises. At last the principal calls my name, and I stand, grinning faintly and apologetically. Although I am six feet one and weigh 190 at the age of seventeen, I feel more like one foot six; for I am black, and inferiority has been hammered into me at school and in my daily life away from home. Three other black boys conspicuously float in this sea of white kids, and the four of us are the most ever to finish high school at one time. There are no black girls. Who needs a diploma to wash clothes and cook in white kitchens?

I accept my sheet of parchment and sit, hand clutching the rolled diploma showing I have completed twelve years of formal study that prepares none of us, white or black, for life in a multiracial, democratic nation. This is a mixed school—mixed in attendance, mixed-up in attitudes. White classmates unquestionably accept superiority as a natural right; we of the black quartet turn and twist, but we can find no way out of the hellhole of inferiority. We are niggers, the scum of the nation, and even our black brothers outside laugh bitterly and derisively as they tell us, "Niggers ain't shit!" Our high school education has prepared us only to exist at a low level within the degrading status quo.

Nevertheless, I *know* I am superior to Negroes reared in Dixie for they have not attended school with whites. I view them with contempt; they are *my* inferiors. Further, although I can never equal the achievements of a Thomas Edison or a George Washington or an Isaac Newton (they were white, weren't they?), I can accomplish as much as any other

Negro. For what had we done in thousands of years of human history that mattered a damn? My white classmates and I learned from our textbooks that my ancestors were naked savages exposed for the first time to uplifting civilization when slave traders brought them from the jungles of Africa to America. Had not their kindly white masters granted these primitive heathens the chance to save their souls by becoming Christians? And had not benign white Northerners unselfishly fought, bled, and died in the Civil War to free us? Yes, I did hear in school about one smart darky, Booker T. Washington, who over-lunched at the White House with the president. But that was it, man; that was all our history found in the books. We were otherwise nonentities, a happy, simple, childlike folk who got along all right as long as we knew our place and didn't get uppity and marry white women like that goddamned nigger, Jack Johnson.

And so, having no black heroes to identify with in this small town on the Kansas prairies, I fell victim to this brainwashing and ran spiritually with the racist white herd, a pitiful black tag-a-long.

But I ran disturbed.

I had done my best to conform to white standards as I knew them. Silently I begged for acceptance by trying to prove I was not like Those Others. Scrupulously I avoided following the known stereotypes—a task doubly difficult when certain stereotypes contradicted each other. No matter how hard I tried to act white, nothing had worked. I was still a big nigger kid tolerated only because state law said we must be tolerated.

I look around at my classmates, knowing this is the last time we will be together. And I am glad. There are only three or four white youths, boys who treated me as an equal and a friend, that I care to remember. From now on the rest can go to hell. My eyes rest briefly on the Class Prophet who, in the class annual, predicted I would become "a small truck farmer." As a student I have been about average, but emotionally I am graduating *magna cum laude* in bitterness.

My twelve years of public schooling have taught me to be white. But I am black. And those who taught me to be white at the same time reject me because of my blackness. The whites had let me look longingly inside their home of equal opportunity, then barred the door. Meanwhile, I have rejected the shabby shack of the only black world I know. I am suspended uncertainly in that limbo between white and black, not yet knowing who I am.

In other words, I am the product of integrated schools that do not integrate. And if I have learned anything of lasting value from those formative years, it is that mixed schooling of itself is only one step toward equality.

2

Obviously when I finished high school in 1923 I knew only the rough outlines of prejudice. But it was enough. I had already learned that white hypocrisy and black oppression were a basic part of the American way of life. And I have never been content with the little corner where the white broom tried to sweep me. I honestly think that had I continued living in my birthplace of Arkansas City I would have eventually become so filled with hate that one day I would have gone berserk and seized a weapon with the intention of killing as many whites as I could reach until I was exterminated by the forces of law and order—also white.

Yet I do not doubt that most whites in my hometown thought they were treating us right, perhaps even too well. Kansas prided itself on being a liberal state and flaunted its tolerance over the neighboring South. They could have pointed out that Negroes voted, attended mixed schools, were not jim crowed on transportation, and not required to address whites as Mr. or Mrs. while in turn being called only by their first names. What more could a nigger want? And had you answered, dignity and respect as a human being, they would not have understood.

Arkansas City during my childhood had a population of around ten thousand with between three and four hundred blacks. There were Mexicans who came up to work in railroad gangs and a smattering of integrated Indians—integrated primarily because they received fat incomes from Oklahoma oil wells. The overwhelming majority of the population was WASP, mainly small merchants, tradesmen and farmers: bedrock of the nation, Kansas Gothic. Physically, the town itself was pleasant enough. Streets were wide, trees plentiful. Large lots surrounded most homes, leaving room in the backyard to grow vegetables and poultry, and on the sides to cultivate fruit trees for family consumption. Farms stepped on city boundaries, and there was a small meat packing plant. Enough vegetables, fruit, grain, beef, and pork were produced to make the community self-sufficient. Located near the juncture of two rivers, the Walnut and the Arkansas (fishing was excellent in both), Indian lore had it that we were safe from tornadoes. Occasionally after heavy rains the rivers overflowed, but since only the poor lived in the lowlands it was not considered a major problem by establishment whites.

Most blacks lived in the noisy, dirty sections hard by the two main railroad tracks, Sante Fe on the east and 'Frisco on the west, not because of residential restrictions but because rent was cheaper. Many owned their small homes. In addition there was a disreputable area known as "the bottoms" which held a miniscule concentration of the city's dusky prostitutes, pimps, gamblers, and bootleggers. Our black community was well-rounded.

Probably because of its location only five miles from the Oklahoma border, Arkansas City had no consistent policy on how to treat Negroes and thus sat uncomfortably impaled on the spike of its own indecision. In some ways it was as blatantly segregated as neighboring Oklahoma of that era; in others it was liberal. Thus we had the anomaly of mixed schools with the silent understanding that black children would not participate in certain activities. Negro teachers were unthinkable. For many years all three movie houses were lily white; the one theatre presenting live shows, with opium dreams of opulence calling itself the Fifth Avenue Opera House, "reserved" the second balcony "for colored only" which was dubbed "nigger heaven." Both city parks were open to everybody, and we could rent boats to row all over the lake at Paris Park but were barred from swimming. (This policy was grudgingly suspended for the moment if a black boater accidentally fell overboard, but even this had better not happen too often.) When the Ku Klux Klan organized a local klavern, many whites would put on nightshirts and parade, then come home and invite black neighbors in for ice cream.

We could buy or rent homes in any part of the town our funds would allow. But we could attend no white church other than the Seventh Day Adventist. We rented store space and operated small businesses in the heart of the small downtown area next door to white merchants, but we could eat in none of their restaurants unless we sat in the kitchen.

Such was the town where I was born of poor parents on 31 December 1905. The family had the supreme proof of honesty. We were supremely poor. I came out at eleven o'clock at night. Another hour and I'd have been a New Year's baby. But you cannot blame my mother for not holding out until midnight. I weighed in at twelve pounds, and she must have been understandably tired of carrying around this burden.

My old man, Sam Davis, floated into town from some place in the state of Arkansas. An itinerant barber and musician (he blew baritone horn, undoubtedly with a heavy seasoning of the blues), he met and married my mother, fathered me, hung around long enough to see what he and God had wrought, then drifted on. They were divorced before I was a year old, and I've never heard of him since. For all I know, the old boy played similar gigs in several towns, and I may be related to a lot of people I never heard of.

Mother was a tall, big woman, cinnamon brown and freckled. She was also mild of disposition, asthmatic, and a compulsive tongue chewer. Her father, Henry Marshall, lived in Wichita. Stocky and bullnecked, his yellow-brown complexion came from a Negro father and a Mexican mother. Like virtually all Afro-Americans—and a high percentage of whites—I am ethnic hash. I have no idea what I may be other than African and one-eighth Mexican. Mother had a younger sister named Hattie, lighter in weight and color, who was a real swinger. Their only brother, Robert Marshall, made his way to Japan around 1910 and never wrote home. It's possible a few cousins may have died when the bomb exploded over Hiroshima and Nagasaki. That's another reason why I hate war. You don't really know what corpse may be your kin.

I was Mother's first and last child. Possibly I discouraged her, for when I was two she left with a white family for California to work as their maid for a couple of years. Since Aunt Hattie had already split the ho-hum prairie scene for Kansas City where there was more action, that left my care and feeding to Mrs. Amanda Porter, my great-grandmother.

Granny had been a slave in Kentucky, losing her first husband, a Northern soldier, early in the Civil War. Promptly marrying again, she lost number two in one of the closing battles. With her luck, she dared not try again. She was one of those *fired,* not freed, by the Emancipation Proclamation as leader-writer Floyd McKissick so aptly puts it.[1] They were kicked out into a hostile world with no severance pay or any provision for making a living. Immediately they became a huge unemployed surplus on the American market. In all fairness, their descendants should still be reimbursed by the descendants of their bosses, North and South, who canned them over a hundred years ago. The cold hard fact is that many offspring of these whites still look upon us from a master-slave point of view. The United States was the only slaveholding nation in the New World that completely dehumanized Africans by considering them as chattels, placing them in the same category as horses, cattle, and furniture. This attitude, still held by too many American whites, helps account for the fact that blacks have won greater acceptance in Brazil and other lands where our forefathers were once held in bondage, but not dehumanized.

Granny had been conditioned to acceptance as an inferior, born to be subservient. A docile product of the system, she was neither antiwhite nor bitter and all her life maintained respect for the children of her former masters, among them a lawyer, C. T. Atkinson, who lived in one of the largest and most pretentious homes near the heart of town and kept a stable of pure-white thoroughbred horses. Granny worked in the Atkinson kitchen, now getting a small amount of pay for services, which as a slave she once performed free, and I went there with her. Since this was the period when Jack Johnson was chasing Tommy Burns all over the planet for a shot at the heavyweight crown, Lawyer Atkinson would often bend over, pretend to spar with me, and tell Granny I was going to grow up to be another Jack Johnson. And do you know, as I look back upon the interracial aspects of my life, in certain respects his prophecy was true.

She told me of incidents while a slave, which remained fresh on her mind. I sat open-mouthed as she related stories she had witnessed, among them the drama of a fellow slave who took an axe, laid his right hand on a chopping block, and deliberately hacked off three fingers so he would have little market value when he learned his owner planned to sell him away from his wife and children. She had also seen bloody fighting in the Civil War and had gazed upon Union soldiers so desperately thirsty they crawled to puddles of urine left by passing horses to moisten their parched lips.

Granny had only one child, my mother's mother, who passed away long before I was born. From then on, both granddaughters lived with her in Arkansas City rather than with their father who had settled in Wichita.

As the widow of a Union soldier, she received a small pension from Uncle Sam. With these funds and by working for "quality white folks," she had been able to build a modest three-room cottage near the northern end of the town's main street. That was my home from as early as I can remember until I went to college. For several years no other blacks lived nearby; we held a monopoly on integrating the neighborhood.

Granny was past seventy when Mother went to California, but she was spry and healthy. She took me on my maiden train ride when I was three, a trip to Kansas City, Missouri, where I remember making my first visit to a saloon, tagging along with several older kids to buy a half-gallon bucket of beer for supper.

There were no open saloons in Kansas; the state was legally dry before I was born. Selling cigarettes or even giving them away was also then against the law. Shows, dances, and sporting events were banned on Sunday. Unless you got your kicks from attending church, there was only one major way to enjoy yourself. I have always been amazed that the state did not have an unusually high birth rate.

Nevertheless, I had my first drink of hard liquor at three, shortly after returning from Kansas City. Being from Kentucky, Granny loved her juice. A deacon in the Second Baptist Church, which she attended regularly, periodically supplied her with a gallon of corn whiskey. One cold night she decided I ought to have a hot toddy before tucking me in. The innovation was so overwhelmingly successful I was soon insisting on a nightly nip. Apparently Granny started having visions of me drinking myself to death before the age of five because she stopped my toddy without prior warning. I won't say I had withdrawal symptoms but I was outstandingly unhappy. Then by chance she discovered the only way I would willingly take castor oil (a cure-all for kid pains then) was as the center of a whiskey sandwich. First liquor, then castor oil, and on top more liquor. Until Granny caught on, I was the sickliest child in town— and also owned the cleanest guts.

Had Granny been in the Garden of Eden, Eve never would have had a chance to take that apple. As soon as that snake appeared, Granny would have immediately clubbed it to death or ran—possibly both. When I was three she gave me such a thorough indoctrination into the pathological fear of serpents, it has remained with me ever since. Graphically she described in detail the attributes of the coach whip snake, which she said ran along beside stagecoaches and whipped horses with its tail until they ran in fright, causing the vehicle to overturn and killing or crippling its occupants; the hoop snake, which took its tail in its mouth and ran along the road like a wheel looking for someone to bite; and the jointed snake, which was so brittle a blow would break it into a dozen motionless pieces until night, when under cover of darkness the parts would reassemble themselves and the snake would crawl away. Granny warned me I must never, never touch any kind of snake because all were poisonous. I was impressed. One day a friend of hers, not knowing how well she had brainwashed me, came by with a gift for me in a closed hand. When I extended mine, he gave me a fistful of crawling, squirming angle worms. In my three-year-old mind, I saw them as snakes and I became hysterical. Granny's friend was abashed, astounded, and penitent—but this traumatic experience further served to underline my already paranoid fear of snakes.

Mother returned when I was four, to my great relief. Granny staunchly believed sparing the rod spoiled the child. During these two years of Mother's absence, Granny had done such an efficient job of beating hell out of me that I gave a minimum of trouble the rest of my childhood. Mother was far less physical. Soon after she returned, Aunt Hattie made one of her trips back home. She and Mother earned money by doing laundry together at home for assorted white families. Our back-yard clotheslines stayed full of drying clothes. Occasionally a garment they no longer needed was tossed in by their employers for me. I was thus expected to wear outmoded clothing to cover my body while their out-worn ideas on black-white relationships were passed on to cover my mind.

One day there descended upon Arkansas City a large contingent of Boganeys from Oklahoma, including father, mother, and assorted sons and daughters, many with their own children. Among them was a son, James Monroe Boganey, then in his late twenties, who had traveled all over the country working at various jobs. Although he was two inches shorter than Mother's five nine, he had a powerful physique and for a short time had been a professional boxer. But he was now ready to settle down. Mother met him at a church social and soon settled him. They were married a few months later, and at the age of four I had my first real father.

Dad, whose formal schooling stopped at the third grade, had an abundant quota of common sense and mother wit. He got a job as common laborer at the material yard of the Santa Fe railroad, a key storage and repair point for the entire system, and worked there some ten years. He moved in with us since by now Aunt Hattie's itchy feet had taken her to St. Louis. Our three rooms were adequate for the four of us but became overcrowded when a brother-in-law of Dad's descended on us for two weeks after arriving from Oklahoma shortly after the rest of the Boganeys packed up and left en masse to invade Coffeyville some one hundred miles to the east.

His name was Gaffney and he was an herb doctor, making his own medicines. He spent hours in the woods hunting specific weeds and grasses, but that was acceptable. What unnerved me was the first time I spotted him picking up and minutely examining fresh excrement from our hens, then selecting choice tidbits for his brews. Immediately I became radiantly healthy, never a moment of sickness until he returned to Oklahoma. I frankly admit I was too chicken to take any of his fowl concoctions, although later I understand he amassed a modest fortune.

I successfully dodged the Gaffney gambit, but I had my share of other home remedies. A doctor was called only in dire emergencies, such as when I had pneumonia at the age of four, often a fatal illness before the age of miracle drugs. For an ordinary chest cold I received a tablespoon of sugar with a half-dozen drops of coal oil, a cup of some queer kind of tea, and a chest rub with genuine goose grease. For a sore throat I gargled with four drops of carbolic acid in a half-cup of hot water. To ward off illness, my first year in school I wore a hunk of vile smelling asafetida hanging from a string around my neck; this was amazingly effective in warding off disease since it kept away other kids who wouldn't get close enough to give me their germs.[2] As for cuts or nails stuck in my foot (during barefoot season I usually wore at least one bandage somewhere), there was a cleaning with hydrogen peroxide followed by a generous dousing with turpentine. A poke from a rusty nail received no special consideration; you merely hoped the old rag you wore for a bandage was clean enough and you wouldn't get lockjaw. This was the accepted practice among the people I knew; if a kid fell from a tree and could make it home, or if he suffered a severe cut and was able to move the injured member without leaving something behind, he received a home remedy. First aid kits consisted mainly of peroxide, turpentine, and clean-looking rags. And somehow we managed to survive.

3

With no other black children living in the neighborhood and oddly enough, no white boys my age, my first preschool playmates were white girls—which established a habit. However, their parents broke it temporarily. Frequent newspaper stories detailed lynchings brought on, the articles solemnly said, because "a burly black brute raped a white woman." Mothers and fathers watched with growing concern as I became noticeably bigger by the month. By the time I was five I was quite large for my age. Now, in their eyes, I had sprouted into a sexual threat to their innocent little darlings and no longer was allowed to play with them. Obviously I was a burly black brute. I was puzzled; I was then too young to understand Caucasian culture.

Fact is, I was completely ignorant of race prejudice when I started school. I had attached no significance to my skin being darker than that of my white girl playmates. True, Granny had been a slave, but I did not know this condition was restricted to those of African ancestry. But I learned fast, on the second day of school.

I was the only Negro child in the first grade. Only five or six were enrolled in the entire school. Most "cullud" children attended the other three. I had already learned how to read and write at home so I had a definite jump on most of the other first graders.

On the second day a white boy grinned and asked very politely, "Do you mind if I call you nigger?" I thought it over briefly. Why should I object? I'd heard that term used by other blacks so I assumed it was acceptable. It seemed to me he wanted only to be my friend. I told him "Uh-huh." "Thanks," he said, then gleefully pointed at me and shouted, "Nigger, nigger, nigger!"

I was momentarily surprised, but then dismissed it as exuberance. When I reached home I told Mother about the nice, friendly little boy who asked permission to call me nigger.

She quit chewing her tongue, then asked quietly, "What did you tell him?"

"I said he could."

Mother clouded up and exploded like a thunderstorm.

"Soon as you get to school tomorrow, you find that nasty little peckerwood an' tell him if he ever calls you nigger again, you'll beat him until he can't see straight. And you'd better!" Then she gave me my first lecture on race relations.

Next day I looked up this boy before class and withdrew permission. And I had my first fistfight.

I also became acquainted with another epithet, but in a somewhat unconventional way. A few days later, on the way home after school, I had a name-calling bout with still another white boy. We stood a half block apart hurling invective at the top of our first-grade voices. After we had both exhausted our oral ammunition (for some reason he never once called me nigger), another white lad who had been looking on came close and suggested confidentially, "Call him a darky."

"A what?" I asked. The word was new to me.

"A darky. Means an old Chinaman."

Sounded like a good idea. Right away I shouted, "You're a real darky!"

A white man had been strolling along the sidewalk and was now almost abreast of my adversary. He stopped suddenly and turned in my direction. Then he looked at my pale oral foe and sharply again at me. I wondered why he had such a queer expression on his face. But he said nothing. He merely shook his head and stumbled on as if in a trance.

"Yah, you old darky!" I shouted again.

The white man hunched his shoulders as if he had been slapped hard on the back and quickened his step. The boy down the block, evidently unable to think of a comeback, hesitated a moment then turned and walked on.

Cocky from my triumph, as soon as I got home I told Mother about this brand new word which had been so devastating.

My story left her both speechless and motionless for several seconds. I had the distinct impression her shoulders fell into a hunch like that of the white man. Then she explained in a somewhat strained voice, "Son, that's a bad word po' white trash calls us. It don't mean an old Chinaman. It really don't."

Well, you learn something new every day.

And I also learned about white violence, at the age of five, when later that fall I was personally selected for a lynching. Both daily papers must have carried another Southern social note about this popular pastime of that era, and a couple of third graders, evidently after hearing their parents discuss it with approval, decided to stage their own junior necktie party. I was on my way home alone, crossing a vacant lot, when these white boys, who had been lying in wait, jumped me. They threw me to the ground and held me down while one lad produced a rope and slipped it over my head. I kicked and screamed. Just as one started to snatch the noose tight around my neck, a white man appeared. He took one look, chased the boys away, freed me, and helped brush dirt and trash off my clothes. He walked with me until I was close to home nearly a mile away, then turned around and went on about his business. I never learned who he was, nor could I single out the embryo lynchers at school next day. Naturally, school officials did not push their probe. I was still alive and unharmed, wasn't I? Besides, I was black.

Like most boys I got into an occasional battle but I never liked to fight just for the hell of it. However, I learned as years passed that I was able to take care of myself more than merely adequately when sufficiently aroused. When I was twenty-one I considered becoming a professional fighter, but this aberration subsided before anything drastic occurred. Fact is, I haven't had a real fist fight since high school. Oh, I've riled plenty of people, but without exception they have been able to rigidly control any inclination to take a poke at me. The fact that my size and looks later frequently caused me to be mistaken for Joe Louis may have had something to do with it.

But let's return to the first grade.

A few weeks after the near lynching I began arriving home unusually early after school let out at 4:00 P.M. Mother noticed I was out of breath, and after this happened several days straight she asked me why. I told her about a white boy in the second grade who chased me home every afternoon. He couldn't catch me, so I was actually benefitting from this enforced exercise: it was helping my speed, wind, and legs. Residents on the route between school and home were now able to set their clocks by me. On the dot I would dash past, leading my pursuer by some twenty feet.

I knew my tormentor's name. Mother told Dad, who worked at the same place as the kid's father. Dad called it to the attention of the white boy's old man and asked him to stop his son from chasing me home.

"Wouldn't think of it," the white man laughed. "You know boys are gonna be boys."

When he came home that night, Dad ordered me to stop running and fight. If I didn't, he promised me, he would personally give me a worse licking than I could possibly get from anybody in the second grade.

Next afternoon the Davis Derby began promptly on schedule. I was running some twenty feet in the lead, when suddenly Dad stepped from behind a tree and stood in the middle of the sidewalk blocking my path. He had quit early that day to look in on the event.

As I said earlier, Dad wasn't big but he was powerful and far more of a menace than my pursuer. I braked and reversed direction so fast that the surprised white kid slammed into me head on and we both went down. I got up swinging and in a couple of minutes had completed a pretty fair job of junior mayhem. My foe had a bloody nose, a scraped eye, plus a few assorted lumps, and a strong case of the weeps. We started running again. This time I was doing the chasing, but Dad caught me and took me home.

Next day at work the white lad's father was incensed and demanded that Dad punish me for beating up his son. He called me a "brute" and a "bully."

"Think nothing of it," Dad said and laughed. "Jus' like you told me yourself, 'boys will be boys.'"

After that I had little trouble the rest of my six years at elementary school, although for a time I was the only black kid enrolled. As I look back now, it's surprising I didn't get ganged up on. Sometimes, even through the fourth grade, I would develop a crush on a little blonde or redheaded classmate and walk beside her, carrying her books. However one day, quite by chance, Mother happened to spot me as I strolled leisurely along, laughing and talking and occasionally pulling on a little doll with long black pigtails and a milk white face who seemed to be enjoying it as much as I. Mother very nearly suffered a heart attack. Following a lengthy lecture by both parents that evening, I ceased this kind of activity.

At home we functioned quite happily without the devices even slum dwellers take for granted today. Our light was from coal oil lamps; and our heating system was a potbellied stove in the front room, a range in the kitchen, and optimism in the middle room. Both stoves ate what seemed gluttonous amounts of fuel since I had to chop the wood and bring it and coal to keep them fed. Water we got from pumps in the yards of neighbors on both sides of our house. I brought it in five gallon buckets; I needed a bath every Saturday night just from carrying water. I was in the sixth grade before we piped in city water, electricity, and gas. We never had a telephone.

I did not realize the extent of our poverty until later. There was little, if any, starvation in my part of Kansas; but almost everybody was poor, some more so than others, except for a few white people because of their oil holdings in neighboring Oklahoma. Material possessions were comparatively scarce. Automobiles were few and costly. This was also before the advent of radios; television sets were not even conceived of except by some dreamers.

As I looked back later, my family was economically in the lower 10 percent. For the first few years of school, in cold weather in place of an overcoat I wore one of Dad's discarded jackets. But I did not mind. Somehow I realized Dad and Mother were doing the best they could with their small, hard-won income. And they saw that I had enough to eat and scraped together enough to provide my necessities.

Obviously our toilet facilities were primitively functional. We had a two-seated privy, furnished with an outdated Sears, Roebuck or Montgomery Ward catalog, in the backyard some forty feet from the house, past the grapevines and with a mulberry tree on one side and dewberry bushes on the other. During winter it seemed miles away but on those summer days when the temperature rose to 110 degrees and the occasional hot breeze blew toward the house, a blind stranger could have found it without directions. When the mercury hovered around zero or below or we had a wild Kansas blizzard, we used our hold-everything-until-the-last-minute technique. We bundled up as if scheduled for a rendezvous at the North Pole, then awaited our internal countdown. We all became proficient at timing ourselves to reach the outhouse at exactly zero, thus keeping our visit short so we could dash back to the warming fire. Come to think of it, those of us who used privies must have been tougher than that brass monkey; nobody ever had anything actually frozen off.

I was in the second grade when one of Granny's friends, also an ex-slave, succumbed to modernity and wed the town's water system to her outhouse. It was just my luck to stop by after school that day and ask to use her toilet.

I paused and briefly considered going on home when I opened the privy door in her backyard and saw this strange contraption with the front end of the wooden seat elevated some three inches. I did not trust this unfamiliar thing but necessity spoke in a commanding voice. Dropping my knickers, I sat gingerly down.

Immediately there was a roar like a dam breaking. I leaped up and ran screaming out, britches sliding down around my ankles. I didn't know whether that thing in there was going to chase me or explode.

Granny's friend hurried out of her kitchen and asked what was wrong. When I excitedly told her, she doubled up laughing. When she got control of herself, she explained the roar was merely the water closet filling, an action starting automatically when the front of the seat was pressed down. It was perfectly harmless, she said, but by then I'd had it scared out of me and didn't need to use the toilet.

4

At seven I turned into a bookworm through sheer necessity. I had learned that, away from school, white and black kids moved in different worlds. Playing with other children my color was a rarity except on those memorable occasions when an entire family visited us or we descended on another family. My family was not yet able to afford a "talking machine." Movie shows were then lily white—although one Saturday night in summer I was downtown with Dad and he stopped in front of a theatre door which had accidentally been left open. On the screen were the closing scenes of a film showing Jack Johnson whipping some White Hope. I shall never forget the look of ecstatic satisfaction on Dad's face as Li'l Arthur kayoed his pale foe.

However, Sundays were full. I went to Baptist Sunday School promptly at nine, then, after a short lull, sat through regular morning services beginning at eleven. This meant hours of listening to a fire and brimstone sermon. On those days when our pastor was in good voice and the amens came loud and often, a three- or four-hour service was not unusual. After that we went to somebody's house for Sunday dinner or they came to ours. Then back at 6:00 P.M. for the Baptist Young Peoples Union and afterwards the regular evening services which seldom ended before 10:30. For many years I spent from seven to nine hours every Sunday in church, rain, snow, or shine.

It was the week days that bothered me. Playing alone in the evening and on Saturday was a real drag. Then one day, wandering around downtown by myself after school, I walked out of curiosity into the public library and discovered books. First the juvenile section. Then I advanced to the adult area and by the age of nine had read both volumes of *Les Misérables*.

I read and lived with King Arthur and his Knights of the Round Table, fought beside Achilles in the Trojan War, and traveled home with Aeneas. I was a companion of Beowulf, Sir Galahad, Sohrab and Rustem, Charlemagne, Ivanhoe; I sought the Golden Fleece with Jason and conquered the known world with Alexander. With hammer and saw and nails and paint, I made a lance and shield and stood alone for hours on our tiny back porch guarding the castle from blackguard (whiteguard?) and villain, or with a different shield and wooden sword I performed sentry duty in our backyard as a Spartan. (These heroes, of course, were white for I had not yet heard of any African heroes.) My imagination kept me busy; forced to play by myself, I made the most of it and was alone no more. I spent so much time at the library that the head librarian, a plump, bespectacled, friendly white woman, called me her "bodyguard."

And, of course, I walked virtually everywhere. The town boasted one dinky streetcar, evidently saved on the ark by a compassionate Noah, which passed our house each half-hour going toward town during daylight and early evening. After that it was put to bed until the next day. I rode it only during a blizzard or heavy rain, paying a nickel. Each morning I walked slightly over a mile to school, walked back home for lunch, and to school again (except in subzero weather when I packed a sandwich), then home again in the afternoon. That was more than four miles. If I were sent back to Clapp's Grocery halfway to school or Sutherland's for a quart of milk, that was more mileage. When I received the added chore of calling each evening for our mail at the general delivery window of the post office, that was still another mile. I accepted this as perfectly natural, although now and then I hitched a ride on a farmer's wagon or a delivery hack just for the fun of it. Later, when I was old enough to run around alone at night, my daily average was at least ten miles, and I believe this laid the basis for good health in later years. However, my early training in learning how to amuse myself made me essentially a loner.

During these young years I began to eagerly await certain annual events. The Emancipation Day picnic and celebration at Wilson Park each August fourth was the largest and most important.[3] Farmers drove in from the country and neighboring Winfield by wagon and buggy with the more affluent coming in Fords, Dodge Brothers, Maxwells, and Saxons. One owned a big Cole 8, the envy of the black community. Many brought with them loaded baskets of food, and there were also barbecued ribs, hamburgers, watermelon hearts, sweet potato pie, ice cream, and soda pop on sale. Faces from near-white to ebony bobbled by in a constant stream. The pack was a moving, laughing sea of black. I especially enjoyed it for I could play with other boys and girls I rarely saw except at an occasional church picnic in summer, usually at Green's Farm, or maybe in the fall when whole families got together and spent a day in the country gathering walnuts and pecans. Other than a few curiosity seekers, the only whites were politicians (Republican of course) who would never dream of letting a mass gathering pass without appearing on the afternoon program to make stilted speeches praising "the progress you people have made since that gr-r-reat Republican, Abraham Lincoln, freed the slaves." Inevitably one would seek to establish real rapport by reminiscing fondly of "my black mammy at whose breast I suckled when I was a baby," and some of the younger listeners, such as Dad, would start angry murmurs.

(Years later, when I thought back to these formative days, I realized how emotionally distant we were from our fellow white Arkansas Citians. As black folk we lived among ourselves in our own three-dimensional sphere, but we existed in only two dimensions in that vaster world of the Caucasian. They accepted our length and breadth but by and large we were mere shadows, incomplete beings lacking depth. We could be ourselves, moving as men and women, only when we closed the door and shut ourselves in our small back room.)

I have a very special reason for remembering 'Mancipation Day in 1917 when I was eleven. This was World War I time with fireworks unavailable. However I learned that by scissoring heads off of long kitchen matches I could fire them in my cap pistol. Dad and I prepared a whole box, and I slipped the snipped heads in my hip pocket to fire at the celebration. This August fourth was a broiling day, over a hundred degrees. In mid-afternoon, with most still unused, I innocently sat down on the iron seat of a swing which had stood for hours in the sun. There was a swoosh and sudden heat on my right hip. I was on fire. Fortunately some resourceful soul emptied a bottle of soda pop over my buttocks and doused the flames; but with my clothing burned to the bare, I immediately went home. For the next week I ate standing up or reclining like those people in paintings of Roman orgies.

Even before I started school, Granny sometimes took me on Saturdays to the heart of town, where in summer Indians came in covered wagons. Tying their horses to hitching posts at Summit and Central, they then fastened their naked children to the wagons with ten-foot ropes and went off to shop. Adults were wrapped in bright blankets, men wearing large Stetson hats and women bareheaded with their blue-black hair hanging in two long, glistening braids. Granny said when she first settled here, gunfights between cowboys and Indians still erupted. This was a tough little town until the big rush south at the opening of the Oklahoma territory to settlers. In the social strata of Arkansas City, Indians were in the middle class, primarily because of the wealthy Osage.

Local whites looked down on members of other tribes, particularly the young attending Chilocco Indian School just across the Oklahoma border who came to town well chaperoned and dressed in conservative uniforms. But the Osage—they were different! Some of those with whom I attended school had incomes reportedly as high as ten thousand dollars per day from oil in neighboring Oklahoma; with this kind of money to spend, nobody dared discriminate against the Osage. They were far friendlier to me than paleface boys and girls. But many of them died young from fast living and fast cars.

At the bottom of the social scale were Negroes and Mexicans— niggers and greasers. And we had an affinity for each other, not only from gringo oppression which we both suffered but because many Mexicans and blacks worked side by side in the railroad yards and became close despite language barriers. I had also learned that down in Oklahoma many Indian tribes had high percentages of African blood, the result of runaway slaves finding sanctuary with red men. There were also a few blacks who had become oil wealthy. And this set the stage for one of the most fantastic stories of my youth.

One day when I was around twelve or thirteen, a young Afro-American in his early twenties, mild as a minnow, came to town and landed a garage job. Self-effacing, he got along well with everybody. After living there a year or so, he made the front pages of both dailies. Headlines shouted the discovery of oil on land he had inherited near Sapulpa, Oklahoma. He had already been offered a cool half-million bucks for his property plus royalties. Immediately, the presidents of both banks became his panting suitors, advancing him fifteen grand for spending change. Auto dealers gave him the pick of their best cars, and he chose a Stutz Bear Cat and a Pierce Arrow. Department stores outfitted him in their best clothing, and he selected a site and had plans drawn up to build a big, fancy, twenty-five-thousand-dollar home. Naturally, he would pay every penny back (with plenty of interest, of course) when he received his money. Leading citizens, with dollars in their eyes, forgot his color as they assured him this was the ideal community to settle in permanently and invest his dough. Even white women, who might have yelled "rape" had he smiled at them before the stories broke, flooded him with letters proposing marriage. He had it made in every direction and for a couple of months was the Black Emperor of Arkansas City.

When the novelty started wearing thin, he announced he was returning to Sapulpa to complete the transaction. A committee of fawning Leading White Citizens chauffeured him to the Sante Fe station and saw that he was comfortably ensconced aboard the jim crow coach (separate accommodations for Southern travel began at Arkansas City).

One week passed, then a second and third. Nobody had heard from him. Finally one banker, impatient at the silence, made a special trip to Sapulpa, returning red-faced and subdued. He could find no trace of the missing "heir." Further, there had been no oil strike. The mild young brother owned no property. Instead a gang of slick promoters had dreamed up the scheme to unload ordinary land at inflated prices. Knowing the pattern of white thinking, they assumed correctly the city's leading citizens would never believe a simple nigger was smart enough to be involved in this kind of confidence game and had made Grade A suckers out of them, unloading land worth no more than twenty-thousand dollars for better than a quarter of a million dollars.

The entire black community howled with glee at one of us pulling a fast one on those smart white pricks. I had grown more sour each year over the treatment given me by the majority purely because of color. Often, after I started attending grade school and when walking alone, I had been stopped by white men, sometimes with their women, who ordered me to dance for them. "All you niggers know how to do the buck and wing. It's just natural for you folks to sing and dance," they would tell me. If they blocked my path, I would stare silently and unsmilingly back until, finding their efforts fruitless, they would step aside and let me pass. Frankly, I have never learned how to tap dance; I'm one of God's chillun who don't got that kind of rhythm.

The Mexicans were as vindictively glad as we when the oil scam was explained. In certain respects, they were treated worse than blacks. They were foreigners and all foreigners were looked down on in this community of native white, farm-oriented Protestant Americans. Further, they were swarthy and Catholic. Unlike us, they didn't belong at all. The dirty greasers would go back home taking their savings with them whenever they felt like it. Hostility toward Mexicans was openly aired. Niggers, on the other hand, were here to stay and overt antagonism rarely showed its face as long as we stayed in what whites called "your place."

Some of the Mexicans had come here with their families, and these were the ones who became especially friendly with fellow black workers. They invited our family to their little shacks for dinners of chili, hot tamales, enchiladas, and frijoles so spicy hot I could hardly eat for crying. I'm sure this developed in me the taste for peppery foods I have retained. That and the barbequed ribs that were also part of my fare. In return, Dad invited them over for feeds of our kind of food: fried chicken, cornbread, black-eyed peas, and sweet potato pie.

One night when I was fourteen there came as guests a Mexican couple who brought along their niece, also fourteen, who had just arrived for a visit. Her name was Teresa, and she was easily the prettiest girl I had ever seen. She could speak no English, and it was just as well; I was so overcome I couldn't have talked anyway. I sat and stared at her long black hair with the sheen of silk, her eyes big and dark and flashing, and her skin softly rich as pale honey. I thought of a luscious ripened plum, and I longed to kiss her all over. I actually could have devoured her, lingering long as I savored each individual atom. When she turned suddenly, caught me gawking, and shyly smiled, she was so beautiful I expected her to vanish. I sat all evening, suspended in space, stunned by her loveliness, and wished I were older so I could ask her then and there to marry me.

Although ordinarily I was quite talented with a knife and fork, that night I could not eat. As soon as they left, Mother started teasing me but I heard little. She had never before seen me show any interest in a girl, and I recall she commented on my resemblance to a colicky calf. But for the most part her remarks bounced off me for already I was looking forward to our next visit with them and another chance to adore Teresa for an evening.

Time passed slowly. Two weeks later (it seemed like two years), we were to go to their house. But a couple of days before, Dad came home and casually mentioned Teresa had gone home to Mexico after her two weeks' visit. Suddenly the sky caved in. For the next few days, I stumbled around like one who is only half-awake among strange ruins. Of course I never saw her again, and for many years after I grew to adulthood I sometimes wondered if she were as beautiful as I had believed.

5

Like most boys, I went fishing several times each summer, usually with Mother and a group of her friends. Only occasionally could Dad accompany us. He worked ten hours daily, six days per week, and to fish meant he had to lay off from his job. If we wanted carp and buffalo fish, we climbed several gates, walked through pastures until we hit the main dirt road east of town, and followed it until we came to the bridge across the Walnut River some four or five miles away. I did not care especially for either variety: too bony. I preferred the large, succulent catfish found in the Arkansas River, equidistant to the west. Catfish were plentiful around both the dam and the headgates. They grew big; many times I saw two men walking along with a huge monster hanging from a pole carried on both men's shoulders. Catfish had fewer bones, and when they were fried in deep fat encrusted in cornmeal and egg I could eat all that were set before me.

Unlike most kids, I really did not care to fish because I was almost certain to run into at least one snake. Although only two varieties around my home were poisonous, copperheads and water moccasins, and so far as I knew nobody had ever died from the bite of either, I lumped all fifty-seven varieties together and tried to keep my distance. In summer this was particularly difficult for on hot days garter and milk snakes invaded our yard or rested underneath the grape, dewberry, and gooseberry vines near the privy. When I went fishing, I spent more time looking around for the crawling creatures than in watching my lines for a bite.

I wouldn't even bait my hooks with fishing worms because their wriggling reminded me of snakes. Either somebody put worms on my hook or I used what was called dough bait, made mainly from flour, water, and cotton.

I greatly preferred hunting to fishing. From late fall to early spring I knew there would be few snakes around. Using a single-shot .22 rifle, I went primarily after cottontail rabbits and became expert enough to bring them down on the run. I enjoyed many good meals of fried rabbit, mashed potatoes and gravy, and hot biscuits dripping with butter and loaded with some of Mother's homemade jellies and jams.

When it was too cold to hunt, I set traps in the underbrush back of our house before the city improved it for residences. These steel traps were placed where small animal traffic seemed heaviest. I visited them each morning and night (unless there was a blizzard) and caught rabbits, an occasional opossum, and many civet cats. Wanting only their hides, I tacked their skins on the back wall of our house until they dried out, then sold them to Old Man Dawson at the tannery for spending change. My first two attempts at skinning civet cats (a two-stripe cousin to a skunk) were di-STINK-ly memorable. My knife slipped, and the entire neighborhood immediately assumed an olfactory character differing from its usual image. Luckily, nobody complained, and soon I was able to skin the small animal speedily, without puncturing the odoriferous sac.

I needed the money from hides for show fare every Saturday. When I was in the third or fourth grade at First Ward School, my entire class was taken to see the silent movie, *Snow White and the Seven Dwarfs*. I was not barred. After a couple of other school-sponsored films at the same theatre, the management realized it had a good thing going and began slanting Saturday shows for school kids all over town. No attempt was made either to bar or give us special seats. When this mixing created no problem, the ban on black attendance in general was lifted. In order to get in on the gravy, the other two film houses rapidly followed suit, although the largest of the trio and the only one with a balcony did reserve the left half "for colored only." Meanwhile I was hooked and began living from Saturday to Saturday to see the next episode of the hair-raising serials. I simply had to learn how Pearl White escaped from that infernal machine in *The Perils of Pauline* and how Eddie Polo avoided falling from that cliff.[4] And the one- and two-reel comedies! Charlie Chaplin, Fatty Arbuckle, the Keystone Cops, and the Mack Sennett bathing beauties daringly showing female legs and knees and sometimes part of the thigh![5]

Occasionally there were black faces in the comedies. At first I thrilled to see people my color on the screen, but rapidly this turned to embarrassment. My face burned when white kids laughed uproariously at niggers running from ghosts and showing the whites of their eyes, stealing chickens and watermelons, or threatening each other with oversized razors big as scythes. That was obviously how we looked to whites, and yet I knew no black in Arkansas City who fit such descriptions. I soon came to prefer all-white movies.

Mother, Dad, and I would attend the show together when there was a new William S. Hart film or a picture as adventurous as *Tarzan* with Elmo Lincoln. We'd talk about it and relive the experience for weeks—especially if the piano player failed to follow the action and romped through "Alexander's Ragtime Band" when the dear old white-haired mother of the heroine lay on her deathbed, gasping her last.

I became a cowboy without horse the summer I was twelve. Previous vacations had been spent working in our gardens. For two years Dad had rented an extra acre nearby and planted it primarily in sweet corn. The second year brought such a bountiful crop that I walked all over town pulling a little wagon and selling roasting ears at fifteen cents a dozen. I made enough to buy most of my school clothes that fall. But in my twelfth year I devoted time primarily to my herd.

Each day I walked fifteen cows to pasture three miles from town and brought them back each evening. Arising at 5:30 every morning except Sunday, I went from house to house gathering my charges from townspeople, mostly white, who liked to keep cattle for their own milk supply. They fed them in their barns during winter, but in summer the owners wanted them to graze. I strode behind my herd with a long stick down the main highway of town to a large pasture owned by Paul Alston, the county's most successful black farmer. Early traffic was usually light, but I had to be ready to drive my herd into ditches on both sides of the road when I heard an auto approach as well as keep them off the tracks over which hourly passed an inter-urban trolley connecting Arkansas City with Winfield, the county seat. When I reached the pasture, I turned them loose for the day and walked back to town unless I was lucky enough to bum a ride. I was free then until 4:00 P.M. when I had to return to the pasture to assemble my herd, drive them back to town, and deliver each to her owner.

Since hitchhiking was uncertain in those days of comparatively few cars, this meant walking a minimum of thirteen miles daily, deliveries and all—if I was lucky. Usually I wasn't that fortunate. Although Kansas is thought of as a flat prairie state, the Alston pasture occupied several square miles of little hills rising as high as fifty feet, sometimes with sheer drops to small ravines. There were many tiny streams and one low, heavily wooded area with high grass. I was especially unhappy when the cows were in this section, for frequently I saw unnerving green snakes slithering through the thick undergrowth or entwined around tree branches. Since my charges were not the only cattle in the pasture, I had the double duty of identifying, isolating, and driving them toward the gate while watching warily for snakes. On high ground I often saw black snakes and bull snakes, but there was room enough to give them a wide berth of at least ten feet. As for the little lizards known as "mountain boomers" which raced from one clump of cactus and rock to another, they bothered me not at all.

I was paid a dollar per month for each cow. This fifteen dollars every thirty days seemed a small fortune, and I was willing to put up with the daily hikes and the snakes for the most money I'd ever had at one time. But one morning in August, I wished I had never seen cows.

As I drove my herd past the town limits, I noticed three white boys around my own age idling along the trolley tracks shooting at birds with a .22 rifle. I was soon ahead of them and had forgotten their presence until I heard a ping and saw dust kick up in the road a few feet from me. I looked back. The white boys were gazing into trees beside the tracks on a diagonal between us. As I watched, one took aim and fired toward the trees and for a second time a .22 pellet kicked up dust less than ten feet away. I yelled back but if they heard me, they gave no indication. I started to walk back toward them and almost immediately heard a Holstein heifer leave the herd and crash through weeds and bushes toward a field bordering the highway. I had no choice but to run and head her off, realizing with a sinking stomach that I couldn't leave my cows long enough to dash back and ask the boys to shoot in another direction. I was forced to walk on, praying I would not get hit. At least twenty times bullets kicked up dust from five to thirty feet away, but luckily neither I nor any of my herd were hit. When I finally locked them in the pasture after what seemed like a twenty-mile walk under fire, the white youths were nowhere in sight. I could never decide if the barrage were malicious or innocently accidental.

Next summer I joined a street-paving gang. Big for my age and growing strong, I saw no reason why I could not pick up six bricks from the wagon and carry them to the bricklayers throughout a full working day. I'd heard grown men call this hard labor, and for the first hour I laughed to myself at their weakness. Then I realized that either the others had speeded up or I had slowed down, and I wondered if somebody hadn't started bringing in bars of lead. After a couple of hours, I was puffing and sweat poured off me. The foreman, a friend of Dad's, came over laughing and told me to take a break. I was glad to oblige. With short rest periods every hour, I managed to make it through the day.

Right after dinner I fell into bed, exhausted. It seemed I had hardly closed my eyes before Mother called me to get up. It was six in the morning. I arose slowly, stifling a groan, for my body was so sore and stiff it felt like a great big boil. Nevertheless I managed to dress and get to the job on time, to the surprise of the entire gang. Frankly, I didn't feel up to it, but I was determined not to be a quitter. I intended to work even if it killed me—and that now seemed possible. After an hour of torture which equaled anything Torquemada[6] could have dreamed up, the foreman suggested I switch to pouring tar. I literally leaped at the chance; I'd have been willing then to fight a tiger with my bare hands rather than tote bricks.

I had to be dressed especially for this job, legs and feet wrapped in several thicknesses of burlap and a pair of thick, padded gauntlets on my hands. The foreman demonstrated how properly to hold a coal scuttle, draw boiling tar through a spigot in the vat, and slosh it over the newly set bricks with little splash. Physically, it was far easier than handling those damned bricks, but this job had its own hazards. Hot tar spattered in all directions, especially if the scuttle was held too high when I let go with a wide sweeping motion through a semicircle. That evening when I got home I had amassed a small army of burns on arms, hands, and legs that turned to blisters overnight. Next morning I was sore in an entirely different way. But through sheer bullheadedness (I told you I was a Capricorn), I nevertheless staggered through the month-long week, then drew my pay and told the gang goodbye. I had proven to myself that at thirteen I could do hard physical labor like a grown man if I wanted to. However I saw no need to run it into the ground. The rest of that summer was spent manicuring white people's lawns.

I also joined the first black Boy Scout troop formed in my home town. Scoutmaster was a young, soft-spoken, dark brown man named Travis Dean who worked for the ice plant. I managed to get together all essential equipment including a pup tent and made my own sleeping bag. I looked forward eagerly to overnight camping trips with only three or four boys. These hikes I considered quite educational for I learned how to roll my own cigarettes and smoke a pipe. In town I had to be careful for fear of being caught, although periodically a bunch of us would go snipe hunting. This meant walking along looking down for only partially smoked cigarette butts or snipes. When we had collected all we needed, we'd make it to some vacant lot or unoccupied house and have a group smoke-in. When the snipes were gone, somebody would pass around Sen-Sen to kill our breath and we'd go home. How we avoided picking up some contagious disease from these discarded butts is still a mystery. But on overnight hikes, away from grownups, we never had to worry about being caught, nor did we smoke snipes.

Since I was still primarily a loner, I diligently studied the Scout manual, getting my Second Class badge in the minimum time, and was soon ready for First Class tests. But there I ran into a problem. The required fourteen-mile hike was a snap; one morning I walked to Winfield, fifteen miles away, intending to return by trolley. Then I thought long and hard over what I could do with that half buck I would spend for fare, and after three hours rest decided to walk back home that afternoon. The problem was in my swimming test.

There was no place for us to swim. The facilities at Paris Park and the new municipal pool were barred to us. We had only the two swiftly moving rivers on both sides of town, and both Mother and Dad had impressed on me their danger. Already two boys I knew had drowned in them that year. (Incidentally, this explains why so many blacks of my generation never learned how to swim.) Scoutmaster Dean dumped the problem in the lap of the citywide scouting council, which had never before faced such a dilemma. After kicking it around for several weeks, that resourceful group brilliantly decided that rather than allow a nigger to pollute the water of their sacred pools, they would waive this requirement and allow me to become a First Class Scout without this basic test. I went on to win merit badges, and so far as I know I may be the only person in America to become an Eagle Scout without learning how to swim.

6

The blues? We were formally introduced when I was eight; even then I had the feeling we weren't really strangers. So when the blues grabbed me and held on, it was like meeting a long-lost brother.

Other major events occurred that same year. Granny suffered a stroke and died. I learned THE difference between boys and girls, and I got my first buddy. Despite my growing affair with books, I did need a close friend my age.

When Granny, then past eighty, became paralyzed and unable to move her left arm and legs, she was placed in the iron bed in the front room beside a window. For seven months her world was condensed to the family, occasional visitors, and what little she could see beyond the glass pane. By day she sat propped against a wooden chair laid across the bed and softened by a pillow. At night the chair was removed and she rested flat on her back. It must have been a grimly monotonous existence, this endless waiting, for she could neither read nor write. Yet she never complained and was convinced until her death that she would recover. I think her determination to regain control of her limbs was motivated largely by her promise to give me the licking of my life "for being so sassy." As for me, I was ambivalent. Despite her mastery of the rod, I loved her and wanted her to recover, but at the same time I did not look longingly toward her promised use of the switch. I confess a feeling of sincere regret tempered with genuine relief when she passed away one morning while I was at school.

Mother had the job of lifting Granny bodily and placing her atop the bedpan. Usually I was sent out of the room, but one afternoon they forgot and I lingered. Finally noticing, they ordered me out—too late. I had made the shattering discovery that everybody was not alike.

I was puzzled. Were all girls this way or just elderly females like Granny? Were they born with this strange physical condition or did it happen when they grew old? I couldn't ask anybody at school since this was summer, and at the time there were no other kids living in the neighborhood. I didn't dare question either parent; once before I had asked Mother where babies come from, and she hemmed and hawed before finally telling me, in the pattern of that period, "You'll find out when you're older." There had also been the time when I saw Aunt Hattie nude from the waist up and stared in wonder at those jiggling globes on her chest until she called Mother who gave me a real bawling out.

But a couple of weeks later a white family moved next door with a boy my age and his four-year-old sister. I asked him about it the day after we got acquainted. He informed me girls were born different and with the directness of eight proved it graphically with his little sister. It was amazing to learn from him that all human females had holes.

"Girls just gotta be different from boys," he explained, "or else they couldn't fuck."

Yes, but what in the world was fuck?

"Oh, that's something grown-ups do."

Since I wasn't adult, I let it drop. But later that day I began brooding. How did they do it? Why? I questioned him again. But he wasn't much help. He knew only that the areas from which people "made water" were somehow involved.

I tried to figure it out for myself. After much pondering, I came up with what I considered the logical answer. Grown-ups must put their mouths on each other down there. That had to be it, and also explained why boys and girls were different: if they were alike, there would be no incentive. I didn't understand why they had to, but presumed I'd know when I became adult. Frankly, I was proud of myself for solving this strange riddle. And more significantly, this undoubtedly triggered my lifelong oral orientation; it had to start somewhere.

Before summer ended the white family moved away to be replaced by Afro-Americans. For the first time, we had our own kind as neighbors. They were the Perrys, and there were five of them: three girls, a boy, and the mother. Mrs. Perry was light brown, wore her hair in a bun, was pigeontoed, and walked as if she were stepping on eggs costing two dollars a dozen. She had the mountainous task of working all day for a white family and trying to rear four kids with only the token help of their father who cooked someplace in Oklahoma and made infrequent trips to see his brood. The girls were Mary, oldest and quiet; Esther, raucous and sexy; and Daisy, cowed by the emotional weight of the others. In between the two younger girls was Donald, a slender hellion who waged a constant fight for masculine identity among all those females and who became my first buddy.

Don and I were both eight, but there the similarity ended. He cussed, found things before they were lost, and played hooky from school. I suppose I was fond of him because he did everything I didn't dare. He was also a good friend to fight with, usually with fists but occasionally with a handy tree limb. But we never let such discomforts as black eyes and bloody noses interfere more than momentarily with the relationship we both needed—particularly when we ran into small gangs of bellicose white boys. It was also Don who helped my theory on copulation.

Gradually I became friendly with other rainbow boys, among them a very dark lad with a high, loud voice. His name, ironically enough, was Solomon, and one day he wised us up on how babies were born.

"It's simple," said Solomon solemnly. "A man gits on top of a woman, sticks his thing in , does it to her an' that's how they gits babies."

"That's all there is to it?" one of us asked.

"Yea, that's all."

"How long you gotta wait before a baby comes?"

Solomon looked patronizingly at his interrogator and with the calm voice of authority replied, "You don't."

"Nah," he sounded exasperated. How could we be so stupid? "They gits birthed right away." He became quite confidential. "One night on Uncle Mack's farm down in Tennessee, I heard a noise in the next room. It was bedsprings creakin'. Uncle Mack and Aunt Millie thought I was asleep. So I gits up an' tiptoes to the door an' peeks in through the keyhole. There they was, moanin' and groanin' and grindin'. But when Uncle Mack is all through an' starts to git up, he can't. He looks down an' there hangin' on to his pecker with both hands was a brand new baby. He'd gone and made hisself another child."

It sounded strange even to imaginative eight- and nine-year olds, but who were we to question the authority of an eyewitness?

That was our concept of procreation until, several days later, older boys set us straight. We went immediately as a kind of committee to Solomon's house to discuss this new information which differed so drastically from what he swore he had seen, but learned he had just been shipped off permanently to—it pains me to say—Uncle Mack's farm in Tennessee.

During the same period that I was acquiring initial sex misinformation, I became conscious of the blues and evolving jazz. It's quite logical to discuss sex and jazz together; the music had developed for dancing, and people went to shindigs for close contact with members of the opposite sex which, with luck and opportunity, might end up in bed. Further, jazz meant both a kind of music as well as the sex act itself. It was obvious what the composer had in mind when he wrote "Jazz Me Blues."

After Granny died, Mother and Dad took me one Friday night to the monthly dance at the little Knights of Pythias Lodge Hall.[7] They had no choice; all the Perrys were out, and there was no place to park me. Neither parent danced. They were both good Baptists, and if you were a Baptist you'd damned well better not dance. But Dad was a lodge officer and had to be present; evidently it was not a sin to listen to dance music. However, if Old Satan lured you to the floor, you'd hear about it next Sunday from the pulpit. Reverend Woods, a heavy-set man with a pockmarked face and a fire alarm voice, would all but read you out of the congregation, and if you were behind in dollar donations even that might happen.

Most of the dancing young belonged to the African Methodist Episcopal Church (AME) which was far less strict. Both congregations carried on an ecclesiastical civil war. Close friends during the week drew battle lines on Sunday. Each was certain his denomination rode the only highway to heaven—although one young man named Ernest Sawyer who belonged to the AME Church would sometimes get drunk Sunday afternoon and attend Baptist services that evening where he would help lead the singing and put a greenback in the collection. But, generally speaking, AMEs were contemptuous of the harsh regulations and total immersion of the Baptist faith; the latter looked upon Methodists and their dainty sprinkling ritual as only a few degrees above complete damnation. A popular story of the period told of a Methodist meeting a Baptist on the street. "When you die, you going to heaven?" the Methodist asked. "Of course," replied the Baptist, "if I don't drown first."

The walk from home to the lodge hall took twenty minutes. I lagged behind so I could look at Dad. When he was togged down he wore a blue serge, box back suit with the coat hanging in a rectangle from his broad shoulders, and the edges of the box were pressed sharp enough to shave with. His trousers were voluminous peg tops tapering to narrow cuffless bottoms breaking once above highly polished, long shoes—"Stetson last" he called them. On his head a derby perched jauntily. He looked as slick as a sweet man from Saint Louis and could have been the sartorial inspiration for "Dying Gambler's Blues."

A small hall was on the second floor of an old wooden building on the northern edge of the business district. Overhead hung paper Japanese lanterns softening the light on ancient former church pews and hard straight-backed chairs lining the walls. A small room on one side of the entrance was set apart for refreshments. Two ice-filled tubs cooled soda pop selling for a nickel. A bowl of hot Mexican chili cost a dime, and a plate of barbecued ribs with cole slaw went for fifteen cents. At the far end of the main hall was a tiny stage. Bass, snare drums, and elementary cymbals sat before an empty chair. Alongside was a battered upright piano. Relaxing on the stool, tossing up a big golden doughnut of a watch and catching it, was an elongated, sadfaced, ginger brown man.

"That's Texas Slim," Dad said. "Sure glad he's here tonight."

Shortly, a big, broad, buffalolike man sat down at the drums and unleashed a quiet roll. Slim pushed his watch into his vest pocket, turned facing the piano, made a couple of brief, exploratory right-hand runs, and began pounding out a slow, bleeding blues.

That was the whole orchestra, piano and "traps," but nothing more was needed. After the first few bars, I was hooked for life. Even at the age of eight, I knew this music was part of me. I'd had the usual exposure to concert and operatic recordings at white neighbors' homes, band recitals at Wilson Park, and the classic songs taught at school; but that was generally boring. I rarely felt even minimal emotional kinship with that kind of music. I did not relate. But the blues—well, this I understood. I dug it in a way impossible with the most brilliant concepts of Wagner and Verdi and Chopin. All that was alien; the blues talked my language. The blues were basic, vital black music; the rapport was natural.

Eventually I noticed couples on the narrow floor, performing what I later learned was the "Hesitation Schottische." The schottische was a dance originating in Scotland, but not even a Scotch-soused Scot could have dreamed what would happen when Duskymerica grabbed hold.

Couples danced in line, moving slowly two abreast. Leaders were a man known as "Foots" and his girlfriend. Foots called the set moves, but the actual rhythm of the dancers is as hard to describe as an old Louis Armstrong trumpet solo. On command they strutted, turned right or left, executed complicated double-time steps, about-faced, tapped toes and heels in unison, danced backward, swayed, then broke into more double-time. Finally Foots shouted, "Slow drag it, everybody," and the couples turned face to face to dance closely with their bodies, feet hardly moving. When the leader yelled, "Quit it an' git wit' it," they returned to their original patterns.

Texas Slim told a basic, gripping story on the keys, and I could have listened all night. At last he stopped, and I came back from wherever you go when something sends you out of this world. I turned and saw Dad looking at me with an odd smile.

"Kinda liked that, didn't you, boy?" he asked. "I'm glad you do. I was beginnin' to think you din't like nothin' but readin' and eatin'."

He told me that white people knew nothing about the blues which he said was "colored folks' music and workin' people's at that." He'd first heard the blues down in Texas, and he liked them because they said what he felt and couldn't express.

Slim and his drummer broke into fast ragtime as a change of pace, but the blues were their meat. They were shuffling slow, shaking medium tempo or hopping fast with roaring bass (later known as boogie woogie), but they were all stewed in the same salty urgency.

Texas Slim also sang in a voice dark as licorice and rough as untanned leather. I still remember the first I ever heard:

My mama tol' me, my papa tol' me too
I say my mama tol' me, my papa tol' me too
Don't let no yelluh woman make a fatmouth outta you.

Afterward I went regularly to the monthly dances, even when I was old enough to stay home alone. Maybe there'd be another piano player floating through town, but unless he could beat it out mean and low-down, he was nowhere. For some six months the duo expanded to a trio with the addition of an itinerant saxophonist who was also indigo steeped, but most of the time it was just piano and trap drums.

As I grew older and more discerning, I discovered that often the sound of an unaccompanied vocal blues was disturbingly close, both rhythmically and harmonically, to the gospel singing at Second Baptist Church, especially at revival meetings and on Testifying Sunday.

Testifying Sunday was the first morning service each month. There was no sermon. Instead members stood up and told how their religion had helped them fight their battles. On a day when the meeting caught fire, it might last five or six hours. Somebody would start a rousing spiritual or jubilee song (they were all a capella, often with a verse sung by the leader of the moment and unison response), a stirring hell and brimstone prayer would follow, and strong religious fervor would cascade over everybody. Inhibitions vanished. Amid a wild but somehow rhyth-mic cacophony of shouts and shrieks, men and women rose in turn, faces lighted by fire within, to speak in praise of their Lord. Brothers cried, sisters wept for joy. Sometimes a sister ran screaming up and down the aisles, falling finally in a faint, her arms and legs jerking convulsively as others nearby fanned her face. Service never stopped; if anything, it in-creased in intensity. "Yes, I know my Redeemer lives" cut through a joyous shout, and others carried on with "Amen!" "Speak, Brother!" Only with the entire assemblage exhausted and wrung out would the meeting end.

There were cynics who swore some of the fainting females planned everything in advance. If, for instance, Sister Brown was sore at Sister White, she'd become filled with the Holy Ghost and run shouting down the aisles until she reached Sister White's pew. Then with a wild cry she'd fling out her arm and clip Sister White on the kisser as she fell in a faint. Of course the victim would be skeptical of Sister Brown's holy seizure, thinking the devil had entered the act, but she had no recourse until next Testifying Sunday when she would become possessed and reap her re-venge by bopping Sister Brown.

I might add that a shouting sister more than once had been known to faint in the arms of a church brother for whom she had an unholy desire. Maybe that's what was meant by applied religion.

From the songs and vocal style heard on Testifying Sunday and at revival meetings, I got the same kind of pulse-quickening charge that shot through me when Texas Slim laid it on. This bothered me for I had been taught that a "sinful song" had nothing in common with spirituals and jubilees. But this was false. Years later I learned that black secular and religious songs were opposite sides of the same cultural coin, and those who sang them unconsciously applied the same strong surviving African-isms, shaping both into a distinctive black music, a major segment of common group heritage. With only a change of verbal content, Mahalia Jackson's spirituals of the period between World Wars I and II could pass for the blues of Texas Slim I had grown to love.[8]

Until white America gave an approving pat, spirituals, blues, and jazz were noisily rejected by Negro "strivers" as a group. Although re-grettable, it was understandable. In the nervous fight of that era for white acceptance, and to prove they were no different, really, from Caucasians except for the happenstance of color, it was then fashionable for souls trying to be "cultured" to condemn such music as "low class" and "a disgrace to our people." They felt that if they showed by actions and interests they were the same as whites, they would be accepted as equals. So they tried mightily to become carbonized Caucasians, doing their utmost to wash away their black identity, both physical and cultural. This opened the door for smart operators (most of them white) to become millionaires by dangling the promise of eradicating physical differences. Sales of skin bleaches, lip thinners, and hair straighteners were gigantic. As a child more than once I had my hair fried with hot combs wielded by friends of Mother's, and during high school I bought several Satin Tops, a chemical process for removing all kinks, from the town's barber. How-ever, I gave this up forever after leaving home.

But I was never caught in the no-blues-trap. Dad, strictly of the laboring class, and Granny, an ex-slave, being farthest down on the social scale, felt no compulsion to indiscriminately copy white culture. They did not fight surviving Africanisms. I was able therefore to avoid the hypocrisy of those who publicly condemned black music while getting their kicks on the sly. Later I observed some of the loudest dusky detrac-tors virtually pat a hole in the floor when they thought nobody was looking.

So I listened all I could. I heard traditional blues verses whose origin nobody knew, as well as the latest compositions making their way to Arkansas City or concocted by those around me. I learned gradually that, to catch on, blues lyrics had to be vital, real, and had to mirror group experiences. I memorized the explicit sex verses which the other boys and I sang over and over among ourselves, not only because we liked them but because they were forbidden by our parents. They were a kind of springboard for our group miseducation about sex.

At the age of puberty, painfully conscious of strong new hungers released in our bodies, we had no grown-ups to give us guidance. In this respect, black parents were as deficient as white parents. Maybe they hoped that, if they closed their eyes and plugged their ears, our need for knowledge would vanish. Of course this didn't happen. Their silence, instead, made it possible for us to accept weird myths and develop our own juicy and expressive vocabulary.

However, one activity was sure to bring a severe lecture from the old man. That was when a boy was caught "playing with himself." To hear an irate father tell it, never in his whole life had he jacked off and it was a "shame and disgrace" to whomp your own. Boys who masturbated "ruined their health," became "weak and sickly," and were likely to end up "in the crazy house." These beliefs, oddly enough, were supported by many physicians, with leading medical authorities writing dissertations and books on this "nefarious evil."

Of course any luckless lad caught in the act would be properly repentant and promise the old man he would never, never do it again. Sometimes he'd even keep the promise for two or three days.

Many boys never admitted indulging, even to their closest friends, but there were a brazen few who kept no secrets from their buddies. Proud of their ability, they often slipped away to a vacant house or some secluded spot and staged contests to see who could ejaculate the greatest distance. And should a new boy between twelve and fourteen come to town and want to join the gang, he would first be initiated by being grabbed and held down on the ground by two or three kids while another masturbated him to climax.

Older youths who had been through all this had a standard routine which worked with the unwary young who swore they never indulged. Two or three would get a green lad of twelve or thirteen alone and ask, "Boy, do you jack off?" The answer was an outraged "No." Whereupon the interrogator gravely said, "That's good, 'cause if you do a hair will start growing in the palm of your hand." Nine times out of ten the younger boy immediately opened his hand to take a quick glance at his palm. The older fellows doubled in derisive laughter. "If you don't jack off, how come you looked at your hand?" one finally gasped, and their victim would drop his eyes and grin sheepishly as he realized he had been tricked. I know, because I was once caught in this fashion. However, I was never discovered performing this act. I'd probably have dropped dead of mortification if anyone had; I was so shy that even in high school I was embarrassed when other lads saw me nude in the shower after physical education classes. This, too, was a manifestation of the inferiority complex being hammered into me by the white world.

All of this, however, was part of growing up, and we learned many things from each other by comparing notes, listening to conversations of older lads, and from an occasional bit accidentally dropped by a parent. Our mothers and fathers would have been shocked into sudden senility had they heard us talking at length among ourselves, but we took great pains to avoid using our expressive jargon around our elders. When a forbidden word accidentally slipped out, it meant a trip to the woodshed. But among ourselves, a large part of our conversation dealt with sex.

Our juicy vocabulary included few dictionary words. Some of what we said would have been unintelligible to whitey. Had anybody said "coitus" in front of us, he would have received a blank stare. But we all knew what it meant to "jazz a jane," "whip that jellyroll to a fare-thee-well," or "get a piece of tail" or ass. A woman had a "pussy," "peehole," "poontang," "sack-a-madam," or "booty" (in school we giggled naughtily when the teacher told how Romans burned and sacked conquered cities after gathering all the booty). She also had a "cock." When we learned whites used that term for the male organ, we felt contempt for their dumbness. The penis was a "prick," "dick," "jock," "peter," or "pecker." It was never a "cock."

I suppose some of the fellows I grew up with have never yet heard of a clitoris, but at an early age we talked about a "purr-tongue" or a "boy-in-the-boat." Since our meaning of the key word was the exact opposite of common parlance elsewhere, a cocksucker logically engaged in cunnilingus. Fellatio was beyond our ken, but we all knew what happened when a person "gobbled the goo." Anybody with both male and female characteristics was a morfydyke, and a bulldagger screwed other women just like a man. All such people, incidentally, were freaks.

Anal intercourse was "cornholing," and funky was not a way of playing jazz music but described the odor of unwashed genitalia. Nobody was ever pregnant. A babe was "knocked up"; when we were quite polite we spoke of her as being "in family way" or "mother way."

If you wanted to drive a gal wild you put on a French Tickler; to avoid "blue balls," a dose, or sores with a strange broad you used either a Fish Skin or a thin rubber called a Merry Widow. But there really wasn't much point in dodging claps; you weren't a man until you'd had at least one dose. Besides, it wasn't any worse than a bad cold. A male with a small penis was "too little in the poop." And the only time you could knock up a gal was right before or during her "monthlies."

From all the secret talk among us and our new desires, most of us were eager for our first piece—and scared to get it. Some found a compromise. They bought big rag dolls that looked like girls or swiped them from their sisters, cut a hole in the proper place, then banged the hell out of them in private. Imagination is a wonderful gift.

Around girls our age we assumed an aggressive boldness. We learned sex verses to blues tunes and retained them far longer than lessons in school. We sang them around young females with salacious snickers, fully aware of who could be trusted not to tell their parents. The young things snickered back, just as salaciously.

To the tune of W. C. Handy's "Hesitation Blues" we'd chant:

> Got a hole in my shoe
> Got a hole in my sock
> A bowlegged woman's
> Got a hole in her cock;
> Oh tell me how long
> Do I have to wait?
> Can I get it now
> Or must I hesitate.

I suppose if some "fast" little chick had sung back: "You don't have to hesitate, I'm ready for you right now," most of us would have fainted from fright. Not all, because a few got in the groove real early, but those who "signified" by singing loudest would have run home and hid.[9]

We had a number of little jingles we habitually sang to each other whenever our gang gathered:

> Before I pay a dollar for cock
> I'll let my dick get hard as a rock

> I'll cut it off an' stick it in the flo'
> An' keep it there 'til booty gits low.

Or maybe it would be:

> Ol' Aunt Dinah sittin' on a rock
> Shavin' all the hairs off her big fat cock
> Razor slipped an' you know what it do?
> It cut that good stuff half in two.

When we were fifteen or so and smoking fairly regularly, we had a special recitation before bumming a "coffin nail" or "pimp stick":

> All you whores come fall in line
> Goin' down to the river to wash your behind
> I ain't lyin' and I ain't jokin'
> One o' you dudes better give me some smokin'.

We also learned how to "hooraw," a vocal pastime consisting of poking fun at another boy's physical peculiarities. You prepared your own comeback while your opponent of the moment spouted off to the uproarious delight of the listeners. Sometimes a victim would become fightin' mad, but usually it ended in a draw with the gang passing on to some other activity.

I recall once when somebody was hoorawing Napoleon Berry, a slow-talking youth who ordinarily was quiet. The topic was ugliness.

"You know," the other guy sounded off, "you ain't ever gonna die. You're just gonna ugly on away from here."

"Talkin' about looking bad," Napoleon came back in a slow drawl, "when you was made it was done on the installment plan. You had to show up on diff'rent days to get all your parts. But somehow you got the days all mixed up. You made a mistake and came on face day for your ass and on ass day for your face. Now you're always constipated 'cause when a good shit gets started it don't know which way to go."

My first opportunity to score with a girl came late in my thirteenth summer, the year I worked on the street-paving gang. The place was Coffeyville, Kansas. Annually Dad received a railroad pass, and I visited his numerous relatives for a week. I liked Coffeyville; I always got a girlfriend as soon as I hit town. The black population was four or five times larger than that of Arkansas City, and Coffeyville itself was twice as big. Furthermore, Dad's kin lived in the heart of the west side ghetto. Because I was a new boy and a stranger, the little neighborhood gals would fall over their young selves to solicit my attention. At home I wasn't interested in any of the available girls, but in Coffeyville I made up for lost time.

This year there was one sassy little chick who staked a strong claim as soon as I arrived. Her name was Irene, and she was a year older than I, light brown, good looking, aggressive, and sexy. She lived a couple of blocks away and during the day took care of a younger brother and sister while her parents worked. Next door to me lived a lad named Ernest who, although only ten, was my main playmate. Everyday we went over to Irene's house.

On the third day Irene announced we were going to play mama and papa. We went back to her parents' bedroom and began roughhousing on the unmade bed. Shortly she shooed out her brother and sister to visit in the next block and sent Ernest on an errand that would tie him up for almost an hour. Now that we were alone, she pulled the sheets back, lay down, grabbed my arm and yanked me over on the bed, then started kissing me. We'd kissed before but they'd been quick pecks, nothing drawn out like this. I felt queer.

In a few moments she stopped and lay flat on her back.

"Get on top of me, face down," she commanded.

"What for?" I asked.

"Well," she said coyly, "I just wanna see how much longer you are than me."

"But I already know," I protested. "I'm two inches taller." Then I got up and sat in a chair until Ernest returned. I knew what she had in mind, but I was just plain scared.

However, this failure did not discourage Irene. The night before I was to return home, she tried again. Ernest and I were playing in front of his house shortly after dark, and I looked up to see Irene and a girlfriend strolling leisurely by, arm in arm and giggling. Irene called Ernest, whispered something to him as both girls giggled even more, then walked on.

Ernest came directly to me.

"I got a message for you. Irene told me to tell you that if you want some, meet her at the Wilcox barn in half an hour."

Well, here it was, my moment of truth. At last I had a chance to do what some of my friends already bragged about. I thought of the time we'd sung those verses to "Hesitation Blues" in front of the girls in Arkansas City. I could take home a story and be a hero with the gang. In my mind I could hear them saying with awe, "ol' Frank got his first piece." Even the older lads would be forced to respect me when the word got around.

But there was one drawback. I simply didn't have the nerve. My knees weakened, and my stomach went in for advanced acrobatics as I contemplated the actual act. Instead of becoming hard with anticipation, I think the poor little thing must have crawled up inside my abdomen to hide in fright.

An hour passed while I played uneasily and halfheartedly with Ernest. Then Irene and her friend, evidently tired of waiting, strolled by again. They stopped on the sidewalk and called me. I started sweating as I walked reluctantly over.

"Frank," Irene began, "didn't you tell Ernest you wanted some of my poontang? I'm ready an' waiting."

I looked at her for one of those eternal moments. I thought, what the devil is wrong with me? A gal I'm nuts about flings it at me, and I'm too big a coward to accept. I wish I was back home!

Finally, I spoke.

"No, I didn't tell Ernest any such thing." And as I uttered the fatal words, I was mentally kicking myself with size fifteen boots as I shrank to four inches high. I despised myself for acting like a sissy, but I could not help it.

Irene and her pal laughed scornfully. "Fraidy cat," Irene said derisively and walked on, wriggling her hips. Her companion looked back at me with complete contempt, as if I were some kind of crawling creature. My face felt as if it were inside a roaring furnace, and I was visibly trembling.

I was so unnerved I was actually sick to my stomach. I had to quit playing and go directly to bed. Next day on the train I called myself every kind of chump I could think of. Then an idea flashed. Since Don Perry and the rest of the gang would not know the truth, why not tell them I had banged my first broad? Then I'd get the reputation anyway. By the time I reached Arkansas City I had my lie ready.

As soon as I saw the fellows, I tried to look both wise and cool. When they asked about my trip, I spouted off about this hot little mama who wouldn't leave me alone.

"Man, I almost had to fight her off," I bragged. "She kept begging me to take her on. She even pulled me in bed and tried to make me get on top of her. She hung around and bothered me all the time I was in Coffeyville."

"What'd you do?" Don asked.

"Well, las' night I broke down an' tapped that thing."

"You mean you actually got a piece?" somebody asked me with awe.

"Of course," I said casually, as if it were a habit with me.

"How was it?"

"Man, it was great!" I rolled my eyes and sighed.

It was just my luck that an older youth of about eighteen, who already had a reputation as a cocksman, chose to wander up and hear part of the conversation.

"How long did you last?" he asked curiously.

Why in hell did a kibitzer have to show up at this precise moment? I hadn't counted on this kind of question. So I fished around wildly in my mind and hooked what I prayed would be a satisfactory answer.

"Oh, 'bout an hour." I tried to sound matter of fact.

"You mean you screwed this jane for 'bout an hour before you shot off?" he asked in a significantly quiet voice.

"More or less," I said, but I realized I didn't sound quite convincing.

He almost ruptured a blood vessel laughing scornfully, and I was wishing he would. Meanwhile I stood looking at him, a silly grin on my face, waiting for some kind of blow to fall.

"You ain't nothing but a bag of wind and you know you's lying," he finally said. "You couldn't last more'n five or maybe ten minutes—an' even that's longer'n most. You might fool these tadpoles," he went on, waving his hand toward the younger boys who by now were laughing just as derisively as they gazed into my flushed and embarrassed face, "but you gotta put down somethin' straighter'n that for an old ace like me. You ain't never had nothin' but ol' Minnie Five Fingers!"

7

I have no nostalgia for my school days. Generally speaking, they were pretty drab. I was almost fanatically religious, accepting the literal fundamentalist interpretation of the Bible put before us by our pastor. I found no conflict between religion and the sex vocabulary I used around other boys for nobody told me it was a sin to use four-letter words. In fact, our pastor had seemingly charted our course in a sexless sea for he never referred to anything erotic except to make an occasional snide remark from the pulpit about "running after other men's wives" when some brother was caught in the wrong place at the wrong time. At twelve I was baptized. Then I taught Sunday school and was assistant BYPU [Baptist Young People's Union] superintendent. Oh, I smoked secretly and took an occasional swig of Choc beer, which was almost the standard drink of that region. Apparently, it was brew originating among the Choctaw Indians, and it kicked like a happy mule.

I was what the town's parents pointed to as a "good boy." None of them ever heard me cuss, and I didn't gamble or steal or get into the kind of mischief usually expected of a teenager. Although I was crazy about jazz and the blues, I neither danced nor dated. For this there was an excellent reason; in girls I desired only the unattainable. Only two interested me. One was a teasin' brown gal, bowlegged but nevertheless very sexy and pretty, named Lillian. She was the girlfriend of a stud called Drummy who was four or five years older than I and one of the wildest and toughest youths in that part of the state, so all I dared do was wish. The other was Alline Brown, a luscious lass who went to school in Kansas City and spent her summers at home with her family. But she was dated regularly by DeFrantz Williams, a year ahead of me in school and with a gift of gab none of the rest of us could match. Frustration here, too. In addition I had this growing oral fixation, an activity condemned by everybody I knew.

Of course there were many white chicks who made my tongue hang out, but I wasn't ready to commit suicide. The town's mores prevented saying hello to a white girl in public even though you had been in the same class together since the first grade. Twice in junior and senior high, black lads were beaten up after school by white boys swearing their dusky victims had "insulted" some Caucasian co-ed. Once in the eighth grade, the principal had to step in and by firm action avert what loomed as a potential gang battle between the handful of black students and a group of honkey youths. I laboriously filed and sharpened a six-inch steel railroad spike which I carried with me until tensions eased. I prepared for violence—which would have been started, as usual, by whites.

With but one or two exceptions, as a group we were tolerated by white kids on campus, but away from the school we were customarily treated as if we were invisible. More than once I surprised white high school couples enthusiastically fornicating at night in secluded areas of both parks; they cowered in fear and guilt until they saw my brown face, then resumed as if they were alone. Once, while delivering handbills, I stepped on a porch and looked through the window at three couples, stripped down to underclothing and drinking. I recognized all of them as students in my classes, but they, too, glanced in my direction then continued as if they had seen nobody. In the boys' lavatory, I would often hear white youths comparing notes and bragging about their conquests, or filling previously used condoms with water to test for leaks with an eye to reuse before discarding.

However, should you by chance see a white girl alone you often became human. One Saturday I ran into an appealing damsel named Hortense I'd been wild about for a couple of years. It was at the drinking fountain in Wilson Park, and nobody else was within a block. She smiled and spoke. I was stunned but recovered quickly. We laughed and talked for at least ten minutes, and when we parted I had to stoop down to touch the moon. Monday I saw her in the hall at school. For the moment forgetting prevailing patterns, I grinned and spoke. She neither changed expression nor opened her mouth. I was again the invisible man.

I had far better luck with jazz than with the janes. The first live band I ever heard was a white five-piece outfit from Kansas City, the Kuhne-Chaquette Jazz Band, which came to Arkansas City to play at some local celebration. Trombone, C-Melody sax, drums, banjo, and accordion comprised this group. Present also were a large string orchestra and a military band, but when the jazz boys cut loose, especially with "Alcoholic Blues," the crowd came running to dig these exciting and strange new sounds. Shortly afterward I visited my grandfather in Wichita and raved for weeks after hearing W. C. Handy and his Orchestra of Memphis with a woman blues singer. Following the exodus from New Orleans when the cops cleaned up Storyville, a band gigged in Arkansas City for a black dance at the pavilion in Paris Park.[10] I don't know its name, but I remember it had two trumpets, trombone, tuba, banjo, piano, and drums. The second trumpet was muted and soft, sounding like a sax and playing what ordinarily would have been the clarinet part; the lead horn sizzled and seared. These cats from the Delta had everybody within earshot shouting and shuffling; since we had the dance floor, whites got up and danced on the grass.

One day I came home from school and almost flipped when I found a phonograph dominating the front room. I think it was a Magnola; anyway, it had a turn-around head for Edison and Pathe discs made with a different kind of groove. Lt. Jim Europe, one of the first blacks to record, was back from World War I and making a name for himself with waxings of "St. Louis Blues," "How Ya Gonna Keep 'Em Down on the Farm," "Memphis Blues," and "It's a Long Way to Tipperary." Almost every nickel I could lay hands on went for records.[11]

I got a personal itch to make music when two blues-playing brothers near my age came to town. Their instrument was steel guitar; they used the bottom of a closed pocketknife to get low-down, whining effects, like on a Hawaiian guitar but immeasurably dirtier. I talked Dad into sending away to Slingerland for a mail-order course in Hawaiian guitar, which included the instrument, intending to rush through the basics so these brothers could teach me to moan and cry on the strings. Unfortunately for me, they moved away just before lesson no. 2 arrived. I learned how to schmaltz my way poorly through several uninteresting pop tunes, but by myself couldn't get the hang of pulling out gully-low blues. Finally I gave it up in disgust and later in Wichita became interested in tenor banjo. Finding one I liked, I traded in my guitar as a down payment; then I was too broke to continue payments and never got the banjo. It ended as a charitable gift to a music store, although I hadn't intended it that way.

But no matter; I could always listen. I was in the tenth grade in 1921, when I heard the fabulous Ma Rainey. She came to town with a carnival, starring in her Georgia Frolics sideshow. Rumor had it that she actually owned the entire carnival and was the wife of the white manager. Could be. Obviously she would have been called out on strikes had she roamed the nation trying to run the works.

Ma Rainey was acknowledged as the greatest blues singer in the world. Opening night of the one week stand the crowd around her tent was so black you had to light another match to see if the first had gone out. And, as usual in an impatient and milling crowd, tempers were short.

"Ow! Git off my feets!" I heard somebody shout.

"Put yo' feet in yo' pocket and nobody'll stand on 'em," came the reply. "There's more of you layin' on the ground than there is stickin' up in the air. Cut you off at the ankles and you's shoot up like a balloon."

"You oughta be the las' person on earth to talk about anybody, the way you looks. If I had your nose fulla nickels, I'd be rich."

"Who you talkin' to?"

"Who! Who! You ain't no owl 'cause your feet sure don't fit no limb."

"I oughta try yo' jaw."

"Can't keep you from tryin' but I bet a fat man I can sho break you of the habit."

"You clowns shut up," another said. "Ev'ry time a bunch of us gits out in public, somebody's gotta cut a hog.[12] No wonder the white folks don't want us around."

"Don't pay 'em no mind," said still another. "They's jus' woofin."[13]

Inside the bulging, breathless tent we watched the corny jokes and dancing until, at last, Ma Rainey appeared.

Ma Rainey was a large, mahogany brown woman. You first noticed her necklace. Made of highly polished five-dollar gold pieces, it glowed brazenly across her mighty bosom under the harsh overhead lights. After becoming adjusted to this fantastic sight, you paid attention to her face. Like the old people said, she was as ugly as homemade sin. But when she opened her mouth and began to sing, she made Mary Pickford seem as nondescript as a scrubwoman. She commanded a big, deep, fat-meat-and-greens voice, rich as pure chocolate, and her words told of common group experiences. It was like everybody shaking out his heart. Way, way low down it was and hurting good.

I remember her first song:

> Trouble in mind, I'm blue
> But I won't be blue always
> The sun's gonna shine
> In my back door some day . . .

She sang others, tension mounting as her lemon-squeezer voice extracted every drop of emotion from each word. One gal jerked to her feet and in a tortured voice rasped, "Great God! Stop her, somebody! I can't stand it no mo'!" We heard her only thickly, as through a dream.

When the show was over, I went out and immediately bought another ticket for a second performance. I scraped together four bits twice that week to go back and hear Ma Rainey, and each time was as thrilling as the first.

If possible, I became even wilder about blues and jazz, so when the *Crisis* magazine carried an advertisement from the new Black Swan Record Company, first of the Negro firms, seeking distributors I wrote in and began selling discs. Every month I bought one copy of each new platter and took them from house to house as demonstrators, getting orders for later delivery. I lived from month to month awaiting new waxings by Ethel Waters. When Trixie Smith came on the scene after winning a national blues singing contest, she, too, became a best-seller. I expanded to add Okeh and Paramount; Ma Rainey, Sara Martin, Mamie Smith, Clara Smith, and other early singing stars now grooved in black homes all over town. My customers wanted vocal blues; I sold few instrumental numbers. They had to buy from me for the white music stores would not stock these labels. The only top-notch black stars generally available were Mamie Smith, Fletcher Henderson, and Johnny Dunn who recorded for Columbia.

I sold records until the 1922 rail strike. Since the railroad was by far our biggest employer, the community suffered. The Santa Fe laid off its black hired hands who then had to hold on to their cash for food and housing. By now my sales had increased enough for me to begin stocking records; I suffered with the rest of Arkansas City since I had over a hundred brand new records I couldn't move, which to me represented a considerable investment. Today they would be worth a small fortune to collectors, but then they were only a headache.

The rail strike brought other changes. In an attempt to bust the lily white rail brotherhoods, Dad and brother laborers were offered jobs as locomotive engineers, flagmen, and brakesmen—duties which they often performed expertly in a pinch but from which they were officially barred by the trade unions. However, Dad convinced the others to turn down these jobs even though they meant two or three times more pay and a chance to get even with the racist brotherhoods. Dad would not play the bosses' game of putting black against white to the detriment of both, pointing out that eventually both would suffer if blacks scabbed. Instead he went into business for himself.

8

Dad opened the Dew Drop Inn, a small cafe in the basement of the Gladstone Hotel downtown. The upper floors were white in this mixed-up burgh but in the basement were two other brownskin businesses, a pool hall and a tailor shop. We didn't go upstairs, and whites didn't descend to the basement, which had outside steps leading directly up to the street. Mother and Dad spent most of their waking hours in the Dew Drop Inn, and I helped after school. And it was here that I met Eatin' John Horton.

Here's what I personally saw Eatin' John put away at different times:

1. One whole case (twelve dozen) of eggs
2. One twelve-pound ham
3. A dozen family-size pies
4. Twelve loaves of bread
5. An entire medium-size stalk of bananas
6. Two one-gallon jugs of water

You don't believe it? That's how Eatin' John made his living, converting scoffers into true believers. Those who considered such feats impossible would bet him he couldn't, only to lose. By the time I saw him, Eatin' John's reputation had extended from Kansas to Colorado, Nebraska, Oklahoma, Wyoming, and Montana, and he was finding it increasingly difficult to locate suckers. Most of the time now he merely went from town to town, charging the curious for eating demonstrations. He had turned down lucrative offers from Sells-Floto, Ringling Brothers, Barnum and Bailey, and Hagenback and Wallace circuses who wanted him for a sideshow attraction.

There was an often-told story that Eatin' John had broken these same circuses of the custom of offering all the lemonade you could drink for a dime. In those days, hawkers would stand beside washtubs full of ice-cold pink lemonade crying their specialty. Rarely could anyone consume more than two glasses even on those broiling days when the mercury stuck at 118 degrees. Through some secret formula, these pitchmen universally had hit upon a way of making their drink so cold you almost had to chip it with an ice pick.

According to the story, Eatin' John asked, "What's that for?"

"Why, it's your lemonade, of course."

"The hell you say! Pour it back."

Whereupon Eatin' John knelt down beside the tub, tilted it, and drained the contents as the hawker and onlookers stared, eyes popping and mouth gaping.

He was not a tremendously big man, standing around five ten, and I doubt that he weighed much over two hundred. His belly was not large, but he was quite broad. He looked like any ordinary black working man. You wondered how he could eat such tremendous amounts. Shortly after consuming these prodigious meals, he would retire and regurgitate. He actually digested little more than a normal man.

When I knew him, he had been hospitalized twice in the aftermath of bets which he had won. Once he ate a quantity of Portland Cement which set on his stomach, and he had to have an operation. Later he drank carbolic acid and again had to spend a few days in a hospital.

I was in Chicago when Eatin' John died around 1928. I recall reading in the New York *Times* a long feature story about his death. For years I saved it to convince those who had doubted my stories about him. I have yet to meet another who was anywhere near his equal at putting away the groceries.

Two other characters hit town and headquartered at the Dew Drop Inn, Big Skeet and Little Skeet. Big Skeet, the older, was quiet and a pool shark so talented he was rumored to have made the old maestro, Willie Hoppe, all but cry uncle. A real hustler, he traveled all around separating suckers from their loose loot. But the glamour boy was Little Skeet.

Little Skeet, around twenty-five, looked like a college lad. A professional gambler, he once let me look through a "magician's catalog" from a Chicago firm showing marked cards, loaded dice, and all kinds of paraphernalia. He often went to Oklahoma for action, once returning with five thousand dollars which he asked Dad to hold. Two weeks later he went back with one grand, sent messengers to Dad twice for the rest, and had to borrow train fare back to Arkansas City. Six days later he flashed a big wad of fifty-dollar bills. But that's the way it is with gamblers— sautéed pheasant breast today, feather soup tomorrow.

With his smooth line of chatter, women both single and married fell for Little Skeet. To top it off, he was a sharp dresser, wearing the first jazz model suit with bell-bottom trousers seen in our town. Shortly afterward, a touring company of the Miller and Lyles Broadway musical *Shuffle Along* (Noble Sissle and Eubie Blake) played at the Opera House with all the male members sporting this new style, and I, too, succumbed.[14]

This was shortly after World War I when Victorian morals started crumbling. Jazz music was the new thing. Rudolph Valentino was the great lover of the silent screen and made women sigh and soil their step-ins. A boy was a "sheik," and a girl was a "sheba." The age of the flapper and bathtub gin had come upon us.

Gals for the first time wore dresses ending inches above their knees. Although not as short as the miniskirts of the 1960s, they were far more shocking, for the break with the long skirts of the past was greater. Parents of that day predicted the wild young generation was going to the dogs. The flappers of the twenties, with short skirts and rolled hose, are the grandmothers of today who predict the wild new generation is going to the dogs.

In the early 1920s dresses were so short many girls were afraid to sit; they had to have leaning places. One woman reportedly told a small boy, "That's a pretty tie you have on, son. Wish I had a dress made out of it." Bobbed hair, with puffs concealing ears, was the popular style, which gave birth to another joke: "Why do girls wear ear puffs?" "So they'll have something new to show the men."

The young male wasn't slighted:

"Ma, what's a sheik?"

"A sheik, my child, is a guy who has to have the drawbridge raised when he floats down the river on his back."

The jazz model suit was the unofficial uniform of the sheik, "lounge lizard," "cake eater," "jelly bean," or "drugstore cowboy." The jacket was long and high-waisted, flaring out from the bottom of the rib cage down. All buttons were close together two or three inches above the navel. If double-breasted, the jacket was ornamental rather than functional, with the two sides touching and held together by auxiliary buttons in the holes. A vest was vitally important, usually two-toned with long points at the bottom. But it was the bell-bottom pants that counted.

In 1966 bell-bottoms made a come back, this time for both sexes. The conservative stylish of the earlier era were content with trousers skin tight at the knee then blooming wide over the shoes, but we of the bronze brigade let our imagination run wild. We opened each trouser leg twelve to fourteen inches from the bottom and sewed in contrasting cloth in red, orange, yellow, or some other vivid color. Often the cloth was accordion-pleated. Also there might be a narrow strip or two of cloth running across the insert and fastened with big buttons on both sides. Some added cords and tassles which flapped as they walked along and a few bought small metal bells which jingled with every step. Top this off with a hat turned up both front and back and a fourteen-inch cigarette holder, and you were a really sharp sheik, bound to attract the attention of the wildest sheba.

There were valid socioeconomic reasons for our flashy extreme styles, just as there were in the 1940s when we, along with Mexicans, Filipinos, and members of other repressed minorities, went in for the most eye-blasting zoot suits. Denied equality by the establishment, our clothing was a form of visual protest. For that reason I felt emotional kinship with the hippies or free people of the 1960s. In the 1920s we were rebelling against the conservative social structure, just as later the free people, the flower children, and new youth, by their nonconformist dress, mod styles, beads, and bells, rebelled against this same establishment which drove us to mass murder in Vietnam and manufactured mental robots in our sick society.

9

In addition to the revolution in morals, music, and dress after World War I, we witnessed another major change in communications. Beginning around 1922, radio broadcasting hit the scene with literally thousands of stations, some as tiny as five watts, sprouting overnight. Radio magazines flooded the newsstands, most filled with articles on how to make your own receiving sets. I made my first crystal set in 1922, winding my own coils around oatmeal boxes, and sat up night after night wearing headphones and moving a cat's whisker over a small piece of galena searching for the closest station in Wichita some fifty miles away. I had plenty of time since I was still basically a loner.

Although I was old enough to associate at will with other youths my age and spent considerable time with them at night and on weekends, these years of learning how to amuse myself alone had developed strong self-consciousness. Usually quiet and retiring, I had little to say around girls with the result that I was seldom invited to parties. Learning that many adults considered me a "queer kid" and socially "backward," even though I was a "good boy," did not flatter my ego. My inferiority complex mushroomed daily.

Through sheer necessity there had been unusually close relationships with the other three members of the black graduating quartet. A few white kids had been friendly, among them a lad named Robert Bays. He lived on the route from First Ward School to the post office, and almost every evening we walked together. Later in both junior and senior high school, he was one of the few whites I still looked upon with real affection. There had also been the Loenickes who lived next door to us for several years. First it was Mrs. Loenicke, a chiropractor, who gratuitously worked the kinks out of many childhood complaints. She also had two friendly daughters. When she left, other Loenickes moved in. This was an entire family (they were all of German ancestry, incidentally) with several sons around my age. Rug makers, they built a small shop operated by the family, frequently with me looking on. Often I accompanied them to the regular services of the Seventh Day Adventist Church, although I saw no logical reason for holding services on Saturday instead of Sunday or for eating cold food between sundown Friday and sundown Saturday. Nevertheless, I went along, with mine the only black face in the congregation, until the family moved elsewhere when I was twelve or thirteen.

Oldest of our quartet was Frank Brown whose father was janitor at the biggest bank in town. Frank also helped out after school and for short periods I filled in. At the very beginning, the senior Brown warned me not to pocket cash left "accidentally" on the floor and in tellers' cages. My honesty was being tested, he said, since supposedly "all niggers steal." Rarely a day passed when I did not gather up paper money, silver, and postage stamps left under wastebaskets, in dark corners, and on counters and place it in a pile where it would be immediately noticed the following morning. Although it did not dent the overall stereotype, undoubtedly the Browns and I disappointed some rabid racists.

At the age of seventeen, I had reached my full upward growth of six feet one inch and weighed 190 pounds. Even today I could hardly be classed as a midget. In 1922 and 1923, when average height and weight were far less than now, I was big enough, as the other boys told me, "to go bear huntin' with your fists." And yet, with generous physical attributes, in a day when all-American guards in college football sometimes weighed no more than 150, I took no part in high school athletics. The same fate befell another of the quartet, Courtland West, who was an inch or two shorter and at least twenty-five pounds heavier, most of it solid flesh obtained through hard work on his old man's farm. We were simply the wrong color. The coaches romanced white boys with far less physical equipment but looked through us. We were black and therefore invisible.

The fourth was Napoleon Berry. He decided on his own to enter the quarter-mile run in the annual interclass track and field meet, and with no formal training finished a close third behind the two regulars on the track team. Obviously he had natural ability and with coaching might have become not only the best in school but possibly a state champion. I suspect the track coach felt greatly relieved when Napoleon, in his only race, did not beat the regulars.

Thus with no possibility of even trying out for school athletic teams, we engaged only in sandlot activities, playing football and baseball among ourselves. When somebody produced a set of boxing gloves, we staged our own tournaments at night on corners under streetlights. Not only were we forced into a narrow social world but we were segregated even in sports—except at those times when black boy and white boy fought each other through anger and hate.

The sole opportunity for organized athletics came the winter before I graduated, and then on a strictly racial basis. Taking over as city YMCA secretary was a new man brought from another town. Seeing no program for black youth, he organized a Hi-Y group among us and, noting we had the talent, a basketball team. He got the high school gym where we could practice at night. I was named manager and substitute center behind Fred Higgins who was my height but much lighter in weight and greyhound fast. Frankly, he was good enough to have played center on the varsity had he been white. There was also a top-notch forward named Leroy Preston, also capable enough for the varsity. The rest of us were merely competent. But through long hours of practice, we whipped together a respectable team and scheduled a game with a black five of similar age from Wichita.

I felt somewhat below par day before the game but nevertheless intended to work out in the final practice that night. I was ready to go to the gym when Mother took one look at my face and kept me at home. I had a big fat case of mumps. To my extreme disgust, I was too sick even to attend the game. However, the contest was an important success although my team lost, mainly through inexperience. It was a great morale booster, not only for the players but for the town's black population, most of whom had never before had any reason to set foot inside the high school gym. Later that year we went to the tournament at Wichita where we lost immediately at the soda fountains. Most of the boys had never before tasted an ice cream soda or a chocolate malt; they so gorged themselves on these unaccustomed gastronomic delights they could hardly move around on the court.

Shortly after the tournament, the secretary was fired by the YMCA board for "spending too much time with them nigger kids. We didn't hire you for that."

There had been only one black youth prior to our graduation to participate in extra-curricular activities. He was DeFrantz Williams who finished in 1922. His forensic ability was so outstanding the teaching staff was forced to take notice. Not only was he by far the best debater in school, he represented Arkansas City in oratorical contests and won a number of honors, including a college scholarship, and was allowed to act in the class play. Later he became a practicing attorney in Chicago.

As for me, I was aware of no special talent. Although I had no incentive to make high grades, I was looked upon as a "bright boy." Fact is, I spent little time studying anything except algebra and geometry. Since

I did not like mathematics, I tried to get it out of the way as quickly as possible and made my highest grades in this field. I had known for some time that I would go to college. Mother had finished the tenth grade— unique for a black girl of her generation in Arkansas City. Dad was determined that I get the formal education denied him. And I had an almost phobic need to get away from most of the whites I knew.

There had not been too much trouble with individual white kids in the few years before I graduated. Because of my size they meticulously avoided any one-on-one confrontation. But when together, a group of three or more, they'd make loud cracks about "niggers," "coons," "dark- ies," "Rastus," "Sambo," or "Snowball." One funny clown might tell the others, "I think it's gonna rain; I see a black cloud." But I learned to keep a poker face and act as if I were deaf. I found through experience that if I socked one, the rest would gang up on me, and they were itching for the opportunity. I also learned that if you ignored them, they would tire of the baiting and clam up. Fighting man to man was the last thing they wanted. And yet they had the audacity to chant: "Two on one. That's nigger fun."

Although I could not participate, I avidly followed the high school athletic teams, often being the only black person present at contests. But I was cured of that, too.

It happened one night during a basketball game as I sat in the midst of white spectators, as usual the only Duskyamerican, intently following the action.[15] Suddenly I found myself shoved hard to the floor. Looking up in surprised disbelief, I saw two young drunks staring belligerently down. I was conscious of giggles and a woman's voice asking, "Why'd you do that? He wasn't bothering you." One of the duo replied, "Why the hell not? Look WHAT he is!" I sprang up fighting mad. Immediately several men grabbed me and asked me to cool down. Nobody seized the drunken pair, and, except for the lone woman, nobody protested their action. I was not released until the pair staggered away and got lost in the crowd. Humiliated and disgusted, I left immediately and never again attended a game.

School officials were not above displaying raw racism. In the tenth grade, water pistols became such a schoolwide nuisance that Principal Funk (that really was his name) one day personally visited all classrooms to confiscate these toys. I was in science class, and, like the rest of the kids, I had one. Using a wicker basket, the principal stopped before each of us and asked for our pistols. He had collected a dozen or more when he came to me. Like the others, I handed mine over. Immediately the head of the school picked it up, aimed at my face, and squeezed the trigger. The class roared, of course, as water dripped from my cheeks. I was the only black student in this class—and I was the only person he humiliated. I never forgave this sadistic act of a white educator in authority making me the laughingstock of white kids.

The curriculum, of course, was designed to uphold white supremacy. In the eighth grade I studied a course called "American Beginnings in Europe." We were taught the history and cultural backgrounds of the Spanish, Portuguese, English, French, Dutch, German, and Italian peoples—every European group whose patterns had any demonstratable effect on American development. This indoctrination continued in senior high. As for my black ancestors, nothing. Seemingly, they existed like animals until slave traders brought a boatload to Jamestown in 1619, and afterwards they were meek bondsmen until Lincoln freed them after the Civil War.[16] Thus, by calculated omission, mixed public schools promoted vicious racism to maintain white supremacy.

And the students learned well these lessons in chauvinism. They were indoctrinated to feel superior not only to blacks but to oriental peoples as well.

One day in my senior year, the instructor in a current history class explained the new Oriental Exclusion Act barring Japanese from becoming American citizens.[17]

"What we should do," he commented, "is tell them we are different and can never assimilate each other's culture. Tell them we realize they are just as good as we are, and we're not barring them because we don't think they're our equals—"

"Don't tell 'em that," interrupted one of the football stars. "I know I'm better'n any Jap or Chink."

"Me, too," chorused others.

The instructor smiled. "I didn't say they really *are* as good as us, I said we ought to tell them that to make them *feel* good."

The rest of the class was satisfied; the instructor had upheld their belief in white supremacy. But I was disturbed. There were no Orientals in town, so how could my pale peers know they were "better" than Chinese or Japanese? Did they presume white skin automatically made them superior to all darker people? I had read somewhere that gunpowder was invented by the Chinese; I knew nothing else other than they were "cruel and mysterious," a conclusion reached by reading Sax Rohmer's *Fu Manchu* terror novels.[18] Of the Japanese I knew even less. However, there was one bright spot. This white chauvinism immediately made me feel kinship with Asians; if not brothers we were at least cousins.

Even older blacks were looked down upon by my young white classmates. Will Logan and his wife, originally from Mississippi, were close friends of my parents. Of course I was taught to call him *Mr.* Logan. He worked for a bank downtown, and more than once I saw white boys from school kick him or rub his balding head "for good luck." Sometimes they jokingly called him, "Will, you old son of a bitch." I also knew he was a tremendous natural fighter, with extraordinarily long arms and great speed, and had seen him in action against other black men. But to the white boys he merely grinned and answered "yessuh" and "nosuh," no matter what liberties they took. Knowing he would not have tolerated such familiarity from me or any of our quartet, I resented this double standard of accepting Uncle Tom status around whites but demanding dignity and respect from us. (However, years later my attitude was softened—but not liquidated—after friends wrote me Will died surprising the town by leaving an estate of around a quarter of a million. Seems that while he grinned and played the buffoon for Mr. Charlie, he carefully went through his boss's wastebasket nightly, rescued notations made by the banker about the condition of certain stocks and bonds, and himself bought and sold through outside agencies on the tips he found. I rejoiced in learning he had put one over on Whitey—but to me that would not be enough compensation for the loss of human dignity.)

Each of us had to work out his own technique for survival in the white world. Will Logan had been conditioned in the vile racist jungle of Mississippi, but it was rotten enough in the more liberal atmosphere of Arkansas City. We were not only outnumbered, but THEY made and administered the law. Determining when to keep quiet and when to stand up and fight back had been as important as anything taught in the classroom. I was learning how to search their faces quickly for one friend among all those pale foes, for there might come a time when my very life would depend on the accuracy of a split-second judgment. And I knew also I could be pushed to the point where I would die before yielding another inch.

What embittered me most was flagrant white hypocrisy. Virtually all aspects of daily life were geared to maintaining white supremacy. And yet, teachers, newspapers, and speakers solemnly preached the doctrine that all men are created equal as they proudly pointed toward the Declaration of Independence and the Constitution. I had come to learn the hard way that they meant only white men. I, and that tenth of the nation like me, did not have equality. Obviously the establishment intended to maintain the status quo until eternity. But why did they lie? Why did they not come out and say flatly what was in their hearts: equality was not for black people? Why did they teach about democracy and then shove me back when I sought my just share? Why is hypocrisy a strong national trait of American whites?

And yet, rotten as the system was, I realized I fared better than my black brothers only a few miles south down in Oklahoma. There segregation at that time was legal. Some towns, like Blackwell, would not allow souls to remain overnight. I'd heard of hamlets with billboards just outside city limits reading, "Nigger, read and run. If you can't read, run anyway." My town, the jumping off place for statutory jim crow, was where placards went up on trains headed south announcing, "This Coach for Colored Only." Dad had told me about Brazos Bottoms in Texas where blacks must have passes signed by Mr. Charley to come to town. He also spoke of a prosperous Negro farmer who bought the first automobile in his county in Texas. Envious whites immediately passed a law barring him from all public thoroughfares. The resourceful farmer, who owned several thousand acres, cleared a road just inside his fence and on Sundays took his family driving on his own land.

All Dixie was hard on blacks. When one boy left to spend the summer in Birmingham, several friends refused to write saying they didn't even want their mail going to Alabama. Some adults said if they owned a plantation in Georgia and one in hell, they'd sell the land in Georgia and live in hell. As for honkies around home, Dad said some of them who tried to act uppity were "so po' they couldn't po' no mo'."

Despite the hard core of vicious young white supremacists in my school, I do not now believe most of my classmates harbored personal animosity toward me or my black peers. Caught in the web of color prejudice spun by the system, they were simply indifferent. Under other mores, some might have become lifelong friends. In later years after my first two books of poetry were published, I heard from a few by mail, and they revealed a warmth I would not have believed existed. The real pity is that during those high school years, like many whites even today, they followed blindly the inhuman trail of racism.

At graduation in 1923 as I sat with my class, I knew I had been "allowed" to attend school with whites only because state law prohibited separate schools in towns that size unless blacks themselves requested them. A few years earlier, Dad had taken the lead in defeating a move by two jobless Negro former teachers to start a separate school. He knew the fallacy of "separate but equal" education; in a tiny town like ours it would have been both a cruel travesty and a tragedy. So I had struggled through to commencement. I had gone to school with some of these boys and girls sitting on the platform with me for twelve years, yet I was on speaking terms with only three or four. But now at last it was over. I was going to Wichita and to college.

I had no idea what I would study in college nor how I would make a living later. At that time, there were no black judges, congressmen, or mayors except in a few all-black villages such as Boley, Oklahoma, and Mound Bayou, Mississippi. Several cities, like Chicago and New York, boasted black alderman. For a black educator to teach in a preponderantly white public school or college was unthinkable. Many plants and industries barred us from the most menial of jobs. Organized labor was lily white. Pro sports, such as baseball, had an unshakable color bar. Tex Rickard, the mogul of boxing, would allow none of us to fight for the heavyweight title.[19] Except as blackface clowns, musicians, and a few jobs singing and dancing, the entertainment world was out of our reach. Financial institutions refused to recognize our existence. Custom and the courts enforced racism: civil rights laws and court decisions banning discrimination were scarce.

Sound black business enterprises were quite limited in number. Law, medicine, dentistry, pharmacy, the ministry, and teaching offered by far the best opportunities for the pitifully small minority who made it through college. Graduate engineers, architects, and scientists usually ended up teaching in some black school, working at service jobs, or, if they were lucky, in the post office. This situation served as the basis for one of my early poems, entitled "Giles Johnson, Ph.D.":

> Giles Johnson
> had four college degrees
> knew the whyfore of this
> the wherefore of that
> could orate in Latin
> or cuss in Greek
> and, having learned such things

> he died of starvation
> because he wouldn't teach
> and he couldn't porter.

Nevertheless, I was going to college. And if eventually I had to make my living as a flunky, I would be an educated flunky living some place other than Arkansas City.

Frank Marshall Davis at age four years

Davis's mother (1924)

Frank Marshall Davis at age nine years

High school graduation portrait (1923)

1923–1926

10

Two days after graduation I went to Wichita to live with my grandfather who had lined up a job for me.

Wichita, of course, had its two worlds, but since the city was many times larger than my hometown the black world was bigger and the color cage had wider walls. I had far more breathing space than in the depressing cell of Arkansas City. For the first time I met black doctors, lawyers, dentists, and other professional people and consorted with those my age attending college. Several small businesses were concentrated in the area immediately north of the courthouse, one of a number of ghettoes roosting on the limbs of this midget metropolis. There was also one genuine, thoroughbred African, called Prince Ranavatona (almost every African I met for many years was "prince") who occupied a kind of twilight status. Whites never fully segregated him as they did Afro-Americans, and blacks never accepted him.

My grandfather was also the only black man sailing in a white sea in his part of town, some three or four blocks south of the end of the closest streetcar line. He owned a miniature in-town farm with chickens, ducks, and a few hogs protected by a strongly fenced backyard guarded by several big, mean dogs which he often used for hunting. These dogs never quite trusted me. For self-preservation I reciprocated, moving slowly and warily when I walked among them. I had the distinct impression they were hoping within their canine minds that I would make some swift and suspicious movement they could interpret as unfriendly, thus giving them their eagerly awaited chance to tear me apart. This was especially trying because the privy was in the backyard, and occasionally I would be in a hurry. But always I took my time, no matter what internal pressures decreed otherwise.

Old Granddad, who incidentally drove a horse and wagon, was as potent as his hundred proof namesake. An evangelizing agnostic, he studied the works of Bob Ingersoll like a preacher studies his Bible.[1] I came under his influence at precisely the right time for I was psychologically ready to defect from the church.

From infancy I'd been taught the power of prayer. When blacks were massacred in the Tulsa riots, I knelt at night and prayed for retribution. When nothing happened, I was puzzled. Later following an especially horrible triple lynching in dear Dixie, with a young black mother bound and burned at the stake while the mob laughed at her cries, I prayed long and earnestly for punishment of the mob members. Apparently this message never got down to the sheriff, for nobody was ever arrested. I became deeply depressed, feeling that somehow God had let me down. Then suddenly it dawned on my that every picture I had seen showed a white Christ, usually blonde, whereas the devil was invariably black—the devil and evil. If this were so, what else could I expect? Why would a white Lord punish those his color, his ethnic brothers? The suspicion formed, tiny at first and then snowballing, that maybe the Christian religion was a device to keep black subservient to white. Very well. Then I was through with it.

Granddad's seeds of agnosticism therefore fell in welcoming soil. He converted me almost immediately, and I began haunting the Wichita Public Library, cramming my mental craw with the writings of both agnostics and atheists. But I did not physically desert the church for many practical reasons: it was the chief social center of black America and I needed the association of other youth. As time passed I cooperated fully with any church program which I believed worked toward realistically solving the problems of daily living.

Granddad also introduced me to Cap Hutcherson, black YMCA secretary who had a way with both groups. White Christians of course wanted our young men to have the benefits of Christian brotherhood so long as it remained on a segregated basis, thus conditioning us for what they felt would be residence through eternity in a jim crow heaven. Cap himself was a heavyset, smiling, vigorous man and an ardent disciple of Booker T. Washington and his black and white philosophy of separate-as-the-fingers-of-the-hand.[2] Although I looked questioningly upon this belief, I liked Cap immediately. His "Cap" was a relic of World War I where he had been one of a handful of black commissioned officers. As a graduate of Tuskegee Institute, he maintained strong ties with the school and introduced me to the *Negro Yearbook,* edited by Monroe Work of Tuskegee.[3] For the first time in my life, I read about some of the black men who contributed significantly to our history. At last I began to develop embryo pride in the accomplishments of our people.

11

I was to take a busboy job at the Wichita Club, playground of the city's elite. The day after arrival, I went to the tiny office of Robert Hill, the headwaiter, who had the comically serious face of a Keystone cop done in light brown skin. His belly, I noticed at once, was several inches larger than his chest, the obvious result of eating the club's rich foods.

"Ever work at a hotel or club before?" he asked.

"Never." This was the first time I'd ever been inside a first-class dining room.

"It won't be hard. Just do what the waiters say and you'll get along, far as it goes and comes to that fact of it."

I blinked. "Pardon me?"

"All you have to do is take out dirty dishes, keep the place clean and things like that, far as it goes and comes to that fact of it."

I didn't ask again. I'd heard right the first time. I soon learned he dropped in this meaningless phrase almost every time he spoke.

He invited me over to his house that same night to meet his two daughters. Five minutes after meeting Roberta, the younger and a dazzler I dug on sight, I asked for a movie date. Getting away from Arkansas City invariably woke up my hormones.

The other busboy at the club was a friendly, long-headed youth named Bill, a couple of years my senior. Bill had two ambitions: to take care of his widowed mother and to become a concert violinist, for which he practiced at every opportunity. Patiently he taught me my duties and did his best to help me adjust to the waiters and kitchen staff, all black except the head chef whose chief assistant was Bully Landrum.

Bully was worthy of special attention. Although past sixty, he was still strong and looked mean enough to subdue a cage of wildcats. In younger days, he had been pimp, gambler, and all-around tough guy. His one weakness was an almost holy reverence for white women. According to Bully, "God didn't make but two beautiful things—a bluebird and a white woman." And when a reigning Hollywood movie queen passed through town and was entertained at the Wichita Club, Bully was able to steal one soul-warming glance. Then he turned away, so the story goes, muttering to himself: "She don't shit—she sugars!"

There were five full-time waiters, plus a dozen or more who came in daily to work the frenzied businessmen's lunch or banquets at night. The hectic midday meal, when it was virtually impossible to keep an accurate tab on food sent to the various dining rooms, was also the time when waiters took off with the delicacies they enjoyed best and hid them for their own feasting when the rush subsided. The huge linen basket behind screens in the main dining room was the hiding place for such choice viands as filet mignon or especially delicious pie. Should the representative of the linen concessionaire make his daily call before lunch was over, waiters would leave customers to dash for the huge basket and rescue goodies hidden in the soiled napkins and tablecloths. Even so, an appreciable amount of forgotten or overlooked food was laundered every day. And I soon learned to drink coffee or iced tea with my meals, after discovering the milk available for the help came from the five gallon containers used for cooking. These containers also doubled as cemeteries for cockroaches.

Almost all the waiters had served overseas fighting the Huns to help make the world safe for democracy—or so they were told. The only real democracy any of them had seen was in France, and all had vivid memories of experiences with the "mamselles" of Paris. Without exception, all gambled occasionally, drank frequently, and "played the dozens" constantly.

The dozens, also known as "taking you down to 12th Street," is oral horseplay consisting of pithy and graphic comments about the sexual activities of the victim's blood relatives, usually female. Such insults are not intended to be taken seriously, and usually those who participate do not become angry. Instead it's a contest to see who can make the most outrageous comments. An anthropologist can trace this singular folk habit back to the songs of derision prevalent among a number of African peoples.

Back home I usually remained silent when other boys started the dozens, which meant I didn't go in for that activity. Now and then I might repeat a rhyme popular among us, but that was as far as I went:

I can tell by the shape of your jaw
A monkey must have been your pa
'Cause you look jus' like your ma.

I was introduced to the Wichita Club variety my first day. The luncheon rush was over, and we sat around the big table reserved for the help to relax and eat.

In came a short waiter with his plate. He looked around, spotted a thin, mournful undertaker type, grinned, and asked pleasantly, "How's yo mammy today?"

"Uh-oh," said another waiter laughing. "Right straight in the dozens!"

"Soon's these jokers git together, they're 12th Street bound," commented another.

"I hear yo' baby sister's in jail again," came back the undertaker type. "She was runnin' a service station with a great big sign, 'Oil an' Ass for Sale.'"

The first threw up his hands in mock supplication. "I was jus' being polite, askin' 'bout your ma, an' you insults me. Jus' for that, nex' time your mother comes aroun' offering me a ten-cent trick, I'll turn her down."

"You ungrateful motherfucker," the other shot back. "If it don't be for me, you wouldn't be alive today. Yo' ma was all set to drown you 'til I step in an' say no. Soon's you was born, you ran up a chandelier. Yo' ma not only couldn't tell whose you was, she couldn't even tell what you was."

"Listen at this grannydodger," said the first. "When you was born, you was las' in a litter of three. The fust two out grabbed yo' ma's titties an' started sucking. That meant they wasn't but one thing left fo' you to eat on. So you ain't no motherfucker, you's a mothersucker."

I joined in the exploding laughter. Immediately the undertaker type, as if he had been awaiting this opportunity, turned to me and asked solemnly, "You play the dozens?"

"No," I answered instantly.

"If you don't play 'em, don't laugh or I'll put you in 'em too."

"Lay off," cut in Bill, the other busboy. "He's new here. He don't go for that crap."

"If he stays 'round here long, he's gonna either play 'em or sing 'em," somebody else said.

I had no intention of engaging in this kind of horseplay, nor did I want to get into a beef my first day on the job. So I clamped on my expressionless poker face, the kind I'd worn around needling white boys at school, and sat painfully through the rest of the meal. It took every drop of self control to remain composed, for I had the feeling they were outdoing themselves to make me laugh and dump me in the dozens.

After a half hour or so they began leaving, singly or in pairs, until there was nobody left except a huge, muscular man I learned had once been a sparring partner for Sam McVey, a leading heavyweight title contender.[4]

"Son," he said, addressing me, "I guess you ain't never been around a gang like this before, have you?"

I shook my head.

"Well, I want you to know these fellows don't mean no harm. It's jus' our way of havin' fun. Sooner or later somebody's gonna slip you in the dozens jus' to see what you'll do. But when it happens, don't git mad. Jus' tell 'em in a nice way you don't play like that an' after while they'll leave you alone."

"But why do they have to play that way?" I asked.

"You ever call a friend of yours a son of a bitch in a jokin' way?" he countered.

"Why, yes," I admitted.

"Your friend get mad?"

"Of course not!"

"Seems to me they ain't much diff'rence. When you call a man a son of a bitch, you call his mother a dog. In the dozens you jus' elaborate an' expand on it more. Both ways you's talking about his females, an' also you're jus' kiddin' 'round. Another thing: you notice two men don't go off an' play the dozens by themselves. It's in front of somebody else."

"I guess you're right," I said, "but why do they make such a production of it?"

He thought deeply for a moment, then replied, "I s'pose because it's a way to feel important. Most of us ain't goin' nowhere in this world; the white folks done saw to that. We ain't ever goin' to do much better than we's doing now, an' that ain't much. But still we all like to feel important. So when a man thinks up somethin' real funny an' the others laugh, he feels good. A man's jus' gotta feel important some kind of way."

As time passed and I lost some of my greenness, I got along well with the crew. I didn't gamble but I would take a drink—although I laid off for a while after a waiter held out a bottle and I snatched it and took a swig before he could grab it back. The bottle, I learned to my burning horror, contained 180 proof alcohol. I couldn't swallow it and I couldn't spit it out; the stuff just sat there flaming. Afterward I nursed a sore throat for several days.

I also learned to leave some kind of tip if you dined at a halfway decent cafe, for I saw what happened to those who did not. The waiters had special treatment for "crabs" who demanded fine service but never left gratuities. On the way from the kitchen with a tray of food, a vengeful waiter lowered his trousers, opened his underwear, bent over, took the dinner plate and wiped it across his bare bottom. If there was no opportunity for this, he spit in the soup and stirred it. He didn't pocket a tip but he got emotional satisfaction.

Later that summer, Bill got me interested in dancing. After a long discussion, he talked me into attending what he called a "funk toss" and induced one of his girlfriends to start me out on a slow drag. By summer's end, when I enrolled at Friends' University, I was making all the hops.[5]

Nineteen twenty-three was the year when I developed a passion for unusual cigarettes. Despite the state law against their sale, they were bootlegged at cigar stores throughout Kansas. A customer went up to a clerk, looked around, then whispered, "Gimme a pack." The clerk, keeping an eye open ostensibly for cops, fished out a package from his pocket, usually Camels, Luckies, Chesterfields, or Fatimas. Standard price was a quarter; they sold in other states for fifteen cents. Of course the police knew what was going on. Since obviously no city could license the sale of illegal merchandise, cigar stores were raided once a year and proprietors fined the equivalent of what elsewhere would be the annual fee for a cigarette license. Nobody gained from this solemn sham except store owners who pocketed extra profits from cigarette-legging.

Such pretense was not necessary at the Wichita Club since its membership included those who ran the local establishment. Cigarettes were openly displayed. I was fascinated by the many varieties and tried them all. Passing up the common brands, I stuffed my pockets with as many as five kinds. I enjoyed casually lighting a Schinasi Natural, Toro, Ivanoff, Richmond Straight Cut, or Murad before people who didn't know they existed. In those days Pall Malls were expensive and came only in fancy red boxes with the long king size in containers of ten. Herbert Tareyton was not then mass-produced and downgraded for the proletariat; Benson & Hedges had many deluxe offerings, and scented Milo Violets were a novelty. My favorite was Churchill Downs, made of Macedonian tobacco, oval-shaped in black paper with a gold tip. I nursed a desire for exotic cigarettes until I was cured for good later in Chicago.

Following a brief trip home to Arkansas City, bad news awaited me when I returned to Wichita. Ol' Granddad, driving his horse and wagon, had been run into by two white women in an auto and lay unconscious at a hospital. Despite his years he was hardy and hung on in a coma for ten days before he died. Both Mother and Dad came for the funeral. Aunt Hattie was finally located in Omaha and made it to Wichita the day after burial, weeping and vowing never to lose touch with her sister again.

He left a widow, a much younger woman, who I had always addressed as Mrs. Marshall. She was evidently born with a sour disposition which curdled more every year. I lived out the school year at my grandfather's house, thankful that college and job kept me away most of the time. It was an old frame building without modern conveniences. I had a room to myself without heat other than that supplied by a lone oil lamp. Many winter mornings when I arose it was so cold I had to break ice in my pitcher to get water to wash my face. By the time spring arrived, I could have felt comfy napping in the big walk-in freezer at the club.

I also began occasionally dating a doll named Willa who influenced me to attend Kansas State College. Like most of the females who interested me then and for the next twenty years, she was older than I. Willa had attended Washburn College in Topeka several terms. And do you know what sold me? Her description of the keen times enjoyed at Kansas State.

Obviously I would go somewhere other than Friends' the following year. It had to be a state school since I couldn't afford a private institution. As I had no desire to become an educator, the three state teachers' colleges were out. After hearing Chancellor Lindley I would go to the University of Kansas only as a last resort.[6] So when Willa sang the praises of Kansas State, this had to be the place.

I sent for a catalog and was stymied. What would I study? Not agriculture or veterinary medicine; I had no interest in either farming or animals. Any kind of engineering required too much math; if I took a degree in commerce and finance, what the hell would I do with it? Now, had jazz been taught I would have enrolled in music, but any other kind of intimacy with sharps and flats was out. I was also the wrong sex for home economics, and I considered a liberal arts course a waste of time. That left only journalism; no math of any kind was required during the four years. And so, just like that, I made my decision. I would learn how to be a newspaperman.

12

Late in June of 1924 I went home for the rest of the summer, but not before falling completely and eternally in love with Lorraine, who had just graduated from Emporia State Teachers College and returned home to Wichita. I had heard of her before Cap Hutcherson introduced us. I fell for her on sight as had been predicted. But what hadn't been expected was that she would fall equally hard for me. Within two weeks, during which I managed to see her every night, we started making long-range plans. I was to get my degree, and she would teach school these four years before we married. My ego jumped way up yonder.

In fact, I was so cocky that shortly after returning to Arkansas City I began dating Alline Brown, whom I had previously considered unattainable, for a month until she left for Saint Louis. I did not consider this disloyal to Lorraine; furthermore, Alline told me more about Kansas State since two fellows she knew were students there.

Because I was one of the pitifully few blacks in the city's history who had been away to college, my status was automatically elevated at home. By going out regularly with the classiest chick in town, it was also assumed that I was now hot stuff. Aspiring jellybeans began coming around to take lessons in bull tossing to impress their flapper friends. In a small way, I had arrived.

According to Kinsey, I was now at the age when my sex drive was strongest. Without knowing it, I had fallen into what Kinsey says is the prevailing pattern of those males who go to college. I did know, however, that the time had come when I had an overpowering compulsion to knock off my first piece. Of course, Lorraine was out of the question; I was in love with her and automatically that made her untouchable. Like so many males then, I wouldn't even think of marrying a gal who consented to unwed intercourse. Nor did I have nerve enough, for all my new-found bravado, to ask anybody else. My best bet was a paid lay. I looked up Don Perry and asked where I could buy some trim, as casually as if I bought it regularly in Wichita.

"The broad you oughta see," he replied, "is Vivian. Man, she just won't don't and only sets you back a one-spot. You ain't gonna find no better tail than that in heaven. But make it morning or mid-afternoon. Her monkey man comes home for lunch then goes back to work, an' I'm damn sure you better not let him catch you there." He gave me her address.

Dad had sold out the Dew Drop Inn and now operated a pool hall. I took over at midday and handled the business for three or four hours while he went home. Next day I decided to call on Vivian before going to the pool hall.

As I walked to her place, all worked up and excited, I thought of an old verse to "Hesitation Blues" I had learned years before:

> Ashes to ashes
> Dust to dust
> Whiskey to drink
> And good booty to bust. . . .

I can remember everything about the way she looked when she opened the door—everything, that is, except her breasts. At that time, back in 1924, the nation had not gone gland glad. Popular styles in women's clothing tried to hide them. Of course you expected a jane to have a set as standard equipment, and occasionally if you thought you could get by with it you'd grab 'em and squeeze (we called it "hunching"), but the broads weren't staging a constant contest for bigger and better bubbies.

Vivian was a tall, well-built, dark brownskin babe, about twenty-five, with a two-inch razor scar on her left cheek which somehow failed to detract from her appearance. She was not particularly feminine but was so flamboyantly female she could make a stud send off steam just by standing close. I was glad to fork over a dollar.

She took a heavy dark quilt, made a pallet on the floor, pulled up her dress (she wore no panties), got on her back, then parted her thighs and raised her knees. I was impatiently eager until I looked down into the ready, waiting portals of a woman. This was the first time in my life I had ever seen this dazzling sight up close. I dropped to my knees in front of her, staring in bug-eyed fascination.

"Whatya gonna do, jus' look at it?" she asked.

I blushed with embarrassment and worked up a sickly grin as I lowered myself clumsily above her—and found I had gone limp. Immediately, I vividly recalled how I had chickened out in Coffeyville five years before, and that was no help. But by lying on her warm body I became stiff enough to enter, then learned I was too nervous to enjoy the sensation, too fearful of failure for success. I moved mechanically for several minutes, maintaining an erection but obtaining no pleasure, wondering why I wasn't getting the kicks I'd expected.

Finally, Vivian spoke.

"That's what I like about white men," she said. "They don't take no time a-tall. You long-winded spades'll wear a woman out."

This was no help emotionally. As I mentally debated whether to act insulted and make a dignified withdrawal, or thrust harder and faster and get my dollar's worth, she spoke again.

"Get up," she commanded, pointing to the clock on the nearby table. "My husband say he's comin' home for early lunch. He oughta be here any time now."

I quit immediately, my clothing straightened almost as soon as I stood erect, and hurried away. I went to her a virgin and left still technically a virgin, remaining in this blissless state far too long. As for Vivian, she became one of my favorite partners that summer at the public dances in Paris Park. But we never mentioned our fiasco.

13

Manhattan, Kansas, smaller in 1924 than Arkansas City, was a pretty, little, tree-filled town existing primarily as an appendage to Kansas State. If you studied farming or veterinary medicine, you called it properly Kansas State Agricultural College; if you were in other courses, you called it Kansas State. Rival schools sneeringly termed it a "cow college" and headline writers abbreviated it to K-Aggies. Later it became Kansas State University.

Black students usually numbered twenty to thirty; Kansas University at Lawrence generally had five times that number. Virtually all the males lived at Phi Beta Sigma Fraternity house, an old three-story frame building supposedly being purchased on monthly installments. A few years later the original owner foreclosed and took back the structure. Seems the intermediary who received the payments, a soul sister, had pocketed the cash.

Living at Sigma house was practical experience in communal existence. A housemother visited us twice a year, but it was run by college boys with no outside help. We slept two to four to a room in bunk beds and maintained rigid rules on cleanliness and noise. Violations received demerits with specific penalties. All monthly expenses, including social events, were added together and divided by the number of residents, each paying an equal amount, usually around eight dollars and on rare occasions as much as fifteen dollars. Most of us worked at white fraternity or sorority houses for our meals and spending change; the rest chipped in for joint chow at dinner and took turns cooking and cleaning the kitchen. Each did his own laundry or mailed it home. We walked to and from campus a mile and a half away. Without regular employment and only an occasional odd job, I got by my freshman year on thirty dollars monthly living expenses, exclusive of fees and books that cost me under fifty dollars per semester. Obviously I made every penny count, but I didn't do without anything I really needed.

Males outnumbered co-eds almost two to one and, except for a few from Kansas City, the co-eds were bowlegged from riding horses on farms. Since there were not even enough of these to meet the demand, we took over the most desirable high school gals. They were flattered by this attention from college men, but the local cats were not amused.

When I said there were twenty to thirty black students at K-State, I mean that was the number classed by the college as Negro. Negro is neither a race nor scientific terminology; it is a label of inferiority for some 12 percent or more of the total American population with known black African ancestry. Persons placed in the category of Negro are then shunted into ghettoes, abused, given poor schools and the worst jobs—if any. A few rise above the herd, either on sheer ability or because they are selected by the white power structure to lead the rest in a manner not offensive to the white majority. But at no time are those called Negroes allowed to forget who they are and their lower position in American society. The designation, Negro, is a brand placed on us by Whitey, a punishment for those who had the poor judgement to descend from obviously African forebears as well as those who look Caucasian but were careless in their selection of an ancestor.

If Negro were a scientific racial designation instead of the designation of an inferior caste, then by logic a person with 50 percent white European and 50 percent black African ancestry could choose whether to be called Negro or Caucasian or else go automatically into another grouping as yet not officially determined. By the same logic, a person with less than 50 percent black African ancestry and the rest white European would have to be designated as Caucasian. But the popular American concept of race is not based on logic. Even though an individual may have only one sixty-fourth African ancestry, if it becomes known, then that person is penalized by being called Negro and shunted aside for discriminatory treatment.

This becomes the height of absurdity when not even the most rabid white supremacist can say with complete assurance that he has no black African ancestry. I know of nobody who can account for every one of his sixty-four ancestors only six generations ago, less than two-hundred years. It does him no good to point to his forefathers in Europe, for productive intermingling between Europeans and Africans had been an accomplished fact for centuries, long before even the rise of ancient Greece, with results reaching into the highest echelons of the aristocracy of northern Europe. Scientists currently estimate that from twenty to twenty-five million Americans calling themselves "pure white" have enough black African ancestry to be classed as Negro according to our prevailing standards. This does not include the millions who have the physical appearance to "pass" for white and leave the black caste never to return.

Only a few decades ago, most of us considered it an insult to be called "black." We willingly accepted "Negro" or "colored." But today the reverse is true, largely because of the unhappy connotations surrounding the work "Negro" and because we are learning to wear black as a badge of honor. Besides, black is as sensible a designation for a group of people ranging from ebony to blonde, tied together by similar experiences and aspirations, as is the word "white," its opposite, for persons ranging in skin tone from brown to light red with none of them actually white—not even from fear when alone and cornered before a confrontation of ultra-Black Power.

Although I frequently use the terms "black" and "Negro" interchangeably, black to me carries the connotation of pride; Negro is primarily a caste classification. Black is subjective, representing joint striving toward the eventual goal of complete liberation; Negro is objective and tells it like it still is.

Returning to my original statement, I do not know how many of us actually attended K-State when I was there. I do know several who had been designated Negro in Kansas City became white at Kansas State, according to my black associates who knew them personally. Of course they were not exposed for we rarely snitch on those of our group who are able to fool Mr. Charley.

However, during my sophomore and junior years, very light complexioned students came to our frat house for lodging several weeks after the fall semester began. They had enrolled as Caucasian and moved into white living quarters, then threw it all overboard to return to the fold. Reared black, they could not take it living with whitey. Our commonly shared experiences and culture, along with general discomfort over living in close quarters with whites, caused them to return voluntarily. I have no way of knowing how many others made the adjustment and remained Caucasian.

14

Freshman Sigma house residents automatically became pledges, with Hell Week, initiation, and membership the second semester if grades and conduct warranted. Pledges not only cleaned the house and tended the furnace but were subject to special rules. Violations meant paddling at regular monthly meetings by upperclassmen, some of whom could bust a barrel stave paddle with a single blow. By the end of my freshmen year all four of us frosh were so calloused we could have received a load of buckshot fired from five feet away without blinking an eye. And we accepted beatings for the sake of belonging, of comradeship—and for the privilege of dishing it out to next year's freshmen.

Swearing was a way of life with us. When we did not cuss one another, it was a sign of anger. Occasionally there would be aggravation lasting perhaps a day or two but never fisticuffs. We were too dependent on each other for violence. And yet there were times when even Job might have lost his cool.

Consider the trials of one Sheridan H. Settler from Council Grove, Kansas, majoring in animal husbandry. His initials were reinterpreted as standing for Shit House except on those occasions when he was called just plain Shit. Since he did not approve, it was his custom not to answer when so addressed.

Those with ready cash usually made loans to whoever ran short pending the next check from home, generally on the first of the month. The first of the month was settling up day; if the lender didn't get it then, he most likely would have to wait another month. And invariably on the first somebody owed Settler.

As soon as his check was cashed, the borrower began repaying. If he owed Settler, he'd make no move until Settler climbed to his third floor room, then he would loudly bellow, "Shit!"

If this was yelled two or three times and Settler did not appear, the shouter would bellow no more. Perhaps later that day or the next, Settler might approach him and suggest repayment.

"But I no longer have it," the reply would come. "I tried to give you your money earlier when I still had it. Didn't you hear me yell for you?"

"No, I didn't hear you call me at all."

"But you *must* have! I knew you were upstairs because I saw you go up. These other brothers heard me call you. I yelled 'Shit' three or four times."

To which Sheridan would reply, "You know damn well that's not my name."

"But that's what we all call you"—said in straightfaced innocence—"and I was trying to be friendly just like all the rest of the fellows. Tell you what"—this spoken confidentially—"the first of next month when I get my check and yell 'Shit' maybe you'd better come running or my money'll get away from me again."

When the next month came, the borrower would again call "Shit!" and this time Sheridan would respond.

"I thought you called me," he'd say on appearing.

"All I said was 'shit'. I was merely expressing disgust. Can't a man yell 'shit' around here without you showing up? You're not the only shit in existence, you know."

Of course everybody present would razz Settler until he withdrew. Whereupon the borrower would call him back, saying "Well, since old Shit is here, I suppose I might as well pay you. But I thought you didn't like for us to call you 'Shit.'"

"I don't."

"Then why in hell do you have to show up when somebody yells 'Shit'!?"

Settler would say nothing. He'd merely pocket the money and go away. He never lost his temper nor was he known to refuse a loan when he had it. There was an unwritten law to lend if you could; besides now and then Settler himself ran short and had to borrow.

Sigma House furnishings included a phonograph and a battered upright piano with a half-inch hole patted into the floor beneath the left pedal. Some of the students could beat out acceptable blues and stomps, and occasionally a visitor, such as Jimmy Johnson who made piano rolls, would pass through Manhattan and give the old box a real workout. For our periodic house dances we alternated between piano and records. Although college rules required permits from the Dean of Women and the housemother as chaperone, about twice monthly we gave "impromptu" dances with neither permit nor housemother. Since we were on our own, we leaned over backward and behaved as decorously as if the parents of each girl were there looking on. As a group we were serious about being there to study instead of swing.

Chapter president was a little dark brown senior named Wilson who finished near the head of his class in civil engineering. On surveying field trips he was assigned to work with a white youth who resented him at first but as time passed gradually warmed to where they discussed everything. One day, having reached the point where he had completely forgotten Wilson's color, he asked:

"Say, did you ever go to bed with a nigger wench?"

Without batting an eye, Wilson replied, "No, I never have. I don't screw anything but white girls."

For one awful moment there was shocked silence as the honkie lad suddenly realized he had been talking to an Afro-American. He paled and firmed his lips, got himself changed to another partner, and never again spoke one word to Wilson.

The campus itself was beautiful with buildings of the same general architectural style, and students themselves were usually agreeable. And they were also cautious.

Never did I wear one of those green caps made for freshmen. Sophomores roamed near the campus, paddles in hand, looking for violators. When they spotted a capless frosh, the cry would arise, "Fresh meat!" and all would dash to the area to paddle the frightened boy, sparing neither black nor white. But me they did not bother, although frequently they grabbed victims all around me. Sometimes I saw them eyeing me speculatively. But instead of running, I slowed my step and put on my meanest scowl as I stared calmly into their faces. I was black and big (I then weighed 210), and I suppose they figured what the hell, it won't hurt to ignore ONE freshman. I do not doubt there were sophomores who would have tackled me had I been large enough to pose as a dark double for gigantic Jess Willard, but, fortunately, they were never around as I strode insolently by. What the paddle wielders didn't know is that had they challenged me, I had no intention of putting up a fight. I depended on my bluff—and it worked.

Mine was the only black face in the journalism department. A couple of years earlier a brown girl had enrolled but dropped out. Here I found no open prejudice. This division, despite its location on the plains of Kansas, enjoyed an excellent national reputation. Nelson Antrim Crawford had recently resigned as head to take a government job in Washington, and the new chief was Charles Elkin Rogers. We developed a fine friendship; I dedicated my second book of poetry, *I Am The American Negro,* to him.

I wrote my first poetry in my freshman year. In an English literature class, taught by Miss Ada Rice, for one assignment we had the choice of writing an essay or an original poem. I had no special interest in verse, but quite by chance in the college library I picked up a magazine containing several pages of experimental poems. I became so excited I immediately composed a short piece and turned it in. At the following session Miss Rice asked me to remain after class.

"It's about that poem you gave me," she said. "Do you have anything else?"

"Why?" I asked in surprise.

"I think you have talent. But I could make a more positive evaluation if I saw more of your work."

Triggered by her interest, I dashed off two more and handed them in next class. These were followed by others. After receiving at least a dozen more, she asked me to type them for submission to Ur Rune Chapter of the American College Quill Club, a national creative writing society. I was one of five accepted that year.

Initiation into this honor group included presentation of a play. Our initial planning meeting was at the home of a voluptuous green-eyed redhead named Blanche Forester who was taking special courses at the college. In her mid-thirties, she had a daughter in high school and was married to a prosperous pharmacist who was also a bank director. She drove a late-model Buick convertible the color of her eyes.

After our meeting and as we prepared to leave, she told me quietly, "Please stay a little longer. I want to talk to you."

I remained. She turned the lights down low, bade me sit beside her on the soft couch in front of the slowly burning logs in the fireplace, then started quoting some of my poetry to me in a throaty voice.

I was knocked out when the first phrase landed. Even today I have a glass jaw when a lovely lady flatters me by memorizing and quoting my verse. Can you imagine how I must have felt at nineteen?

We developed a very pleasant platonic relationship revolving around literature, although I was uncomfortably conscious of her physical appeal. Later when I returned to Kansas State after an absence of two and a half years, Blanche had gone to Hollywood. Her daughter had elected to follow in her mother's footsteps and was now in the journalism school.

On campus I was a mild curiosity after word got around that I had made the Quill Club, and I was described as "the poet who looks like a prizefighter." But the most illustrious of our small black group was Louis Edwin Fry from Texas. He took his degree in architectural engineering and, besides receiving a number of awards in Beaux Arts competition, was the first Afro-American at K-State elected to Phi Kappa Phi, national scholastic honor society. He set such a high standard that many white students were embarrassed at being in his classes. They didn't want to work as hard as they had to with him around. His grades were so consistently topflight he rarely had to take a final exam. When he returned later to study for his master's degree, the head of the engineering school often consulted him on difficult problems.

Yet Louis, for all his brilliance, was considered the "dumber" of two brothers.

The other was Francis who sought a degree in electrical engineering. He was not in school during my time, but his reputation was already well established. His record might have been perfect but for two weaknesses: horror of study and love of sleep.

Francis shunned early classes as if they had been invented for his special torture. He either cut them completely or arrived just before the end of the period to learn the next assignment. In a few rare instances he had been induced to bring in the body at the proper time, but he immediately went sleep. However in such courses as advanced calculus and theory of equations the instructor was grateful even for that. On those days when he had little success in getting across new concepts to his class, he looked around in desperation for Fry. If Francis was present, he'd be napping. The instructor would awaken him and ask that he explain the problem. Francis would stretch, yawn, walk to the blackboard and present the material so simply even an idiot would understand, then return to his seat and resume his snooze. In one course he showed up only at the time of the six weeks, mid-semester, and final exams, yet he received an A grade.

For several years after Francis took a course in wiring, the instructor reportedly told his class at the start of each final exam:

"Your problem is to convert this motor completely from AC to DC wiring. Don't tell me three hours are not long enough. Recently I had a colored boy named Francis Fry who was given the same problem. Ten minutes after the exam began, he came to my desk. I thought he wanted further instruction. Instead he told me he'd finished. Naturally, I thought he was kidding, but he insisted he was through. You may be sure I went over his work minutely, looking for some mistake. But it was perfect. Now, if this colored boy could do it in ten minutes, you white boys ought to finish the job in three hours."

Despite the general air of liberality, there were two extremely sore spots: athletics and ROTC. Kansas State belonged to the old Missouri Valley Conference which had a "gentleman's agreement" barring black athletes if member schools refused to play against them. Missouri and Oklahoma universities were lily white and Kansas U., with racist Lindley as Chancellor, was a spiritual brother. (In view of the black All-Americans who, starting in the 1950s, won their reputations at these schools, this may seem hard to believe, but in the 1920s it was a living fact.) Only one member school, Iowa State, dared challenge this policy when it came up with a star tackle in 1926 named, I believe, Holiday. He was six foot four, weighed a muscular 225, and spoke in a high tenor voice. Even today he would be a giant but in that era of smaller men he was a bronze curiosity—and so tough nobody could embalm him.

He was allowed to play only three games his entire first season, but one of these and by far the most important was against Nebraska, perennial conference champion whose battles with Knute Rockne's Irish were headliners. Nebraska, intending to get rid of Holiday in a hurry, aimed its first three power plays at him, and three times Cornhusker backs were thrown for losses of five to ten yards. That third play broke his hand, but Nebraska never knew for no more plays came even to his side of the line the rest of the day. Because of his sensational play in those three games, he was chosen All-Conference tackle and next year, 1927, was selected All-Midwest by Walter Eckersall of the Chicago *Tribune.* Had he attended a more highly publicized school in a metropolitan center, undoubtedly he would have won national fame.

Several black athletes could have easily made the Kansas State varsity in football. Four of our scant number had captained their mixed high school teams and another had been a star punter at Wiley College in Texas. While I doubt that I could have made the team as a regular, I resented not having an opportunity to try. Later, as a staff columnist in the student newspaper, I blasted this gentleman's agreement—to the mortification of the athletic department.

The ROTC, of course, maintained the official racist policy of the U.S. Army. Since this was required training at all federal land grant colleges, we were tolerated but only at a low level. We all took two years of training; but no matter how talented, we could not even rise to corporal, and advanced study was out of the question.

Nevertheless, the ROTC was a boon to those of us, black and white, who had to count our pennies. For one dollar per semester we received a full uniform (World War I surplus) with no restrictions on its use, and we could replace any worn-out article by returning the remnants to the commissary. Many of us, both white and black, wore our uniforms most of the week to save wear and tear on our regular clothes.

15

Late in October of 1924 Lorraine came to Manhattan to visit me on her way back to her teaching post in Salina following a state teachers' convention in Topeka. As she boarded the train she saw another young teacher she had just met. Lorraine sat beside her and they talked.

"Where are you going?" Lorraine asked.

"To Manhattan. I'm going to visit my boyfriend over the weekend. He attends Kansas State."

"How nice," Lorraine said. "I'm going there too. What's your friend's name?"

"Frank Davis."

"It's what?"

"Frank Davis."

Lorraine's jaw dropped in surprised disbelief.

"What's wrong?" her companion asked.

"I don't know yet, but something is. Quite. The guy I'm going to see is Frank Davis."

They stared at each other incredulously as the train roared on, both wondering who does that rat think he is, Rudolph Valentino?

Finally the other said slowly, "I never thought he'd have the gall to pull a dirty trick like that. Not Jimmy!"

"Who?" Lorraine asked.

"Why, Jimmy, of course. What do you call him?"

"What's his full name?"

"James Frank Davis. Most people call him Frank, but I call him Jimmy."

"Wait a minute," Lorraine said. "This James Frank Davis—how does he look? How big is he? Where's he from?"

"You ought to know! He's five feet six and comes from Nashville. Why do you ask a question like that?"

Lorraine sighed her relief. "The Frank Davis I'm going to see is Frank Marshall Davis. And he's over six feet and comes from southern Kansas."

That was the story they told as soon as Jimmy and I saw them that afternoon. Jimmy, an engineering student with an unusually large head, had been dubbed "Atlas" by fraternity brothers who called me "Heavy" from my first day among them. Despite our similar names, nobody had expected any real complications although several times we had accidentally opened each other's mail.

The odds against this must be astronomical. Of only two dozen black students, two males known as Frank Davis lived in the same frat house and had as girlfriends two teachers boarding the same train to visit them at the same time. From then on he called himself James F. Davis and I went on record as F. Marshall Davis. Then, with the perversity typical of humankind, I was referred to as "Little D" and little Jimmy was called "Big D"—which habitually confused strangers meeting us for the first time.

That night we had an "impromptu" dance at the frat house honoring the visitors. Afterward Jimmy and I took our dates to the private residence where most soul sisters stayed when in Manhattan, then settled on opposite ends of the long porch, covered and dark, to neck. The weather was still warm enough for us to remain outdoors without discomfort.

I'll never forget that night.

I was so in love with Lorraine I wouldn't have dreamt of touching her sexually. We hugged and kissed in exquisite torture, carefully avoiding contact with what were known as each other's "private parts." With all this tremendous stimulation, our libidos strained at the chains. We were the two horniest virgins you ever saw, burbling in our own frustrated juices.

"I'd follow you to the end of the world," she told me looking ecstatically into space. Then she turned her beautiful and intelligent eyes toward me, whispering, "I'd do anything you want me to do—anything!"

I got the obvious message flashed in three-foot letters. I also got a whopping "hard." John Henry could have used it in place of that fourteen-pound hammer. But the greater the ache, the more ashamed I became. She was willing to give herself to me, but I was just too damned noble to take advantage of what must be a moment of weakness. Besides, if I truly loved her, I reasoned, I should be above such carnal thoughts. It was all right to want to go to bed with an ordinary girl, but true love should soar beyond such earthiness. There must be something wrong with me, some serious flaw or I wouldn't let sheer animal desire shove its dirty snout into what should be a clean and pure romance. After we were married, perhaps we could engage in an occasional genteel intimacy, but to want her now (no matter how she felt) was an insult. Obviously I was a victim of the prevailing Puritan hangups of the day.

At times, mind simply will not win over matter, and this was one of them. The most incisive mental flagellation did not diminish my biological urge. I called myself every imaginable name, but I remained hard. About 4:00 A.M., I gave up and went home, ashamed of my still persistent erection. Later Lorraine thanked me for "not taking advantage" of her that night. I felt like a brother of Sir Galahad, proud that I had been strong enough to uphold our joint honor and virtue.

Jimmy had a roommate, Paul Orville Brooks from Boley, Oklahoma. Next day he asked me, "How come you studs didn't get in until way after this morning? What'd you do, fuck 'em all night?"

Righteous wrath flooded me. The very idea, daring to talk like that about a girl like Lorraine! I called him into another room and spoke to him privately and seriously.

"I want you to know," I said, "that Lorraine is not that low, common kind of woman. Why, we're engaged to be married. As long as you live, don't you ever dare say anything like that again."

I was five inches taller, fifty pounds heavier, and obviously upset. Paul peered up into my face and, being a realist, said nothing. He merely nodded his head.

Later one of the frat members told me Paul had said afterward, "Heavy got mad because I asked him if he'd been screwing his girl all night. For sure, that must be holy pussy."

I thought immediately of taking Paul aside for an even more serious talk but threw up my hands and thought, what the hell, let it go. Words won't harm me anyway.

16

I stayed in Manhattan over the Christmas vacation. Dad gave me the choice of coming home or saving my round-trip fare for the Sigma initiation and fraternity pin when the first semester ended. The house was empty except for Harry Hazel, another freshman, who had been discharged from the cavalry at Fort Riley earlier that year and was working his way through college. For lack of any other way to pass time, I began playing around with Hazel's saxophone, a brass C-Melody Buescher with a busted key. Hazel never used it anyway. I became so interested I bought a book on how to play the sax and started teaching myself. I also bought sheet music, and by the time classes resumed in the new year I surprised the entire gang by sitting down and blowing "Japanese Sandman."

Stronger reactions soon replaced their initial surprise. Beneath their outward veneer, most of the brothers were undoubtedly antimusic at heart. Only this could explain why, on assembling the instrument for practice, I often discovered somebody had hidden the mouthpiece. I soon learned it was wasted time to ask where it was, no matter how politely, for nobody ever knew. Finally I quit asking and automatically began a long and patient search. On these evenings when I failed to locate it, I would hear such unkind comments as "Well, one night of peace anyway" but I chose to ignore them. Despite such handicaps, by the end of the second semester I was doing rather well (an opinion not unanimously shared at the frat house) and had visions of eventually leading my own jazz band after getting a sax with a full set of keys. Meanwhile I played platters over and over, trying to copy the breaks by a particularly interesting reedman with Fletcher Henderson. Years later I learned he was Coleman Hawkins.[7]

In January I was ready for Hell Week and initiation. Some brothers had expected me to flunk. When most were cramming for finals, I read cowboy magazines or stayed up late at night with another frosh logging long-distance radio stations. When I brought in my final grades, including an A in chemistry, they were gassed. I was sassy. My chemistry instructor, a recent graduate of the University of Alabama who spent many class periods praising Dr. George Washington Carver, the black wizard of

Tuskegee, told the two soul sisters in my class to see me if they needed special help away from campus. As a result I became so over-confident that in the second semester I flunked Chemistry II.

17

I knew Hell Week would live up to its name. With all the practical jokers present, living there day to day had its hazards. One night I woke up in a darkened room to answer what I understood to be a long-distance call from Lorraine, and found I had been lashed firmly to the bed with stout ropes. There was the night Mays, an upperclassman, wore a new suit to visit his girl. When he returned after midnight all doors and windows had been locked, and nobody could be roused to let him in. The lone open entrance was the basement coal shute which, in complete disgust, he finally had to use. Then there was Frank "The Beak" Greene, another frosh, who swore he had the softest bed in the house. Habitually he took a running start and dived into what he called "the feathers." One night another student and I placed two large wooden draftsmen's boards under his sheets, smoothed them out, then stood around and waited until he leaped into bed (landing with a mighty thud). Of course we were sympathetic and shared his rage all next week at the unidentified bastards as he nursed a sore nose, knees, and elbows.

I slept in the bottom half of a double-decker shared with Wilson, chapter president. One night he turned off the room light, climbed on his bunk, and slid his bare feet beneath the covers. His feet contacted a hairbrush, an old football helmet, and an assortment of cold turkey bones. I knew he was a crack engineering student, but I looked on in awe as his body described an artistic arc returning to the floor.

"What the goddamned hell is that?" he asked in a voice several octaves higher than normal.

I would have convinced him I knew nothing of this dastardly deed had I not inadvertently mentioned the number of bones in his bed.

I thus expected a bad time not only from Wilson but from two other upperclassmen, Victor "Tit Head" Reef and Theodore "Mouse" Miller. Reef, a potential chemical engineer who looked like a refugee from Lebanon, possessed a unique characteristic nobody in the house ever let him forget. On the back of his head, beneath the hair, was a peculiar fleshy protuberance with a fantastically real resemblance to a female nipple. I loved to sneak up behind him and rub it—to his great disgust. Miller, studying electrical engineering, strongly resembled an emaciated rodent and did not care at all for his nickname. Nor was his attitude improved when one day I found a dead mouse in his trunk and solemnly accused him of murdering a relative. So I prepared myself for the worst.

I read the special list of rules with some apprehension:

> All pledges are to rise and stand at attention when a member enters the room. This applies even though you are in bed asleep.

> All pledges must carry an egg and a rock of equal size in the same pocket. (In one day I learned to hard-boil the egg.)

> Each pledge must have on his person at all times six kitchen matches.

> When ascending stairs at Sigma house, each pledge must go up three steps then back down two. When descending, the reverse must be followed.

> Entry and exit from the building must be only through the designated second-story window. You must do the Lon Chaney (a walk imitating the star in the movie, *Hunchback of Notre Dame*) from house to sidewalk, and the Black Bottom (a dance step) from sidewalk to house on reentering.

The morning after Hell Week started, I was sent to the grocery store. I climbed through the window to the porch roof and looked down. The ground, twelve feet below, was frozen. I knew I had to jump, but the idea was not appealing. Somebody called, "Come on, break your neck and get it over with." Behind me upperclassmen said pointedly they wanted me to go to the store today, not next year. Finally I sighed and jumped. Other than a stinging in both feet, I was unharmed. But I arranged to borrow a ladder for the week before I returned.

We received special assignments late every night. That first night Harry Hazel and I were ordered to bring in a live bird, a live fish, or a pure black tomcat by morning. We started out at midnight with the thermometer registering 12 above. Knowing it was an impossible assignment, we headed straight for one of Manhattan's two small railroad stations to keep warm. After an hour or so the agent chased us out and we went immediately to the other. When, eventually, we were asked to leave there we returned to the first but found it closed. When we walked back to the second it was locked tight. One of us conceived the brilliant idea of getting arrested; we would then have a legitimate reason for failing our assignments. Accordingly, we walked to the town's best residential district and began singing at the tops of our voices. Although it was 3:00 A.M. nobody even switched on a light. Then we stood on opposite sides of the street and swore as loudly and colorfully as we could. Still no one paid us any attention; townspeople had been conditioned to expect anything during Hell Week. Finally, hoarse and almost frozen, we walked dejectedly back to the frat house about 5:00 A.M. The citizens had let us down.

Next night, I was sent out alone about 10 P.M. to bring back a quart of sheep manure. I was at a loss until I remembered the college kept a herd of sheep on an experimental farm somewhere west of the campus. I wandered around for three hours, finally found it, filled my pot, and returned home, shivering and thinking that without doubt, this is the coldest shit in town. (Next year, incoming frosh got wind of this caper and prepared in advance by hiding a gallon in the basement. Then the weather turned unseasonably warm, and the whole house got wind of it.)

My next assignment was with Hazel. Each of us was to bring back a highway sign reading at least five miles to Manhattan. It was just our luck to choose the road which evidently was serving as a convention site for canine malcontents. We both retreated until we obtained arsenals of clubs and rocks. We found our first marker six miles from town and the next one seven and a half. Fortunately, the temperature had risen to about thirty degrees. Otherwise, this fifteen-mile hike would have left us perambulating icebergs.

During this week every pledge had to go to the town's cemetery once at midnight. This did not frighten me. I recognized the moaning as wind sighing through tall trees and the glimpses of white as reflections from tombstones. I carried a large box of kitchen matches which I struck as I went from grave to grave looking for a specific headstone where I would find instructions. I must have read the names of at least half the people in the cemetery before I found what I wanted. It was a note telling me to look for my next orders by a certain tree on the opposite bank of the stream bordering the far edge of the cemetery. I went there. The river was about thirty feet wide, and there was no way to cross. Trying to wade in icy water of unknown depth was not appealing. I walked down the bank, hoping for stepping stones and a narrow neck where I could cross. Instead it got wider. I had no choice but to backtrack to the highway bridge, a mile and a half away, cross, then come back to the tree—a round-trip of three miles. Then when I got the note, it instructed me to look under the steps of my frat house and bring in what I found. I was disgusted.

Next night, Hazel was sent alone to the cemetery, and the entire campus heard about it the following day. He was to pick up his instructions in a culvert on the far side of the graveyard. Purely by amazing coincidence, a white frat had a similar assignment for one of its pledges. At roughly the same time, both freshmen sallied forth alone and, by chance, began crawling through opposite ends of the pitch black culvert, each thinking he was the only live human within blocks. Feeling their way quietly and cautiously, their hands suddenly came in contact with moving flesh.

Although they were both college men, in one fraction of a second they lost all traces of cumulative culture and reverted to the primitive. They yelled. They swore. They grabbed. And it was fortunate for both that the culvert was too small for full physical action, or they'd have nursed more than minor contusions when they returned to the twentieth century. Still, the experience had one bright result. For the rest of the year, they became good personal friends.

Culmination of this week of paddlings and special tasks was initiation. Strong-arm grads came from as far away as Omaha and St. Louis. There were four of us frosh, wearing old clothes and blindfolded. We went through the rites singly. First I was told to show love for my new brothers by partaking of their excrement. My hand was guided to a slop jar on the floor. This in itself was revolting. But when I picked up the vessel and heard splashing, I froze, trying to gather courage to raise it to my mouth. Then I thought, might as well get it over with and tilted the pot. A lump brushed my lips. I shuddered in revulsion. Surely the goddamned bastards wouldn't actually give me THAT! I was debating whether at this late moment to say to hell with the initiation, I don't care about joining the frat, when I received a couple of explosive swats with paddles. I was told I couldn't back out now so I might as well go ahead and drink. I took a small sip, but I was far from happy. Later I learned the concoction was unsweetened lukewarm tea with a few biscuits and hot dogs afloat.

Now I received a stimulant for my "long journey across the burning desert." I recalled what had happened at a white frat when a pledge was fed a raw oyster. He swallowed it easily. But he didn't notice there was a thread attached; when it was suddenly jerked, back came the oyster escorted by remnants of his latest meal.

And after sampling the stimulant, I would rather have had the oyster with thread. It was a heaping tablespoon of the vilest concoction I ever tasted: cold bacon grease, crushed Nature's Remedy tablets, and vinegar. It wouldn't go down, and the brothers wouldn't let me spit it out. I had to hold it in my mouth until the rites ended. Then I had two areas to soothe, for the "burning desert" was a storm of paddles as I crawled blindly about on hands and knees. There must have been enough splintered wood to feed a bonfire. When it was over, all four of us dashed madly to wash out our mouths with soap and sit in cold water.

And in the solemn following ceremony, I forgot the bruises in the sheer joy of becoming a member of the frat. Now I could wear the Sigma pin. And what was equally important, I had a year to plan my revenge on next year's crop of freshmen.

18

Many of us who attended college in the 1920s owe our education to railroads and white people's tips. Service jobs were the chief summer employment. When I learned Hazel had applied and been accepted by Union Pacific in Kansas City as a dining car waiter, I also applied and was asked to report to the commissary three days after college closed. Hazel was so broke he sold me his sax for four dollars. Together we went to Kansas City, and next day we were to go to Ogden, Utah, to work on the Oregon Short Line Branch. That night I went to Paseo Dancing Academy, a big gaudy ballroom with huge revolving chandeliers, to catch one of the classic Battles of Jazz between the bands of Benny Moten and George Lee.

Together they ruled the K. C. jazz kingdom. Moten's band originally leaned heavily on New Orleans jazz but soon slid into a groove of its own, influenced by the Texas eight-to-the-bar piano style filtering north through Oklahoma. Emphasis was on driving rhythm with strong riffs providing a blazing base for hot solos, much as the left hand of a boogie-woogie pianist lays the foundation for swooping flights by the right. Of course in 1925 this style had not reached its full development; that was to come ten years later, after Moten died and Count Basie formed a band liberally laced with Motenites.

In 1925 Moten could hold his own with most bands and was justly famous throughout the Midwest. Nevertheless, he had a strong rival in the smaller group led by George Lee.

We wanted Lee that year for our annual spring party at Kansas State. This was our one major event. We planned and lived for it all year. Guests came for a three-day weekend by train and car from as far as Denver, Omaha, Oklahoma City, and St. Louis; one year Roy Wilkins, later national head of the N.A.A.C.P., attended while vacationing from Minnesota University where he studied journalism. The big dance was Saturday night on campus followed by smaller after-parties until dawn. Of course Lorraine came from Salina.

However we couldn't meet Lee's price and settled for a lesser but highly competent band from Topeka. As for Lee, he played every instrument in his outfit. His sister, Julia, who in the 1940s won belated fame on records as a blues singer, was regular pianist and vocalist, but the big star was George. Ordinarily he blew soprano and baritone sax; but on special numbers he soloed in turn on piano, trombone, trumpet, and drums as well as reeds. The broads flipped. Their jazz battles were basically a contest between Moten's musicianship and Lee's showmanship.

Next day Hazel and I "deadheaded" out of Kansas City for Utah: that is, our travel and meals were provided by the railroad. Back we went through Manhattan and monotonous miles of ripening wheat and finally the rising foothills of the Rockies. This was my first sight of mountains. From Denver to Ogden I looked as if I were watching a tennis match as I tried to see out windows on both sides of the day coach.

We were housed in the Porters and Waiters Club near the Ogden Union Station and given vouchers for meals at a nearby restaurant. Since the railroad was completely responsible until we made our initial trips, the commissary assigned us immediately. Hazel left next day, and twenty-four hours later I was sent on a run to Idaho and Oregon, returning by way of Salt Lake City with a stopover there of several hours. On this five-day trip I learned the compact organization of a dining car. Every inch of space was efficiently utilized. At night we folded the tables, stacked chairs, and then removed cots from floor compartments, hung curtains, and converted into a rail dormitory. But I got little sleep. Next to me was a second cook who several times nightly snored the grand finale to the *Overture of 1812* with explosive snorts that would give an inferiority complex to real cannon.

Now that I had made a run and was on the payroll, Union Pacific assumed no more responsibility. From then on, all expenses had to come from my pocket. I was to report daily for possible assignment. Each morning I went to the commissary, lazed around several hours with a dozen other impatiently waiting waiters, then was told to go home and come back next day. This was in the dark ages before dining car unions.

I had picked up a few dollars from tips on my run and had a little money left over from home, but rent and food soon reduced this almost to nothing. The Porters and Waiters Club was a drag unless you drank, shot pool, or gambled; and I could afford none of these. When I tired of hanging around I walked.

Ogden was especially beautiful in early morning, when a fresh sun poured honey-bright rays on snow-covered mountains crouching nearby. Physically this was a delightful city. I would have liked it better had it not been in Utah.

Church and state were almost indistinguishable. The Mormon religion controlled the government. Like Kansas, Utah also banned cigarette sales but for religious reasons. This I could have accepted. But I could not accept the attitude toward blacks.

It was not the vicious hate prevalent in Dixie, but a cold indifferent contempt conditioned by Mormon interpretation of the Bible. They believed our black skins were a curse, a punishment from God for all descendants of Ham who laughed at Noah's naked drunkenness.[8] Of course some of us individually were "good darkies," but, as a group, the best we could hope for after death was eternal abode in a jim crow ghetto outside the pearly gates. The more fortunate might be selected as celestial garbage men to rid the golden streets at night of old cartons of milk and honey. The Mormons didn't really hate us; they just didn't give a damn. And yet, years later in Honolulu I numbered several individual Mormons among my best and most reliable friends.

Despite the prevailing attitude, a number of blacks had settled in Ogden. Steadily employed dining car workers and Pullman porters after several days on the road usually had money to spend and craved action. These permanent residents helped them lighten their pockets. Three brownskin prostitutes had rented a house near the club and were virtually coining money. In their large front room were tables for blackjack and poker. Customers gambled while awaiting their turns with the gals. If a sucker went broke meanwhile, the whores had already pocketed a sizeable portion of his cash through cutting the games and selling bootleg liquor. Cops ignored this house and its virtual wide-open operations, apparently on the theory that it was better for niggers to go to bed with their own women instead of crossing the color line.

After two weeks of daily disappointment at the commissary, I gave up in disgust. I drew my pay at the same time as a couple of California college men returning to Los Angeles and one or two older fellows getting jobs as dishwashers and porters in Ogden restaurants. I never saw Hazel again.

On the way back I stopped off in Denver to take in a dance near Five Points and to pawn my sax. Elementary mathematics told me that returning to Kansas City was unwise since I did not have train fare home. I hocked the sax for fifteen dollars so I was still eleven dollars ahead. Taking a map, I selected what seemed the closest town to Wichita on the Union Pacific line and jumped train. There I bought a ticket on one of those panting little locals which puffed to a stop every time a trail crossed the tracks. I considered getting off and walking, but that would have put me in Wichita ahead of my suitcase.

Lorraine lost her cool when she returned home from mailing a letter to me in Ogden and found me sitting on her front porch. However, I stayed in Wichita only a couple of days. It was now too late to get a summer job so I went home to Arkansas City, arriving just in time to see Dad pay one man a dollar not to kill another.

It was the aftermath of several eight-ball games at the pool parlor which Foots (who used to lead the "Hesitation Schottische") had won from a younger guy named Cecil.

"At two bits a game," Foots announced, "you owes me a buck."

"Man, you'll get your money," Cecil said.

"I wants it right now."

"I ain't got it now."

"You mean you done lost an' ain't gonna pay me?"

"Not now I ain't."

"Then I'm gonna git me a dolluh's worth of your ass."

"Man, you ain't bad, you jus' smells bad," Cecil retorted angrily. "Since you think you's so tough, I ain't gonna pay you a goddamn cent now or any other time."

Foots didn't say another word. He got that cold, mean look on his face which we knew from long experience spelled trouble. Then he turned on his heel and walked rapidly out the door toward his house a block away. We watched him through the window. There were four of us left in the pool hall in addition to Cecil. In the past Foots, a heavy and powerful man, had beaten a number of foes unconscious and had cut one severely. He was understood to have shot a man to death down in Oklahoma. Accordingly, we tried to reason with Cecil.

"I wouldn't give that motherfucking bastard a dollar now even if he promised to show me the Statue of Liberty doing the hootchy-kootchy," Cecil said. "Why, man, I wouldn't even piss up his ass if his guts was on fire."

Through the window we watched Foots coming back toward us. He had a double-barrelled shotgun in the crook of his right arm.

"Fella, git outa here!" Dad pleaded. "That fool's fixin' to blow your brains out!"

I suppose that when the chips are down, a man who has been kicked around all his life, who knows nothing but the mean heartbreaking blues and is breathing only from force of habit, doesn't give a damn whether he dies today or tomorrow. The wagon can come anytime; it doesn't really matter whether he goes this day or the next. Cecil continued leaning against the pool table looking completely unconcerned as Foots came closer.

"I ain't scared of that black son of a bitch," he said in a matter of fact voice.

Foots opened the door, came in, his face cold and hard, and started to aim his shotgun at Cecil from ten feet away, with no more emotion than if he were drawing a bead on a sitting rabbit or a sleeping snake. Cecil neither moved nor changed expression. The rest of us scrambled to the far side of the room. That is, all but Dad. Reaching in his pants pocket, he yanked out a dollar bill and waved it in front of Foots, pleading, "For God's sake, don't shoot! Here's a dollar. Take it an' go!"

Foots lowered the gun, reached out and took the greenback, then turned and left without saying a word. I was trembling as we watched him through the window until he reached his house. Then Cecil spoke:

"Any of you clowns wanna play a game of rotation?"

That summer, about a week later, I had my first and only run-in with the local police department. It happened around midnight. I had closed the pool hall and had walked to within two blocks of home when a cruising car slowed and came to a stop near me on the dark street.

"Where'n hell you goin' this time of night?" a voice asked.

I looked toward the black sedan. I saw two white men sitting on the front seat and another in back. There was no identification on the vehicle.

"What business is it of yours?" I shot back.

"Don't get smart, boy. We're police," one of the men said, getting out and flashing a badge. I spotted a holstered gun on his right side. "I'm police chief here. Now, what th' hell you doing in this neighborhood this time of night?"

"I live here," I said, "a couple of blocks down the street."

"How come I ain't never seen you before?"

"I've been away to college. Just got home a week ago."

"Yeah?" the chief sounded skeptical. "Well, you git your black ass in this car with us. A white lady on th' next street over phoned there was somebody prowling around her yard. We aim to take you there an' see if she can identify you. She got a good look at him."

"Am I supposed to fit the description?" I asked.

"Shut up an' git in the car," the chief said, motioning toward the back seat.

I entered and sat beside the officer who kept an eye turned in my direction, evidently to see that I didn't make a break for it. Nobody spoke during the five-block ride to the complainant's house. The chief and an aide marched me to her front porch and knocked on the door.

"Ain't this him?" the chief asked hopefully when the woman answered.

She peered at me and shook her head. "I told you he was short and stocky. He warn't tall like this'n."

"Are you sure? Maybe you made a mistake."

"No. The prowler didn't look nothin' like this boy."

"Okay, lady." The chief sounded keenly disappointed, as if he had been deprived of the anticipated pleasure of working me over in company with his brother officers. It wasn't every day they had a chance to whip a big black nigger, and a college nigger at that. He motioned to me, "Git back in the car."

About a block away we stopped.

"What'd you say you was doin' around here this time of night?" the chief asked.

By now I, of course, was angry. Obviously I had been picked up not because I fit the description of the prowler, but because I was the first black they saw.

"I told you I was on my way home," I said.

"Where do you live?"

"At 1014 North Summit Street."

The chief turned to his companions. "I didn't know any damn niggers lived in this part of town, did you?"

"There's a darky family livin' down here somewhere," one answered.

I boiled inside, but I was helpless. At that moment I would have given twenty years off my life had I been able to bind all three together, throw them motionless on the ground in front of me, and for a whole hour piss in their faces.

"All right, boy, git out an' go on home," the chief said, opening the car door.

I went home, resolving from then on to spend as little time in Arkansas City as I possibly could. This was my birthplace, but it wasn't my town.

19

That fall of 1925 I hit the campus with what was, in the language of that day, the "cat's meow." It was a pair of Oxford Bags, a new style of trouser with legs large enough for guests. Mine were biscuit tan with each leg a flopping twenty-three inches wide from crotch to bottom ending in a big two inch cuff. I bought them as I passed through Wichita. A men's shop there had just stocked its first shipment. They were not available at Kansas State for at least two weeks after the fall semester opened. Judging from the stares they attracted on campus, many students undoubtedly thought they were some weird coon style until they were displayed at the smartest male clothing stores.

I especially liked the way they flopped around when I danced the Charleston. By now I was admittedly expert. I even entered the local contest ending a week's appearance at a Manhattan theatre by Ginger Rogers and her Redheaded Girl Revue. Later to become one of Hollywood's top dancers and glamour queens, Ginger had just entered show business after winning a statewide Charleston contest in her native Texas. She was quite young, around fifteen at the time, but already she had enough appeal to head a little road show playing small towns in that part of the country. Ginger herself helped judge the contest which closed her troupe's performance.

No, I did not win. The best dancer for miles around was my frat brother, Mouse Miller, who also beat out an adequate piano and was a natural comedian. Most of us thought he should have gone on the stage instead of studying electrical engineering, although later he became an inspector for Uncle Sam, assigned to installations throughout the Pacific area. Our belief in Miller's potential was strengthened when a crazy little broad, who had danced professionally in Harlem and Chicago, settled temporarily in Manhattan and teamed with Mouse. We called her "Hey Hey" after the rhythm and commonly used expression of most Charleston dances.

She proved her value during the annual Aggie Orpheum that spring. This was a contest, held two consecutive nights in the college auditorium, at which campus organizations presented vaudeville acts competing for cash prizes. That year Sigma house entered for the first time. Fry, the brilliant architectural student, was also an accomplished tenor banjoist. He played several jazz numbers with Mouse on piano, then made a series of lightning charcoal sketches which started out as one subject then completely changed into something else. For our final number Mouse, Hey Hey, Frank Greene, and I danced the Charleston together and as encore I soloed. My frat brothers figured that seeing Old Heavy gyrate and perform the fancy steps expected of a hundred-pounder would slay 'em, and they were right. We brought down the house.

Purely by chance that first night, we followed a white student act featuring the Charleston and by comparison the ofay kids looked like rank beginners. ("You know, my dear, colored people are natural dancers. They're *born* with rhythm, you know.") We carved 'em so completely that our pale competitors wanted to withdraw but were talked into going through with the second night's show only on the condition that our acts be completely separated. On the final night, they opened the show and we closed it.

Judges awarded us second place, although the audience booed loud and long believing we clearly deserved top prize. For several weeks afterward, white students stopped us on campus to tell us they believed we had been cheated. As for me personally, I found I was now being described as "the poet who looks like a prizefighter and Charlestons like hell." I was able to pick up some badly needed cash by teaching some of my steps to a number of white girls at several of the sorority houses.

This was also the year we formed a quartet to sing spirituals. I remembered the repertoire of the Hi-Y group in Wichita and handled bass. Frankly, we were pretty horrible, but the white churches were wild about us. After all, we were the only group in town who could render "the plaintive music of our darker brothers in Christ, those songs which comforted them during the dark days of slavery." Fact is, all we really had to do was open our mouths and make a noise; our audiences had wholeheartedly accepted the stereotype that "all Negroes know how to sing."

That summer I was able to get my old job back at the Wichita Club and I met my new great love, Gladys, on a blind date. The everlasting flame with Lorraine had already burned out; evidently they'd started making eternities shorter. Gladys was firey, slender but shapely, light brownskin, and quite good looking. Although she was two years younger than I, after due consideration I refused to hold that against her and went overboard in a hurry. She was studying music in Wichita with the intention of becoming a concert pianist. Within weeks we reached the when-we-get-married stage.

Mother died that summer, in 1926.

She became ill on a trip to Texas and rushed home for hospitalization, but it was too late. Her appendix had ruptured, and peritonitis had already set in. I was called home and reached Arkansas City only a few hours before her passing, when she was already in a coma.

As you have gathered by now, I am in many ways unconventional, a black maverick. I am quite unorthodox even in my attitude toward death.

To me death is so final and inevitable that I look upon tears as ridiculous. It's not that I oppose weeping; under certain conditions I have cried copiously and undoubtedly will continue to do so. But this is in anger, frustration, or extreme joy—an emotional reaction to a condition which may be controlled by me or other humans. Not so with death. I may be horrified or incensed or sickened at the way death comes but never at death itself. I know of nobody who does not move toward an eventual rendezvous with this finality from the first moment of breathing. Since we have not yet discovered a way to escape death, why weep? So I accepted my mother's passing as I did that of Granny and Old Granddad and of close friends throughout life: I missed them for selfish reasons, but I knew all along that some day there had to be a parting, a period to the sentence, an ending of the chapter, and a final closing of the book.

A month after I returned to college in the fall of 1926, I heard from Aunt Hattie. After Ol' Granddad died she had again sworn to keep in touch with Mother and, as usual, had not. Dad finally located her in Joliet, Illinois, and Aunt Hattie was magnificently remorseful over not being able to attend the funeral of "my own dear sister." From now on, for sure, she was going to keep in touch with me; I could depend on that since I was her "only living relative." She had married (her third husband) a Clarence W. Reynolds from whom she was now separated.

She not only wrote me regularly but contacted her estranged mate, who lived in Chicago, and had him begin writing to me. Within a short time, they built in me a gnawing hunger for the Windy City. Reynolds, a Spanish-American war veteran, worked as a Pullman porter but had long been a frustrated journalist. He told me about South Side newspapers and mailed me copies.

I went into an intensive huddle with myself.

There wasn't anything wrong at Kansas State. I was satisfied, especially when I was in the journalism building where I considered myself well integrated. This wasn't always true elsewhere—except at exam time. On such days, when I took a seat, I would suddenly find myself surrounded by pink dolls who heretofore hadn't seemed to acknowledge my existence. They would break out their most charming smiles and say quite frankly: "I'm expecting you to help me with some of these answers today." Invariably, I would nod gravely back. When stumped and the prof wasn't looking, a coed would nudge me and look expectant. Whereupon I would whisper, "That beats me, too," even though I knew the answer perfectly. I remembered a blues recording by Mamie Smith:

> I'm gonna tell you like the Chinaman tol' the Jew
> Say I'm gonna tell you like the Chinaman tol' the Jew:
> "If you no likee me then me no likee you."

The journalism building was different. Very. I had excellent relationships with all and was treated like any other student. In fact, one instructor, a very attractive German girl who had graduated from Northwestern the previous June and was teaching for a year at Kansas State, told me privately and pointedly she was going to teach in China next year; and after I got my degree, she was sure I could get an appointment on the staff where she would be.

But Chicago was a seductive siren. I had no desire to teach in China or anywhere else. Both Aunt Hattie and Uncle Clarence had flooded me with all the black weeklies they could find, and I had read enough to know by now I was a far better writer than most they then employed. Further, my technical training was now aimed mainly toward eventually working on a daily and there were none in Afro-America. I was fully aware also that any job would be with the black press and at a comparatively low pay scale; no matter how well qualified or imposing my record at Kansas State, the white press was locked against me.

In fact, in a rash moment the previous summer I had applied at the Wichita *Beacon* for a job as a reporter until the fall semester started. I knew of white students who had obtained similar work elsewhere on Kansas newspapers—students who were, according to the teaching staff, far inferior to me as embryonic journalists. Further, the *Beacon* managing editor was a personal friend of one of my favorite profs who had taken a special interest in me. I suppose inwardly the *Beacon* executive was amazed at my audacity, although outwardly he kept his cool. He explained the staff was full with a long waiting list; there simply was no room for a summer reporter. He was quite pleasant, and I accepted his explanation at face value.

A day or two later I mentioned to a soul brother that I had been down to the *Beacon* to apply for a job but had not been accepted.

"That's too bad," he said, "I understand their janitor jobs pay pretty well. You could've saved a lot for college this fall."

I opened my mouth, then decided to keep quiet. So rigid were employment barriers, I think I might have ruined his day had I said I asked for a reporting job.

One day that fall Dr. Willard, vice president of Kansas State and dean of men, called me to his office.

"You have a nice record in your department and of course you expect to graduate next year," he began. "Tell me, what will you do when you get your degree? Are there any colored newspapers?"

I was taken aback. It had never occurred to me that an educator of his standing could be so ignorant of black America. Yet in a way I could appreciate his concern. He assumed correctly there was virtually no chance of my being hired by a white newspaper. At that time there were only two black newsmen to my knowledge on white dailies in the entire United States: Eugene Gordon on the Boston *Post* and Lester A. Walton, later U.S. Minister of Liberia, on the New York *World*.

"We have a few," I said, not cracking a smile. "Something like two hundred." My figures were from the *Negro Yearbook* which had provided me with facts and information on Afro-America not available to me elsewhere; my sense of identity and pride in black achievement had taken root and grown strong in the few years since high school.

"Is that so?" he said, looking both relieved and surprised. "I didn't realize you people had any presses. Then maybe you *can* get work."

I didn't tell him I was thinking of dropping out of college. I saved that information for Professor Rogers just before the Christmas holidays.

"Why not stay out for a while, if you think you must, and plan on coming back later for your degree," he suggested. "When you're ready to return, let me know and I'll do everything to get you any financial help you might need."

I spent a week of the Christmas vacation in Wichita to be with Gladys and the other week at home with Dad. Knowing he might try to dissuade me, I didn't tell him I was going to Chicago at the end of the first semester, preferring to wait until it was an accomplished fact. Besides, I became twenty-one while at home and believed that since I was now legally a man, I should not expect further support from him even to finish college.

Since then I have never been back to Arkansas City, nor have I been homesick. I could never be homesick for that town. Sure, I'd like to see childhood friends, but that's all. I have too many bitter memories from discrimination. I am glad to call any place home where I can live decently. I cannot feel nostalgia for any special patch of earth hemmed in by prejudice. How many older Afro-Americans of sound mind long to go back to Lynchem, Mississippi, or Shootem, Alabama? If ever I find a soul brother or sister sincerely singing "Way Down Upon the Swanee River," "Old Folks at Home," or "Carry Me Back To Ol' Virginny," I shall place a panic call for the men in white; such a person would be so mentally deranged he would constitute a serious threat to the community.

But don't get me wrong. Arkansas City was no better or worse than a thousand other places under the Stars and Stripes. It was then far superior to others in Dixie. What I am saying is that most communities stink. Most of us are not homesick for the kind of racism we faced in the place of our birth.

I stopped over in Kansas City on my way to Chicago to hear Bennie Moten again and call on a teacher who had attended our last spring party. She was quite dark, with a complexion rich and creamy like pure butter, and the most beautiful teeth I have ever seen. However, she did not go to public dances, so I went alone to the Paseo Dancing Academy.

The Moten men were stomping up a storm to the noisy crowd. The huge revolving chandeliers showered the dancers with confetti of light spangles while the band burned them with smoking hot jazz. As I stood on the sidelines, a young fellow about my size came up to talk. I recognized him as a Kansas Citian who brought two-gallon jugs of liquor down to one of our parties at Kansas State. His name, too, was Davis, and he had poise plus a friendly flow of gab. Later he moved to Cleveland and was elected to the city council.

"Look at these birds and the way they dance, and you can tell what kind of work they do," he said. "See that dude there with the real mean look? I bet he's a chauffeur for some big white doctor and hasn't had much sleep all week."

He pointed to at least a dozen others and speculated not only about their jobs but their personal habits. We called over two or three at different times and after short conversations learned one was a packing-house worker, another a bellhop, and the first a doctor's chauffeur as Davis had surmised. He looked triumphantly at me.

"How's that, man? Thirty-eight and two, huh?" he said, using the latest hip talk of that day.

"Forty all over the world," I shot back.

1927–1929

20

Monotonous miles of freight cars and passenger coaches on a web of twisting endless tracks below, and above snakes of smoke slithering from factory chimneys and blending with the gray winter day. This was the Chicago I saw as my train rumbled toward Dearborn Street Station. I was excited for this was a mighty monster of a metropolis. I could toss in the population of both Kansas Cities, Denver, Wichita, Ogden, Salt Lake City, and every other city I'd seen, and it wouldn't fill half of Chicago. I knew there were more than a quarter of a million blacks, more than two and a half times as many as lived in all Kansas.

I had only thirty-six dollars and didn't know anybody. I was coming in on hope and faith. I hoped my uncle, whom I had never met and who would not be back for a couple of days, would help me find a newspaper job. Even if that failed, I had faith in my ability to get along. You're like that at twenty-one when you leave college. You got the world in a jug, Lawd, stopper in your hand. You got the River Jordan flowing through your veins, and the gals oughta stand in line waiting to be baptized. You've got confidence oozing from your pores.

I knew I had three assets. First, I was big and seemed strong; my hands with their long slender fingers looked artistic and bespoke sensitivity. Second, I owned a deep voice which appealed to some women. And, finally, I was a college-trained journalist. On the other hand, I still had my inferiority complex and was usually quite shy and withdrawn around women.

I left the station and walked past patches of grimy snow toward State Street. This was a dirty, busy edge of downtown. On State Street, a short distance away, I stopped and looked north. Elevated trains roped in the south edge of the Loop. Beyond I saw sooty buildings strain upward. So these were skyscrapers and that was the main business district. And I was disappointed. The buildings were tall, yes, but I wanted them even higher. Really now, what *did* I expect? Steel and stone creasing the sky above as far as eye could see? After all, wasn't that ridiculous?

A streetcar clanged along. In Kansas City somebody had told me which to take to reach the Wabash Avenue YMCA. I studied the signs, and when the right one came I hopped it; somebody had also told me I'd have to move fast or I'd be left behind. I stared intently at block after block of dirty buildings; they were old and decrepit but they were new to me. Then, around 26th, I saw more and more rainbow faces, and by the time I left the trolley at 38th I was merely another swimmer in an endless soul sea.

A short block east squatted the Wabash Y, a building dingy as the rest. I registered, paid a week's rent, grabbed breakfast in the cafeteria, then set out walking to explore nearby Chicago.

Walking slowly north on State Street toward 35th I heard the loud belches of the overstuffed city, but rising above this cacophony was the swooping sound of loudspeakers blaring the new Bix Beiderbecke-Frankie Trumbauer recording, "Singin' the Blues." The melody rushed at me from a half dozen little record shops in three blocks. I didn't mind because I liked the number. But at the same time it had the disturbing effect of reminding me of the sax I'd hocked in Denver.

On 35th I walked east looking for Fannon's Drugstore where Uncle Clarence received his mail. I would meet him there day after next. I passed hundreds of blacks, all in a hurry; here they rarely lazed along. I found Fannon's but nearby of equally great importance was the shouting sign of a cabaret. It was the Sunset, and there were pictures of entertainers and a huge photograph of Louis Armstrong who played there nightly with his band. Across the street, another sign said Plantation Cafe. That was where King Oliver and his Creole Jazz Band blew nightly.[1] I had records by both groups and was frantic to hear them in person. But my pocketbook told me no. Maybe later, but not now.

At a nearby newsstand I bought a copy of a small magazine, *The Light and Heebie Jeebies,* telling all about South Side night life.[2]

An advertisement for the weekly Dancing Class at the Alvin Dansant caught my eye. Admission was only seventy-five cents. That night I went and met and danced with two sister schoolteachers originally from Phoenix, Arizona, but mainly I listened to a band led by a hot trumpeter named Thigpen who called himself the "young Louis Armstrong." Although Satchmo was then only twenty-seven, he had already become a legend. Thigpen's horn whetted my appetite for the real thing, so when I left the Dansant I went immediately to the Sunset and stood outside on the sidewalk. I saw no one enter but ofays and a few sharply dressed black studs who plunked down a cover of $1.50 each. But I did hear a searing high horn, joyous and defiant, snipping wild and crazy patterns of rhythmic sound. I stood there spellbound until I was actually shaking from the cold before returning to the Y.

Next evening I went to the Vendome Theatre on State near 31st. The movie was inconsequential; I wanted to hear Erskine Tate's band. Louis played there nightly before doubling at the Sunset. Following the new, forgotten film, a spotlight ran its finger over the orchestra pit. I heard a brief semiclassical program before the band launched into a jazz concert, and from the first note I was conscious that Satchmo was not the only master. A phenomenal percussionist named Jimmy Bertrand, who could pass for white, played an actual melody on the kettledrums; an amazing pianist named Teddy Weatherford sounded as if he invented the ivories, and a little alto saxist, Stomp Evans, took wild solos sitting on the back of his chair and turning in a half circle. This band just wouldn't behave; it was really forty, a knockout.

On the following day I went to Fannon's to wait for Uncle Clarence. After a half hour he showed up. He was a little guy, dark as a raisin, past fifty. After preliminary amenities, I mentioned that Aunt Hattie quit writing after I told her I was coming to Chicago. I wondered why.

He looked at me gravely, as if making up his mind, then said, "You may as well know the truth. She quit writing because she doesn't want you to see her the way she is now." He took a deep breath. "I did all I could to help her, but it wasn't no use. Bad friends jus' drug her down to nothin'. I hate to say it to her own flesh and blood, but she's a whiskey head. She'll do anything for a bottle."

I knew instinctively he was telling the truth, and I sensed he was carrying a mighty torch for Aunt Hattie. So that was it. Very well, there was nothing I could do. Afterward I didn't mention Aunt Hattie. Some six months or so later, I heard from his friends that she had died of acute alcoholism and Clarence had borrowed money to give her a decent burial.

Clarence had arranged for me to meet Lucius Harper, managing editor of the Chicago *Defender,* so next day I joined him at the drugstore with samples of my feature articles and news stories. As we walked down 35th, he tugged my arm, saying, "Here comes a guy I want you to meet."

We stopped in front of a solemn, yellow skinned, keenly dressed man.

"Shake hands," my uncle said, "with Jelly Roll Morton."

The famous pianist, who claimed he invented jazz, pumped my hand without smiling. After a few innocuous pleasantries he sauntered on. My uncle said, "That's the greatest piano player in the world." He paused, then added, "And one of the biggest pimps."

I was impressed to know Clarence was on speaking terms with Jelly Roll. The last record I'd bought before leaving K-State was his waxing of "Black Bottom Stomp" and "The Chant" which we'd almost worn out at a frat house hop.

At the big *Defender* office on Indiana Avenue I was introduced to Lucius Harper. He had the sleek look and facial features of a well-fed Italian gangster. He seemed genuinely impressed as he read my material taking time to digest every word of two features based on material in the *Negro Yearbook* which contained material Harper said he "didn't know." But there was no opening now on the editorial staff; nobody left the *Defender* except by request. However, give him time and he'd try his damnedest to work me into the picture.

I waited for a week or two but nothing happened. I knew there were few trained black journalists around; I doubt whether there were a dozen in the entire nation. The *Defender's* city editor, Dewey Jones, had a degree from the Medill School of Journalism at Northwestern; I believe he was the only college-trained black in all of Chicago at that time. There were a tiny few scattered elsewhere about America. My cash had virtually disappeared. Then Willard Townsend, one of Clarence's friends I had met at Fannon's, told me of two newspapermen who were starting the National News & Feature Service. Townsend, who later founded the Red Caps Union, took me to the new Waverly Building at 35th and Michigan, not yet formally open, where Perry Thompson and Henry Brown had an office on the second floor. Both were enthusiastic about my work and promised me that if I stuck with them we could all make money together. They were planning to syndicate a magazine section to the Afro-American press. With my talent, they said, I would be a key figure. Meanwhile they would assure me of living expenses until the magazine got rolling. Their picture looked so good I immediately joined with them. That night I wrote to Dad, who had been wondering what the hell had happened to me, to tell him that I had a job.

21

Here is the South Side newspaper scene in 1927. First and foremost was the *Defender,* then the largest in the nation. Next came the *Whip,* and in third place was the *Bee.* Some distance behind was the *World,* and limping along far back was the *Broad Axe.*

The *Broad Axe* was known as a "tri-weekly"; it tried to come out weekly but rarely made it except at election time. Like virtually all our press, it was Republican. A black Democratic newspaper before Franklin D. Roosevelt was almost on a par with the second coming of Christ.

Sometime before I arrived, the editor of the *Broad Axe* had made a unique contribution to history.[3] Trying to cash a check at Lincoln State Bank, then a prominent institution near 31st and State, he had been turned down. Furious, he swore to get even.

So burned up was he that the following week he got out enough papers to cover South Side newsstands. In shouting black letters three inches high was a scare headline legible thirty feet away:

LINCOLN BANK FAILS

Beneath in small type was:

TO CASH CHECK

An immediate run started on the bank. Depositors took one hasty look at the huge headline, dropped everything, and made a beeline for Lincoln State. These were the days before Uncle Sam insured deposits. The street in front was jammed with people shoving and pushing to get inside and take out their money. Alarmed bank officials were both frantic and puzzled until someone produced a copy of the *Broad Axe.* Of course they were outraged and demanded the editor's arrest for printing false information and started a run on their institution, a criminal offense.

But the editor calmly folded his arms and laughed. He pointed out he had merely told the truth. Lincoln Bank HAD failed to cash a check. It was all there in print. There was no law, he reminded them, requiring all pertinent facts to appear in the same size type. He had them, and the bank officials knew it. They could do nothing but fruitlessly fume. And it is a matter of record that Lincoln Bank was never the same thereafter, closing its doors within the next few months.

The Chicago *World,* edited by Jake Tipper who regularly ran for some office each election and just as regularly lost, usually showed its face every week. Sometimes, however, there would be no change in content except on the front page. A nosey person could look inside and see whether the editorial staff had been paid the previous week. No wages, no change in reading matter.

Jake, a fast-talking, heavy, but energetic dark man, rarely noticed news content, concentrating almost wholly on ads. During one election campaign, he was said to have grabbed the latest copy of the *World* from the press and hotfooted it to the office of Judge Lyle, a well-known jurist, to sell him a big advertising layout for the next issue. Judge Lyle picked up the paper, glanced at the front page, read the main headline, stiffened, and angrily threw it back at Tipper. The banner, written by Carey B. Lewis, city editor who was no fan of Judge Lyle, read: JUDGE LYLE IS A SISSY. When Jake saw the streamer, he almost exploded. Apologizing profusely and promising to immediately fire whoever was responsible, he also gave his word to right this grave wrong in the next issue. So seven days later he returned and proudly presented that week's edition bearing another larger streamer: JUDGE LYLE IS NOT A SISSY. But this did not placate the judge, who pointed out this might have the opposite effect on those who had not seen the first headline. However, Jake talked his way out of this, although he did not get as large an ad as he had expected.

Tipper also operated a job printing shop. Realizing he had to pay his printers or they would quit, he developed a system for taking care of his most essential employees. Rarely having enough on deposit to cover his entire payroll, he gave checks early to the favored few, then engaged the rest of the staff in a lengthy discussion until the lucky ones cashed their checks and returned. Then he distributed checks to all, including "dummies" to those he had paid earlier, and disappeared until Monday.

Anthony Overton published the *Bee.* A financier, originally from Kansas, he owned the thriving Overton Hygenic Company which manufactured hair straighteners and cosmetics; was chief stockholder in Victory Mutual Life Insurance Company; and president of Douglas National, America's only black-owned national bank. All were housed in his own office building at 36th and State. The *Bee* was virtually a house organ to glorify his business interests. This *Bee* had no stinger. Overton wanted nothing controversial in its columns. There were enough sacred cows to stock a Texas ranch. In addition Overton, a small, stoop-shouldered, medium-brown man, felt he had been ordained from on high to keep any money that came his way. Judging from the salaries he paid, he was surprisingly successful.

The *Whip* was the South Side's most militant journal. Only seven columns wide instead of the standard eight, its owners were trying to cut into *Defender* circulation and win community support with its aggressive "Don't Spend Your Money Where You Can't Work" campaign. Three men owned it: Joseph D. Bibb, Patrick B. Prescott, and A. C. MacNeal. Bibb, an attorney, was editor; MacNeal was general manager. Both were Harvard graduates and light enough to pass. Prescott, also a lawyer, had graduated from the University of Chicago, published a number of short stories, and was son-in-law of Bishop Archibald Carey, an AME prelate who was the nonwhite member of the three-man Chicago Civil Service Commission. Prescott was managing editor, but neither he nor Bibb spent much time at the *Whip* which, although operating a separate job printing plant, was itself printed each Wednesday at a large white commercial shop on the West Side.

Perry Thompson had recently been city editor for the *Whip*. From Fisk University in Nashville where he'd majored in chemistry, he'd drifted into journalism and shown an uncanny ability to get news. Once, however, he became too nosey and stepped on highly sensitive gangster toes in a series of articles. By mail he received a special delivery package containing only a solitary, highly polished .38 bullet. He got the message immediately. The articles stopped.

The *Defender* was at least two laps ahead of all competition. It was the brain baby of Robert Sengstacke Abbott, a stocky dark man from Georgia who came to Chicago "wearing a boot and a shoe." Starting with only a pushcart and a dream, he became one of the nation's wealthiest Afro-Americans. During World War I, his income mushroomed beyond his wildest hopes. Gathering a competent staff, he pounded with all his might at Dixie discrimination. Using such slogans as "American race prejudice must be destroyed," he urged his readers to come North with such apparent success that the *Defender* was banned in many parts of the South. The *Defender* then went underground. Sales zoomed, particularly when distributors, serving also as reporters, wrote gossipy notes from their home communities, and for the first time many Afro-Americans saw their names in print. Lucius Harper also devised fake casualty lists following floods and other disasters which, prominently displayed on the front page,

attracted even more readers. Money orders and checks poured in so profusely that the business office in desperation set up barrels as temporary
receptacles for the morning mail, later emptying and tallying results.

With all that cash floating in, palms were sticky. Abbott, a realist who
knew what was going on, reputedly called his key personnel together one
day and said, in effect:

"I know some *Defender* money is finding its way into pockets where
it doesn't belong. I could worry myself sick trying to watch, but I won't.
Instead, I'm going to draw twenty-five hundred dollars weekly for myself,
insist that all *Defender* obligations be met on time and that a certain
percentage above operating expenses be set aside as reserve, and let you
fellows fight over the rest." Remember, this was a day when apartments
rented for forty dollars monthly, a good wage was thirty-five dollars
weekly, and a brand new Ford cost less than one thousand dollars.

General manager for the *Defender* was a diminutive, stern faced,
wavy haired lawyer, Nathan K. McGill, known as "little Napoleon," who
ruled with a stainless steel hand. It was unclear whether his mission was
to try to wrest control from Abbott or defang the overly ambitious by
promoting friction. What was certain, however, was that he could have
taught Machiavelli a thing or two about chicanery. He successfully kept
employees guessing as to how long they would hold jobs, and the petty
jealousies he encouraged were just big enough to stop them from banding
effectively together. Periodically he would mastermind a general house-
cleaning from which not even the managing editor was exempt. Editors,
after serving fifteen to twenty years had been known to leave the office
Saturday at peace with the world and arrive home to find telegrams stating
they had been fired. In due course, some were rehired, perhaps after an
interval of several years. Others were so disgusted that no offers, no matter
how lucrative, could lure them back. Eventually McGill himself, who had
comfortably feathered his own nest, was sacked and spent the rest of his
days and bankroll fighting Abbott and his successors and starting rival
newspapers which soon failed.

Abbott lived in a manner commensurate with his income. His home
boasted several servants, and he had his own chauffeur. But he also put
money back into the newspaper. During the Great Depression when
both advertising and circulation nosedived, he personally poured in
over three hundred thousand dollars—according to estimates—to keep
operating.

He also had idiosyncrasies, among them an abhorrence of the word "Negro," and its use was banned except in those rare instances when it was absolutely necessary, such as part of an official name. Instead, Race man or Race woman was substituted, giving rise to staff parodies such as:

> "Eeny, meeny, miney mo,
> Catch a Race man by the toe——"

A few other newspapers appeared only as election time hustles. Their owners extracted campaign money from white candidates who knew no better. With these it was no more than a racket.

Except for a few at the *Defender*, pay was pitifully low for editors and reporters. I do not know whether publishers expected writers to supplement their small income by easing "inspired" articles into news columns, or if they cynically believed their staffs would do this no matter how big their paychecks and thus rationalized their failure to fork over larger salaries. But there was one unspoken law: don't take too much or get caught. That was why Perry Thompson left the *Whip*.

Small and soft-spoken, Perry wrote like a male sob sister. He also threw off sincerity like a lilac exuding perfume—a real asset in selling a proposition. His partner, Henry Brown, loud and very black, had once been a topnotch boxer and was a talented cartoonist and sports writer. Now and then, he wrote and drew for the daily Chicago *Journal* and monthly *Ring Magazine*.

Either one could con the feathers off a chicken; together they could bullshit a greyhound into climbing a tree. They had already jived Mr. Waverly, the wealthy white owner of the Waverly Building, into letting them occupy the best office before the building was formally opened, paid only one month's rent, remained more than a year as tenants, and once borrowed two hundred dollars from their landlord. Later they split up and moved to two other offices in the building, one a storefront. Waverly also had a Deusenberg agency, and I believe Thompson and Brown did have some remnants of a conscience or they would have talked him out of one of the most expensive cars made in America. Of course, could be Waverly just liked black people for he once told me I could have a Deusenberg for one hundred dollars down and whatever I could pay per month. Fortunately for one of us, I never had that much at one time during this period.

22

South Siders, as I saw them, could be divided into three general classes: stragglers, strugglers, and schemers. Of course some had arrived and did not fit these categories: people such as Abbott, Overton, Jesse Binga of Binga State Bank, and several dozen others in business, politics and the professions. But they were exceptions.

Stragglers, of course, were the numerical majority. Except for churches they were generally unorganized—and at this time the church gave little leadership in solving social and economic problems. Most labor unions were lily white. The great bulk of South Siders were merely breathing out their minutes until their numbers were called, many times in a brawl. Unable to overcome the handicaps of a black skin in the battle for survival, they looked forward to nothing but sex, liquor, gambling, and hard times. They were buried beneath the hopeless blues.

Strugglers busted their brains to get ahead. They struggled to buy apartment buildings or late model cars, to put a little away in the bank, or give their children a good education. They established small beachheads in the struggle for success, either in the hostile white world or among their own people. Their mental fingers grasped the thin edge of a dream.

Schemers were a breed apart. They wanted a maximum of money with a minimum of effort. If they had a good thing going, they guarded it closely. To them, honest work was only for mules or fools. These were the policy kings, gamblers, pimps, con artists, petty politicians, fortune tellers, promoters, self-anointed holy men, and anybody else trying to make a fast buck.[4] Some were technically legitimate in their operations; others were flagrantly outside the law. Most of those I knew in my early Chicago days were schemers.

I soon learned that Perry Thompson and Henry Brown were no more than schemers. Mrs. Thompson was steadily employed as a cateress, and Mrs. Brown was a registered nurse. What Perry and Henry finagled from their wives and what they picked up in small hustles kept them going as they waited for a miracle to start the National News & Feature Service. Obviously there was little for me. But in all fairness, Perry saw to it that I didn't quite starve.

One financial "angel" of the embryonic service was Jack Swade, a big-time pimp and gambler who drove a flashy green Lincoln. Several times when I was absolutely flat Perry wrote a note and told me to take it to Jack. When I found him, he read the message, handed me a ten-dollar or twenty-dollar bill from an elephant-choking roll, and made the same comment: "Perry told me to give it to you. I don't know why."

J. Levirt "St. Louis" Kelly also frequented the office. A lean, dapper man with quick movements and piercing eyes, he was in a number of rackets, including policy and prostitution, and was a rival of Swade's. Once he briefly published a Democratic newspaper which Thompson edited. But he was not asked to help back this new project, and it rankled.

However, his main ambition was to be acclaimed "the toughest man on the South Side." He aspired to the toga recently worn by one Shug Burrell, undisputed king of the badsters—until he was shot to death by a mild-mannered waiter he had bullied once too often at the Sunset Cafe. Ironically enough, Kelly himself became a labor czar and two decades later was also killed with a gun.

Shug's reputation was well known, and nobody in his right mind had dared cross him. Once while driving his car on Indiana near 47th, he accidentally bumped the auto ahead of him at an intersection. The driver came back a fighting man and spouting a stream of flaming invective. Shug laughed, and the other snapped open a switchblade knife.

"What the hell you mean laughing, you black son of a bitch," the irate driver roared. "I'll cut out your balls and throw 'em in your face."

Shug, still sitting calmly in his car, asked, "You know who I am?"

"No, an' I don't give a good goddamn."

"You better. I'm Shug Burrell."

The belligerent driver's jaw dropped. He swallowed hard and broke the world record for knife closing.

"Why'n hell didn't you say so in the first place," he said, hurrying back to his car. "Honest, Mr. Burrell, I didn't mean no harm."

"St. Louis" dreamed of evoking similar terror at the mention of his name, but never quite made it. He carried a .30 Luger pistol shoved down the front of his trousers and knew how to use it. Shortly before I met him, he had shot a collar button into some luckless guy's neck.

I was too much of a young fool to be impressed by the Kelly reputation. One night while Uncle Clarence and I were having dinner at a cafeteria on 35th, Kelly came in and began kidding me about the proposed news service. I was aware of his irritation over Jack Swade being in on the deal instead of him. I listened without comment until he brought up the poor financial condition of Perry and Henry and pointed out if the three of us worked for him, we wouldn't be broke.

"You know, that really would be a happy solution," I cut in. "You supply the cash, which we haven't got, and we supply the brains, which you haven't got."

He froze and looked at me as if I were No. 1 candidate for immediate extermination. I stared calmly back at him. Suddenly he turned on his heel and stalked out.

"Goddamn it, boy, but you were a lucky jackass," Uncle Clarence said. "It's a wonder he didn't take out his Luger and drill you. I was so sure he was gonna go for you that I grabbed a bottle. I was gonna try to brain him if he started to reach for his gun."

Frankly, I hadn't been the least bit scared. After that we always spoke when we met, but he was never cordial. Perry told me later that "St. Louis" thought I was an "educated fool." And me with only two and a half years of college!

Another partial backer of our project was a unique character named Eugene F. Mann. Mann looked like a dirty Caucasian, usually sported a two-day growth of beard, dressed poorly, squinted nervously through bifocals, was thin as a bed slat, and fired talk like a Gatling gun. He refused to let any associate know where he lived. Should his address be learned, he would pack up and move next day.

Mann also had the dubious distinction of fathering that bane of crowded city living, the kitchenette apartment. A good many years earlier he conceived the idea of chopping a large apartment into a number of small independent units, each with its own tiny cooking space, and a community bathroom; the landlord was thereby able to double and triple his rental income for the same amount of space.

However, Mann earned the major part of his living as a philanthropist. Each year he threw a gigantic Christmas dinner for hundreds of down-and-outers. Obviously, a sizeable hunk of cash was required to provide the needy with all they could eat. Mann personally promoted the annual event, going all over Chicago soliciting food and funds from sympathetic businessmen. His kindheartedness, his unselfishness in devoting so much time to the poor unfortunates won his praise and feature articles in the white and black press. It also won him enough to live on comfortably throughout the year.

Mann also had nerve.

In the spring of 1927, he and Perry Thompson toured Dixie in Mann's jalopy to personally sell Afro-American editors on the proposed magazine section. Mann, who had never been South before, behaved exactly as he would in Chicago. Paying no attention to Perry's warning, he strode boldly into white restaurants in South Carolina, Georgia, and Alabama and demanded service. If the proprietors told him he'd have to eat in the kitchen or take a sandwich outside, he bawled them out and left in a huff. Thompson, meanwhile, cringed in the car awaiting for all hell to break loose. I suppose Mann's audacity so astounded the Crackers they made no attempt to "put him in his place." On the return trip to Illinois, when funds were low, Mann went into his supply of extra tools kept for this purpose and traded them at service stations for oil and gas. If the operator objected, Mann wouldn't leave and continued laying down such a heavy verbal barrage that the proprietor would finally make a deal to get rid of him. When they got back to Chicago, Perry vowed no amount of money could induce him to drive South again with "That mad Mann."

Luther J. Pollard was another fast-talker. Advertising salesman deluxe, he could jive a crippled Siamese cat into visiting a dog show. At all times he carried a hundred dollar bill in his wallet and was reputedly the first black to produce commercial motion pictures—one- and two-reel comedies with all-Negro casts. He was also responsible, months later, for getting me a job on the *Whip*.

But it was his brother, Fritz, who was by far the best known. Sports followers were quite familiar with the name Fritz Pollard of Brown University, who was, I think, the first black selected as an All-American halfback by Grantland Rice and who probably got more mileage out of this high honor than anybody else in history. His sensational touchdown runs against Yale, Harvard, and other Ivy League schools in the World War I era brought him a living for several decades; Brown lists him as an all-time great. Many influential white youths from Chicago, New York, and elsewhere were in on his various ventures and bailed him out when he got in over his head.

Fritz was another early tenant of the Waverly Building, renting space for a coal company office several doors away from us. When I met him he weighed around 165 but was well built, quite strong, amazingly fast and tough. He had also been a sprinter and as a boxer was talented enough to serve as instructor for soldiers during World War I.

One day, he told me, after teaching assorted rookies ring technique, a rugged looking fellow approached him and said:

"I think I learned a lot from yo' class, an' I was wondering if you'd mind sparring with me an' teaching me some more."

Fritz didn't mind so they donned gloves. After a few moments of feinting, Fritz was socked with a hard left hook he hadn't seen coming.

Accidents will happen, Fritz told himself, and he'd better be more careful. But a few seconds later he was shaken by a hard right cross landing flush on his chin. Well now, he thought, this has got to stop. Better teach this young punk not to get fresh with the instructor.

Completely serious by now, he went after his opponent with all he had. But no matter how hard he tried, he couldn't land a solid blow. He tried every trick he knew, but nothing worked. Meanwhile he was again bopped hard several times.

Suddenly, his adversary stopped.

"I enjoyed that workout," he grinned, "but I think I done had enough for today."

By then Fritz was winded from his fruitless exertion, but nevertheless panted out his praise. "You're damned good. A natural. Soon as the war's over you ought to fight professionally; I think you'd get somewhere. What's your name?"

The other guy laughed real hard.

"I'm Panama Joe Gans," he said, revealing to Fritz for the first time that he had been sparring with one of the greatest fighters of the century.[5]

I was present at a fight in Fritz's coal office between Fritz and Dick Hudson, a big bruiser who dwarfed me and who had been an outstanding college tackle at either Drake or Creighton University. Dick, incidentally, was also a schemer, specializing in handling athletic teams and promoting sports events. Despite their friendship, he and Fritz often got into vigorous rhubarbs.

I don't know what started it this time. I happened to walk into the coal office just as a boiling Dick invited Fritz to fight. There were four or five fellows standing around listening to the beef.

Fritz, who sincerely believed nights were made for playing, had come to the office without sleep and was trying to snap out of a hangover. Nevertheless, he got up from his desk, walked over, caught Hudson with a hard left hook to the nose and, as Dick tried to counter with a right, fell to the floor. He lay there for at least two minutes while Dick implored him to get up and fight like a man. Suddenly he sprang up, caught the surprised Hudson with another fast hook, and dropped back to the floor still untouched. Dick roared with frustrated fury. This routine went on for several minutes, with Pollard rising as from the deep, bopping his slower opponent who outweighed him by at least seventy-five pounds, then diving for safety before Hudson could hit him in return.

We were all fascinated by this unique hit-and-fall technique, unveiled before us for the first time, and which was driving Dick wild. No one knows how long it might have continued had we not heard an approaching police siren stop in front of the building. Some neighbors, alarmed by the commotion, had called the cops. Hudson, bleeding from nose and mouth, scooted down the back stairs and when officers arrived, nobody knew anything about any fight.

Fritz looked at the lot of us reproachfully and with deep disgust when the policemen left.

"The only reason I took a poke at Dick, with the way I feel today, was because I didn't believe you clowns would actually let us fight. If I hadn't felt certain you guys would stop it right away, I wouldn't have taken him on." He shook his head sadly. "You birds sure picked a hell of a time to let me down."

I came to know Fritz quite well. Despite beliefs prevalent in some circles at the time, he did not live on liquor. He drank only on special occasions, such as the arrival of another day. To prepare properly for this event, he handed me fifty cents virtually every day to go out and buy a half pint of corn whiskey. My pay was a couple of swigs, and he'd down the rest. Then I stumbled on a crummy joint in the alley under the elevated track between 34th and 35th where I could buy a half-pint for fifteen cents if I brought my own bottle. That was no problem; almost anywhere you went on the South Side you'd find an assortment of empty half-pint bottles staring solemnly in your direction. I'd pick up one, wash it, and buy this cheap booze. I pocketed thirty-five cents on this petty hustle, enough to feed me for a day.

Fritz never got beyond the first taste. Invariably he contorted his face in disgust, spit out the whiskey, and snorted: "What the hell's wrong with that goddamn bootlegger, selling me this rotgut crap?" Then he passed the bottle to me, saying, "Here, you can have it all if you want it." At that time I could down almost anything without changing expression or suffering any after effects. This meant I had free liquor plus eating money. Of course I'd go to Fritz's regular bootlegger every third or fourth trip; I knew better than to ruin a good thing by bringing him fifteen-cent swill all the time.

Another in this bouquet of unusual people was a talented but eccentric African named Santie Sabalala.[6] Santie had been taken to England as a member of a Kaffir Boys Choir and had been educated in London and at the Case School of Applied Science in Cleveland. Slender, quite black, and intense, he had already attracted attention as a writer. His short stories had appeared in *Adventure Magazine,* and Harriet Monroe had devoted four pages of *Poetry Magazine* to his excellent free verse about Africa.

However, Santie possessed two strong peculiarities which did not win friends, and I use "strong" advisedly. Those who met him once could walk into a darkened room of average size and tell that Santie was present. He had an air about him caused by his bitter and uncompromising war against soap and water. Not only did he refuse to take baths, but he was determined to see that his clothing likewise refrained. His other peculiarity, which he would discuss as long as he had an audience, was the delusion that the Insull interests, which then virtually monopolized midwest utilities, were trying to rob him of thousands of acres of virgin timberland in Michigan. Several years after I met him, he was placed in a mental hospital for a while and on his release swore he had been railroaded there by the Insull interests who, he said, would have a better chance to steal his property with him out of the way. Once, before his enforced vacation and after meeting Lucia Mae Pitts, an attractive young poet, he asked me to arrange a marriage with her "in name only" as protection for himself while he completed "certain important financial transactions." In return Miss Pitts, who was then working at the Regal Theatre, would have full use of his "Rolls Royce town car with chauffeur," and after his business was completed she could get a divorce and receive "a substantial cash settlement" for her trouble. The deal never went through because, among other things, he couldn't find his Rolls Royce.

Sometime before I met him, Santie had worked briefly as a janitor at Douglas National Bank. Following a heated argument with the bank's president, Anthony Overton, he was fired but swore to get even. Next Saturday morning when business was at its briskest, he smuggled in a homemade stink bomb and set it off. The bank transacted no more business that day.

Not long after I arrived in Chicago, Black Patti Records came into existence with offices in the Overton Building.[7] Heading this venture was J. Mayo "Ink" Williams, outstanding end on the Brown grid team in the post-Fritz Pollard days. Williams later joined forces with Decca Records where he rounded up and exploited many of the firm's "race" artists.[8] Santie and "Ink" had cooked up a deal for Black Patti in which Santie was to organize a group of native Africans to record songs of the bush. I was one of the "native Africans" in his choir of nine or ten male voices— along with an assistant Wabash YMCA secretary and several others of similar jungle background. For several weeks we rehearsed diligently, phonetically learning tribal, hunting, and fertility songs, along with fierce war chants. Finally Santie was satisfied. We could now jointly intone words with the proper inflection (we never learned their exact meaning) and tomorrow, he announced, we would meet at the Y at 10:00 A.M. and go to the Black Patti studio three blocks away for an audition.

Next day we met and waited. An hour later Santie showed up visibly disappointed. The deal was off. There would be no audition. That morning, he told us, the still fledgling Black Patti Records had gone bankrupt. Thus was America deprived of a chance to hear rare and authentic music of the Dark Continent from the throats of assorted Chicagoans.

Although Santie was born in Africa, his knowledge of that continent did not begin to compare with that of Capt. Harry Dean who knew more about Africa, its peoples, and customs than any other person I have ever met.[9] He was one of America's rarest breed: a black sea captain. White-haired, with a face like a tan Pinnochio, he came from "free stock" in Philadelphia and had followed family tradition by going to sea when he was fourteen. He went first to England where he got a job as a cabin boy on a sailing vessel bound for Africa. Somewhere around Arabia he was taken off the schooner by a group of Arab tribesmen who insisted he was a prince who had been kidnapped by the British. Eventually escaping, he made his way across Ethiopia and back to England and, finally, home.

But the sea was in his blood. (By the way, how does one stay healthy with salt water coursing through his veins?) Years later he obtained his own sailing ship, built in Scandinavia, which he named the *Pedro Gorino*. He told me he had sailed completely around Africa seventeen times, crossed it from north to south twenty-four times and from east to west thirty-three times. Once he brought a fortune in ostrich feathers and other items to the United States with the dream of establishing a vast trading business. After spending months contacting wealthy Afro-Americans in various cities from coast to coast, he found his potential fortune had dwindled to almost nothing through losses in traveling, theft, and the leaving of samples which were never returned. "The damn fools just couldn't see they had a gold mine," he told me.

As Capt. Dean came to know the peoples of Africa, he began giving all possible aid in their continuing fight against European oppression, secretly bringing them shipments of arms and ammunition. Eventually the British caught him with a load of guns and confiscated his vessel.

He was in his late sixties and ill when I first met him. There were rumors that he had been fed some slow-acting poison strange to American medicine. Doctors could provide little relief to his almost constant pain. His sole palliative was a pint of olive oil consumed daily. Although gentle by nature, he was stubborn as a block of granite; virtually penniless, he nevertheless had burning pride. He would rather starve than accept anything with the mildest hint of charity. More than once I heard friends plead long and earnestly that it would be a favor to them, before he would accept dinner or money for rent.

Capt. Dean was personally acquainted with important people all over the world. He was awaiting a grant to sustain him for a year while his life story was written. Impressed with what he saw of my work, he wanted me to write his book. But when funds were allotted, it was stipulated he was to work with Sterling North, then a rising young white writer associated with the University of Chicago. The completed book, called *The Pedro Gorino,* was published a couple of years later by one of the major publishing houses.[10]

I introduced Sabalala to Capt. Dean one day at the office, and after learning Santie's place of origin, the old sea captain chatted with him at length in his native tongue. Capt. Dean not only had visited Sabalala's homeland but was a personal friend of the chief of his tribe.

One of the frequent visitors to our office was a Hindu who rented a large brownstone mansion on Michigan Boulevard near the Loop. Here he manufactured incense and perfume on the upper floors and operated a restaurant on the ground level featuring curries and other East Indian specialties. Always turbaned at his place of business, when he moved about the South Side he wore an ordinary hat and resembled any other light-complexioned black man. Still another occasional caller was a short, chunky Russian youth named Dimitri Stakoff. I recall that he had only four stubby fingers on his left hand and spoke with a thick accent. Each time I saw him he insisted that we go out together that night and "find some Jewish girls," but we never got around to it.

Ever hear of James A. "Billboard" Jackson? He was known in black theatrical circles as Billboard Jackson because he had served as correspondent for this bible of the show world. A recognized authority on souls behind the footlights, he was no longer active in the entertainment field and had focused his attention on building up black industry and trade. Later, under President Hoover, he was appointed a small business specialist in the Department of Commerce. Tall, white haired, heavy jowled, dignified in appearance, and light brown in color, he looked like anything but a former minstrel man, but he was conceded to have been one of the best. He spent hours providing me with background on the theatre and its personalities.

It was during this period that I met and became well acquainted with Jack Johnson.[11] The ex-heavyweight champion was then operating a gym on 35th Street, a few blocks from our office and close to the Sunset Cafe. Perry Thompson had asked me to get a five-spot from him to cover mailing a special publicity release to the Duskyamerican press. Since I was broke as usual, I decided to try for something for myself.

As I walked in, he was standing by the ring, puffing on a cigar and thoughtfully watching one of his fighters shadowbox. His enormous head was bald; he kept it shaved and wore only a beret.

"I'm supposed to pick up fifteen dollars," I told him after introducing myself.

"How come it's that much?" he asked.

"We're mailing out this special article on you to every Negro newspaper in the nation," I explained. "In order to impress them with its importance, we're sending it special delivery,"

"That's a hell of a lot of money for postage," he protested.

"But there's a hell of a lot of papers."

He puffed steadily, searching my face. I suppose I looked reasonably honest for he finally counted out a ten and a five from a sizeable roll. I passed the fin on to Perry and went downtown.

I told you earlier of my weakness for unusual cigarettes. It had been a long time since I splurged, but this was going to be the day. I walked along North Michigan Avenue looking in the windows of quality tobacco stores. Finally a variety of cigarette I had never seen before caught my eye. I stopped and went in.

"Gimme a package of Cerise No. 2," I said casually to the clerk. I tried to look as if this were my regular brand.

He gave me the package, and I handed him the ten. He hit the cash register and counted out my change.

It was exactly $7.25.

I was again glad for the poker face developed during my high school days, but it was an effort and I almost didn't make it. I looked slowly around, as if I wanted to see if there were anything else I needed before letting my gaze take in the cash register. There had been no mistake. It read $2.75.

But I would have died before losing face in front of the white clerk and customers in this swank shop by asking for my money back. I simply had to go through with it, although I was somewhat barren of enthusiasm.

A half block away I carefully opened the small box. They were Russian cigarettes, made in England with tan paper and straw tips. I counted twenty-six in the package. And if you ask me, they weren't worth nearly eleven cents each. But they did last me six months. I never smoked them casually; puffing each one became a special ritual in which I thought of nothing but how best to enjoy each inhalation. No pot was ever smoked with as much reverence and loving care. And after I finished the last one, I saved the box for years. Since then, I have somehow never had a desire to barge in and buy another package of exotic cigarettes.

Shortly after I tricked him out of ten dollars, Jack Johnson opened an office in the Waverly Building a few doors down the hall from ours. This he used in connection with sales and distribution of his newly published autobiography. Even at his age of nearly fifty, the former great champion was still capable of holding his own in the ring against the best for four or five rounds. He still had his punch, his timing, and his unequaled defensive skill, but his legs couldn't take it now. Nevertheless, he was convinced he could whip Jack Dempsey any day and itched to put on the gloves with the Manassa Mauler. When Dempsey was training for the second Tunney fight, Li'l Arthur showed up at his camp one day volunteering to act as his "sparring partner." But Jack Kearns, Dempsey's manager, would have none of it. He not only turned down the offer but had Johnson escorted away from the camp.

Jack told me about his fight with Jess Willard and the controversial knockout in that Havana ring.

"Did you ever see an unconscious fighter shade his eyes from the sun?" he asked, referring to the photo showing him lying on his back with one opened hand above his head.

He had been in voluntary exile as a fugitive from justice, he told me. A warrant for violation of the Mann Act was ready for him anytime he set foot on U.S. soil. Whites were furious that an Afro-American was champ and that he had beaten all their white hopes; that, in addition, he should have a white wife and other white women chasing him was almost more than they could take. But he had tired of roaming around and wanted to come home. So a deal was cooked up whereby he could return to the United States and serve only a nominal prison term if he would let the heavyweight title be "restored" to the white race.

A championship bout was arranged for Havana, and Willard was to win the crown. Jack was also to get a nice bundle of the long green. But through bitter experience, Jack had learned not to trust Whitey. Taking no chances, he said, he insisted that he be paid in full before "losing" the title. To insure against being double-crossed, he ordered one of his trusted friends to remain with the promoter until he collected every penny.

According to prearranged plans, his friend was to return to a reserved seat near the champion's corner as soon as he collected. He was not there when the fight began. Before starting each round, Jack looked to see if payment had been made. The bout went on for twenty-five rounds before the seat was occupied. When Li'l Arthur glanced over this time, his friend grinned and nodded. The following canto, Willard landed the "kayo" punch. It was as simple as that, the former champion said.

There have been many stories about this fight, including some by writers who swear Big Jess whipped Johnson in a fair match. I do not claim that what Jack told me was the gospel truth; but in view of our patterns of prejudice and what followed later, it was quite logical. It is a matter of record that Johnson came back to the United States shortly after he lost the crown and served a nominal term in the federal prison at Leavenworth where he was treated like an honored guest rather than a criminal.

I came within a hair's breadth once of seeing Li'l Arthur in unscheduled action. His near foe was a wild stud named Bob Haynes who actually challenged the former champ to a fistfight—and meant it.

Haynes was one of the fastest and most accurate linotypists I have ever seen. At this time he operated his own typesetting shop at 36th and State where he had a machine geared specially to capitalize on his fantastic speed. He also believed he had a divine directive to get rid of all the liquor in Chicago by personal consumption. Bob was such a steady customer that he had a charge account with most of the bootleggers on the South Side. However, his intake was usually several bottles ahead of his income. In order to leave his shop, he first took a sheet of paper and plotted a course that would not take him past too many of the bootleggers he owed.

One night Haynes, partially loaded as usual, picked up a broad and brought her upstairs into the Waverly building. When he pushed her into the woman's lavatory and started in himself, she screamed. Bob cussed. Jack Johnson happened to be in his office with his wife. The loud swearing and shrieking brought all of us, including the former titleholder, into the hall.

"Fellow, I wish you wouldn't swear like that," Jack said. "My wife's in there." He nodded toward his office.

"What the hell you gonna do about it?" Bob asked belligerently.

"I'm just asking you not to swear in front of my wife," Jack replied evenly.

"Why, goddamn you, I'll kick your ass," Bob shouted, letting go of the woman who immediately scooted down the steps and out the front door.

Haynes, who weighed only around one seventy-five, put up his dukes and began circling around Johnson, looking for an opening. He knew he was taking on what many authorities consider the greatest heavyweight in boxing history, but he just didn't give a damn. I stood dumbfounded, not believing my eyes. Perry and Henry were equally astounded. But Perry got hold of himself just in time to let out a yell and run toward the ex-champ, shouting:

"Don't hit him, don't hit him, he's a friend of mine! He's been drinking and doesn't know what he's doing!"

Jack said, "He really must be crazy," as he turned, walked back into his office, and closed the door. Meanwhile Henry and Perry and I grabbed Bob and hustled him down the steps while we tried to explain how close he had come to committing suicide. But Haynes refused to be impressed, muttering, "I don't give a damn who he is. I'll even try the Angel Gabriel one time anyway."

Bob was like that. He'd take on anybody, anywhere, anytime. Once I saw a crowd in front of a poolroom in a really tough neighborhood. As I came closer, I spotted Bob Haynes standing in the center with folded arms. Circling him was an irate, mean-looking stud with an open knife.

"Hell, no, I ain't gonna pay you for those games I lost," Bob was telling him. "And you better put that little frogsticker of yours away before I get mad and kick your teeth down your goddamn throat."

And believe it or not, when Haynes took a step toward the other guy, he backed off, closed the knife, put it in his pocket, and walked away without another word.

Years later Bob went to work as linotypist for the *Afro-American* newspapers in Baltimore. One Christmas, dissatisfied with the amount of his bonus, he went down to the plant, took a sledgehammer, and smashed every linotype in the shop. His brother, a sedate and successful Chicago attorney who was also chief counsel for the National Baptist Convention, Inc., had to fly to the Maryland metropolis to straighten things out.

"Gentle Jimmy" Gentry, who specialized in night club productions and beauty contests and also published a theatrical sheet, along with Rudolf Johnson, his sidekick, made our scene quite as often, as did Gus Ivory, a commercial artist. But the schemer who made them all sit up and take notice was U.S. Stamps from St. Louis. He breezed in just prior to the 1927 primary elections, formerly president (mainly on paper) of the Green Donkey Club, brought out one issue of *Kick,* its "official organ," then walked into City Hall and came out with several grand to "help swing the election" with his "mass organization" and "widely read publication." Some of the old hustlers literally cried at the way this young, newly arrived upstart had all but swiped the gravy off their plates. But that was only the beginning for Stamps. During the next two decades, he organized insurance companies, burial societies, fraternal orders, and you-name-it, including one bright scheme in 1930, along with artist Gus Ivory, to beat the Depression with artistic slogans to be sold for hanging in business places. That is, he organized these schemes when he wasn't in jail.

23

Meanwhile I was learning the very exacting technique of how to live on practically nothing.

Well-wishers suggested I get on the police force, take a civil service exam for postal work, or try my luck in the boxing ring. I speedily vetoed all three. I intended to make it as a newspaperman or starve to death trying. There were moments when it seemed the alternative was winning out.

Once I went without a bit of food for three whole days. Not long after that I ate for an entire week on thirty-five cents. This was when you could buy three doughnuts for a nickel, so I rationed myself to a trio of sinkers per day. I rapidly learned how to get the most of my food money. While living at the Wabash Y, I was introduced to a filling twenty-cent meal of beans and bacon cooked to the consistency of mashed potatoes, then topped with gravy. The fellow who wised me was Walter Barnes, who lived across the hall and kept me awake nights practicing his clarinet. Later Walter formed a big dance band and was on the verge of the real big time when one night at a dance in Mississippi the building caught fire and burned rapidly to the ground. Hundreds died or were badly injured in the holocaust, including Barnes and many of his musicians.

In college I had developed the habit of going without breakfast in order to sleep a little longer. I was therefore accustomed to only two meals per day. Sometimes late in the morning I went to Foote's Cafeteria near 35th and State where I got three steaming hot biscuits, a generous dab of butter, and hot coffee for a dime. Often at night I patronized the sandwich wagons which seemed to sprout out of the ground all over the South Side. It was a toss-up whether to spend a dime for a fried fish sandwich and battle the tiny bones for a good half hour, or buy a fried tripe sandwich. Each tripe sandwich was like a strange new adventure; you never knew what to expect. They all looked the same from the outside: tripe boiled, covered with batter, and cooked in a skillet until brown, then smothered with sliced onions and hot sauce and slapped between two slices of bread. You took that first bite with fear and apprehension. If your teeth came solidly and easily together, you had a good one and could enjoy yourself. But if they bounced back, woe be unto you! The tripe had been insufficiently boiled before frying, and it was like trying to chew a rubber inner tube. At such times I walked unhappily along masticating bread, onions, and hot sauce. Finally, my jaws weary, I would fling away the tripe triumphant, bitten into but unbowed. Years later I realized it would have been ideal for repairing blown-out tires.

Man, I learned, is an exceedingly perverse creature. Acquaintances kept my pockets loaded with cigars or cigarettes and my belly filled with booze even while I tottered on the crumbling brink of starvation.

"Come on, let's get a drink," some acquaintance would say.

"I'm broke."

"What the hell, I don't want you to buy. The drinks are on me."

"I'd rather have a hamburger on you," I'd reply.

"Aw hell, man, you can eat anytime. I want somebody to drink with."

So we'd toddle off to a speakeasy or a good-time flat, and the clown would load me up on corn liquor. He might even buy me a pack of cigarettes or a handful of cigars if he saw I had nothing of my own to smoke. But food? No, man, no!

I'd end up with a gurgling gut, but still hungry as hell. Fortunately, I had an excellent constitution. Never did I become ill from not eating or through guzzling on any empty stomach, nor did I get drunk. I was able to surround any liquid set before me, no matter how bad, without showing the customary effect. I might feel enough to stagger, but it showed itself only in a faster walk. The higher I got, the more rapid my steps, but that was all. Those who knew me swore I had a cast-iron stomach.

In fact, the only time I've ever been sick from liquor was in 1932 in

Atlanta when a mortician friend threw a party out in the country and provided the liquid refreshment—and to this day I'm not certain he wasn't trying to drum up business. He made his own potables combining alcohol with various nonintoxicating flavorings. Being economical, he used empty containers which he had in abundance: old formaldehyde bottles. The odor lingered and evidently some of the original contents. Of the more than thirty guests present, some of whom were serious drinkers with endless thirsts, nobody would touch the stuff, following the first whiff, except me and another jerk. Within an hour we were both so ill we had to be rushed home and put to bed. However, I can say that for once I was truly pickled.

Actually, I didn't have to starve in those early Chicago days. Several family friends who knew me from childhood, among them Mr. and Mrs. Colonel Austin, now lived on the South Side and constantly begged me to eat with them. A practical person would have dropped around when hungry. But being an oddball by nature, that's the time I usually stayed away. If by chance I happened to be visiting them at mealtime, I would turn down a sincere invitation if I were flat broke and almost starved, accepting only when I had money in my pocket and could afford to eat in a restaurant.

Can you explain me? I, for one, can't.

Also I could have written Dad for money. He had accepted the idea of my quitting college and trying my luck in Chicago. But because I had made this decision alone, I intended to go it alone. Twice, however, I was forced to break down. The first time was when I had to give up a room in a private home because I couldn't pay my rent and had to sleep in the office for a couple of weeks; and second followed my week on doughnuts.

But most of the time I treaded water, writing stories for future use while waiting for Perry and Henry to get the show on the road. During the primary elections, they were sidetracked as Henry made drawings and Perry wrote campaign literature for various candidates. I acted as errand boy and in the process met Ed Wright, political boss of the South Side and the only man I have ever seen who exuded such intellectual strength that I felt overwhelmed and mentally inferior. I went down to his Loop office to get a check for political printing and looked on with awe as this black man subtracted the amount from a bank balance showing more than thirty-six thousand dollars.

Undoubtedly my extensive walking as a child and in college gave me the physical strength to survive during those dark days in Chicago. I

walked all over the South Side to save carfare and developed the habit of
looking at the sidewalk in the hope of finding loose change. I had fair
success, and one rainy night hit a junior jackpot. Staring back at me from
the wet cement was a beautiful ten-dollar bill. I was ecstatic. Hurrying to
the nearest cafe, I ordered a real feast, my first meal of the day. I need not
tell you how many crushed cigarette packages, especially the green Luckies, I had hopefully picked up and thrown away in disgust before I made
my strike. But with a satisfied stomach, I became dissatisfied. I bemoaned
my luck in not finding a fifty instead of a mere ten.

24

Chicago, late winter, early spring, 1927. A broad-shouldered brute of a
burgh, dirty and rough. New Yorkers called it an overgrown country
town, and they were right. But despite its coarseness, its blatant vulgarity,
its raw corruption, I soon came to love it.

Gangland ruled. Mobsters chose which laws to observe, which to
flout. They killed and went unpunished. Judges were for sale at so much
per dozen. Prohibition was a sorry joke. Make the big payoff and run your
racket, any racket. Cops strolled into speakeasies or thinly disguised saloons and drank openly with the customers. Some police made four or
five times as much in graft as they drew in salary. Mayor William Hale
Thompson—Big Bill, the Builder, he called himself—smiled benignly
from his throne at city hall and went back to his one-man war with King
George V of England, deceased for over a hundred years.[12]

Policy barons peeled and ate the South Side like a ripe banana. But
they were black; Al Capone, Bugs Moran, and the others did not muscle
in on this rich racket. And the policy kings made millions from the pennies
of the strugglers and the strivers. The black citizenry threw in its loose
cash before exploding from the ghetto in the morning to labor for white
people; they paid again at night when they returned to the crowded flats
and tenements of the colored compound. Always the dream of a lucky hit
and extra dollars to spend; let me catch policy one time, Lawd, and I'll
get well.

A quarter million souls strained at the restrictive covenant buckle
fastening the Black Belt. There'd been a race riot in the early 1920s, and
now we used only certain beaches. Slowly we were inundating previously
all-white communities; 55th Street was giving way. Whites still operated

many businesses along Garfield Boulevard; not long before a black male had been gunned down for having the audacity to enter the Golden Lily Cafe with a blonde woman. Before too long, the tan-tide would flow to 63rd and beyond.

Prostitutes preyed in packs. Size? Take your choice. Fat or lean, short or tall. Color? Tar to tantalizing tan. Frolic with your friendly neighborhood whore for two iron men. Have yourself a ball, pretty papa. (And when the Depression came, screw a hungry gal for a bowl of chili or a plate of stew. Room? Why waste money on a room? Go to the nearest alley or stop in a quiet entryway. Now bend over, gal, hoist your dress and earn your fee.)

One night on South Parkway between 39th and 41st Streets, I counted twenty-four—and this on only one side of the street. Often two or three hung around each of the four corners of an intersection. Obviously they paid off or they would not have been in the same place night after night soliciting any male.

With such widespread graft and corruption, vice was comparatively highly moral.

To utilize every inch of space, many old apartment buildings were constructed at the edge of the sidewalk with overhanging windows. This was ideal for the stay-at-home sisters. Sitting in front of a large window, a hooker used a pencil or ruler to tap on the pane and attract attention. As a green newcomer, I knew nothing of this practice. I looked up the first time I heard an insistent tap-tap to find woman in lounging clothes smiling and beckoning me to come to her apartment. Curious and not knowing what she could possibly want, I went in.

"I'm ready for you, daddy," she said as she opened the door.

"Ready for what?" I innocently asked.

"Don't you want a good time? It's only two dollars," she replied, pulling aside her negligee and exposing a bare brown breast to excite me.

It worked. But hell, I didn't even have a dollar.

"Okay, okay, if you ain't got two dollars, how about a buck and a half? You're young an' look like a pigmeat anyway. Ain'tcha got that, sweetie?"

I was flat broke, I told her.

"Then why'n hell didya waste my time comin' up here?" she asked angrily, snatching her negligee over her teasing titty, in the manner of a merchant returning a suit to the rack when he sees it's no sale. "I mighta missed a good trick while I was jus' fartin' around with you."

"But you called me in," I protested. "You tapped on the window. How'd I know what you wanted?"

"Ain'tcha never heard nobody tap on a window before? Are you all that goddamn dumb?"

I explained I was new in town and where I came from nothing like that ever happened.

"Well, you're in Chicago now, buddy boy, an' next time somebody taps don't you go in unless you mean business. Now haul ass."

I left.

From then on, I paid no attention when I heard a light rap on a pane or a voice softly calling, "Come here daddy." Finally a lot of the hookers came to know me on sight because of my nightly walks and didn't bother to say anything. But some poor stiffs were not as lucky. Frequently a desperate whore short of her quota would snatch the hat off some reasonably well-dressed sucker and dash into a building. He had the choice of going on his way bareheaded or chasing her. If he followed, he had still another choice: redeeming his hat by paying for a piece or trying forcefully to take it back—which might result in the broad screaming and her pimp or a gang showing up to beat or cut hell out of him.

Oh yes, Chicago was quite a town.

25

By contrast with the raw, savage strength of Chicago, I looked upon New York as a slick sissy although I had never been there.

I, of course, was aware of the Harlem Literary Renaissance of the early 1920s. I had read Carl Van Vechten's *Nigger Heaven,* some of the short stories of Rudolph Fisher and Jean Toomer, and the poetry of Langston Hughes and Countee Cullen. I had heard of Claude McKay at Kansas State; he attended there for a brief period after coming from the West Indies. But other than Fenton Johnson, I knew of no black bards in the Windy City. I had read and reread the work of Carl Sandburg whom I considered the nation's greatest poet, the Edgar Lee Masters of *Spoon River Anthology* fame, and the jazzlike rhythms of Vachel Lindsay, although I did not like his chauvinism. My debt to all three was obvious to anybody who read my own poems. I did not identify with those I considered Eastern writers.

But I could find only the first weak contractions of a movement which might later give birth to literary creativity on the South Side. There was no contact with the white writers of that period; our worlds were still separate. I recall an abortive attempt to start a writer's group back in 1927. Fenton Johnson, a small, dark brown, very retiring man who had been one of the pioneers in the free verse revolution of the previous decade, was among those attending. Lucia Mae Pitts, a young woman showing real promise in this field, and Barefield Gordon, a University of Chicago student who wrote very proper sonnets and was an uncle of Frank Yerby, who had not yet started writing, were two others. But the dominant figure was a dapper, graying man known as Judge Moore who had the most caustic tongue I have ever heard. He gloried in shooting his opinions like napalm. Nothing pleased him except possibly his own work. Nobody dared criticize his mediocre efforts for fear of being orally annihilated. I never read anything before this assemblage. I think it burned itself to death through a blaze set by Judge Moore's tongue.

In the main I had to depend on myself, and I had plenty of time to write. You know, starving poet in a garret turning out deathless literature. But how could a two-hundred pounder convince anybody he was starving?

This lack of communication between poets, and the realization there was nothing in Chicago even remotely resembling the Harlem Renaissance, firmed my ambition to do for the Windy City in verse what others had done for Harlem. I felt there were all kinds of materials shouting for attention. If ever I became well known, I intended that it be for my portraits of the South Side. In order not to come under the influence of mighty Gotham, I have in my life spent less than a week in New York, and that was in 1943. It was some ten years after I arrived in Chicago, before I established any significant relationships with white Chicago writers.

I also learned in 1927 of a group called the Inter-Collegiate Club composed of current and recent college students. I joined. The president was a smooth young man named Frederick H. Hammarubi Robb, who today would undoubtedly be a leading black activist; as it was he got into trouble with Uncle Sam during World War II for aiding the Black Dragon Society of Japan.[13] The club was preparing an ambitious yearbook intended to reflect all spheres of black achievement in the metropolitan area. When it became known that verse of mine had appeared in the *Crisis* magazine, I was asked to contribute several poems. The results were a disaster. Either the printer suffered from temporary insanity or the proof-

reader stepped out when my copy appeared, for the published results were
such a jumble of pied type that they made Gertrude Stein seem as clear as
a first-grade reader.[14]

Nevertheless, I wrote my first long poem during this period, an effort
which years later resulted in a close association with the most fantastic
woman I have ever met:[15]

Chicago's Congo
(Sonata for an Orchestra)

Chicago is an overgrown woman
    wearing her skyscrapers
    like a necklace . . .
Chicago's blood is kaleidoscopic
Chicago's heart has a hundred auricles

* * *

    From the Congo
    to Chicago
    is a long trek
    —as the crow flies

Sing to me of a red warrior moon victorious in a Congo Sky
    . . . show me a round dollar moon in the ragged blue purse
    of Chicago's heavens . . . tell me of a hundred spoil laden
    blacks tramping home from the raid . . . point me out a
    hundred brown men riding the elevated home on payday . . .
    pick me the winners . . . in Chicago? . . . in the Congo?

Skyscraper pinnacles rip great holes in the rubber balloon
    bag of the sky . . . do spears kill quicker than printed words?
    . . . midnight lies and cobra fangs . . . ask me if civilization
    produces new forms of biting and tearing and killing . . .
    see three million whites and two hundred thousand blacks
    civilized in Chicago

    From the Congo
    to Chicago
    is a long trek
    —as the crow flies

* * *

I'm a grown-up man today in Chicago
My bones are thick and stout

(when I move to new districts bombings
    couldn't break them)
My flesh is smooth and firm
    (look—the wounds you give me heal quickly)
See how the muscles ripple under my night-black skin
My strength comes not from resting
You should be proud of me Chicago
I've got a lion's heart and a six-shooter
I've got a fighter's fist and five newspapers
I've got an eye for beauty and another for cash
Nothing you've got I can't have

A song dashes its rhythms in my face like April rain
My song is a song of steel and bamboo, of brick flats and
        reed huts, of steamboats and slim canoes, of murder
        trials and jackal packs, of con men and pythons
My tune I get from automobiles and lions roaring, from the
        rustle of bank notes in a teller's window and the rustle
        of leaves in Transvaal trees
I ask you to find a better song, a louder song, a sweeter
        song—
Here's something Wagner couldn't do

State Street is a wide gray band across Chicago's forehead
At night a white face mother moon clothes skyscrapers in
        gray silk
At night when clocks yawn and hours get lazy
At night when the jungle's a symphony in grays . . .
Oh mother moon, mother of earth, bringer of silver gifts
Bring a veil of stardust to wrap this Congo in
Bring a shawl of moonmist to clothe Chicago's body

                        *   *   *

Between the covers of books lie the bones of yesterdays
Today is a new dollar
And
My city is money mad

                        *   *   *

Across the street from the Ebenezer Baptist Church
        women with cast-iron faces peddle love
In the flat above Williams Funeral Home
        six couples sway to the St. Louis Blues
Two doors away from the South Side Bank

three penny-brown men scorch their guts with
four bit whiskey
Dr. Jackson buys a Lincoln
His neighbor buys second hand shoes
　　　—the artist who paints this town must
　　　use a checkered canvas . . .

Tired looking houses of brown stone
Ramshackle flats with sightless eyes
A surface car throws a handful of white sparks at cracked
　　　red bricks
An L train roars oaths at backyard clotheslines
Mornings on South Parkway flats sit like silent cats watching
　　　the little green mice of buses running up and down
　　　the boulevard
And only grass has heard the secrets of vacant lots

*　*　*

This song has no tune. You cannot hum it.
This song has no words. You cannot sing it.
This song everybody knows, nobody knows.
It is in a pattern of brown faces at the Wabash Y.M.C.A.,
　　　a 35th Street gambling place, a Parkway theatre
　　　—you get it or you don't
It is a melody of everything and nothing

I saw twelve stars sitting along the edge of a four-story flat
I saw a moon held by leafless tree fingers
I heard a shot tear huge holes in the blanket of silence
Later—just a little later—the moon got away and
　　　the stars stepped back into the sky

There will always be new wordless songs, new humless tunes
Chicago sings these songs each day
Chicago who wears her skyscrapers like a necklace . . .

However, the bulk of my writing was for bread and beans. Trans-
lated, that means I prepared articles for use in the *National Magazine*
when and if it ever appeared.[16] Henry Brown illustrated some of the
material. And I wrote my first short story which Perry pounced on and
filed.

In the hope of obtaining a little eating money, I hacked out a second short story with *The Light and Heebie Jeebies* in mind and took it forthwith to Percival Prattis, the owlish looking editor who was also responsible for getting out Associated Negro Press releases.

ANP, operated by Claude Barnett, a suave, six foot five, slender, and resourceful man with a quiet way and big feet, was located in a small, crowded office only a few doors from the *Defender,* but so far as Robert Sengstacke Abbott was concerned it didn't exist.[17] There was no official relationship between ANP, the standard news gathering and distributing agency for the nation's soul sheets, and the *Defender* which scorned any affiliation. This condition existed until Abbott died some years later.

Prattis bought my short story for four dollars, and I was set not only to eat for a week but to take in a couple of shows, including the Metropolitan Theatre near 47th and South Parkway where Sammy Stewart's band gave a performance similar to that of Erskine Tate's at the Vendome.

The Regal Theatre had not yet opened. That entire corner was only a huge hole and plans. The South Center Department Store, Walgreen Drugs, and the Savoy Ballroom were still months away from reality. Nevertheless this area was already the South Side's main drag. The Met was therefore more conveniently located than the Vendome on State near 31st, but both theatres and bands had their rabid partisans. Sometimes heads were cracked as a climax to arguments over who was better, Stewart or Tate.

Sammy himself was a dapper little chap with a waxed Kaiser Bill mustache. He loved to meander down the street with a pair of sleek white Russian wolfhounds. Personally effeminate in his mannerisms, his music nevertheless had a hard masculinity. Against Armstrong, Teddy Weatherford, Stomp Evans, and Jimmy Bertrand, Stewart could toss such stars as Tommy Ladnier or Freddy Keppard on cornet, Jerome Carrington on piano, and Vance Dixon on alto sax. When Vance took a solo blowing sax and clarinet simultaneously, or when he thrust his right hand behind his back to finger his sax, the crowd shouted "Clean cookin' papa," "Oh, it's tight like that," and "Look at that zig! He just won't don't!" As for Keppard, this fabulous New Orleansian was the most powerful horn man I ever heard. I have stood on the far southeast corner of 47th and South Parkway and over the roar of dashing buses, streetcars, and autos heard him take a solo in the Met. I was present one night when he blew the mute from his horn to the far side of the orchestra pit some thirty feet away.

All gleaming gold and polished purple was another night at the Met. After Sammy and his men concluded their concert, we in the audience sat back to see some now forgotten silent film of that era. It had unreeled for perhaps ten minutes when Carey B. Lewis, who managed the theatre, barged down the isle with a broad, fat freighter of a man in tow. Lewis berthed and anchored him at the pipe organ, turned on the little light, and stepped back. The big boat of a man began to beat it out. Like strange wild birds the notes soared and zoomed through the theatre for a dozen bars. The audience unleashed such a tremendous wave of shouting and handclapping that the projectionist was forced to turn off the movie and aim a spotlight full on the organist.

It was Fats Waller.

Fats sat in the beer-colored light, grinning like an affable Satan as he freed his imps of jazz. He had not yet developed his vocal style of wrapping his brown woolen voice around Tin Pan Alleyisms and twisting them into caricatures.[18] In this period he was strictly instrumental, and his pipe organ recording of *St. Louis Blues* had caught fire in the nation's Congos. Jazz on a pipe organ was audaciously new.

He played for almost an hour before the film could be shown. Two days later he was hired at the Vendome, the Met's twin sister, and for several weeks it was a solid nightly ball with Waller plus Tate's band along with Satchmo. Then Fats disappeared as suddenly as he had arrived. He had fled to Chicago because of wife trouble and to avoid paying alimony. When her attorneys caught up with him, he returned to Harlem.

But even without Fats, Chicago had a bulging bag of jazz. Many of the Crescent City's top musicians settled here after Storyville closed. Once I listed some thirty orchestras, and this was far from complete. Several excellent groups rarely, if ever, played for dusky dancers, among them Doc Cook and his Doctors of Syncopation blasting away at White City; others, such as Hugh Swift, were heard by us over the radio. Dance halls abounded, most of them featuring regular Dancing Classes similar to the one I attended my first night in Chicago. All had regular bands and a regular following; they were almost like social clubs open to the general public. In addition, 31st and 35th Streets were loaded with cabarets featuring topnotch entertainers, high brown chorus lines and hot orchestras. Ethel Waters headlined her own *Calico Girl Revue* at the Cafe De Paris on 31st featuring the subdued music of Dave Payton's Orchestra. Sammy Stewart doubled at the Dreamland on State near 35th; such now legendary figures as Jimmy Noone, Johnny and Baby Dodds, and a young fellow named Earl Hines were heard nightly.

The South Side jumped. All you needed was dough to rise with it.

26

Journalitis is a disease afflicting persons who dream of power or think they have a message. It is rarely fatal, although it can have a permanently debilitating effect upon the purse unless the victim has a generous share of know-how. Certain cynics aver that the only business harder to make money in than a daily newspaper is a livery stable at the downtown corner of State and Randolph, busiest in Chicago.

Nevertheless, one morning in April, Perry Thompson burst excitedly into the office with the news that two South Side realtors, Pace and Alexander, who also had their hands in a policy wheel operation, had been floored with journalitis. They were preparing to launch a daily newspaper.

We had recently heard that another victim of this peculiar ailment planned to start a daily. However, he didn't have enough capital. There had been no talk of the Pace and Alexander venture. We dashed immediately to 38th and Indiana and found a gleaming new flatbed press, linotypes, and mechanical equipment being installed on the first floor of an old apartment building. Tons of newsprint had been delivered and stored. However, they had overlooked one little detail in their planning. Pace and Alexander had made absolutely no provision to hire an editorial staff to get the damned thing out.

Any idiot knows it is impossible to sell a blank newspaper. Gently but firmly we brought this to the attention of Messrs. Pace and Alexander, and this should have been our tip-off. Yet when they not only agreed but casually mentioned they had enough funds to insure operation at a 90 percent loss for more than a year, expediency overwhelmed our common sense. Pace and Alexander might not be capable of publishing a paper, but they could assure us of three square meals a day for the next twelve months. Perry and Henry speedily talked the owners into letting us take over the entire editorial operation.

It was easy to recruit a staff from dissatisfied or nonworking newspapermen. The daily was to be called the Chicago *Evening Bulletin.* Perry Thompson was combined managing and city editor, Henry Brown was sports editor and cartoonist, and I was night city editor and columnist. A half-dozen others were hired, and we were all set. In addition, the weekend edition would carry the *National Magazine,* so at last we had a live outlet.

My pay was thirty-five dollars weekly. That was a very good salary in 1927 and looked like a million after months of existing on practically nothing. However, it seemed ironic that I had quit college because I felt my technical courses were not preparing me to work on a weekly, yet my first real job was on a daily.

Within three weeks we were ready to make our debut. We realized that a half-dozen or more earlier attempts to establish a black daily had ended in failure, but we were undaunted. The earlier efforts flopped through lack of finances, and knowledge. But didn't we have enough green stuff to last a year? We never doubted our ability.

Our fist headline, stretched across all eight columns, read: LINDBERGH REACHES PARIS. To tell the truth, the Lone Eagle hadn't made it yet. But we kept abreast of radio reports as he made his historic solo flight across the Atlantic. Finally, Perry said, "Hell, if he's that close, he'll be there by the time we hit the streets. Let 'er roll!'"

At last I was in harness.

An editor is, first of all, a reporter. A reporter is an odd amalgam of opposites. He is a voyeur, peeping and prying into the naked lives of others. He is a parasite, living off the blood and meat of fellow humans. He is a great gray wolf, lurking in the shadows, always set to pounce upon those who stray too far from the pack of social acceptance. And yet, at the same time, he is a policeman armed with the authority of the printed page to protect the public. He is an overworked Saint George, slaying some new dragon in virtually every issue of his rag. He is a street sweeper, cleaning the highway of filth and dung left by the constantly passing parade.

And for what?

Certainly not for money. Any preacher or pimp of comparable ability commands a far better income. Of course, there are a few material advantages: free entry to this and that, a press card permitting the bearer to pass police lines and get shot at by thugs or buried under burning walls. You also have the opportunity to rap with and nab the lowdown on glamour girls and murderesses as well as ask personal and insolent questions of politicians, businessmen, and extraordinary screwballs. Maybe at times you feel like a missionary saving your little world from seven kinds of spotted devils, or maybe it's a kind of ego-kissing satisfaction derived from the belief you've written a bitch of a story and because some readers have taken the time to toss you gleaming pearls of praise.

That's the way it was with me, although then I couldn't have phrased it. I knew only that I was happy to work in the field of my choice, and I gladly put in twelve to sixteen hours every day. Mornings and early afternoon I covered police stations, a few court cases, and interviewed people; late afternoon and evening I wrote my stories and daily humorous column, rewrote or edited stories by others, and helped lay out the next edition. In those days before the Newspaper Guild, most newsmen accepted the proposition that they were available twenty-four hours daily anyway.

All went well for three weeks, until Perry discovered he didn't have as much material for the *National Magazine* as he thought. Around ten o'clock on a Friday night, he wondered if I could write a short story to help fill up space—and I was just crazy enough to deliver. It so happened that I had a plot I'd intended to work out when I got around to it. By 2:00 A.M. I had whipped out a complete whodunit involving a pair of dusky detectives. I am not a fiction writer, but this hack effort was so well received by our readers (I suppose it was a reaction to the chauvinistic Octavius Roy Cohen stories then appearing in the *Saturday Evening Post*) that from then on I had to turn out a weekly story woven around this duo of sepia sleuths.[19] I was tiring of this chore when it was eliminated by a new development: lack of money.

Instead of enough finances to operate on a 90 percent loss for a year, Pace and Alexander didn't have enough green stuff to carry them from May through the summer. The clinical treatment for journalitis is costly.

First inkling that all was not well came in the second month of publication. Ordinarily the ghost walked each Saturday at noon, but he didn't crawl this time until around five o'clock when he came up with half of each check and an explanation that the *Evening Bulletin* funds were temporarily tied up but would be available next payday.

Billboard Jackson quit immediately. He had been, at best, lukewarm about the *Bulletin,* joining the staff only out of consideration for Perry. With the theatrical editor gone, I was asked to take on show business reporting due to my known interest in jazz.

Next week I put in my regular time during the day and in the evening began making the rounds of theatres and nightclubs, arriving home around 4:00 A.M., snatching three hours of shut-eye, and reporting back to the office at nine. I enjoyed meeting and talking with top names in the entertainment field; but when, at the end of a week, I found I had lost nine pounds and had fallen asleep listening to Satchmo raise the dead at the Sunset, I cut my hours. From then on, I came to work at noon.

One of my favorite places was the Grand Theatre, across the street from the Vendome, where Butterbeans and Susie, the ageless comedy team, often appeared. Butterbeans wore a suit so tight it looked as if he had been buttered to slide his skinny frame inside. Quite often I made the Saturday midnight shows at the Indiana on 43rd which brought in featured acts from all over Chicagoland. Billy Mitchell, an off-color comedian, and his trained dog called Professor Toby were regulars. Because of some peculiar structure of his leg bones, Billy was able to turn his feet in opposite directions and walk grotesquely, or he ran across the stage on the inside of his ankles. But his following was primarily because of such songs as "Two Old Maids In a Folding Bed," for which he had innumerable verses:

> Two old maids in a folding bed
> One turned over to the other and said
> "I gotta have some yum-yum-yum
> Yum-yum-yum, yum-yum-yum
> Before you go to sleep."

The theatre where I spent most of my time was the Apollo on 47th near Vincennes. Frankie "Half Pint" Jaxon was producer, and I became one of his staunchest fans when he asked permission to use material from my humorous column in his next show. His top stars also appeared as headline attractions at cabarets. Among them was Jimmy Ferguson, a comedian who later became known as Baron Lee when he led the Mills Blue Rhythm Band, and Jazz Lips Richardson, comic and acrobat with phenomenally powerful fingers who usually ended his act by supporting his body on one thumb. A supple gal named Rookie Davis led the chorus, and Tiny Parham provided the music. Tiny, a huge happy hulk who resembled a mustached hippopotamus with horn-rimmed glasses, picked powerful piano and pipe organ, but the management finally fired him. Seems that the Apollo could rent costumes for all its cast except Tiny; his had to be tailor-made to cover his three hundred and fifty pounds.

Two of the brightest girl stars in the nightclub firmament were Mae Alix, "Queen of the Splits," and Blanche Calloway, singer. Mae, voluptuous and curvesome, would make a running slide across the floor of the Sunset and end in a split at the exact spot where some customer had tossed a greenback. She retained this limberness years later, even after she put on fifty pounds and became sloppy fat. As for Blanche, at the time she completely overshadowed her younger brother, Cab, who was then attending law school during the day and paying his way by taking juvenile leads in cafe shows and singing romantic songs.

I covered the opening of the Apex Club, a small but classy upstairs cafe not far from the Sunset. Featured was the band of Jimmy Noone, the famous New Orleans clarinetist, who had with him on piano the young wizard from Pittsburgh, Earl Hines. But the star was Ollie Powers, an excellent entertainer and drummer who died a few years later. Manager of the Apex was Julian Black, best known in years to come as the man behind Joe Louis.

That summer I also saw the controversial second Tunney-Dempsey fight at Soldier Field. Frankly, I did not care who won. Since Jack Johnson, the door to the richest prize in boxing had been slammed and bolted in the faces of black contenders. Tex Rickard, czar of the mahouts of mayhem, had vowed that no Afro-American would ever again compete for the heavyweight title. So such wallopers as Harry Wills, George Godfrey, and Big Bill Tate stood hungrily on the outside. Maybe at their peak, none of them could have licked Tunney or Dempsey, but as logical contenders they merited the chance to try.

Nevertheless, I went. Henry Brown gave me one of his working press tickets, and I shifted my schedule to go. I was among the few receiving a real closeup view of the famous long count. We got out an extra edition, phoning the results to Perry Thompson who rushed the *Bulletin* to the streets a good half-hour before the big citywide dailies could truck theirs from the Loop to the South Side. But as soon as drivers for the *Tribune* and *Herald-American* saw our sheet on the stands, they dumped the *Bulletin* on the ground or covered it with their own. And there wasn't a damned thing we could do about it, not in gang-ridden Chicago of 1927 which only a few years before had sat silently by while circulation men killed or maimed each other in a civil war to control newsstands.

Meanwhile the *Bulletin*'s finances grew worse weekly. We still received promises, but a full check was only a wild dream. One by one, members of the mechanical and editorial staff got disgusted and quit, some leaving Chicago. Several of us stayed, however, due to wishful thinking and a lack of other immediate job possibilities. We hoped for some miracle that would permit Pace and Alexander to come up with our mounting back pay and continue operation. Each Saturday those still working in the composing room would come up to the editorial quarters for a joint vigil. If, by two o'clock, neither owner had materialized with cash we sat solemnly down to write angry letters of resignation. It became a joke and a ritual; we had a kind of contest to see who could write the most devastating farewell note. Yet we knew that when either Pace or Alexander showed up around four or five, looking harassed and pitifully imploring us to stay with them a little while longer, we'd take that part of our pay that was available, shake our heads, and tear up our resignations.

In late summer the *Evening Sun,* whose publication had been announced long before the *Bulletin,* hit the streets. A city which formerly had no black dailies now found itself with two. But not for long. The *Sun's* owner had even less cash than Pace and Alexander; as a result, the *Sun* set almost as soon as it rose. Shortly after its demise, the *Bulletin* quietly expired when its publishers were unable to raise the price of even one more roll of newsprint. Henry, Perry, and I returned to our National News & Feature Service office in the Waverly Building.

27

It was early October 1927. I sat alone in the office dourly contemplating the coming winter with no prospect of work. The blues poured over me; the broke and penniless blues with the smell of cold weather strong in the air. I felt so low a snake's ass would have looked like a star.

Suddenly the door opened. I looked up slowly. In walked Dad accompanied by a small dark woman named Edith. I stared, completely speechless. When I returned to normalcy, he said somebody had passed the word along that I wasn't doing too well, so he sold our little house to come to Chicago. Edith, I learned, had recently been writing his letters to me.

After one good look, Dad hustled me to the nearest penny scale. I weighed one seventy-nine, a drop of thirty-one pounds from when I last saw him at Christmas. Following a big fat meal, he took me to a men's store and bought a supply of new clothes, then handed over some folding money. I did not utter one word of protest.

He married Edith soon after coming to Chicago. Only eight years older than I and some fifteen inches shorter, she got a tremendous jolt out of solemnly introducing me to friends as her "son" and observing their double-takes.

Around Thanksgiving the Savoy Ballroom opened featuring continuous nightly dancing by two big bands, the hot and ready New Orleans group of Charles Elgar and the comparatively inhibited orchestra led by Clarence Black on violin. Elgar's roaring jazz brought me back night after night. Zutty Singleton pounded the drums, and both Darnell Howard and Omer Simeon starred on reeds. These two had a fantastic version of Trixie Smith's famous "My Man Rocks Me with One Steady Roll" in which they stood and blew chorus after wild chorus of unison clarinet in much the same way that King Oliver and Louis Armstrong had worked on cornet.

The Savoy at its opening was a palace of a place. Carpets, thick and deep, covered the aisles and the seating area, which was furnished with expensive overstuffed settees and lounging chairs. Lights and hardware were equally impressive. Several years later, the management put down linoleum on the floor, bought much cheaper wicker chairs and couches, and erected soft drink bars.

All but the hardiest Dancing Classes folded soon after the Savoy began operating. They could compete in neither appearance nor attractions. The Savoy opened every night at 8:00 p.m., with closing time usually 1:00 or 2:00 a.m. Holidays offered continuous dancing for thirty-six hours, with music from as many as six different big bands. Fletcher Henderson and other visiting outfits made occasional appearances in the early days, but there were so many topnotchers in Chicago that imports were not needed to draw big crowds.

In this period, when the pinktoe public accepted Paul Whiteman as the "King of Jazz," one of his trumpeters was popularly touted as Satchmo's rival. His name was Louis Panico, and he had developed a strong following due to his nightly radio time. Many who had never heard of Armstrong swore by Panico and his version of "Wabash Blues." Even an amazingly large number of Duskyamericans, influenced by Caucasian concepts, were Panico camp followers. It was a natural for the Savoy to arrange a battle of jazz between the two horn-men named Louis.

The duel was set for a Sunday afternoon in the summer of 1928. Copious publicity had jammed the joint. Panico, as guest, blew first. He was in superb form, and as he finished his set and the crowd cheered, he couldn't hide a triumphant smirk.

Then came Satchmo's turn.

His band cut loose with some fast stomp, and after a couple of choruses the Reverend Satchelmouth leisurely arose with horn in hand and, pointing its bell toward the ceiling, began his sermon. As his rainbow notes zinged in crazy curves toward the stratosphere, the crowd gave a huge collective gasp, and by the time the first number ended, it was no longer a contest. Panico had been carved and slashed into confetti, and

everybody at the Savoy knew Armstrong was the king of them all. I heard
Satch from 1927 until his death, and at no time did he surpass the performance that Sunday. If old Gabe had been down here snooping around,
he'd have smashed his own horn through unholy envy. I have often
regretted that tape recording had not then been invented.

I felt sincerely sorry for Panico. After his second set, the crowd
wouldn't even come back to the dance floor, preferring to talk and social-
ize until Armstrong returned. The big white boss of the Savoy was so hot
over this rebuff of Panico you could have broiled pork chops on his head.
Panico cut his appearance short, leaving disgusted, defeated after less than
an hour, never again to play before a South Side audience.

28

Luther J. Pollard called one morning early in 1928 and asked me to contact
Joe Bibb at the Chicago *Whip*.

"That is, if you want a job," he added.

"Of course I want a job," I told him.

"It's waiting for you. Fact is, you'd have been hired long before now
but the owners were suspicious after you hooked up with Perry Thompson and Henry Brown. They figured you'd learned how to be as venal as
these past masters. But I told them you were okay and didn't try any of
their tricks."

I went to work next day. The *Whip* occupied a small office upstairs
over a cigar store at 31st and State. The job printing plant was located a
block away. Wednesday was press day in order to get on the stands no
later than Thursday morning and thus get the jump on the *Defender*
which came out every Friday.

Al Monroe was sports and theatrical editor; Mrs. Lovelyn Evans
handled society news, and Bibb himself wrote the thundering editorials.
Two of us comprised the news staff, me and a young fellow named Edwin
Drummond Sheen (Wassamatter? You never heard of a black Irishman?)
who had recently received his master's degree in English literature and
was working on his Ph.D. When I saw him ten years later he was still
working on his doctorate, but I was later relieved to learn he finally
finished it somewhere around World War II. Sheen, who had won a
national short story contest conducted by *Crisis* magazine, was, incidentally, the most even-tempered person I have ever met.

My regular news beat was the 35th Street and the Pekin Inn police stations, along with the municipal court at the latter and occasionally a case at a higher court. In addition, I wrote a regular column based on my observations around town. With my pay of fifteen dollars weekly went the title of "Assistant City Editor." Later, through hard work, industry, perseverance, brilliance, ability, and recognition of my sheer genius, I got a raise to eighteen dollars. But in all fairness, I received it regularly and living expenses were low. I couldn't afford to keep a mistress; but at the Greek restaurant a few doors away, I bought a complete meal including soup, roast, and two vegetables, salad, coffee, and dessert for thirty-five cents.

Also as a reporter in constant contact with police and the courts, certain other necessities cost me nothing. I spent no money for hootch as long as I was with the *Whip*. Since Prohibition was unpopular, cops rarely raided liquor joints unless they were repeatedly reported as nuisances, or to replenish their own private stocks. Nearly all kept anywhere from a quart to a gallon in their station lockers for their own use. They were also required to hold the evidence in those rare cases when bootleggers were bound over to the grand jury. When the liquor was of above-average quality, it often mysteriously changed to colored water when brought months later into trial court as evidence. More than one defendant went free when a smart defense attorney insisted on chemical analysis of the "booze." Since police also liked to keep on the good side of the press, I could always bum a half-pint from some cop. That is, when I did not actually get it in court.

There was a routine which seldom varied when a bootlegging case came up before whatever judge might be sitting at Pekin Inn Court.

Arresting officers came before the bench, bringing the evidence in one or more gallon bottles.

"Is that stuff any good?" the city or state's attorney asked with a grin. "If so, save me some."

Invariably, this brought a titter from the crowd. Spectators assumed the officials were kidding. An attorney sworn to uphold the law couldn't possibly be serious. They'd have been shocked had they known what really happened.

When the case was disposed of by the dropping of charges, a small fine, or by holding the defendant for further action, the bailiff confiscated the liquor and carried it to the judge's chambers. I put away my pencil and notes and followed. There we sampled the concoction, the bailiff and

I. If I found it satisfactory, I filled my bottle (I carried an empty pint container for this specific purpose) and returned to my reporter's perch in front of the bench. Later, when court adjourned, both the city's and state's attorneys scurried in to taste the booze and take what they wanted. Incidentally, certain bootleg joints known to provide good corn whiskey were raided only when the cops tired of inferior stuff; it was a kind of payoff for being allowed to operate.

Only one judge refused to cooperate. This was Judge Albert George, first Afro-American elected to that post in Chicago. He was trying his best to establish a record beyond reproach by white racist elements of the GOP, but in doing so he won the antagonism of many South Side lawyers who worked vigorously for his defeat next election. When Judge George hurt them in the pocketbook, they forgot racial loyalty. Many of these brown barristers derived the bulk of their fees from policy wheels and stations who paid them to get operators and writers back on the street soon after arrest. Inasmuch as raids were rarely conducted with warrants, quashing the evidence on the ground that it had been illegally obtained was a monotonously routine procedure for defense counsel. Cash brought in was confiscated, usually for some charity, and the prisoners were freed in time to dash back to work for the next policy drawings. But Judge George refused to cooperate. Anybody arrested in a police raid was bound over to the grand jury, no matter how the evidence had been obtained. Judge George was not reelected.

After a couple of months on the *Whip,* I made my first trip to Morals Court at City Hall. I was covering a story involving the latest caper of Tack Annie, a notoriously tough sister who made her living strong-arming white men who prowled 35th Street at night looking for a good time or to "change their luck." She had been arrested by Big Six, one of the few officers capable of handling her. Tack Annie looked no different from any other streetwalker, but she was at least as strong as the average man and knew all the dirty tricks of gutter brawling. When she lured her drooling victim into an alley or dark hallway and grabbed him, he was usually so surprised he offered only feeble resistance. But Big Six could haul her in, just as he could handle anybody else. He stood six feet six and weighed two hundred and sixty, virtually all of it solid muscle. He had been known to clean out the toughest dives on the South Side using nothing but his fists.

Waiting for Tack Annie's case to be called, I went up in front of the bench and took out pencil and paper to make notes on any other potential story. Morals Court was the clearinghouse for all of the city's sex cases involving women. Any young female, incidentally, found alone on ghetto streets late at night was likely to be picked up by cruising white cops as a prostitute; those suffering from extreme Negrophobia also arrested white girls riding in cars with black men until a married couple sued and won heavy damages for false arrest. Under a seldom used statute forbidding fornication, officers occasionally raided hotels and nabbed luckless broads in bed with their lovers.

As I stood listening to a case, I felt a tug on my coat sleeve and turned to find a well-stacked, high-brown babe by my side. She was obviously quite nervous.

"What you writing?" she asked.

"News," I replied. "I'm a reporter. For the *Whip*."

She hesitated, then asked, "Can you sit in back with me for a few minutes? I wanna talk to you."

I followed her, and as soon as we sat down she went straight to the point.

"I got a case coming up today. You gonna write about it?"

"Of course," I said, "if it's news."

"But I can't afford to have my name in the paper," she protested. "My husband would kill me when he comes in off the road. If he didn't read it himself, somebody'd be bound to tell him."

"That's too bad," I said.

"Of course it's my fault," she went on, "goin' out goodtimin' with that jellybean. But a girl can't stay home by herself all the time when her husband's gone five nights straight waitin' table on a diner."

"That's right," I agreed.

She sighed. "An' it was just my bad luck to get caught in a room at the Trenier."

"What a shame," I commiserated. "I bet there hadn't been a raid on that hotel in five years."

She looked at me, forcing a nervous smile. "You look like a nice guy. You ain't gonna print that in the *Whip,* are you?"

"I'm sorry, but news is news."

She was silent for several moments, as if coming to a decision. Then she spoke. "I'm supposed to be pretty good lookin'. You think so?"

"I'll go along with that," I said, and I meant it.

"Then there oughta be some way I could keep the story out."

I was silent. There are times to talk and times to keep your big mouth shut.

"Tell you what," she said, taking my arm, leaning real close and looking directly into my eyes. Her breath was on my face and her perfume in my nostrils. I felt myself responding naturally. "How 'bout coming by my apartment tonight around nine? Ain't gonna be nobody home but me. You think maybe we can find a way of keepin' that little ol' story out of the *Whip?*"

I nodded my head, and she gave me her address on Forrestville.

Although I took pride in having played it cool, I was mighty impatient for nine o'clock to roll around. From the look of things, tonight I at long last would end my virgin status. Once since Lorraine, I almost made out in Lawrence with a tall, dark co-ed who attended the University of Kansas and lived at home with her family. A group of us had driven to Lawrence to attend a Kappa Alpha Psi fraternity dance my last fall at Kansas State. Jo was my date; I had met her at our own spring party and liked her. But since I had no marital intentions, I considered her fair game.

She was sensual looking with cotton-soft lips, and when I took her home we started a torrid petting session in her darkened living room. We both became horny in a hurry, and she sank back on the couch. Just as I started to push inside her vestibule, her mother spoke from her bedroom.

"It's mighty quiet out there. Has the young man gone?"

"No, Mom, he's still here."

Naturally I froze.

"How come you so quiet?"

"We're reading something together. Some of his poems. He writes poetry."

"Ain't it kinda dark in there to read?"

"We got good eyes, Mom."

"Maybe I'd better come out and turn on more lights. You oughtn't to strain your eyes."

Jo sighed and threw out her arms helplessly. "That's okay, Mom, I'll turn 'em on. No need of you getting out of bed."

"I don't mind. I gotta get up anyhow to put away something I forgot in the kitchen."

Jo looked at me, smiled wryly, and shook her head. Already it was the end of the line and I hadn't really gotten on. I resented being dispossessed before I occupied the premises. Reluctantly but hastily we parted.

Within moments her mother came into the living room and found me standing in polite conversation with her daughter. I could have sworn her smile was slyly triumphant. Shortly afterward I left.

That had been my last real opportunity until now. I did not care for a cold cash transaction, and the cost of romancing in Chicago was beyond my means. So I was a celibate. Since I had never known any other state, it wasn't too difficult. You can't miss a Rolls Royce unless you've owned one.

All right, so here at last was a Rolls Royce ready and waiting.

That night the woman I'd met at Morals Court opened the door to her apartment on Forrestville wearing a thin kimona and apparently nothing beneath but herself. I felt frantic but tried my best to look calm.

"Sure glad you came," she said smiling. "I'll do anything to keep that mess out of the paper!"

"Anything?" I echoed. I couldn't help it, but my voice broke.

"Of course." She came close and put her arms around my neck. A pungent perfume drew back a fist and walloped me. Later I learned it was Black Narcissus. "The deal's still on, isn't it?"

"By all means." I tried not to sound too fervent, but for some reason I seemed to have lost control of my voice.

"How'll I know that after I give you some you won't print it anyway?"

"You'll just have to trust me," I said. "All I can do is promise to keep my word."

"You know something? I think I *can* trust you." She smiled, pulled my head down, and kissed me hard, thrusting her body against mine and twisting her hips. "Come on in the bedroom." She led me back into the small apartment, opened the door to a little room, and sat me down on the side of the bed. Throwing off her kimona, she stood before me completely naked.

"Do you like me?" she asked, turning slowly around. Obviously she was proud of her shape and her pride was justified. But in a way it was wasted on me. By now I'd have been ready for King Kong's rejected daughter; you know, the one that didn't uphold the family standard of beauty.

"Baby, you're hell all over," I told her, my eyes racing everywhere.

She laughed and got on the bed. I snatched off my clothes and joined her. I wasn't nervous but I was inexperienced. However, any intelligent fool can get the hang of it in a hurry. I'd had enough detailed descriptions from associates to know the proper procedure.

I made up in enthusiasm what I lacked in technique. And if the lady was disappointed, she was smart enough not to show it. Neither time. I suppose you really could call it blackmail: after all I was black and male.

But to keep the record straight, her story was so trivial I had no intention of using it in the *Whip* anyway.

Now that I knew another advantage of being a member of the working press and hoping this kind of lightning would strike more than once, I made a number of other reportorial visits to Morals Court when I could so arrange my schedule, and on three other occasions I allowed myself to be horizontally persuaded to leave out stories I had not intended to print. A lot of good things are presented to a reporter with pencil and paper, particularly when he's observed in court by cheating wives so frightened on arrest in hotel rooms that they make the grave error of giving police their correct names and addresses.

In fact, several times I received frantic phone calls from nervous broads who were so afraid some scandal about them would appear in the *Whip* that they gave me stories I otherwise would never have known— and then begged me not to write them.

Occasionally at night I rode with detectives in their Cadillac squad cars. Cadillac was the official police car; I understood a dealership was held by a close relative of a high city official. This dealer made a mint. All of these Cadillacs were specially built, seven-passenger sedans designed for the Age of Capone—bulletproof glass, nearly puncture-proof tires, a built-in arsenal behind the front seat holding sawed-off shotguns, Thompson submachine guns, tear gas equipment, etc. In theory this was to be used to battle gangsters. Actually it was no more than an excuse to dip greedy paws deeper into city funds. Police simply didn't fight mobsters; such would have been against the unwritten law. Any officer who dared molest a member of an organized gang faced the loss of his job.

By cruising with the cops, I was able to get spot coverage of murders, fires, accidents, and similar crime news in which the *Whip* specialized. A few times, incidentally, I was on the scene long before police, right when a homicide was taking place.

I remember one killing in an apartment on Wabash Avenue. As I walked along the street one late spring night I heard a man yell, "No, baby, no!" followed by six rapid revolver shots. Sensing a mint-fresh story, I dashed in and up to the flat; there was no locked door at the entrance activated by an electric button. Calmly standing, gun in hand, over the lifeless body of her husband was a big, brown, busty babe who told me without emotion that she had just bumped off her spouse. She sat down and I talked with her until police arrived, called by a neighbor. It seemed her husband wouldn't agree to give her up so she could marry some other dude who struck her fancy. She settled the matter for all time by getting a pistol divorce.

Aha, I thought, here is one wench who will get the works when she's tried for murder. It was as clear cut a case as I had ever known. I followed her arrest, arraignment, indictment, and trial. And do you know what finally happened? She went completely free, without even a slap on the wrist.

And all because she had Wendell Green as defense counsel.

Wendell Green was the most brilliant criminal lawyer I ever saw in action. For him to lose a case was almost as rare as a snail outrunning a jackrabbit. He had become a major headache to the best men on the state's attorney's staff, for they never knew what surprise he would pull in court. A small, medium-brown man, he became a giant before the bench. I saw him make judges so angry they lost their dignity and shook with rage in their black robes, but they could do nothing because they knew Green had the law on his side. He could also play on a jury like Heifetz on a violin.

A story was told of how Green got a black lad exonerated on the charge of killing a white cop in a holdup—one of the hardest raps to beat. At the trial, after the state (with Green's sly help) had built its case on the firing of the death gun, a .32 calibre revolver, from a distance of sixty feet, the brown barrister, who had been examining the weapon after lengthily and eloquently insisting it would not be fatal from that distance, wheeled suddenly and fired twice at a bailiff less than thirty feet away. In the ensuing pandemonium, with the bailiff milk white from fright, he rested his case and walked out. The obvious fact that the lawyer had secretly loaded the revolver with blanks did not overcome the impact of his dramatic act, and the jury found the defendant not guilty.

Later Wendell Green became a civil service commissioner and, finally, a judge, his great ambition. You may be sure nobody was happier to see him out of the field as a practicing barrister than the office of the state's attorney.

29

In February of 1928 the Regal Theatre opened and packed them in from the start. Rotund Dave Peyton conducted the symphony orchestra. But most South Siders came to hear jazz, and the hot unit was led by a New York import, Fess Williams, incidentally the uncle of the late great bass player, Charles Mingus. Fess was a combination of musician, leader, and clown and even without these special assets would still have been a hit because of the band he fronted. Most of the top stars were lured from other groups, including Louis Armstrong who quit the Vendome. There was speculation as to how Erskine Tate would fare without his trumpet ace, but that resourceful leader uncovered a fine replacement in Reuben Reeves and the Vendome continue to draw well. Fess Williams also emceed the lavish stage extravaganzas at the Regal, which included as a regular feature the Regalettes, a dancing chorus of the loveliest soul sisters available. Later the emcee chores were taken over by Shelton Brooks, best known as the author of "Some of These Days," the song Sophie Tucker made famous—and vice versa.

With the Regal and Savoy side by side, entertainment emphasis shifted from 35th to 47th and South Parkway. This was one of those rare instances in which fate advantageously pulled the strings. The quadren-nial convention of the AME Church was held in Chicago that summer at the Eighth Regiment Armory near 35th and Giles. A rare South Side cleanup in that area was launched, but little needed to be done since virtually all the neighborhood cabarets were already closed.

I covered various phases of that convention and received an eye-popping course in the operations of that august body. I saw as much power politics in the bishopric campaign as occur at any Republican or Demo-cratic national convention. Candidates rented entire houses for campaign headquarters and draped them with wildly shouting streamers. Candy for the lady delegates and cigars for the men were available around the clock. Privately, candidates made any kind of deal they could afford. Even in 1928 the estimated cost of a good fight for election was at least fifteen hundred dollars. And let me say that some of the venerable prelates when aroused could out-cuss a misanthropic truck driver suffering from both hives and ulcers. As for the younger delegates, including certain ministers, they made a beeline for the Savoy immediately following the final evening benediction. Many whores bragged they had the best week of their careers.

If you think I've got it in for the AMEs, you're wrong. I was editing a paper in Atlanta in the early 1930s when the National Baptist Conven-tion, Inc., met there, and I killed a spicy story about a well-known Baptist minister who broke his leg jumping from a second-story window when cops raided a brothel. After all, religion is a poor substitute for biological needs—especially when you're a long way from home and don't think you'll be found out.

Incidentally, I had hoped through the father-in-law of Pat Prescott, one of the *Whip* owners, to get a civil service job. The father-in-law, Bishop Archibald Carey, ordinarily would have been able to grant me a soft spot, supplying enough cash for me to attend the Medill School of Journalism at Northwestern while working on the *Whip*. In this graft-ridden town, anybody with the proper connections ordinarily had it made. I knew that the pastor of a leading South Side church was on the city payroll for three hundred dollars monthly; his job consisted only of signing his paycheck. I was looking forward to an appointment as "lake level inspector." This paid two hundred dollars monthly (with a kickback of fifty dollars) for taking a look each morning at Lake Michigan and phoning in whether the water seemed high, low, or normal.

It was just my luck for the Chicago *Daily News* to launch, at this time, a crusade for civic betterment.[20] In a series of sensational front-page articles, the leading afternoon sheet exposed graft and corruption at City Hall. Key administration figures suddenly decided this was the time to take vacations; some left for "business trips" in Canada and the West Indies. While I am all for honesty in government, I do wish the *News* had chosen another period for its crusade. By the time the series petered out and conditions returned to abnormal, with millions again being squandered, I had left the *Whip*.

30

As I left the El station on 41st Street around midnight one warm summer evening, I saw S. Quay Herndon standing in front of the Boston Cafe looking like a darker but more angelic brother of Mephisto. He was something of a fixture around cabarets, selling advertising and writing a nightlife column for *The Light and Heebie Jeebies*. As a result we had become jug buddies, habitually draining every drop either of us might have on him.

"Howya doing?" he asked.

"Not so hot. As usual, white folks got all the money."

"Whatcha got on?"

"Nothin'. I'm gonna grab me a nightful of shuteye."

"That can wait. This is the time we oughta settle it once and for all."

"Settle what?" I asked.

"Settle which one of us can down the most liquor. We've been cleanin' each other out whenever we meet at a hot spot, and neither of us bats an eye. You got me wondering who can drink the most. Now, you don't work tomorrow and neither do I. My landlady runs a buffet flat and keeps a gang of it stashed around. Tonight let's settle it once and for all."

We walked a couple of blocks to his living quarters. From his landlady he got a pint of clear corn whiskey and two white coffee cups. We killed that in record time. He ordered a second. It did not disappear as swiftly as the first, but it didn't tarry. When Herndon called for a third pint, the landlady eyed us as if we were a new species of animal brought back by an explorer.

Our conversation drifted to politics as we leisurely reduced number three. Oscar DePriest had recently been elected to the House of Representatives from Chicago, the first black congressman since Reconstruction.[21] A tall man, tan colored, his high mane of gray hair made him seem bigger than he actually was. Owning a powerful voice and knowing how to use it effectively, he and Roscoe Conkling Simmons (his foes called him "Cackling" Simmons) were the orators of that day. Rough and rugged, he had slugged his way to the top in South Side politics and had been an alderman before taking on the white Democratic incumbent and defeating him for a seat in Congress. Knowing that many Southern congressman had virtually flipped their racist lids when they learned a black would sit among them, both Herndon and I agreed a better choice would have been almost impossible. DePriest had already gotten into beefs with several of the more vicious white supremacists and had stood his ground. He was a verbal match for any of them, and we knew none dared attack him physically. Although we realized he could accomplish little legislatively, we were quite satisfied at last to have somebody in Congress to speak up for us; in that respect, Oscar DePriest represented the whole black America rather than a district in Illinois. That was something to drink to.

When the third pint died, neither of us showed any symptoms of being even mildly high. Since we didn't want the bout to end in a draw, we again called for a bottle.

The landlady came in wearing a "I'll-be-goddamned-if-it's-so" expression and asked:

"What you cookies doin'—bathin' in it?"

"We're thirsty," Herndon said.

"But this'll make a half gallon," she protested, "and there ain't but two of you."

"We're trying to decide whether we like it," I explained.

This left her wordless. She turned and walked out, muttering under her breath. She was gone so long I asked Herndon if there were any women roomers in the flat.

"No," he said. "Why?"

I told him about a story uncovered two days earlier at Pekin Inn Court. Police testified they had raided a flat at 29th and Federal where the landlady boasted she could provide a bottle any time of the day. Should a customer call when her supply was low, she sat him in the living room, secretly took a basin, called on any of her three women roomers who might be in, and asked her to urinate in the pan. Mixing this with 180-proof alcohol kept in reserve for just such an emergency, she bottled and sold it. Nobody could tell its composition by looking. It had strength, body, and a distinctive flavor, often even an amber color. One of the arresting officers opined this concoction might actually be an improvement over the rotgut she ordinarily sold.

I wondered aloud how prevalent this practice might be on the South Side. And then there came a sudden thought: could this be the secret of that fifteen-cent stuff I bought for Fritz Pollard? I would never know—and maybe it was better that way.

The fourth pint came and went. I looked at Herndon. He didn't seem the least bit drunk. As for myself, I felt a slight glow but I was not too far from normal. No reason in the world why we couldn't down another. Herndon called the landlady.

"I ain't got none left," she said. "You damn fools done drunk it all up 'cept maybe a half-pint. Want that?"

"Well, if that's all you got," Herndon said. "But next time try to keep enough on hand for two people. All you had tonight was about right for one of us."

We split it evenly between the coffee cups and drained every drop. The clock now said 4:00 A.M.

"You feel all right?" Herndon asked.

"Fine. How's 'bout you?"

"Couldn't be better. But since we're out of booze and can't get any more this time of morning, I guess it's a draw. We still don't know who's champ."

"Yeah. But I could eat. How 'bout dirtyin' a plate at the Boston?"

We went to the Boston Cafe with no sign of a stagger, had bacon and eggs and coffee, then went our separate ways. I felt fine, completely at peace with the world, and dropped off to sleep as soon as I hit the bed.

But when I woke up some time around noon, I paid my dues.

It was no hangover, but a feeling, a mental state I've never had before or since. I felt plopped down into the middle of a strange world in which humans were not humans. They no longer had even the illusion of civilization. Now there was nothing but stark antagonism. Sometime before the day was over, I would be killed. The excuse would be trivial, or maybe it would be from the sheer joy of wanton slaughter. Not knowing who my executioner might be, I walked gingerly, fearfully, and anxiously searching each face. It could be man, woman, or a child. At each street corner I hesitated, looking in all directions, before I stepped off the curb and then dashed across, hoping to reach the other side before somebody squashed me with a car. By nightfall my nerves were threadbare. I went home early, locked myself in my room, thankful that by some miracle I was still alive.

31

The *Whip* was constantly hard pressed for cash. Despite its militant Don't-Spend-Your-Money-Where-You-Can't-Work campaign, its circulation was only a fraction of the *Defender*'s. The *Whip* had broken down many South Side employment barriers, but those who profited were not regular readers nor did they become subscribers. In a retrenchment move that fall, I was laid off along with two others with a promise to be rehired when business improved. Actually, it never did, and the paper folded a year or two later. But I couldn't wait anyway. In October I went out to Gary, Indiana, the steel-making suburb, to work on the Gary *American* as managing editor.[22]

The Gary *American* had been started by a fast-talking whiz who could have sold Greta Garbo on quitting movies to become a stripteaser in a skid row burlesque house. But he didn't stay anywhere long and soon split for Kansas City after involving A. B. Whitlock, Gary's lone black alderman, and Fritz W. Alexander, a young attorney who sported a Kaiser Bill mustache, so deeply in its operation they decided to keep it going. He also left his editor, Chauncey Townsend, a journalism graduate from the University of Southern California.

Gary's population was one hundred thousand, of which some twenty thousand were black, the largest homogeneous group in the city. Many had come North to work in the steel mills. Blacks outnumbered native-born whites. Most Caucasians were immigrants from Southern and Central Europe. For the most part, however, they had left their national prejudices at home, even though many could speak no English. It was not uncommon to see a Lithuanian church standing next to a Polish center, or to find Italians, Greeks, Slavs, and Mexicans living side by side. This was a rich and almost virgin field for a serious sociologist.

I was in Gary only a short time before I wrote this poem:

Gary, Indiana

In Gary
The Mills
feast
on ore and men . . .

Like potbellied hoboes
the mills snore
lying face upward
on the north horizon
their breath
like winter exhalation
fogs redly
the night sky
capers madly
on a black stage
hoboes
yes
hoboes
their stomachs filled
with ore
and men
hoboes
yes
they'll hit the road tomorrow
if the food runs low

The mills are always hungry
what a beast
they make steel in their bellies

it's hard to tell
men from steel

To the south
the town
squats on sand—
a lanky woman
the steel mills'
concubine

A hundred thousand people
Europe in America
Africa in Indiana
an extension of Mexico
the Orient transplanted
another Babel
all different
all alike
steel faced men
iron featured women
and plenty of women
for the steel faced men

A mayor
yes
and a city council
and officials
and graft
sure
and banks
and stores
and places
they eat the crumbs
the hoboes drop
and grow potbellies

Suffering
now and then
in the town
in hoboes
get indigestion
now and then
and don't feast
on ore and men

> Well
> anyway
> old judge Gary
> knew his stuff . . .

Fritz Alexander was conservative, but A. B. Whitlock stayed in orbit. He looked like a lanky, sunburned po' white sharecropper with African features. Sharp and resourceful, he won national recognition a couple of years earlier when he masterminded the settling of a school strike by white students (sons of immigrants!) who objected when black kids were assigned to a previously lily white public school. Townsend, who was himself becoming a slick operator, sold advertising and helped lay out the sheet. I did most of the reporting and editing, wrote all the editorials and a regular column (I've been columnist on every paper I ever wrote for) and made the front-page layout. An office girl who doubled as society editor completed the full-time staff. Small town, small paper, small staff. Actual printing took place at a shop in Indiana Harbor a few miles away.

I saw Gary for the first time in October and voted in the national election in November. Even a fugitive from justice on the run from New York to California could have voted in Indiana in those days. I marked my ballot for Hoover; like virtually all souls, I lived by the words of the great Frederick Douglass who in the past century had declared, "The Republican party is the ship, all else is the sea." Clearly did I remember the often repeated words of our leaders: "I'd rather vote for a Republican dog than the best Democrat who ever lived." And believe me, we helped elect our share of dogs! But using elementary logic, we felt justified. Dixie was controlled by Democrats. Dixie hated black people. Ergo, Democrats hated black Americans.

That fall I covered a black Democratic rally of less than a hundred at which Ferdinand Moton, civil service commissioner from Harlem, was imported to orate for Al Smith. Most of those present came for free eats and several kegs of bootleg beer; I was there to ridicule the event in writing. Evidently I was successful for I received congratulatory letters from cities as widely separated as Denver, Seattle, and New York where I did not know we had readers.

I was able to vote after less than a month's residence because registration was a fraud. In Chicago the political bosses got their voters' lists from tombstones in cemeteries. In Gary clerks visited homes, knocked on doors, and merely asked landlords, "Who lives here?" The landlord rattled off any names he chose, and that was it. There were instances of fifteen or twenty "persons" living in a shanty. So far as I know, these registration lists were never challenged. Some individuals were registered from several precincts, thus allowing them to make a kind of grand voting tour on election day.

The *American* paid me twenty dollars weekly, an improvement of two dollars over the *Whip*. Living cost less in Gary, but each Saturday I went by bus over to Chicago (fare thirty-five cents) returning Sunday night or Monday morning. I did little socializing in Gary except for an occasional date with Willa Brown, then a new schoolteacher but later to become Afro-America's foremost aviatrix.

Usually on Sunday I rode the streetcar way out to Morgan Park where Dad and Edith now lived. Dad operated a pool hall, and on Sunday I ran it to give him a day off. I could keep any income over five dollars which was prorated overhead. I regularly pocketed ten to fifteen dollars for myself.

Almost without fail I went Saturday and Sunday nights to the Savoy Ballroom. In Harlem the Savoy was the home of happy feet; in Chicago I found it a happy hunting ground for chicks. The Savoy in Harlem had more of a mixed clientele; white Dixie belles alone in Gotham were known to make a virtual beeline there to sample black forbidden fruit. Few ofays frequented the Chicago Savoy and then usually in parties keeping to themselves. But there were enough Duskyamerican dolls ranging from blonde to black to please any palate. Most of these young broads were as interested as the slick studs in making a connection. It was all quite simple. When I saw a gal whose looks I liked, I asked her to dance if she seemed free at the moment. If she liked the way I looked, we'd take it from there.

That's how I met Julia. Her complexion looked as delicious as a chocolate bar and her teeth were startlingly white, but it was her eyes that turned me on. They were big and soft and must have been taken from an ancient Egyptian drawing. I stalked her several weeks before catching her alone one Sunday night returning from the powder room. We danced. I shot her a fast line and made a date for Tuesday night.

I came in from Gary and sped straight to her address on 42nd near South Parkway in a dejected stone building squatting helplessly with no pretense of gentility. There was no buzzer at the entrance. I walked up to the second floor. Before I could ring the bell, the door opened and a young man, who looked as if he had recently left the rural South, came out. Two smiling women stood just inside the flat. One said, "Come back soon," and the other postscripted, "Be sure an' tell your friends about us." The young man mumbled, "Sho will," grinned, and started down the steps. Both gals turned to me, smiling speculatively.

"Is Julia in?" I asked.

"She's inside," one said and yelled, "Julia!" They lost interest and stepped aside. I heard one tell the other, "That down home papa was the first trick I had tonight." The other replied, "That so? I ain't had but two."

Before I could fully digest this, Julia appeared wearing a short yellow dress hugging her as close as nineteen is to twenty.

"Oh, hello, honey," she said, in a voice with soft warm arms that grabbed and hung on. "I hoped you wouldn't forget. Let's go to my room where we can be alone." She opened a door leading off the hallway.

Hanging from her ceiling must have been the only tenth-of-a-watt light bulb ever made. I became mildly irritated; I not only like to see what I'm doing but I also want to visually enjoy an appealing woman. Eons dragged by, it seemed, before objects took form in the near-black room; finally I recognized a big double bed, a chair, and a dresser piled high with many kinds of dolls. Julia, meanwhile, stood beside me chattering away about nothing in particular.

Silently I turned and placed my arms around her, fervently hoping she was not like the pair in the hall. I kissed her and scouting hands reported she wore nothing under the skintight dress. I was so aroused I didn't care what she might be; I wanted to get in bed with her forthwith. I reached down swiftly and pulled her dress as high as her belly before she could twist away, giggling nervously.

I wanted for her to say something.

"If you want it," she said hesitantly, "it'll cost you two bucks."

"Two bucks?" I echoed. I fell from the peak of expectancy and was angry with myself for having hoped she was not a whore. "I didn't know you were in business," I said as cuttingly as I could.

"The two dollars," she explained evenly, "is not for me. It's for use of the room. My landlady won't let you do *anything* without trying to make herself some money from it."

This only partially pacified me. "Just the same, I don't like it. I didn't come here expecting to treated like a trick by you or your landlady."

"If I looked on you as a trick," she shot back, "I wouldn't have let you kiss me. I *like* you."

That got me. I thought, hell, what's two bucks for a room. Maybe she's not one of *them* after all, and even if she is, maybe she really does like me. Combine male ego with wishful thinking, and you can rationalize your way around all kinds of barriers.

I reached in my pocket for a pair of singles and started to hand them over when I heard a woman's voice outside the door say, "Tell him to come back later. She's busy now."

Automatically I assumed that "she" was Julia and this was a trick calling for her horizontal services. This made her a full-fledged prostitute. My desire dropped to zero. Unh unh. None for me.

Julia seemed to read my mind.

"Honey," she said, "why don't we take a little walk? The night air might do us good."

She piloted me down the stairs and up the street, talking easily and constantly, allowing me to say little, filling any potential holes of silence with chunks of chatter about the Savoy, Louis Armstrong, and dancing. Two blocks away she stopped in front of a small eating joint featuring french fried shrimps and asked me to buy her some, saying, "They're awfully good." She was right. They came with a sauce made of that liquid fire the devil hands the tormented thirsty, yet tastes so heavenly a saint would hock his halo for another spoonful.

"I guess you think I'm pretty awful," she said as we munched our second order.

"Well," I said slowly, fishing for the right words to describe my mixed feelings. I could not deny that physically she was devastating. For that alone I couldn't call her awful.

"I'm gonna be married a year from now," she went on. "He's in show business. A dancer." She named a member of a well-known duo of vaudeville and cabaret hoofers. "So you'll know I'm shootin' it to you straight, here's his last letter." She took a folded special delivery envelope from her purse, showed the return address as Small's Paradise in New York, and had me read the extremely affectionate salutation and ending on the long letter.

"He sends me a hundred dollars a month to live on. I can make it on that," she continued, and I nodded. "Reason we're waiting to get married is because it'll take that long to be completely free of his present wife. He's paying her off now, so much per month."

"You love him?" I asked curiously.

"So long as he thinks so, what's the difference? I'm going to be a hell of a good wife. I can be content with him the rest of my life." She paused. "But if something should happen, I don't want to be left holdin' the bag. So I salt away as much as I can of the hundred he sends, along with anything else I can get hold of. It's like insurance."

"Why don't you get a regular job?" I asked.

"I spent two years at Philander Smith College in Arkansas before Daddy's money ran out. That was just long enough for me not to learn how to do anything. I wouldn't take a job in a store or a restaurant or a laundry at fifteen dollars a week unless I was starving, and you know that's the usual pay. Besides, he doesn't want me to work. He's likely to call long distance any time. He doesn't mind if I'm at the Savoy or a show or out for a bite to eat, but that's about the only kind of excuse he'll accept if I'm not here when he telephones."

"So what you're doing now is okay?"

"What *am* I doing now?" she asked innocently.

She had me there. I couldn't blurt out she was a whore purely on circumstantial evidence. I simply wasn't callous enough to make that kind of accusation to a doll who looked at me with the kind of eyes that rocked Pharoah. I said nothing.

"You know," she went on, "I DO like you. We could have a good time together, if you'd loosen up." Julia laughed and rose. "Would you mind taking me home?"

Still ambivalent, I left her at her door. From her looks alone, she was worth far more in bed than I could ever hope to pay, but I was not in the mood to buy.

On the bus back to Gary I suddenly remembered the prevailing South Side price was a pair of frogskins even when the broad provided the crib.[23] So what did she mean, the landlady wanted two bucks for the room?

Still—

I saw her at the Savoy several times thereafter, and each time she looked at me with question marks in those big, soft, Egyptian eyes. I knew I was about to crumble. I was on the verge of saying, "All right, baby, I don't care what you are. You move me so much I'm coming to see you with money in my hand," when I was snatched away just in time. And all because I picked up another gal at the Savoy.

Her name was Eleanor, and she was a recent divorcee. No glamour gal, but she had warmth and sensuality. I was attracted the moment I saw her. I asked for a dance, and we clicked immediately. Tall and tobacco brown, with a blend of African and Indian features, she worked as a furrier in the Loop. Unfortunately, she lived in Evanston which meant a two-and-a-half-hour trip from Gary to see her unless we met at the Savoy. Since we both loved dancing, this was no problem.

As months passed, she spoke more and more of matrimony. I had to mention I was engaged to a girl named Gladys back in Kansas. This stalled her only momentarily, for she pointed out Gladys was seven hundred miles away and she was right here. I gave no encouragement except under special circumstances, such as being in bed together. She tried to pin me down when I pinned her down, asking passionately, "Sweetheart, you are going to marry me, aren't you?" Not caring to argue at such intense moments, I would have agreed to walk the water from New York to London. To have peace for a piece, I mumbled, "yes." I hoped she'd realize the emptiness of a promise under this kind of duress. It must have properly impressed her, for I always changed the subject when she mentioned matrimony under ordinary circumstances. Further, she was the first to provide a consistent outlet for my hitherto repressed oral desires, so I did fully enjoy the relationship.

32

Despite the paucity of pay, a newspaperman received other kinds of compensation. A working press pass signed by the chief of police insured the bearer a certain respect and deference, even from Mr. Charlie and the police. Sometimes a reporter threw his weight around, as when a *Defender* reporter named Poindexter, late for an assignment at the 48th Street Municipal Court, dashed up to a stranger sitting in a parked car on 35th, flashed his press pass and ordered the driver to rush him to his destination. The poor soul, seeing the police chief's signature, roared through heavy traffic and ran red lights to perform what he thought was his duty as a good citizen. Ed Jourdain, later Evanston's sole black alderman, in his reportorial days was known to have flagged down a squad car loaded with cops, flashed his press pass, and then lectured them on the dangers of fast driving. The officers fumed but passed it off as a joke, for they never knew when they might need a good word in print.

One night Chauncey Townsend and I drove home from Chicago to Gary by a different route. It was midnight, and Townsend was twenty miles above the speed limit when we heard a siren and were forced to the roadside by a motorcycle patrolman.

"Where you think you're going? To a fire?" he asked sarcastically. I have often asked if this standard quip is part of Lesson One in the Officer's Manual.

"No, we're just in a hurry to get home and to bed," Townsend said.

"Yeah? Well now ain't that just too bad. Turn around and follow me."

He drove back five miles to a small building, unlocked the door, and had us enter. It was a miniature police station, and he seated himself across the tiny desk from us.

"Who do you think you are, speeding like hell?" he began.

We said nothing. Townsend produced his press pass and laid it before the white officer. I followed suit.

He looked at them, and his eyes bugged. It was probably the first time in his life he had ever seen black reporters.

"We've been working on a big story," Townsend said, cued by the officer's awed expression. "Been on it since six o'clock yesterday morning. We gotta get some rest and get right back on it again early today. Now you've made us lose a lot of time. Do you realize you're gumming up something of special interest to the administration?"

The patrolman fidgeted uneasily, forced a grin, and apologized.

"I'm sorry I stopped you gentlemen," he said, "but you *were* goin' kinda fast and how'd I know who you were? I was only doing my duty."

Townsend looked at me. "He was only doing his duty," he repeated sarcastically.

The cop squirmed. "Tell you what?" he said, suddenly inspired. "I'll escort you back to where I stopped you. Drive as fast as you wanna. But about three miles farther on you'll see three big signboards on the right side of the highway. I suggest you slow down 'cause that's where my partner waits, and I'd hate to have him inconvenience you gentlemen."

With his siren crying, he escorted us back at over a mile a minute, then waved goodbye as we sped on. I had the impression he'd consider himself lucky if we didn't report him to his superiors.

33

Gary election campaigns were on the same low level as voter registration. The dirt of Chicago politics settled in neighboring Indiana where it gathered additional pollution. A candidate customarily searched his voting district for someone with a name similar to that of his most popular rival, then entered him in the primary race hoping to split the opposition vote. Of course this did not work if your most formidable rival was named Funkhouser, for where would you find another?

When A. B. Whitlock came up for reelection as alderman in the 1929 spring primaries, he concluded his strongest opponent was a certain businessman and used an entirely different technique to destroy him.

Buried in police files was a record of this rival's arrest some years before for "annoying white women." As a city official, Whitlock had access to this material. Borrowing the arrest sheet, he reproduced thousands of photostatic copies for distribution in the ward with distinctly different accompanying messages. White voters read: "Would you elect to represent you in the city council a Negro who has such uncontrollable sexual desires that police had to take him into custody for molesting white women?"

Black voters got the following: "Surely you cannot vote for a candidate who is so dissatisfied with our own women that he sneaks off and tries to cross the color line by bothering white women. How many times that we do not know about has this happened both before and after he was arrested?"

At last election day came.

Because of the ridiculous registration, candidates customarily hired truckloads of out-of-town floaters to be herded from precinct to precinct. At each polling place, they assumed the names of non-existent voters who had been officially listed by the neighborhood registrars. After making their rounds and casting their ballots in all the polling places within a ward, they were then rented to a candidate in a different district for a similar round of voting. A nondescript floater with no outstanding marks of identification could make a good bundle by hitting every polling place in Gary.

Of course this was illegal, but since it was common practice candidates did not protest. Instead, if an office-seeker could afford it, he hired guards to watch highways leading into town. Should several vehicles loaded with men approach Gary, these guards stopped them at gunpoint. If they were identified as hirelings of a rival, they were herded to some out of the way place and detained until polls closed in late afternoon. However, despite all vigilance, some of the opponent's drifters always managed to slip through.

Even when a candidate paid floaters, there was no assurance that a rival would not give these hirelings a larger amount to vote for him. Whitlock rented a group after they finished their chores in another ward for the incumbent alderman. After the final tally, he noted to his disgust that in one tiny precinct his total was actually less than the number he had directly paid for. I don't believe he ever learned who double-crossed him.

However, Whitlock did receive several multiple votes he hadn't bought. Around eleven o'clock that morning a very agitated Townsend ran into the office, out of breath, and in scared tones pleaded:

"Hide me! I was helping Whitlock by voting in several precincts. But as I was coming out of the fourth polling place one of his enemies recognized me and yelled for the cops. I got away as fast as I could and ran here. You gotta hide me until this thing cools down. I don't want to go to jail!"

Under a small throw rug in Fritz Alexander's law office was a trapdoor leading to the basement. There in the cool and quiet of old crates, discarded office equipment and records, and a nosey family of housekeeping rats were a chair and a couch maintained for anybody who wanted to get away from it all. It was a perfect hideout.

Townsend scooted down, I replaced the rug, and we sat around awaiting developments. But nobody came nor did anybody bother to telephone. In Gary of 1929, why worry about such a minor matter as quadruple voting?

It did occur to me, however, that this was an ideal time for Townsend to communicate with the infinite. An editor, no matter how small the publication, rarely has a chance to make with a Buddha act. I felt, therefore, properly benign—nay, even sanctimonious—when each hour I lifted the door and yelled down that a couple of officers had called and would return again. He might have believed he was wasting his time had I not given him justification for remaining hidden. After all, a man would rather feel wanted than neglected. He remained secluded for some eight hours, well past 7:00 P.M., and I honestly felt the rest did him a lot of good. Unfortunately, some blabbermouth told him later that nobody had snitched to the police about his illegal voting and no cops had visited the *American* office, with the result that for some days after hearing this revelation Townsend was pensive and uncommunicative, speaking to me only when absolutely necessary. I had the strong impression he was not grateful.

Whitlock successfully eliminated the businessman he had looked upon as his most formidable opponent. The photostats of that arrest sheet did the job. Nevertheless, Whitlock was defeated in the primaries. And by a young upstart he had almost completely ignored, so little did he think of his chances.

The young upstart was named Wilbur Hardaway. In his twenties, he won because he got the high school vote. Yeah, that's what I said, the high school vote.

Hardaway ran around with the older high school kids and those who had recently finished, played pool with the boys, belonged to their social clubs, and in every way was a genuine buddy. With the ridiculous registration system and schools closed on election day, it was easy for high school boys and girls (with the connivance of polling place officials who didn't like Whitlock) to vote for Hardaway en masse, giving him a winning margin. And thus Gary got a new black alderman who, incidentally, was reelected for several terms.

During the primaries at East Chicago, Indiana, I took on a special and unique assignment. The owner of the white commercial plant in Indiana Harbor (part of East Chicago) which printed the *American* also edited a weekly newspaper. He had chosen to support an aspirant who had visions of unseating the incumbent mayor.

"Our campaign," he told me, "is being waged against the wholesale corruption of the present city administration. We know that each week thousands of dollars in bribes go to the mayor—a no good skunk if ever there was one—the chief of police, and assorted detectives. This big payoff comes from the gang which controls vice in East Chicago. We're going to blast this whole rotten mess wide open. We're going to expose the tie-up between responsible civic officials and organized crime. You can help us by finding out where, when, how much, and to whom these payoffs are made. Are you willing to work for our side?"

Of course I was willing. At twenty dollars per night plus all expenses, how could I refuse?

On the outskirts of East Chicago was a well-known roadhouse operated by a notorious black racketeer who had reportedly knocked off several guys and had beaten the rap. I was well acquainted with the joint, having gone there several times. On the first floor were two bars running wide open despite Prohibition. There was also a small cabaret with a five-piece band which was the first mixed jazz aggregation I had ever seen. Tables were small and rough. For a buck you could buy a half-pint of clear corn liquor served in a water glass with two smaller glasses and ice. The cabaret was usually loaded with floozies; when a half-pint came to a table so did a couple of the gals, drawn like flies to molasses. On my initial visit, to insure solitude I picked up the water glass containing the half pint, looked around at the chippies expectantly licking their chops, and drained it. They got up and left.

Also on the ground floor of the roadhouse was a small cafe, and upstairs were rooms for transients. If you didn't bring your own broad, there was always available day and night a supply of reasonably priced black, Mexican, European, and white American whores. Interestingly enough, there were no separate Ladies' and Gents' washrooms; everybody used the same facilities like one big happy family. This system had its merits. Occasionally an occupant would "forget" to lock the washroom door and suddenly find guests; this not only helped men and women become better acquainted but often led to renting of rooms. The operator of this bustling business had a nice fat income. The biggest single operation in East Chicago, the payoff had to be huge.

The roadhouse also offered bottled in bond liquor (supposedly from Canada) at seven and a half dollars per half pint. I was instructed to be a real sport, buy the best booze, and take on a few lay-for-pay babes. The opposition to the existing administration was willing to spend plenty of money so long as results were forthcoming.

Of course this campaign was not being undertaken to give the city clean government; civic virtue was not the real motivation. By now I'd seen enough of politics to realize that the aspirant wanted to unseat the present mayor in order to bring in his own vultures. He wanted the rake-off himself. Already he had made arrangements for another Cicero gang to come in and take over if he won the election, ousting the present setup. The king is dead; long live the king!

I assumed correctly that Whitlock had or could get every iota of information I needed. Without stirring from Gary, I obtained from him the names of the East Chicago cops who collected the payoffs, when and where, how much, and by whom. All of this was frontpaged in a series of articles in the weekly. I collected my twenty bucks plus expenses averaging forty dollars for each of a listed five nights work. The three hundred iron men constituted a real windfall. Both my employers and I were thoroughly satisfied.

Despite the exposé, the incumbent won the spring primary and I forgot all about it. In late winter I had written to C. E. Rogers telling him I wanted to return to Kansas State and get my degree. Immediately, Professor Rogers had set the ball rolling. A faculty committee was formed to find me a scholarship. They finally came up with a Sigma Delta Chi perpetual scholarship (meaning I was supposed to pay back the funds when I could) which would take care of all fees, a job with the college publicity staff to provide me with money for current expenses, and a promise from various profs to lend me all necessary textbooks. By mid-summer I was all set—and lucky it was that it had all been worked out.

Early in August two strange white men walked into the *American* office and said they wanted to speak privately with me. They showed FBI credentials and came straight to the point.

"Last spring a series of articles about graft in the city administration of East Chicago appeared in a weekly newspaper in Indiana Harbor," they said. "We have learned you gathered the information. Our own investigation shows that what you reported is substantially correct. Now, we want to know where and from whom you got your information."

"As a reporter, my source of news is confidential," I replied. "Besides, what's so important about it anyway?"

"That exposure and our own investigation shows that federal law has been violated. We're gathering evidence on the hookup between organized vice and the East Chicago city government to be presented before a federal grand jury meeting at South Bend this fall. We shall expect you to appear and testify as to what you know."

"As a newspaperman, I shall refuse to testify."

"If you won't appear voluntarily, we shall be forced to subpoena you."

"Then you'll just have to subpoena me."

They left.

Next day I received a special delivery letter postmarked Chicago. It read: "You are hereby warned that you had better not appear before the grand jury in South Bend and testify, subpoena or not. If you appear it will be the last thing you ever do." It was signed "Aiello Brothers."

The Aiello Brothers were one of the many gangs with headquarters in Cicero, Illinois. Not as big or powerful as Al Capone's mob, they nevertheless had their working agreement and were tough enough and strong enough to control certain specified territories. Furthermore, an Aiello bullet was just as deadly as a Capone slug. While I considered myself protected by constitutional guarantees against revealing the source of confidential information and had no intention of talking if carried bodily before the federal grand jury, I had no way of knowing how familiar the Aiellos might be with the rights of reporters. They might not be aware of this unique position of a working newspaperman, and I knew of no way to inform them.

Although I had learned that the Aiello Brothers were involved in the East Chicago graft arrangements, the gang had not been mentioned in my articles. I had plenty of reasons to keep their name out of the exposé—reasons like the possibility of being confronted with a fistfull of automatic. I had pointedly ignored them, but it now looked as if they would not return the favor.

I also marveled at the speed and efficiency of the underworld spy system which brought me a threat only twenty-four hours following a confidential visit from the FBI. Having lived in Chicagoland for two and a half years and reading of the fate of people the gangs merely suspected of talking to officials, and with the St. Valentine's Day massacre only a few months old and still unsolved, I was properly impressed by the letter. I did not look forward with glee to the prospect of being taken for a ride and being dumped lifeless beside a country road or crammed into a culvert. This was not the kind of future I had planned at college.

A gangland threat is one of the most forceful means I know for inducing a rapid decision. That evening I told people I had a job offer from Philadelphia and within a week split the Gary scene. Although I knew it would be a few months before I could expect a subpoena from the grand jury, I preferred not being a sitting duck for the Aiello gang. I felt safer elsewhere—any elsewhere. I spent a few quiet days on the South Side, primarily with Eleanor, visited Gladys at her home in Kansas, and arrived in Manhattan four days in advance of the start of fall semester. I kept an eye on the happenings in Indiana. I do not doubt that the FBI could have found me had this organization believed it essential to try to force me to violate my reportorial credo, but they had dug up overwhelming evidence elsewhere. I recall reading where one witness who appeared before the grand jury at South Bend was discovered a few days later thoroughly dead from a half-dozen well-placed bullet holes. I kept the clipping several years as a reminder that there could have been two of us.

Oh yes, the mayor of East Chicago, chief of police, and a few other officials were indicted, tried, convicted, and served prison terms. I thought you might like to know.

1929–1930

34

When I returned to my frat house after two and a half years away, I was pleasantly surprised to learn two frat brothers, Louis Edwin Fry and Alva Watson, had also chosen 1929 to come back, the brilliant Fry to get his master's degree in architectural engineering and Watson his bachelor's in veterinary medicine.

I found myself something of a celebrity, junior grade. The student newspaper interviewed me and published a long front-page story headed "Negro Poet and Journalist Again Enrolls at Kansas State." I was asked to write a regular column which I frequently used to blast the policy of the lily white athletic conference. I was given a job on the college publicity staff. Various other jobs were thrown my way, enough to make me self-supporting.

The previous year Sigma had won the Aggie Orpheum, in which I had once appeared, largely through the efforts of one William Johnson, a natural actor and comedian who so impressed the department of speech that a production of Eugene O'Neill's *The Emperor Jones* had been scheduled to showcase his talents. However, Johnson did not return that fall. Somebody got the bright idea I could enact the role, so I read the part and was tentatively drafted. Fortunately for the future of dramatics at Kansas State, Bill Johnson returned the second semester before rehearsals began, and I accepted a minor part, that of Lem the Native Chief.

However, I did let Bill talk me into acting in a play he was to direct and produce as an assignment for a course in drama. He chose *The Man Who Died at 12 O'Clock* by Paul Green, and I agreed to take the main role. Other students were used as stagehands. Climax of the comedy comes when the clock strikes twelve and the devil appears. Everything before that builds to this high point. To be sure all was in order, the student stage manager tested the clock before the curtain rose.

The play moved along to its dramatic peak. At last the moment came when I fell to my knees to pray. The clock was to strike twelve as I finished. I ended my prayer but nothing happened. So I continued kneeling in the center of a long, loud silence. Wondering what the hell was wrong, I turned my head slowly to cock an eye at the clock. It said five minutes to twelve. After testing, the stage manager had forgotten to reset the hands properly.

I froze. What in the world could I do on my knees for five minutes? The audience tittered, knowing something had gone haywire. I tried to ad-lib a prayer in keeping with Paul Green's script. By now I was visibly perspiring, and my knees ached. At that moment I would have welcomed anything to get me off the spot, even a visit from the Aiello gang back in Chicagoland. Unable to think of another ad lib, I again glanced at the clock. Only two minutes had passed. Completely disgusted, I rose slowly to rest my knees and walked around, cussing to myself, then announced to the spectators, "Well, I guess I'll have to pray some more. The first one didn't seem to take." As the audience roared, I got back on my knees. Mechanically I repeated the prayer, mentally kicking myself for letting Bill Johnson talk me into this and trying to think of an excruciating torture for that bastard of a stage manager who didn't have sense enough to reset the clock. When I finished Green's short prayer for the second time and the clock still hadn't struck, I thought to hell with it all and motioned for the devil to walk on stage. The audience, by now half hysterical, applauded the appearance of my self-service Satan—and even I realized it was ridiculous for me to show surprise and fright as the script demanded. Then just as I began speaking my lines there sounded a steady bong-bong an even dozen times. When the noise ended, I turned to the spectators and with a straight face announced "That's what I was waiting for." I don't think anybody heard the remainder of the play. Still, the show had been a howling success—although not in the way the author intended.

The year before, a practical streak had shown itself in freshman hazing. During Hell Week a freshman was sent one evening to the largest restaurant in town to preach a sermon and take a collection, returning with enough to buy badly needed coal. When we lost our frat house and moved to smaller quarters, there was no central heating plant. Instead there were two small stoves in the biggest rooms. We hit upon the plan of requiring each resident in turn to supply a sack of coal. Since we lacked funds, the only solution was to borrow from others—better known as stealing. During the day we kept our eyes open for backyard coal piles and at night made quiet raids. When neighbors noticed their fuel dwindling at an unusual rate, they began staying up late with loaded shotguns. Realizing we had been favoring those who lived nearby, we immediately established a no-discrimination rule and visited other parts of town. Luck was with us; nobody was caught all year. Only one student refused to cooperate. On those nights when he would not bring in his quota, he was barred from all heated areas, even when the mercury dropped to zero or below.

By the end of the school year in 1930, I was fully aware of the Depression which had been growing since the previous fall. Dad had lost all of what little cash he had when his bank crashed. Even though I had not depended on him financially, I wondered if I could make it back next fall for my final courses. I'd had an excellent year scholastically. My two and a half years of practical newspaper experience not only handed me an edge in class but gave me a special standing among students, none of whom had been to Chicago. I had seen the special book of gangland photographs, too gory for the public but privately printed by the Chicago *Tribune* for distribution to select persons, that graphically portrayed the bloody violence of gang warfare. Using these and experiences of other reporters as a basis, I often held a group of students spellbound while I talked, as if from personal experience, about the mob bosses and their hired gunmen.

I needed a half year for my degree. But my graduation requirements included courses which were offered only in the spring. I left Kansas State at the end of the school year, intending to find a job and work through summer and fall, then return in 1931 for the second semester to finish up and graduate. I did not know in June of 1930 that I would become an educational casualty of the Depression.

35

That summer I tried railroading again at the suggestion of a frat brother named Harry White who was so light complexioned he was nicknamed "Half." He had worked for Union Pacific and got me a job as a dining car waiter on the run between Kansas City and Cheyenne, Wyoming. Meanwhile I roomed at his parents' home on the Kansas side.

I was assigned to a friendly and helpful crew. It included a couple of college men, one a dentist with offices in K. C. A practical psychologist, he had built up a large practice through the simple scam of being available only on the two days between runs. His office girl was on duty daily; when a patient called she expressed regret that the doctor's schedule was so full she could not arrange an immediate appointment.

Impressed, the patient would admiringly tell his friends, "You know my dentist? He must be mighty good. He stays so busy you have to call a week ahead of time to get an appointment."

Human nature being what it is, those wanting work done on their teeth would ignore dentists who could give them immediate attention. They preferred waiting for the expert who obviously was unusually proficient because of his full schedule. So this astute practitioner was doing quite well, Depression notwithstanding. He earned enough as a waiter to take care of regular living expenses; his office activity on the two days between runs alone brought an income at least equal to the take of most of those working full-time at the dental profession. His pattern was virtually foolproof since there was little chance of his patients finding out he was also holding down a service job. Few souls ate in a diner on those rare occasions when they might travel west on his train.

A similar pattern existed in Chicago, but from necessity instead of choice. During the Depression and its drastically reduced incomes, a number of South Side doctors and lawyers kept regular daytime office hours but at night donned overalls to work on city garbage trucks in white residential areas far from possible contact with their patients. Black college graduates in general were grateful for the lowest menial jobs in order to eat. Virtually any large railroad station had enough well-educated Afro-Americans with degrees working as porters and redcaps to staff a first-rate college.

But back to Kansas City.

Judging from the pay and tips on my first few runs, I seemed assured of earning enough to return to Kansas State. The head of the commissary department in Kansas City seemed to like me. However, I was listed as an extra waiter. When one of the regular members of another crew became ill, I was assigned to take his place.

It was my bad luck that this crew comprised a bunch of old Uncle Toms who disliked college men, the kind described as having worked on the diner so long they thought they owned the railroad. I was at least twenty years younger than any of the others, and these fibrous fossils showed their resentment as soon as I stepped aboard to help stock the diner in the U. P. yard. I was painfully conscious of growing tension.

Finally the emotional pot came to a boil east of Denver after I took the orders of two Australian passengers for steaks, medium rare.

I shouted the order to the chef and went back to serve my other customers. A few minutes later I returned and asked him for my steaks.

"Keep your drawers on, they're comin' up," he bellowed.

Five minutes went by. The Aussies called me, and I again went to the kitchen to ask for my order.

"Goddamn it, wait your turn!" the chef yelled. "You ain't got the only order in here."

After another long wait, the Australians protested to the steward, a southern white man from Arkansas, who went directly to the chef and asked about the order.

"He ain't asked for no steaks," the chef lied.

Calling me to come with him to the little aisle running beside the kitchen and leading to the dining area, the steward asked angrily, "Why did you tell a damned lie about ordering them steaks when you know good an' well you didn't?"

"But I'm not lying," I told him. "I went back twice after placing my original order and each time the chef told me to wait."

The steward shook his head. "You know goddamned well you didn't put in no such order. You're just trying to act like you think you're smarter'n the rest of these boys 'cause you're a college nigger."

As I said earlier, I don't like to fight. I don't even remember socking the steward, but there he was, crumpled on the floor of the swaying vestibule, and my right hand tingled. As a matter of fact, not since then have I hit another man with my fist.

The steward climbed slowly to his feet, rubbing his jaw. I stood motionless, waiting. He looked at me but said nothing, turned and walked back into the dining area. I followed. He called another waiter to take the steaks to the Aussies, then went to his small office and closed the door. I resumed my own duties. Later I learned he wired ahead to division headquarters in Denver asking them to fire me immediately, but no action was taken until I returned to K.C. I gave the head of the commissary a full report. He asked me to come back to work with my first crew as if nothing had happened. But when I went down to board the diner a few days later, he sadly showed me a telegram from Denver ordering my immediate discharge. And that was the end of my days as a dining car waiter.

36

I hung around Kansas City long enough to collect my paycheck from the Union Pacific, then visited in Marion, Kansas with Gladys, who laid down the ultimatum that the next time I tried to leave her home she was going with me as my wife. I returned to Chicago and out to the Gary *American.*

During my year away, the newspaper had managed to obtain a small plant at an auction and was struggling to beat the Depression. I was promised eighteen dollars a week, and some weeks all I got was eighteen promises. I helped make up pages on the imposing stone and lugged some of the heavy forms down to the basement where I locked them on the flat bed press. Later I carried them back upstairs to be broken down. Working at the plant and living in a corner of the basement he'd fixed up for this purpose was an itinerant white printer who maintained a huge, bottomless pot of salt pork and navy beans, which he ate three times daily. When the level dropped, he added fresh beans, plus a teaspoon of baking soda for a preservative. It was comforting to know I could be assured of at least a belly full of beans.

In 1930 any kind of food was important, for the economic picture grew worse daily. Checks were looked on with suspicion. Instead of being returned marked "No Funds," they just as frequently came back stamped "No Bank." Only one bank remained open in Gary, and that one solely because it was owned by the steel mills. That summer a state legislator went to a special short session at the capitol a wealthy man, but was wiped out so suddenly in the crashing market he had to bum a ride home. In Chicago both black banks, in addition to scores outside the Loop district, went broke. All over the Windy City it was a common sight to see the ragged and hungry that winter fighting with numb fingers over garbage thrown away by restaurants and markets; the dailies carried many stories of men and women and children frozen to death sleeping in the doorways and vestibules of apartment houses in sub-zero weather. And in a master stroke of good public relations, Al Capone set up soup kitchens for the hungry.

When I first came to Chicago in 1927, the Knights of Pythias had begun erecting a tall temple and office building at 37th and State. During the Depression it was virtually abandoned, becoming instead apartments for the aloof Moors, a nationalist sect similar to the Black Muslims, which later attracted many followers in the ghettoes of Chicago and Detroit.

In this trying period, farmers in Kansas and Nebraska and Iowa burned wheat and corn by the bushel as fuel because they could not sell their harvests. Many wore rags because they had no money for clothing. Meanwhile down South the starving farm population warmed their houses by burning cotton—and went hungry. They could not sell their major crop to buy corn and wheat from the Midwest. And in the big urban centers, the ordinary working people went without both clothing and food.

This situation was utterly ridiculous, yet it was no laughing matter. Why was our economy so cockeyed that both food and cotton were destroyed while millions of citizens desperately needed both? It seemed to me that even a fool should be able to work out a simple trade in which the food went south and the cotton came north. How could we label ourselves the greatest nation on earth when our destiny was in the hands of hopeless idiots?

I felt then as I do now that every human being has a right to adequate food, shelter, education, medical care, and dignity. I do not believe that any society which, having the means to do so, fails to provide these essentials is so sacred it cannot be changed. We have a collective obligation to revise any system which does not insure a decent standard of living for all. There is no such thing as a holy mandate from heaven to perpetuate poverty.

But no matter what my dissatisfaction with the power structure, we had to live with it somehow. We at the Gary *American* had to maneuver to get along. Even when an advertiser bought space in our columns, we never knew if he'd stay in business long enough to pay us. So we returned to the old days of barter and trade. We ran ads for restaurants in exchange for meal tickets; space sold to a clothing store brought me a much needed new suit and accessories.

I had resumed my relationship with Eleanor, although by now it was not so constant or demanding; she had given up the idea I was ever going to marry her. I prowled the Savoy as often as finances permitted and heard Noble Sissle and his orchestra which had recently returned from a long stay in Paris. Featured with him was a clarinetist and saxophonist who, rumor had it, was "found" by Sissle in Paris and was appearing in America for the first time. Later I learned this musician was Sidney Bechet, one of the New Orleans giants of jazz who had merely been making his home in Europe for the past several years. Sissle stepped aside, and Bechet came down front to lead the band on two wildly winging numbers, "St. Louis

Blues" and "Tiger Rag." There was some question about Bechet's real age when he died in 1959; but when I first saw him in 1930 his hair was gray and members of the Sissle band called him "the old man."

By now Cab Calloway had launched his meteoric career as a band leader. He fronted a group called the Missourians and was about to break into the big time. That followed when he went to Harlem and the Cotton Club and introduced the world to "Minnie the Moocher." During my first Gary period, I had heard the fantastic new jungle band of Duke Ellington broadcasting on a nationwide hookup from the Cotton Club in Harlem. After my first awe-inspiring introduction, I tried to be near a radio for all his air shots; I was unable to decide who was better, Ellington or Fletcher Henderson. Several times late at night I also tuned in a Detroit station broadcasting music by a white band, that of Jean Goldkette. What brought me to attention and caused me to fish for this station was the only cornet I had heard that I considered near Satchmo's class. Later I found out this unbelievable musician was named Bix Beiderbecke.[1]

1931–1934

37

In January of 1931 a stocky, medium brown young man about four years my senior walked into the *American* office accompanied by an obviously younger brother.

"You're Davis," he informed me. "I wanta talk to you. Let's go have breakfast."

He was brusque almost to the point of being uncouth. But I was curious. I accompanied him to the best black eatery in town. On the way I learned his named was W. A. Scott.

"I came out here to see you," he said, "because I was told you're the kind of man I want. I'm looking for an editor for my paper in Atlanta, Georgia."

I blinked. Me go South? Why, I'd crossed the border into Oklahoma less than a dozen times when I lived in Arkansas City. The North was bad enough. The South was impossible. But on the other hand, maybe I could draw a regular paycheck.

"What's your proposition?" I asked.

"Twenty-five per week to start. If you're what I want, I'll raise you to thirty-five. Remember, it costs much less to live in Atlanta than around Chicago."

In 1931 in Chicago, a regular twenty-five bucks sounded big as the Wrigley Building and thirty-five was fantastic. During the Depression, many family heads would have been ecstatic to draw a regular wage of fifteen per week.

"Who told you about me?" I asked.

"I came to Chicago just to look for an editor. Claude Barnett at the Associated Negro Press said you were just the man. So I came over here to see you."

"You spoke about papers in Atlanta. What do you mean?"

"I've got a semi-weekly, the Atlanta *World*. I've also got one in Birmingham, another in Memphis, one in Chattanooga, and a couple more. They're all printed at my plant in Atlanta. That's my headquarters. We're getting ready to bring the Atlanta *World* out three times a week."

I was astounded. Frankly, I'd never heard of his operations. But if he could live up to his promises, it might be worth risking a trip to the bowels of Dixie. I told him I'd think it over and let him know in two weeks.

Next day I went to see Barnett. The Atlanta *World* was evidently in sound financial condition and rapidly growing, I was told, but sadly needed an editor.

I thought of all the wild yarns I'd heard about Dixie. That was where we were not allowed to enter a store and ask for John Ruskin cigars; we had to request *Mr.* John Ruskin. We weren't permitted to drink milk unless we first colored it with ink; it was also against the law to lay your black bodies down on white sheets. A Negro farmer with a team of one black and one white horse plowing his field could shout to the darker, "Giddap, you black son of a bitch," but woe unto him if he did not remove his hat and respectfully address the other, "Won't you please giddap, Mr. White Horse?" In Florida you dare not say "Miami" to a white person; it had to be "Yourami."

I asked others about living in Dixie.

"You'll get along all right if you remember where you are," said Lucius Harper of the *Defender*, who was born in Rome, Georgia. "In fact, it's easier than living in Chicago. Down South you know ahead of time what you can do and where you can go. Up here in Chicago you're never certain. Maybe they'll treat you right one place, then throw you out if you dare show your face next door."

"Jus' don't start nothin' you can't finish," said another. "Remember, if you get in trouble in Atlanta you can run north for a hell of a long time and you'll still be down South in Tennessee or Kentucky. But at the same time, there's ten million blacks still livin' down there and they've learned how to get along."

For a long week I lived the undecided blues. But I could see only darkness in the economic outlook around Chicago, and finally I wrote to Scott that I was coming and asked him to send me a ticket. I went around giving long-faced goodbyes as if I were leaving for another planet.

And so, Depression-driven, I arrived in Atlanta feeling as if I had voluntarily gone to prison for the sake of regular food and shelter. Yet in reality your attitude depended on your frame of reference. To me I was going to a place rigidly hemmed in by bars and restrictions; to my people in the little hate-filled backwoods hamlets of the state, Atlanta represented freedom, a city of refuge.

I left the jim crow railroad coach, walked through the jim crow waiting room, and took a jim crow taxi for the jim crow Butler St. YMCA, two blocks from the *World* office. I walked over to the newspaper plant on Auburn Avenue, the jim crow main street of jim crow Atlanta. Still, to all outward appearances, this was not too greatly different from Chicago. In Chicago segregation was enforced by custom; in Atlanta it was legalized.

Yet this difference was vitally important. In Chicago we could dream of some day escaping by climbing over or burrowing under the high walls of the ghetto. In Atlanta it was impossible. The walls were not only guarded by shotguns and fire and rope, but the slick smooth sides were studded with spikes and sharp knives. Even a black Houdini would have been kept captive.

Any possibility of substantial change seemed hopeless. Atlanta prided itself on its numerous colleges, yet there was virtually no communication between white and black institutions on either a student or faculty level. Transportation, housing, entertainment, and religion were rigidly separated. Black contact with the police was that of target with marksman. We did not vote. Even facilities in downtown stores were segregated.

Had somebody predicted in Atlanta in 1931 that by 1970 homes all over the country would watch news, shows, sporting events, and movies in color through a little box called television, and that we could sit in our living rooms and watch men die in a war ten thousand miles away and see others walk on the moon, he would have received no more than tolerant smiles.

But had the same prophet predicted that in thirty-five years there would be desegregated schooling, service in Mr. Charlie's best restaurants, blacks staying as guests at the leading hotels, Afro-Americans in the state legislature, and even a black mayor of Atlanta, he would have been hustled off to the nuthouse at Milledgeville as hopelessly insane. We have come a long way since 1931—but we still have a long way to go.

The *World* shared a building with the city's black bank. A long and narrow hall, with little cubbyhole offices built on one side, led up a couple of steps to the large printing quarters, running the width of the building, in the rear. But above all, it had the feeling of being alive, of people getting things done. There was the staccato sound of busy people, hopeful people, and the steel song of the tireless linotypes, and the raucous, rhythmic roar of the press, pouring thoughts into the paper.

W. A. Scott (usually called just W. A.) led me around and introduced me to his family and staff, commenting to key personnel, "He's one of these high-powered newspapermen from Chicago. We're gonna see what he can do down here." The office was stuffed with Scotts. Three brothers, two sisters, mother, and number one wife worked here. I say "number one" advisedly, for she occupied a unique role as mother of his two sons. Already he had divorced wife number two and was in his third marriage. A fourth brother was up north in Illinois attending a university, and a fifth, oldest of the lot, was a college professor in Virginia. However, family ties played little part in W. A.'s attitudes; he was as tough with his kin as with any other employee. More than once in the months that followed, his mother, a very sweet lady who had not let rearing a rambunctious brood sour her spirit, asked me to see if I could persuade W. A. "not to be so hard on his family."

But there were people other than the Scotts in key positions. With a gift for organizing, he had a well-functioning and sizeable mechanical staff, advertising department, and circulation department. However, the editorial department stank.

If ever a prize is given to the worst newspaper in America, I have a strong contender in the Atlanta *World* as it was when I took over. I inherited two reporters who could not write. One was Gene White, a dapper fashion plate attending Morris Brown College. The other, Milton Randolph, I had known slightly at the old Inter-Collegiate Club in Chicago. Except for police reports and accounts of the latest shootings and cuttings treated at Grady Hospital, the city institution, there was little general news. The paper was "edited" by the plant foreman who grabbed Associated Negro Press releases as they came in twice weekly, checked what caught his eye, then turned these articles over to the linotypists who transferred everything, including the heads, into type. In the last issue prior to my arrival, the *World* had finally gotten around to printing a noncrime story from Atlanta which had gone all the way to Chicago and returned via ANP before local people could read it, several weeks after it had happened.

It was immediately evident that the *World* was not growing because of either appearance or general news coverage. What, then, was the reason for its success?

Simply, the normal desire of people for dignity. Black Atlantans were able to read accounts of their social activities, and at a frequency greater than once a week. Blacks didn't get their names in the white press unless they committed crimes. But the *World* devoted column after column to club news, social notes, and religious activities. And, of equal importance, they were Mr. and Mrs. They were hungry enough to read any publication which supplied emotional sustenance, no matter how poorly edited.

The sports section was easily the most readable part of the *World*. Two Clark College students, both athletes, produced these pages. One was Lucious Jones, a comparably normal youth, and the other was Ric Roberts, wild and unpredictable but who was also an excellent cartoonist and commercial artist. Contributing an occasional article was J. C. Chunn who occupied a menial position at the Atlanta *Constitution,* the morning daily.

Two mail carriers were regular contributors. One, named Reynolds, authored a popular, small, front-page feature known as "Deacon Jones," consisting of earthy black philosophy. The other contributed occasional verse. He was Thomas Jefferson Flanagan and was so entranced by his Irish name that he sometimes wore a flowing green Windsor tie and shoes with four leaf clovers decorating the toes. He split his loyalty between Emancipation and Saint Patrick's days.

The *World* was started in 1928 on less than five hundred dollars. W. A., a graduate of Morehouse where he had been a star back on the football team, first produced a Negro business directory and then decided to enter the newspaper field. Until then, Atlanta had been served after a fashion by the Atlanta *Independent,* owned and edited by Benjamin Davis, Sr., fraternal leader and Republican National Committeeman from Georgia. He was also the father of Ben Davis, Jr., a lawyer who became a Communist leader and New York City councilman.

The *Independent* was little more than a personal sheet. The *World* caught on after W. A., correctly analyzing the situation, switched from a weekly to a twice-weekly publication. Since then it had grown so greatly, with W. A. keeping a sharp eye on advertising and circulation, that he realized the time had come to get an editor. It is the inalienable right of every newspaper to have an editor.

On my first day there, he told me, "Doc, I want a paper I can put up beside the Pittsburgh *Courier* and not be ashamed. Think you can deliver?"[1]

"Of course," I said, "but I do need a little time to get some order out of this editorial chaos. It's a hell of a mess. You've got the basics, but it looks as if nobody here knows anything about getting out a real sheet."

"That's what I got you for, Doc. She's all yours."

Any change would have been an improvement. But I was expected not only to upgrade the product but place it on a par with one of the best-looking weeklies of the era. I had exactly three days to whip up a style sheet, obtain samples of all available type for a headline schedule, indoctrinate the foreman in the process of making up a newspaper, and try to teach my reporters how to write. They were cooperative, and they tried hard. But the experience was especially trying for me. They never learned. In desperation, I personally rewrote all their general news and partially revised some sports articles, then stood over the composing room workers to see that my layouts were followed. A couple of hours before my first issue was to appear, W. A. began impatiently pacing back and forth awaiting results.

At last the first copy rolled off the press. He snatched it, looked at the front page, then raced through the remainder of the eight pages. He grinned, turned, thumped me on the back and said gleefully, "That's it, Doc! That's what I want!" Grabbing up a dozen or more copies, he tucked them under one arm and set off down Auburn Avenue personally distributing them among his friends.

For the first couple of months I spent from fourteen to sixteen hours daily at the plant, cutting down on Sunday to six or eight, in an attempt to get the kind of newspaper I wanted. Gratifying results showed in everything but the work of my reporters; I still had to rewrite most of their stories. Usually I ate at a nearby restaurant operated by a Spanish Jew reared in Georgia; the mixture of accents was worth traveling miles to hear. This meant I had little contact with whites during my period of adjustment to the South; for this I was thankful. However, I did run into a totally unexpected problem; many Atlantans professed an inability to understand my mixture of Kansas and Chicago accents.

Like the rest of the nation, this city complained about the hard times resulting from the Depression. However, the Georgia metropolis was a boomtown compared with Chicago. The economic picture did not become seriously muddied until many months after I arrived in Atlanta, although I assure you there was no connection.

Daily, W. A. grew more fascinating. He was a strong, positive man with imagination and a natural knack for business. He would willingly try anything once if he thought it had a fair chance of success, although he explained he never went into anything unless he had prepared an escape route in advance. A lightning quick thinker, he could jump into the air and have a new program planned by the time he landed. If somebody confronted him with a proposition, he was ready immediately with a different one giving himself the advantage.

He also had his faults. Loud, ruthless, domineering, cold-blooded, and a confirmed egotist, he created many enemies. I think we got along fantastically well together because he realized he knew nothing about the editorial side of newspaper work and respected my ability. He was usually at odds with some member of his family. He thought nothing of firing one of his brothers and ordering him out of the office, although later after a family conference W. A. might put him back on the payroll. His chief adversary was his older brother, Aurelius, the college professor; they had been bitter rivals since childhood. The competition between them often flared into open hostility when Aurelius visited Atlanta, and sometimes it dropped me uncomfortably into the middle of a family squabble, as when W. A. implored me to help him physically eject Aurelius from the office. I would not have intervened, considering this beyond my duties as editor, had not two of the younger Scotts muttered threats as to what they would do if I aided W. A. Since I took this as a personal challenge, I helped him. Later the family fight was patched up, as usual.

He drove a car with the same daredevil spirit that characterized his business activities. I was scared when I first rode with him but I learned he was safe driver despite the appearance of recklessness. He maneuvered an auto the same way he once ran on a broken field with a football. His judgment was phenomenal; invariably he accurately gauged whether he had space to squeeze between a truck and a streetcar. Unfortunately, other employees who tried to ape the boss in company cars suffered smash-ups.

Less than a month after I reached Atlanta, the *World* changed to a triweekly. The Birmingham and Memphis *Worlds* remained semiweeklies, and the Chattanooga paper was suspended. These three, owned outright by W. A., were the key members of the Scott Newspaper Syndicate (SNS). An enterprising person in any city could found a newspaper, name it, and become a member of SNS by contracting to purchase so many copies weekly. Each newspaper was allowed a certain number of columns of local news depending upon its circulation as well as, naturally, its own local advertisements; the rest of the material was common to all the publications. At one time, membership totalled more than fifty newspapers from New Orleans to Florida and extended through the Carolinas, Tennessee, Alabama, and Georgia. The only sizeable Georgia city without an SNS publication was Macon. There, the owners of the daily Macon *Telegraph* had shown more business acumen than the usual white Southerner by putting out a special black edition with a page edited by Minnie

Singleton and containing only Afro-American news in which dignity was observed.

Meanwhile, in Chicago a rotogravure section was launched for syndication throughout America. Scott subscribed. When the venture folded shortly afterward, W. A. immediately started his own for SNS use, allowing each publication a quota of local pictures commensurate with its circulation. This feature, popularly termed "the brown sheet," became a major circulation builder as people struggled to get their pictures in this section.

The expanding Atlanta *World* program demanded additional trained personnel. More refugees from the depression-plagued North gladly came South. One was E. N. Davis, a small, prematurely bald journalism graduate from the University of Illinois whom I had met in Chicago. He was assigned to edit the Birmingham *World*. Another journalism graduate named L. Herbert Hennigan was sent to the Memphis *World;* later he became a publication specialist with the U. S. Department of Agriculture in Washington. A Chicago woman, Beulah Mitchell Hill, well known as a music critic, was imported as head proofreader and editor of the rotogravure section. A later addition was Cliff MacKay, who still later became an editor of the Baltimore *Afro-American*.[2] He hooked up with us after leaving the Chicago *Defender,* where he had served as theatrical reporter. MacKay had been a victim of a *Defender* shake-up. Lucia Pitts, the poet and my old Chicago friend, came in as secretary to W. A., and Carl Beckwith, whom I had known when he was employed at the *Whip*'s job plant, was added as mechanical superintendent. Lucile Bluford, later managing editor of the Kansas City *Call* and a leader in the fight to break the color barriers at the University of Missouri School of Journalism, also joined our staff.[3]

For the first couple of months, what free time I had was spent in my room at the Butler Y listening to the radio. Regularly, late at night, I picked up a Chicago station broadcasting Louis Armstrong and his band from a spot called the Show Boat. I never tired of his brilliant version of "The Peanut Vendor." Sometimes I also grabbed an earful of Fletcher Henderson at the Roseland or Duke Ellington at the Cotton Club.

38

Because of my inexperience in Dixie, W. A. cautioned me to "take it easy" editorially. Accordingly, I was quite innocuous until I became acclimated, reserving any pointed comment for my column, "Touring the World." In each edition I also wrote a rhymed summary of the news for a small front-page box called "Jazzin' the News." However, after the first month or so, W. A. paid little attention to the editorial page. His primary interest lay in closely watching the income from ads and circulation; he had developed an excellent home-delivery system, and carriers were watched by hawk-eyed supervisors. But after my breaking-in period, I refused to remain silent. Some particularly nasty bit of racism invariably forced me to write an angry editorial, to the consternation of some of W. A.'s close associates who would fearfully point it out to him.

W. A. would read it and hurry back to the office.

Calling me aside and pointing to the editorial, he'd come on with, "Doc, you gotta be more careful. You can get us all in a mess of trouble with some of these crazy white folks. You're not up North now, so take it easy."

"Okay," I'd agree, and for the next few issues, which I knew he would carefully read, I'd be as blithe and happy-happy as Pollyanna. Then gradually I'd start swinging again at the racists until another particularly vitriolic editorial was called to his attention. We went through this routine at least a dozen times.

Several weeks after I reached Atlanta, a story broke which so inflamed me I threw all caution to the wind. I learned the great and sovereign state of Georgia was preparing to "punish" a fourteen year old black kid.

What was Georgia going to do? Kill him in the electric chair, all nice and proper and legal. What had he done? He had entered a home in a rural community where a white man and his wife lay sleeping. Although he had been caught before he had a chance to steal anything and had not molested either one of the couple, nevertheless he had been tried and sentenced to death by electrocution.

The South went in heavily for capital punishment. A long list of acts called for the supreme penalty. This kind of legalized killing has long been used against the blacks as an object lesson to "keep them in their place." Helpless Afro-Americans for generations have been railroaded to the gallows and electric chair on evidence that would have freed white prisoners. The use of capital punishment as a racist weapon against my people is enough, all by itself, to make me completely opposed to this form of socially sanctioned murder. Throughout Dixie, and in parts of the North, lie the barren bones of humans who were put to death mainly because they were black and helpless; how can I support capital punishment when one of its major uses has been as a ready servant of racism?

I learned of this outrageous story only the day before the scheduled execution. I knew that a white boy of fourteen, under similar circumstances, at the most might have been sent to a reform school, although more than likely he merely would have been placed on probation; and this realization embittered me. It was too late for any kind of preventive action. I could move only in a kind of stupefied horror until I received the news that the switch had been thrown, that this child had become another premeditated sacrifice on the altar of white supremacy. I became sick to my stomach. And I vomited all my anger in a front-page double-column editorial in the next issue of the *World*. For the convenience of any Caucasian who wanted to take issue, and to keep W. A. from trembling with fright, I signed my name.

Gene White, whose beat was the police station, got scared as soon as he read it. He was so apprehensive of what police reaction might be (cops read the *World* as soon as it appeared, to keep an eye on blacks) that he waited until late at night to go to the station, after the officers who knew him were off duty. He planned to slip in, hurriedly scan the arrest sheet, then quietly sneak out.

But just as he was turning to leave, he told me later, a voice roared;

"Hi, Gene. How's the *World* reporter?"

He said he found himself suddenly trembling and perspiring as he thought, "Well, this is it. They got me now."

He turned slowly around. A white newsman from one of the dailies was striding closer.

"Who's this guy Frank Marshall Davis anyway?" he asked Gene.

"He's a new guy from up North. He hasn't been here long enough to understand everything down here yet," Gene apologized. "So please don't blame him—"

"Blame him? Hell, I want to shake his hand. I feel the same way he does. That guy's got guts. Tell him I agree with him wholeheartedly."

It was a greatly relieved Gene who came back to the office to tell me his story.

I learned, as time passed, that many Southern whites had respect for blacks with the courage to fight back. Not enough to even begin to swing the verdict in our favor, but a significant percentage. I believed that those of us in a position to be heard and act should do all within our power to smash the rigid color barriers. And I am convinced that the Atlanta *World*, the *Black Dispatch* in Oklahoma City, and the *Informer* in Houston, by intelligently blasting away at racism, at least split much of the kindling which was ignited a quarter of a century later by the Reverend Martin Luther King, Jr., and turned into a roaring fire that burned down legal segregation in Dixie.[4]

I found out also that a soul who has a reputation for not taking any crap from anybody would be left alone unless whites formed a mob. Word speedily got around, "Better leave that 'un alone. He's a crazy nigger." One outlying section of Atlanta had been the scene of a bloody race riot before I arrived. Duskyamerican denizens of this area acquitted themselves so well that cops shunned it unless in squads because so many "bad niggers" lived there.

The street transportation company had learned to keep its rabid racist employees off trolley cars serving colored compounds. There had been instances in which operators of these streetcars had been seriously hurt or killed at the ends of their runs. Black victims of especially vicious hate tactics said nothing in return to the operators. They waited silently until the vehicle reached the end of the line, everybody got off, and the motor-man-conductor stepped down into the night to switch the overhead trolley for the return trip. Then all hell broke loose in those few seconds of complete darkness. "Unidentified assailants" would beat, cut, or shoot the Negrophobist and leave him bleeding and senseless on the ground as they noiselessly disappeared. Police investigation was fruitless; nobody ever knew anything about the incident.

I personally avoided as much as possible the jungle of white Atlanta with its beasts of prejudice, preferring the comparative safety of the black ghetto. Of course there were times when of necessity I had to venture forth, and then I observed "The Rules." I entered streetcars through the front door, sat in back, and exited through the rear; if I went to a white theatre, I waited in a jim crow line at the side of the building, entered through a separate door, and mountain-climbed to "nigger heaven." If I had to buy clothing in a white downtown store, I grew accustomed to the janitor putting aside his broom or mop to wait on me. Otherwise I had little occasion to be around Caucasians since few came to the *World* office.

Only once, despite W. A.'s fears, did I draw white threats, and that was after the infamous Scottsboro case shocked the rest of the planet.[5] In 1931 seven black boys were forcibly removed from a freight train in Alabama and in a farcical trial were quickly sentenced to die for "raping" two white girl hoboes aboard the same train. This would have been a stirring victory for our mass production technique had not protests poured in from all parts of the globe. Later one of the "rape victims," Ruby Bates, toured the nation under Communist auspices and told the world she and her companion, Victoria Price, had lied to save themselves from vagrancy charges. Medical examination proved that at least one of the boys was physically incapable of sexual relations, and the idea of the others criminally assaulting two white girls on a freight train in Alabama loaded with prejudiced white male vagrants was too preposterous to be believed by anybody but a confirmed irrational racist. The case journeyed several times all the way up to the U.S. Supreme Court, and out of it was established, for the first time since Reconstruction, the principle that Afro-Americans must be permitted to serve on juries.

When the story broke, the seven frightened kids were painted as "monsters" by the Dixie dailies. Now, a black newsman learned in kindergarten that the white press, especially that of the South, was often strongly biased in reports involving the two major ethnic groups; in fact, presentation of the black version of news events was one of the prime reasons for the existence of our press. The *World,* therefore, dug up the facts to counteract the white lynch hysteria.

One day I received a letter, written in pencil and postmarked Birmingham, which read:

> Lay off that junk in your little nigger paper if you know what's good for you. Them niggers is guilty and you know it. If you keep on printing that junk you'll die just like they're going to.
>
> Ku Klux Klan

The sheet was decorated with crude drawings of flaming crosses.

I kept this letter as a souvenir for several years before eventually losing it. I showed it to a number of persons in the *World* office but not to W. A.; I didn't want to scare him. I continued with the coverage of the case exactly as before and never again received any kind of warning.

In fact, my only threats came from other souls, and these came particularly after the *World* ran an editorial against carrying concealed weapons, especially switchblade knives. Each Saturday night and Sunday, along with every other kind of assaults—virtually all of blacks by other blacks—occurred murders, averaging at least two per week.

After a particularly active weekend, in which more than a hundred assault cases were treated at Grady, I wrote and signed a front-page editorial pointing out that the lynchers and hair-trigger cops were pikers compared with what we did to ourselves. We were far more proficient at injuring and decimating our numbers than were Caucasians. Our casualty list came primarily from fighting each other. I opined we should not devote our energies exclusively to the passage of federal antilynching legislation (at that time a major goal of Afro-Americans) and the prosecution of so-called law officers who took target practice on us; we ought to, with comparable vigor, develop a greater respect for human life in general and insist upon the apprehension and punishment of those who maimed and murdered their own ethnic brothers. Since the most popular weapon used in our intrafraternal warfare was a switchblade knife, I suggested as a first step the passage and enforcement of a city ordinance outlawing the possession of this lethal device.

It was this suggestion that triggered the eruption.

Next morning, shortly after the *World* hit the streets, I began receiving telephone calls from irate readers who heatedly supported toting these deadly pocket weapons. Within a couple of days I was deluged with letters containing the same viewpoint. Some writers were so incensed they promised to come down to the *World* office and personally carve me into souvenir strips if ever the police tried to prevent their carrying those trusty switchblades. And do you know, I did not receive one letter or telephone call backing my position?

As these readers explained it, they needed to carry the knives for protection from "po' white trash" (although rarely did I hear of a soul cutting a honky despite endless provocation) because they couldn't afford pistols, and because they needed to protect their laundry hung for drying on backyard clotheslines when they had to go into the house—although frankly I have yet to hear of a clothesnapper being caught wethanded and made to see the error of his ways with a few well-chosen slashes.

Being a stubborn cuss, I refused to "take low." Instead, I pointed to the unwritten code which seemed to guide white officials: if a nigger kills a white man, that's murder and automatically means the death penalty; if whitey kills a nigger that's justifiable homicide; and if one nigger kills another, that's good riddance. I reiterated we had absolutely no justification for arming ourselves with switchblades and again demanded the banning of this weapon by law. Of course the city administration ignored my request and after the first flurry, there were no more threats from readers.

What depressed me most about Dixie in the early 1930s was the wantonness with which we maimed each other as well as the mass acceptance of racism. I did not expect blacks to form mobs and lynch Caucasians in retaliation. Apart from all other considerations, there was the big fundamental fact that law enforcement agents and National Guardsmen were white and under the direction of strict segregationists; nothing would have pleased many of these sadists as much as official orders to shoot us.

Nevertheless, we did have the right to start legal action against murderers in official uniforms. Whether we obtained convictions was not the key issue. What we would have demonstrated was a willingness to fight back, and even if it were no more than an inconvenience to the accused, it would serve as a deterrent—with the strength of the deterrent determined by the numbers of those who pooled their resources to take action. There was no way to convince me that several thousand outraged blacks would not have had a sobering effect on future policies of the establishment. Later, in the 1950s and 1960s, it worked in Dixie.

But instead we then did nothing.

The *World* carried many stories of murders by law officers. Readers merely shook their heads in disgust, perhaps weeping bitterly when alone. But the overt reaction, unless a relative was a victim, was simply, "That's a crying shame, but it's not my little red wagon."

One killing was so brutal even W. A. became fighting mad. A constable went to a farm near Atlanta to arrest a black boy accused of stealing a white man's wagon. Dressed in ordinary clothes and showing no credentials, he tried to walk in and search the farmhouse. The youth's mother and sister barred the way. Drawing his gun, the constable shot and killed both women. This double murder was listed as "justifiable homicide."

W. A. was so incensed he requested a front-page editorial calling for donations to prosecute the officer. The *World* itself put in the first fifty dollars and asked for contributions from each reader. Scott sent special-delivery letters to every black minister in Atlanta asking that, in next Sunday's service, he speak out against this atrocity and take up a special collection to help finance the prosecution. And of all the pastors in Atlanta, only two acknowledged the letter and tried to raise money. Our drive failed.

One was the Reverend J. Raymond Henderson, pastor of Greater Wheat Street Baptist Church and uncompromising foe of racism. The other was a Colored Methodist Episcopal (CME) church elder, a Reverend Martin, equally militant and who later died suddenly under mysterious circumstances.

Unlike other pastors, Rev. Henderson barred separation in his church. Instead of reserving a special section for "white friends" who might want to attend musical programs ("Ooh, doncha jus' love them darky spirituals?"), Rev. Henderson announced Caucasians were welcome at all services but must sit any place they could find a seat.

Following an especially heinous slaughter of an unarmed black by a trigger-happy cop in Atlanta, the minister asked for and received front-page space for a series of articles calling for the arrest and prosecution of the officer and launched the proposed fund with a contribution of twenty-five dollars. Several of us at the *World* added various amounts. And that was the sum total of money raised. The police department was incensed, but none dared seek revenge on the prominent pastor.

As a group in 1931, we were black defeatists. When you stuck your neck out, you did it alone. We were grateful for any victories, but if you lost the reaction was "you should known you couldn't do that in the South." Credit the post-World War II new black breed and the bus boycott victory of the late Martin Luther King, Jr., in Montgomery with goosing us into mass militant action.

Rev. Henderson was still a thorn in the side of the white power structure when I left Atlanta. But Whitey found a way to get rid of him. Greater Wheat Street Baptist Church held services in the basement while trying to raise enough money to complete the structure. One day a number of wealthy whites quietly let the deacon board know they would supply enough money to finish the building if Rev. Henderson were relieved of his duties. Among Baptists the deacon board controls the hiring and firing of pastors. Rev. Henderson, when next heard of, was heading a church in Los Angeles, and Greater Wheat Street dedicated a magnificent temple.

39

In 1932 the Angelo Herndon trial captured world headlines, second only to the Scottsboro case.[6] A young black Communist, Herndon led a march of starving black and white depression victims on the Georgia state capitol to demand food and shelter—an act of unbelievable courage. For this offense to the status quo, he was arrested and sentenced to death by the white power structure under an antiquated antisedition law dating from the 1870s.

This intended act of legal barbarism was so outrageous that even students and professors from white Emory University and Georgia Tech, who usually lived all their lives in another world, actively joined in the Herndon defense. I met and talked with several who came to the *World* office and was impressed with their sincerity. Herndon, whom I came to know personally when he was freed on bail pending an appeal, was a youth of intelligence and sincerity. As for bravery, he possessed this in superabundance to take on state officials in the heyday of Governor Gene Talmadge.

The CME churchman, Rev. Martin, stuck close to Herndon through the long months of the case until the antisedition law was declared unconstitutional by the U.S. Supreme Court. The defendant was freed. Knowing that the establishment still might try to harm him, Herndon was placed aboard the first train out of Atlanta. Riding with him as far as Baltimore as a kind of bodyguard was Rev. Martin. A few months later, this bold religious leader died suddenly from a mysterious stomach ailment. Some observers, I among them, believed he might have been poisoned in retaliation for his active support of Herndon. I saw Herndon in Chicago shortly afterward. He told me the Hearst Press had offered him a fat fee to "tell all," but he turned down such propositions. His quarrel, he said, was with certain individuals, not the ideology.

The Herndon case also shaped the future of the late Ben Davis, Jr. Ben Davis, Sr., was not only a black leader but also well fixed and had sent his son to Amherst where Ben, Jr., starred on the tennis team. I met young Ben shortly after he returned to Atlanta to begin practicing law. We were both around the same age and size; since we both had the same last name, this sometimes led to a confusion of identities.

Because of his father's prominence and connections, the junior Davis could have had a comfortable income and jim crow respectability had he chosen to play ball with the system. But he was no compromiser. Incensed by Georgia's effort to liquidate Herndon, Ben devoted all his energies to the defense. Daily he grew more disgusted with the entire white supremacy setup and its systematic degrading of black Americans. His determined fight for civil rights led him into the Communist Party, election to the City Council of New York, and later to prison under the Smith Act. He died in 1964.

As a practicing attorney, Ben believed, he should have access to the state law library like white barristers in Georgia. Officials thought otherwise. He finally wrote to the governor demanding this right as a citizen and lawyer. I need not tell how far he got.

Not only Ben but a number of other young Afro-Americans, incensed by the Herndon case, joined the Communist Party. Many were students at the five black colleges—Morehouse, Morris Brown, Atlanta, Clark, and Spelman. One or two were crackpots, among them Marcus, who penned long rambling letters to the *World* on, first, the Herndon case and then on other branches of human activity. When I refused to print them as composed, he started calling me at all hours of the night to utter dire threats.

Once he got me out of bed at 3:00 A.M.

"This is the Avenger," he announced dramatically over the telephone. "I want you to know that because you refuse to print Marcus's letters, you will be one of the first liquidated, comes the revolution."

He spoke sincerely with no effort to disguise his voice. Obviously he was nuts. Of all the many admitted Communists I have met, he was the only one to seriously invoke that phrase, "comes the revolution."

"Kindly go to hell," I said, hanging up the telephone.

Twice more at fifteen minute intervals it rang. I was certain it was Marcus and did not answer. But I was irritated.

Next morning as I ate breakfast at the restaurant operated by the Spanish Jew, one of the helpers, a Morehouse student, asked me, "Did you get a call about three o'clock?"

"That I did."

"Were you threatened with liquidation, comes the revolution?"

"That I was."

"Do you know who made the call?"

"Of course. That damned fool, Marcus. Why?"

"He called from here. I guess you musta hung up on him. He was cussing a blue streak and tried twice to call you back, but nobody answered."

"Yeah. Once was enough."

"You gonna do anything about him annoying you? Gonna feed him a face fulla fist?"

"I don't intend to touch him," I said, "but I assure you he'll be taken care of. He won't get away with waking me in the middle of the night for nothing."

I had no intention of anything more severe than bawling the hell out of Marcus next time I saw him. But fate stepped in.

Two days later, before I had a chance to see Marcus, he was found dead in an alley in a tough part of town. Some unknown person had brained him with a brick.

When I walked into the cafe, my Morehouse friend along with the restaurant crew looked at me with awe.

"It sure doesn't pay to get on your bad side," he said.

I shrugged my shoulders.

"Of course I don't think you did it," he went on, "but just the same, gah-ud damn!"

40

Atlanta was the site of the most humiliating experience of my life.

I have roughhoused most of my years. I suppose I have been trying to compensate for the frustration of early childhood when I so often had no playmates. Frequently at night, when dignity was no longer necessary, I took part in wild horseplay with other staff members.

One this particular evening I was chasing my reporter, Milton Randolph, through the office. We ran into the mechanical department, circled the presses and the imposing stones, then started back down front to the news and business rooms. A partition containing a doorway that I could just pass through without stooping separated the editorial area from the business division. Since I was gaining on him, Randolph snatched a chair into my path to slow me down. Instead of stopping to push it aside, I tried to leap over it and go through the doorway at the same time.

I really should have known better.

Oh, I made it through all right. My momentum saw to that. But my head struck the two-by-six crossbar at the top of the doorway and I landed flat on my back, bleeding profusely from a wound in the center of my cranium. I got up, looking around in surprise. Immediately, Randolph and the shop foreman rushed me to Grady Hospital. However, I never lost consciousness. I admit I'm just naturally hardheaded.

At Grady, which of course had an all-white staff, I was turned over to a young interne who shaved the injured area and prepared to suture it. He was told I was editor of the Atlanta *World*. Meanwhile, he kept up a steady flow of chatter. Finally he asked me a direct question.

"Yes," I answered.

He froze, scalpel in one hand, medication in the other, and in a strange, rasping voice asked, "What did you say?"

"I said 'yes,'" I replied in surprise because his question had been unimportant anyway.

Very slowly and deliberately, the young doctor put down his instruments, looked first at my companions, then at me, and said: "I expect niggers to say 'Yes, sir' and 'No, sir' when they address a white man. You know I'm in control in this room. I can fix your wound, or I can put something in it that will take care of you permanently. Your life is in my hands. Now again, what did you say?"

You don't have much of a choice at a time like this. Of course, I could have been a defiant fool, maintaining my pride, but what would I have gained? The satisfaction that I had stood up to one little nothing of a racist as I breathed my last? With his knowledge of drugs and poisons, there was nothing to prevent him introducing some substance into my tissues that could result in speedy or painful death. I thought of his Oath of Hippocrates but knew this did not apply to niggers; in the warped minds of many Caucasians, even those with numerous university degrees, we were less than human. And I knew that this interne would be able to scientifically murder me in front of my associates from the *World* and go completely free; what white official would accept their statements over that of any reasonably responsible white person, particularly one with the prestige of a medical doctor? Even though he knew I edited the *World* and was therefore somewhat intelligent, I was black; therefore, I was a nigger and trash.

There flashed through my mind in this one agonizing moment, while he waited, memory of the assault on Roland Hayes, the world-famous tenor. He had returned to his birthplace at Rome, Georgia, an internationally acclaimed artist, had entered a shoe store, and had been severely beaten by some little white snip of a clerk to whom Hayes had not shown the proper respect.[7] Brice Taylor, a black All-American football player for the University of Southern California in the 1920s, had been fired from his job as coach of a southern black college team when he was overheard addressing a blonde former classmate, who lived in the Dixie college town, by his first name. No matter how renowned in the rest of creation, in Dixie our best were lower than the lowest white.

Since I was a child I had studiously avoided saying "Yes, sir" and "No, sir." It was a reaction to Granny's insistence that all white males be addressed in this manner. I had come to look on it as a sound of servility left over from slavery. Even in the South I had thus far gotten around this expected response by the simple device of telling Caucasians "That's right" or "I don't think so."

Now, because of one mental lapse, I was cornered. There was no way out unless I chose to gamble with my life. I steeled myself. And the emotional hurt surpassed by far the ache in my split head as I said: "Yes, sir."

The young doctor said no more, and neither did any of us. He took nine stitches, bandaged me, and we left.

I was so helpless, frustrated, and angry that I entirely forgot about the wound. I returned to the office, finished my work, went home, and came back on schedule next day, losing no time from the job except to have my injury treated—but from then on by a black physician.

Through generations, Dixie had worked up a sizeable Book of Etiquette on Race Relations designed to keep the Afro-American "in his place."

A male Duskyamerican may have reached the venerable age of a hundred, but he was still a "boy"; this attempt to consign us to perpetual childhood was back of our insistence, even among the very young, of addressing each other as "man" and was a group way of compensating. Evidently we were like the lower animals; we could mate, but we did not marry for no white supremacist referred to our women as "Mrs." An Afro-American could be called "Doctor" or "Professor" or "Reverend," but the Dixiecrat mind rejected "Mr." and "Mrs." The racist also placed himself in an illogical position by calling our older folk "aunt" or "uncle"; one must assume they were more willing to admit close kinship than render elementary courtesy.

I recall a blues verse that sardonically pictured relationships in Dixie, especially in rural areas:

> Nigger an' a white man playin' seven up
> Nigger win the money but scared to pick it up.

Miscegenation was still primarily a one-way street in the South. A white man could bed black women with impunity, but the reverse was a signal for violence. In fact, more than one black man has been murdered for consorting with a black woman looked upon by some honky as his private possession. Conversely, there have been lynchings because some white gal literally threw herself at a brother and, to save her own hide when the relationship was exposed, yelled rape.

Because it was against both the law and custom, relationships between mahogany males and chalk chicks had an almost irresistible fascination for many Southerners. Ric Roberts, the *World* cartoonist who could draw fabulous females, picked up sizeable fees from leading white Atlanta businessmen for creating large pictures of gorgeous nude blondes and gigantic well-tooled black males engaging in every imaginable kind of sex activity. These high priests of Nordic supremacy perversely got tremendous erotic kicks from looking at pictures of intimacies that would have made them pop their blood vessels had they witnessed them in the flesh.

Despite the mores, many white realists knew there was some consorting between soul studs and ofay broads, especially in hotels. It was reasonable to believe that a bellboy who provided a gal for guests would, in time, want to sample the commodity and the girl herself would become actively curious about her agent; this was elementary common sense, although most guests never thought it through. There was one white doctor who insisted he could always tell when one of his white female patients had slept with a black man; he swore that for several days afterward she was listless and unable to show genuine interest in white males.

This widespread belief in the sexual prowess of "black bucks" was undoubtedly a major reason why Southern white males might murder a soul stud if he was heard to make even a verbal pass at a white woman; they did not really feel they must "protect the honor of white womanhood," but they had an almost pathological fear that by comparison they would be judged sexually inferior. Naturally, such thinking influenced police action.

One night Ric Roberts, dark brown of complexion, was driving around town with his girlfriend, very high yellow and from a small town in Georgia. Under subdued light, she could be mistaken for Caucasian.

A patrol car containing two cracker cops ordered Ric to the curb.

"Boy, what you doin' with that white woman in youah cah?" one officer asked him, shining a flashlight in their faces.

"She's not white," Ric protested.

"Of course not," the young woman chimed in. "I'm colored."

"You're both lyin'," the cop said. "Dontcha think I know a white woman when I see one?"

It took some fast talking by Ric and his companion, who told where she lived in her hometown, what kind of work her father did, what school she attended, and where she stopped in Atlanta, to convince the cops they had made a mistake.

At last, grudgingly, the officers let them go but not before growling a warning to Ric:

"If you run around with a gal this light, it proves you must like white women. So, nigger, you bettuh be careful."

Speaking generally of Dixie etiquette, George Schuyler, the late iconoclastic columnist of the Pittsburgh *Courier,* told me how he had defied the patterns in Mississippi.[8] He stopped off at the *World* in 1932 on his way back to NAACP headquarters in New York, which had sent him into this haven of the hateleers for a special investigation.

It happened in a small town where he had stayed for several days. Each week the NAACP wired his salary and expenses. He was at his lodging house when the telegram was delivered.

Schuyler went to the general store which housed just about everything including the post office and Western Union and stood at the window. Of course the lone storekeeper waited on all the whites before finally coming over to Schuyler. George meanwhile had kept his hat on his head in direct violation of custom which decreed blacks were to talk to their "superiors" hat in hand.

"You new around here, boy?" the storekeeper asked, keeping his eyes glued to George's hat.

Schuyler replied he was "just visiting" and handed over the telegram. The white man was astonished at the size of the check since souls in that area rarely, if ever, got their hands on that much money at one time. Curious, he asked questions as he counted out the bills.

"You one of them college professors?" he asked.

George pocketed the funds, edged near the door, and replied, "Who ever heard of a 'boy' being a college professor?" Then he walked rapidly out the exit and disappeared before the white man could recover from the shock of this impertinence.

Schuyler told me he went to his room, grabbed his suitcase, and hurried to the railway station to wait for the next train out, just in case the storekeeper decided to round up a mob of his cronies to find that "sassy nigger" and teach him a lesson.

41

One morning, some two months after I began editing the *World,* a young woman named Thelma Boyd walked into the office to start work as a clerk in the business department. She had just arrived from Florida. W. A. Scott had roomed at her home in Jacksonville where he had published a business directory before coming to Atlanta.

A divorcee, three years my senior, just over five feet tall, golden brown in color, and exuding a soft sexuality, I went for her in a hurry. Before long we were dating virtually every night, in addition to seeing

each other at the office during the day. But despite this disturbing development, I was going to marry Gladys back in Kansas. Now that I had a
decent job, we planned to wed that summer.

Roy Wilkins wrote from Kansas City asking if I would replace him
as managing editor of the Kansas City *Call,* one of the nation's largest and
most influential weeklies.[9] He was going to NAACP headquarters in New
York as assistant to Walter White whom he later succeeded as secretary. I
accepted. I didn't like Kansas City, but after Atlanta even that hotbed of
prejudice seemed more liveable. Further, it would solve the Thelma problem. If I went to Kansas City, I would go down to Gladys's home, marry
her, and set up housekeeping in K.C. It was becoming clearer by the day
that it would not be wise to bring Gladys to Atlanta.

C. A. Franklin, *Call* owner, and I arrived at a salary schedule by mail.
I agreed to arrive in Kansas City in June a couple of weeks before Roy left
for New York so he could break me in. I wrote to Gladys telling when I
would come for her. Everything seemed settled.

But I reckoned without W. A. Scott.

I had already told him I was quitting. Two weeks before I was
scheduled to leave, he called me aside.

"Doc, you still going to leave the *World?*" he asked.

"That's right. In two weeks."

"Well, Doc, if you're going to leave I want you to quit now instead of
waiting two weeks."

I looked at him without comment.

"You see, Doc, there's Henigan in Memphis. I can bring him over
here to take your place, and I got another man who wants a job that I can
send to Memphis. If I gotta make changes, I want to get it over with."

I still said nothing.

"Of course, now, if you should make up your mind to stay here I
think I can squeeze you out more money every week but it's gotta be just
between us. You know I already pay you more'n anybody else in the
organization and if word ever got around you were making something on
top of that I'd have trouble with the rest of the crew. Besides, I have big
plans here at the *World.* Y'know, you've got a real future here—"

"How much more?" I cut in.

"I'll make it ten bucks now, and if you're here another year I'll add
another five." He paused for effect. "Think it over, and let me know what
you're gonna do day after tomorrow."

I thought it over for two days. I was still curious over what we might be able to accomplish together at this challenging *World*. Of course I could have agreed to remain and then cut out in two weeks as I'd originally planned. What decided for me was my involvement with Thelma and the realization I was no longer keen on marrying Gladys.

At twenty-five, I felt a compulsion to marry. And the pendulum had swung to the other extreme. Only a few years before, I would have been horrified at the idea of matrimony with a woman willing to sleep with me without a wedding ring; now I demanded practical demonstration before-hand of coital compatibility.

I often wonder what would have happened had there been a chance for full comparison between Thelma and Gladys. I knew what to expect of Thelma and was pleased; Gladys was an unknown quantity. Also of major importance was the fact that Thelma could not bear children. Many men marry with the expectation of fathering a family. But I abhorred the idea of bringing offspring into a world which treated blacks as if we were filth. I felt it was better to remain unborn than grow up learning we were automatically pigeonholed by Caucasians as inferior. I was already embittered by prejudice before reaching Atlanta; now I felt helpless frustration. I could see no way out. This was no fit legacy for children.

However, I did feel a moral obligation to marry Gladys. We had looked forward to it for five years. But ethics were no match for emotional involvement. I decided to remain in Atlanta, but then I faced the distasteful task of telling Gladys there would be no wedding.

I wrote her saying I had changed my mind and would remain in Georgia. Marriage, I wrote, was out of the question because it would be unfair to her. I had just learned from my doctor I had an incurable disease and had been given only a few years to live. She airmailed a reply stating some of her girlfriends had already given her bridal showers and, if I were sick, she would be happy to come to Atlanta and nurse me the rest of my days.

I felt, justifiably, like a real heel.

Nevertheless, I tried another approach. In desperation I told her that since being in Atlanta I had discovered I was a homosexual and therefore unable to fulfill the duties of a husband. Whereupon she replied that she believed that, if she were with me, she would eventually get me out of this unnatural condition, and wouldn't I please give her a chance to try?

With that I surrendered. I told her bluntly I was going to marry another woman and expressed my sincere regrets at how things had turned out. Meanwhile I had written to Wilkins and Franklin telling them my change in plans. Immediately, they reached over to Memphis and yanked Henigan for the Kansas City vacancy.

Thelma and I got married one Sunday in June by an Episcopalian minister who had attended Howard University in Washington, D.C., and who was a member of my fraternity, Phi Beta Sigma. Before the ceremony, he told me in confidence and without blinking an eye that this frat had been known on campus as "the cock and pussy club." Well, all Greek letter societies have their own traditions to live up to.

42

Smart Atlanta bootleggers had developed a unique technique for staying out of jail. They simply did not keep the stuff at home. Instead, if you went to a residence to buy a "sixteen" (local jargon for a pint because it contains sixteen ounces), the bootlegger would first look around to see if the coast was clear and then lead you away from his door to the nearest drain in a street gutter. Tied to the bars with long, stout strings and dangling below would be a number of bottles of moonshine. He'd haul one up, exchange it for your cash, and that was that. Of course somebody always kept an eye on the gutter through a curtained window, but this extra trouble was worth it to avoid being caught with the illicit goods and slapped in jail. And, of course, if some nosey cop happened along at the wrong time, nobody owned the liquor or knew how in the world it ever got down there in the gutter.

However, shortly after I married and moved into an apartment, I acquired one of the town's better bootleggers who provided deliver service. A quite ordinary looking guy, he showed up at the *World* one day and asked if I wanted to buy some good imported liquor at special prices.

"Of course," I said. "What've you got and how special?"

He rattled off a list which included Gilbey's Gin, Johnny Walker Scotch, Four Roses Bourbon, and Bacardi Rum. All of this had been run in through Florida, and there was plenty available at what were quite reasonable prices. I bought several bottles and sent him around to friends at the Atlanta Life Insurance home offices a few blocks away, who I knew appreciated good stuff. He sold several cases.

From then on, he made weekly deliveries to me. I would have leaped at the chance to buy any potable which did not suggest close kinship with a bug spray. I have never decided which was worse, Kansas or Atlanta corn liquor. After a couple of months, when we had reached friendly familiarity, he asked me, "What do you do with your empty bottles?"

"Throw 'em away, of course."

His face broke into a sheepish grin.

"Tell you what I'd like you to do," he said. "You save me the bottles, but don't let nobody know, and from now on I'll sell you anything you want at half-price. You've thrown a lot of business my way, so I feel I owe you something anyhow."

"You mean you're gonna use the bottles over?" I asked.

"Sure. You didn't *really* think that stuff was imported, did you?"

Fact is, I hadn't given it a thought. I merely knew it was far better than the rest of the booze I'd had in Atlanta. But when he put it that way, I couldn't lose face by letting on I had been sucker enough to think it was what the bottle said it was.

"I'd been wondering how long you'd still pretend it was genuine," I replied. "By the way, where do you get it? It's still the best stuff I've found in Georgia." On that point, I was telling the truth.

"We put it together out in the country. The joker I work with sure knows his stuff."

Later on I bought a couple of charred kegs and filled them with raw corn whiskey to which I added nonalcoholic flavorings. However, I never let it age long enough. I was always ready for it long before it was ready for me.

I learned that almost anything could happen at the *World* office in addition to itinerant bootleggers wandering in.

Around midnight one warm summer evening, a reporter and I were working in the front office with the door open when in walked a noisy, prowling pack of male homosexuals. There were eleven or twelve in the group, three my size and larger. All took turns describing graphically and in minute detail what they would like to do to us. We listened in speechless amazement, without becoming interested, until they evidently decided the time for talk had ended and advanced upon us with action in mind. Since we couldn't beat 'em and had no desire to join 'em, we retreated hastily to the shop for reinforcements. When we returned with some half-dozen members of the night crew, our uninvited guests reluctantly left after telling us they'd return the following night. From then on we locked the front door after 10:00 P.M.

Just two mornings later a character came to the office and told the receptionist he was looking for a home with one of the single male employees. He was a good cook, he said, could sew and darn well and was an excellent housekeeper. His name? With a perfectly serious face he replied, "Florence Nightingale." However, there were no takers. If there is a moral to this story, coming from a newspaperman, it is that it doesn't always pay to advertise.

To keep the record straight, I have neither contempt for nor antagonism against the homosexual, either male or female. I sincerely believe that any activity engaged in by two consenting persons of legal age should have the same status as copulation between husband and wife. I am unalterably opposed to any attempt at regimentation of the sex drive into the rigid outlets customarily prescribed by our religious traditions. Of course, this idea is rejected by many psychiatrists for eventually, should such practices become socially acceptable, much of our nationwide neuroticism would end, thus reducing the number of their patients and the total of their fees.

Frankly, I think those headshrinkers who attempt to narrowly limit sex activity are doing our entire social order a great disservice. You know what a perversion or deviation is, don't you? It's any kind of sex act with which the psychiatrist has no sympathy. Contemporary American society still treats homosexuals as it does other unpopular minorities such as blacks—with hate, scorn, and discrimination. During the dramatic civil rights demonstrations of the 1960s, I often thought we ought to form a united front with joint sit-ins at cafes. In my mind I envisioned the result: an indignant white restaurant manager frantically phoning the police, "Get here in a hurry! We got niggers at the counters and our washrooms are loaded with fairies and lesbians!" Or perhaps there might have been a joint March on Washington waving banners: "Blacks and Homos, Arise!"

43

The numbers game was popular in Atlanta just as it was in New York and up and down the East Coast. Chicago, of course, was a policy town. Should you not know the difference between these rackets, let me explain. In policy, the numbers are usually inserted in small capsules, placed in a wheellike drum, which is turned for mixing. Then the first selected (at random, theoretically) are the winning combination. After the drawing, they are printed on slips of paper, distributed at various stations, and given to writers. A wheel may have three for four drawings a day, often known as "classes," thus giving the operators a triple or quadruple shot at the public's money. In the numbers game, the winning combination generally consists of three digits in the total stock market sales or some daily statistic carried in the newspapers.

One morning I received an agitated phone call from a subscriber who insisted he wanted to see me privately on a street corner near the *World* office at one o'clock. "It'll be worth your while," he added.

I met him at the designated time and place. He was small and inoffensive looking, and as soon as he saw me he pulled out a ten spot.

"This is for you," he said. "All I want is the winning numbah for t'morrow."

I stared incredulously. "How in hell can I give you a winning number?" I asked.

"C'mon now," he grinned. "I know you's gifted that way. I heard all about it. I done heard you could tell the day befo' what numbah was gonna fall. Tell you what: I'll give you this ten dollahs an' if th' numbah you give me falls in two days I'll give you half of what I wins. I also got friends willin to pay fo' a good numbah any day."

"Don't you suppose," I asked, "that if I could tell up front what was gonna fall, I'd play it myself and get rich?"

He looked at me for several seconds before it sank in. Then he mumbled, "Nevah thought of that," turned, and slowly walked away.

Of course I could have taken his cash and rattled off any number. There was always the chance he might look for me with murder in mind if it didn't come out; but if through sheer luck it fell, I could have raked in the cash as word got around and people came in droves to buy a "sure hit." I'd seen it happen in Chicago when a woman who called herself "Madame Zephyr" set up shop on Indiana Avenue near 36th and sold "gigs" (combinations of winning numbers) to policy players at five bucks. In collusion with the operator of a certain wheel, she had arranged to have one of her gigs win. The news sprinted through the South Side. Within a month Madame Zephyr was able to buy a Cadillac and a six-flat building, and the owner of the wheel had tripled his already fantastic take. She operated for more than a year on the strength of this fixed hit and one or two others which, by the sheer laws of chance, happened to win and retired with her pile to California.

Old and young, they were caught in the net of the numbers game, eagerly awaiting news each afternoon of what fell, hoping to make a monster killing for an investment of a few cents.

I had occasion to visit a friend at Grady Hospital. The black section had big dormitory-type wards shared by as many as twenty-five patients. As I stepped into one of the men's wards, an elderly, innocuous looking patient, who was at least seventy-five, greeted me from his bed near the door.

"How do, son," he said.

I spoke in return, smiled, and asked how he was feeling. I had never seen him before.

"Tol'able, son, jus' tol'able," he said in a slow, tired voice.

"Have a bad day?" I asked politely.

"When you gits my age, mos' days is bad," he said in his dragging, dispirited monotone. "I got rhumatiz pow'ful bad. Can't hardly walk. My ticker's playin' out, and I jus' don't seem to have no appetite fo' any kind of eatin'. What's mo', my daughtuh an' her husband's done busted up, an' she got five chillun she don't know how she gonna take care of. Son, what fell today?"

44

A year after coming to Atlanta, with the *World* finally running smoothly, W. A. popped his head in my little office and said, "Doc, I want you to bring out a daily in about a month."

I looked slowly around, as the words sunk in, but he had already vanished.

Well now, I thought, a daily! Who does he think I am? Merlin the Magician? Of course, I believed I could be the first person in the history of Duskyamerica to successfully edit a black daily. My sad experience with the Chicago *Evening Bulletin* had shown me what pitfalls to avoid. Still, the idea of a daily was not a complete surprise. Some subscribers had already asked for it.

As soon as possible I cornered W. A. and told him what I'd need. We arrived at a budget, and immediately I contacted various agencies including United Press and King Features Syndicate. I contracted for several comic strips I had regularly read in Chicago dailies but which Atlanta sheets had ignored. I arranged for the Associated Negro Press to wire important stories in addition to the regular twice-weekly mailed releases. A UP leased wire was available at 250 dollars weekly, but I made no decision pending an indication whether member papers could supply us with enough news. However, I did arrange for daily worldwide picture service. I planned a daily summary of important national and world news to keep our readers informed, but the emphasis of necessity would be on news of our own black world.

Within a month I brought the first issue of the Atlanta *Daily World.* The public welcomed this venture. Our circulation immediately increased, and some readers cancelled their subscriptions to the three white dailies. Fortunately for us, the Atlanta *Journal* came out around this time with a belittling story describing an annual event in another part of the state at which "darkies" were in pain because this was the only time in the year when they wore shoes. Next day I ran a front-page editorial pointing out black Atlantans were not required to buy the *Journal* and pay for insults. Within two days, for the first time in history, white girls representing the white dailies called up prominent Afro-Americans such as Forrester B. Washington, director of the Atlanta School of Social Work, and Jesse O. Thomas, head of the local Urban League, asking if they liked their newspaper, if delivery service were satisfactory, and inviting them to contact management any time they were dissatisfied. Obviously we at the *Daily World* had made our presence felt.

Our reporters, incidentally, had amazing empathy with their counterparts on white dailies, particularly Cliff MacKay who was volunteered use of the press room and telephone at city hall. For one brief period, Police Chief Sturdivant was so irked with the white press that, in spite, he signed reporters' passes to be given wholesale to *Daily World* employees.

Within a few months the *Daily World* was operating smoothly. Each weekday night, E. N. Davis brought out the *Daily World* while during the day I concentrated on SNS papers, editorials, and my column, in addition to overall supervision. Saturday night, I personally took care of the larger Sunday edition. During this period W. A. attended a publishers' convention, met Carl Murphy, big boss of the Baltimore and Washington *Afro-American* newspapers, and started a feud which continued until W. A.'s death.[10] At one time W. A. seriously considered opening a plant and starting a morning newspaper for one city and an afternoon daily for the other in order to place one of his newspapers in spite on the Murphy doorstep twice a day.

Meanwhile the Depression finally hit Atlanta hard. Even white street peddlers on Auburn Avenue began addressing us as "Sir." The disgusted electorate threw out Herbert Hoover and elected Franklin D. Roosevelt. But, just as he took office, all banks closed. W. A. Scott, ever alert to grab an extra dollar any kind of way, dashed next door and drew out enough cash to take care of his payroll for the next four weeks. Then he paid his staff only half our salaries on the theory it was better to get half our pay than to receive full checks which nobody could cash.

One weekend Thelma drove me to Tuskegee to visit her sister, Basiline, wife of Albon L. Holsey, special assistant to the president of the school and founder of the ill-fated Colored Merchants Association stores. Rural Georgia and Alabama would be far more beautiful if they were not in Georgia and Alabama. But on the way back I received one of the greatest surprises of my life.

We stopped in some nameless hamlet around eight o'clock Sunday night and pulled into a combination general store and service station to buy gas. Three or four crackers, including a shirt-sleeved deputy with a bright star, loafed on the porch.

The apparent owner asked, "What'll it be?"

"Ten gallons of gas."

He arose and strode around to the side of the car. I tensed, wondering how I had violated the ethics of living jim crow.

"Ah' sorry, suh," he said with his thick drawl, "but Ah cain't sell you no gas now. We got a local ordinance which won't let nobody sell nothin' durin' church meetin' time in the mawnin' and at night. But if you need gas right bad, go two miles straight the way you's headed an' turn right about a quatah of a mile. That's Jake's place. He's outside the city limits an' he can sell you gas any time."

I heard all he said, but I was still hung up on that "sir." A white man calling me that in the Georgia sticks? Something must be wrong. I turned toward the deputy. He had a great friendly grin riding his face.

"I'm sorry," I told the store owner, "but will you please repeat those directions?"

"Yes, suh, you bet," he replied. I had heard correctly. That "sir" was no mistake. The mountain had crawled on its knees to Mohammed.

To be sure I was still in Georgia, I drove around until I came to another service station. At the moment I would have welcomed being called coon or nigger for then I would have been in touch with reality. But at the second station (there were only two in this tiny town), the owner was as polite as the first. I drove away talking to myself. Back in Atlanta I was hesitant about revealing these experiences.

My friends would have sworn I had concocted a fairy tale.

But a few months later, in a small town twenty miles away, several members of Blanche Calloway's band were severely beaten by infuriated whites for attempting to use the rest room while their bus was taking on gas. And in north Georgia, near the Tennessee border, Juliette Derricotte and several companions died following a car crash because no white ambulance would carry them to a hospital. Miss Derricotte, internationally known and the highest black figure on the national YWCA staff, was forced to lie critically injured on a public highway until a black ambulance could be summoned from thirty miles away to haul her to a hospital with facilities for black citizens. By then it was too late.

At least the rest of Georgia had preserved its racist image.

45

I missed the live jazz of Chicago, but I did find new kicks in what was to me a strange area: college football games. I had been reared on the usual repertoire of Sousa marches and similar numbers at grid games, but then I had never seen a black contest. When I attended my first in Atlanta, it came as a distinct shock to hear school bands start swinging and the partisans chant and stomp in a strongly rhythmic blues vein. And of course at that time the 'Bama State Collegians, led by Erskine Hawkins, were a favorite on all campuses.

Most of my jazz enjoyment was via radio. A sensational new group, the Mills Brothers, airing over NBC, had Atlanta singing praises along with the rest of the nation.[11] It was hard to believe they used only their voices to realistically imitate musical instruments. In an effort to compete, the rival CBS network with great fanfare introduced the Three Keys. They were good but not in the same league as the Mills Brothers and soon faded. The most popular band of the period was Cab Calloway's. Few people missed his broadcasts. Also on the rise was Jimmie Lunceford, who developed a following through his audio exposure from the Cotton Club in New York.[12]

Two bands dominated the local scene, but when a New York name band came to town they played before turnaway crowds. Women virtually panicked when Claude Hopkins appeared with oriental-looking Orlando Roberson singing romantic vocals. But my personal high spot was the night Bennie Moten played.

Several times I had heard Bennie on the air and realized his band was even greater than when I last heard it in Kansas City. At this time, he was on tour and a local promoter booked him for a one-nighter and then, seemingly upset by his own audacity, resolved to keep it a secret. Since Atlantans generally were not familiar with midwestern bands, the dance at the Odd Fellows Temple began with the orchestra outnumbering the paying customers.

Nevertheless the band jumped and wailed as if it were a command performance. Buster Moten lead the group on accordion. Count Basie ignited the ivories, and Eddie Durham, who had revitalized the organization, doubled on trombone and guitar; Walter Page plucked bass, and Harlan Leonard blew alto, with rotund Jimmie Rushing belting vocals. The band was loaded with star talent, but my immediate favorite was Hot Lips Page on trumpet.

Climax of the night was their version of "St. Louis Blues." It dug in from the first note and grew hotter each bar. Then, to top it all, Lips stood up and seared the stratosphere as he improvised thirty-four consecutive choruses. This was the greatest blowing I'd heard since the battle of the Louies at the Savoy when Satchmo annihilated Panico. Page proved himself to be one of the all-time greats on his instrument.

46

One Tuesday morning in 1933 I was standing near the receptionist when in walked a tall, handsome, brownskin man wearing a wing collar and having the air of a swashbuckler. Behind him was a shorter white man.

"I'm Colonel Hubert Julian," he told me.

Naturally I'd heard about him. He was the Black Eagle who not long before took off with tremendous publicity from a New York airport on a nonstop flight to Africa—and ended up in the Harlem River. Later he had been given command of Emperor Haile Selassie's Royal Ethiopian Air Force, consisting of one plane, which he promptly wrecked in Addis Ababa. Many souls now laughed at his name, but he was immune to barbs. He had continued to go his suave, audacious way, living in headlines.[13]

"We flew in this morning," he explained, nodding toward his white companion. "He's the pilot. We came in a Bellanca plane I'm trying to raise money to buy. I intend to fly it nonstop to Spain."

"How come you didn't fly it yourself?" I asked.

"My license permits me to fly this craft internationally only. I don't have a license to fly it in the United States."

As I digested this, he went on:

"The Bellanca is out at the Atlanta airport now. What I want to do is put on a show next Saturday to raise money to buy this craft. Will you give me publicity? Every penny will go straight to the Bellanca people. How about it?"

I gave a speedy yes. At least here was something different for the front page. I was cynical over Julian's ability to get a plane safely into the air and back down again, but this was too good a potential story to pass up. Even that of itself would be a lure. I'd get him a crowd; it was up to him to produce or make another fool of himself. So for the next few days, as reader interest mounted, I headlined the coming Saturday exhibition. Meanwhile Julian and his pilot wired for special clearance to let him fly the Bellanca.

Saturday the honkies stared in amazing disbelief as black Atlantans literally invaded the airport. A crowd of several thousand was waiting expectantly as Julian came to me and told me quietly he had been denied clearance to fly the Bellanca over Georgia. Many of the gathering, drawn to the field by curiosity seasoned with skepticism, laid down a barrage of I-told-you-so when word was passed around.

"I'll see if I can borrow one of the airplanes here," the Black Eagle volunteered.

Well, it was his neck. He went off and returned fifteen to twenty minutes later with the news that a plane was available, but its use required a deposit of five thousand dollars to pay for any possible damage. *World* staff members and I accompanied the colonel to look at the craft.

"Junk," he snorted after inspection. "The damn thing is not worth over twenty-five hundred dollars, and I'm being generous at that. But this is the only one they'll let me use."

"Think you can fly it?"

"Of course I can fly it! That is, if you'll put up five grand?"

We looked around at the spectators. A good many had already left in disappointment. Then we looked at the white airport crew. Their faces were uniformly contemptuous and cynical. That cinched it.

Five of us, including William Kelley, circulation manager, and one of the Scotts made out checks for one thousand dollars each and turned them over to the airport manager. Only the Scott check was good. If something happened to the plane and the manager tried to cash them, four of us were chain-gang bound and we knew it. We were painfully aware of Julian's record for cracking up, but this was a chance we had to take. We were willing to risk our freedom to wipe those sneers off cracker faces and give black Atlantans the pride of seeing a brother take a plane into the sky.

Nevertheless, we tried to be prudent. Calling Black Eagle aside, we earnestly implored him to go up into the air, not too high, circle the field a couple of times so everybody could see he was alone in that crate, then ease back down.

He nodded his head in agreement.

The Black Eagle got into the little junk pile and zoomed off. Souls on the verge of driving away came back and got out of their cars. Virtually all the honkies stopped and froze to immobility as they watched the strange sight of a black man flying a plane. Only the crackers knew what kind of unsafe craft it was.

But Julian did not level off after climbing a few hundred feet into the air. He went up at least three thousand feet, then began a nosedive. The five of us looked at one another in real anguish, thinking of those bogus checks. The Black Eagle could break his fool neck if he wanted to, but he had no business messing with our freedom.

At about five hundred feet he straightened out, and we sighed with relief in unison. I sneaked a quick glance at the closest cracker airport attendants, and they looked as if they didn't believe what they saw. Not in the junk pile now overhead.

Of course we expected him to come in for a landing. I thought if that wreck holds together when he sets it down, we can dash over and get our checks back and everybody will be happy.

But instead of coming in, he shot back up into the sky, giving the popping little engine full throttle. Our stomachs collectively flew back up with him. Up high he went into a number of fancy Immelmann turns, spun several times, and performed all kinds of dangerous maneuvers. Then when he was only a couple of hundred feet off the ground, he leveled off and raced across the field upside down. I was certain my hair must have turned gray from the ordeal of watching. All five of us cussed loudly but fruitlessly, calling ourselves every known kind of jackass for voluntarily offering ourselves as candidates for a prison farm. We had reached the point where we didn't give a damn what happened to the Black Eagle. Had there been some way to yank the craft away and give it back to the airport manager, leaving Julian still flapping around in the air, we would have gladly done it. He had convinced us all he was a fine flyer, as well as an excellent stunt pilot, so what in hell was he still trying to prove?

Finally, after what seemed like the passage of two millenniums, he returned to earth, landing the junk heap so beautifully that the airport manager felt compelled to tell us with awe and admiration that he had never seen anybody set down more smoothly.

Collectively we sighed with relief and ran over to Julian to praise him for his exhibition and then bawl him out for doing tricks and scaring us out of our wits. We pulled up short when we saw his face completely covered with a thick, dripping layer of oil.

"That scrap heap even had a broken feed line," he explained, wiping off the muck.

"Then why did you do all that fancy stuff?" I asked. "Didn't that make it even more dangerous?"

"Of course. But I couldn't let you down. I just wanted to show you I was at home in the air."

He had proved his point, even though it left five spectators on the verge of a nervous breakdown. We retrieved our checks and immediately tore them up. From then on when anybody doubted Col. Hubert Julian's ability to actually pilot a plane I could tell them I knew personally of his proficiency, for I had risked time on a Georgia chain-gang so he could prove it.

47

The letter, in an unfamiliar, feminine handwriting, bore a return address on Chicago's Gold Coast. It was mixed in with my regular mail this spring morning in 1933. Opening this innocent-looking envelope was like opening Pandora's Box, for it introduced me to the most fantastic female I have ever known.

Her name was Frances. Recently she had become acquainted with people on the South Side, where she by accident stumbled across a copy of *Abbott's Monthly* containing my poem, "Chicago's Congo." She was so amazed, considering me a "masculine extension" of herself, that she could not rest until she learned how to contact me. Before I had time to answer her first letter, she wrote two more, telling me all about herself. She said her father had once run for president on a Silver ticket.[14] Frances was thirty-four, of mixed Indian and Caucasian ancestry, had a twelve-year-old son, and was currently married to a yachtsman who was "a husband in name only." Pictures were included.

I was speedily turned on. During my two years in Atlanta I had written no poetry. But under her interest and stimulus, the creative flame was rekindled. I sent her new work for suggestions and criticism, and she sent me samples of her own. Soon she told me I ought to ready my work for publication. She would find a publisher.

A relationship based on a mutual appreciation for poetry rapidly changed character. Daily I received lengthy letters; by late spring she started calling me long distance at least once a week. She loved jazz music and Duke Ellington especially, was ultra-sophisticated, and lived the kind of Bohemian life I had long dreamed of having.

Frankly, I was completely vulnerable to the overtures of an aggressive white woman. Raw from the biting lash of Dixie racism, it soothed me to smile to myself and think, "You crackers believe I'm some kind of ape, but emotionally involved with me is one of your own precious women, and a woman of obvious culture at that." Undoubtedly Governor Gene Talmadge would die of apoplexy if he knew one of his black untouchables was called regularly from Chicago by one of his ethnic sisters. I admit freely that revenge against the white world was originally a major ingredient in my relationship with Frances. But as I came to know her, this angle vanished.

Yet this did not affect my basic attitude toward Thelma. Despite her many attributes, she did not fill all my emotional and intellectual needs, and I doubted that any one woman could. Thelma did not relate to me in a creative way, whereas Frances was able to walk inside my poetry and make herself at home. I felt a need for both. In a monogamous society, I therefore had to maneuver as best I could.

The World's Fair opened in Chicago late that spring. Since I had been away two and a half years, I told Thelma I was going to visit Dad and Edith for a couple of weeks in late summer.

Of course I spent most of my vacation with Frances, who had told her husband she was visiting friends in Michigan. She had already gone out voluntarily to meet Dad and Edith. I also met her son, who took a liking to me, as well as a number of her personal friends who evidently had come to expect anything from her. Within two days she announced she wanted to take me to Paris. Although I often dreamed of living in this mecca of creative artists, a place without the awful stench of American color prejudice, I had no intention of breaking with Thelma. I preferred keeping the existing arrangement and returned to Atlanta.

Also I was interested in seeing what W. A. would get into next. Scott had temporarily shelved the idea of dailies for Baltimore and Washington.

Instead he dreamed of a chain of grocery stores all over Dixie. Although this was not my field, I knew I would be of value in promoting such a challenging venture. Meanwhile he had rid himself of wife number three, Ella Ramsey, a beauty shop operator. Later he married Agnes Maddox, a quiet young woman who worked in the office.

Despite his power, W. A. was frowned upon by the black social register. A gal ruined her reputation merely by riding alone with him in his car. The Maddox family did not look with glee upon their new in-law. Shortly W. A. began carrying a gun.

Retaining grudges, he was determined to kick his third wife out of the Odd Fellows Building where her beauty parlor was located. To do this he would have to buy the edifice, largest black building in Dixie. He made a big down payment preparatory to taking title. That same night around two o'clock I was awakened by Bill Kelley, circulation manager. Scott had been shot and was in the hospital. I dressed hurriedly and accompanied Kelley there.

W. A. fully expected to recover. He would not reveal to us the name of his assailant, intending to "take care of him" when he got well. Instead he died within a few days. A year or so later a brother of his last wife was arrested and tried, but won freedom. Officially the murder is still unsolved.

After much maneuvering, the estate was settled. Cornelius Scott, a younger brother who had attended the University of Illinois, became general manager. Competent and likeable, he lacked the daring and vision of W. A., and I gradually lost interest in the *World*. Another factor, of course, is that I no longer received the extra fifteen dollars weekly, although during the Depression a weekly paycheck of thirty-five dollars was an enviable income. Living costs were unbelievably low; I paid only ten bucks for one of the finest all-worsted wool suits I ever owned.

Meanwhile I realized that the longer I stayed in Atlanta, the more docile I became. Now I accepted with Dixie patience indignities which burned me up when I first arrived. I was in danger of allowing southern racism to erode my manhood. Also Frances was bombarding me with pleas to return to Chicago. Somehow she had won the ear of Congressman Arthur W. Mitchell, who rode the Roosevelt landslide and ousted Oscar DePriest. If I came back, she said, she would get me on his staff at a good salary. Then, after my book came out, we would go to Paris.

I still had no desire to break with Thelma, but I did want to retain my thing with Frances. That summer I again vacationed in Chicago, the same week she again "visited" friends in Michigan. But the night before I was to return to Georgia, Frances pulled out a detailed dossier on my wife's amorous escapades obtained by hiring a detective agency. It was a traumatic shock, as Frances had anticipated, for like most husbands then, I was hung up on the double standard. I felt perfectly justified in owning a harem and also righteously indignant if my spouse looked twice at another male. This cinched it. I decided to remain in Chicago and sent a wire to the *World* and Thelma.

I noticed, however, that Frances suddenly became excessively jealous. A couple of weeks passed before I learned the reason. She'd had the poor judgement to bet a brownskin beauty from the famous Cotton Club chorus, then visiting a sister in Chicago, that the chorine could not seduce me. I need not tell you Frances lost with a bang, if you'll pardon the pun. She said later it wasn't the hundred dollars, it was the principle of the thing.

Actually I was glad of what I considered a legitimate excuse to remain in the Windy City. Despite its dirt and brutality, the Lake Michigan metropolis was far and away my favorite town. Frances, who had recently sold a small business she owned, was delighted. Now, she said, she could devote her full time to helping me put finishing touches to my first book. First of all she convinced her husband we needed an office on the South Side where I could do public relations work and help her revise a trunk full of her own manuscripts ("You know, darling, I told you how amazingly alike our styles of writing are. Frank's the only one in the whole world who could help me," she told him). Renting half the office occupied by a hard-up attorney in the Regal Building at 47th and South Parkway, we set up shop where we "worked" virtually every evening until around midnight.

Usually we dined each night at Poro College where she had managed to meet and become friendly with Madame Mallone, founder of that system of beauty culture.[15] Once she persuaded a Loop woman's advertising club to hold its monthly dinner meeting at Poro where she treated the guests to such exotic mental fare as a talk by Jack Johnson (who she had also contrived to meet) and a reading of some of my poems. Although of course Li'l Arthur was well past his prime, his reputation still fascinated women.

She introduced me to W. C. Handy who was then in Chicago preparing for the annual Chicago *Tribune* 1934 music festival at colossal Soldier Field. We spent a number of memorable evenings with the noted composer, who was even then almost totally blind, and for several years afterward I carried on a sporadic correspondence with him. The "Father of the Blues" was one of the warmest and friendliest persons I have ever met, with a rare portfolio of stories based on personal experiences, all of which he told beautifully.

He spoke of the early part of the century when he toured Mississippi as leader of a small dance band playing for rednecks. One of the favorite tunes of the day was "If The Man In The Moon Was A Coon." He received many requests nightly for this number replete with a unison vocal by the musicians. This created no special problems early in the evening, but as the hour grew late and the male dancers became drunk, they would gather in front of the band waiting. As the singers finished the line, "if the man in the moon was a coon, what would you do," the listeners, almost as if on signal, would draw revolvers and empty them—at the moon. The point was obvious.

He insisted that few blacks in small southern towns had ever sat through a complete showing of the film *Birth Of A Nation*. "And for a very good reason," he explained. "Of course all the colored people had to sit way up high in the top balcony. There never was any trouble during the first part of the movie. But as you know, it becomes more inciting as it grinds along. At last would come that sequence, supposedly during Reconstruction, showing black men chasing white women through fields. Invariably ofay men in the audience, sitting on the first floor, would turn and look menacingly up at black faces peering down from the balcony. The closer black men in the film came to catching the frightened and screaming white women, the meaner would grow the faces of these white men downstairs and the more frequent their increasingly baleful glances back and up. And by the time a black man on the screen finally laid his paws on the poor helpless white woman, the audience down below would be hopping mad. They'd rise up in their seats as one and turn toward the balcony with fire in their eyes—only to find the balcony suddenly empty. The colored people were no fools. They knew the time had come to 'take low.'"

We spent many evenings together, Frances and I, at the little cabarets between 22nd and 35th, particularly a cozy spot featuring Bertha "Chippie" Hill, the famous earthy blues shouter, along with a female impersonator who called himself "The Sepia Mae West." His real name was Dick Barrows, and he came from southern California where he had attended medical school before detouring into the entertainment field.

Built like a wrestler or a Big Ten football tackle, he had on occasion bare-handedly cleaned out the cafe where he appeared when angered by heck-lers. His great joy, however, was his extensive wardrobe of costly and exquisite gowns. Coiffured, rouged, bejewelled, and bedecked in filmy silk and satin, his transvestite king-size version of the movie queen was unquestionably spectacular. He also created confusion; although he re-putedly had a weakness for half-pint males, he shacked up with a very sexy German girl.

A month or so after receiving my telegram, Thelma arrived in Chi-cago. Frances had already told me that Thelma was not willing to accept my telegram breaking off our relationship and intended to discuss our situation in person. She also knew when Thelma was leaving Atlanta and would reach Chicago; her private eye was on the job. When Thelma arrived, I avoided her for several days and then, over Frances's violent and frantic objections, we met.

I was still quite fond of Thelma, and had not decided what position to take. But when she told me she had known all along of my affair with Frances (her friends at the *World* office kept her informed of the daily letters and frequent long-distance calls) and had remained silent expecting me to get over it, my sense of the ludicrous forced me to reject the wronged-husband role. We decided to resume living together at a later date. Meanwhile she would return to Atlanta where she now had a job.

It had also occurred to me I could not logically oppose one kind of discrimination and support another. If I fought privilege based on color, I could not conscientiously demand privilege based on sex. To a modern, emancipated woman, male chauvinism is as offensive as white chauvinism to a black American. If I objected to being treated as if I were owned by Caucasians, a woman could rightfully object to being treated as a male possession. From then on, I rejected the double standard.

Generally speaking, black women have long been more sexually liberated than their male counterparts. During slavery they were not only forced to bed their masters but breed with powerful studs, like cattle, in the hope of producing physically strong offspring; but this was forced behavior. I refer instead to a more realistic attitude toward sex as a surviv-ing Africanism and to the economics of black existence. Traditionally, white women have married for security after being taught coitus was a dirty ordeal to which they must submit. This systematic repression of natural urges resulted in frigidity from which white women have escaped in sizeable numbers only since the spread of the continuing sex revolt.

There had been far less of this hang-up in the black world. With Afro-American males customarily the last hired and first fired, with vast numbers both underemployed and underpaid when they have jobs, prospects of marrying for security are far fewer. Our women, knowing for generations that usually they must work to help make ends meet and because they often were forced to raise their families alone, long ago developed sexual independence. The economic facts of life dictated that the soul sister should satisfy her natural desires for sex just as she took care of natural desires for food and sleep, instead of waiting for some knight in shining armor to carry her off to a castle where she could live happily ever after sheltered from the cruel outside world. It is no coincidence that sexual freedom among white women has increased as they broke away from home and took jobs; the two seem to go hand in hand. There has never been much black frigidity except among women of the small middle class who have blindly aped white cultural patterns, no matter how absurd, for they were the only ones likely to get husbands with whom they could trade virginity for security.

That is why Bessie Smith could sing, and black women share her feeling, in "Young Women's Blues," recorded in 1926:

> I'm a young woman and ain't done runnin' round
>
> . . . .
>
> I ain't gonna marry, ain't gonna settle down
> I'm gonna drink good moonshine an' run these browns down
>
> . . . .
>
> I'm a good woman an' I can get plenty of men. . . .

Ideas such as these had little practical application to the mainstream of white life at that time. Today, over fifty years later, with barriers lowered they begin to have general validity in the white world. Caucasian erotic attitudes are growing closer to those long held by blacks.

Editor of the Atlanta *World*. Photograph used with permission of the Frank Marshall Davis Estate.

1935–1948

48

Frances found a publisher on the North Side, Norman W. Forgue, owner of the Black Cat Press. From his background he was one of the last persons one would associate with fine books. A smiling young Irishman, he was an ex-sailor and had been welterweight boxing champion of the U.S. Navy. As a civilian, his passion was for creating beautiful books. He had the attitude of an artist; he would rather produce an aesthetically pleasing book than hit the best-seller lists with a tome that looked mass-made. Although Forgue had only meager resources, he agreed to publish my volume on a royalty basis. If it made a few dollars, well and good, but if not he would have the satisfaction of bringing out the kind of fine book he felt the contents demanded.

I met Hal, Frances's husband. Many a normally intelligent Caucasian husband often loses his mental balance when introduced to a black male by his wife. Either he sees the soul stud as a rapist of all white women, or he finds it impossible to believe his mate would even dream of having an affair with one so obviously his inferior. Hal belonged to the second category. He seemed genuinely glad to know me, particularly after my book was published. Somehow he had the idea that I was "the first Negro ever to write a book."

This superior attitude had its virtues, for I was able to walk above suspicion. However, I do not doubt that Frances would have found a way to handle anything which arose. Not only was she in control of most situations, but she had herself been a former newspaperwoman and knew enough about local, national, and world figures to issue her own *Confidential*. I was particularly fascinated by her reminiscences about a Judge Frank Comerford, then deceased, who had been an outstandingly successful criminal lawyer. He had married the widowed heiress to an automobile fortune, only to request an annulment when, on his wedding night, he learned he was expected to share the bridal suite with the ashes of her deceased husband resting in a golden urn on the dresser.

A dignified, stern, and powerful-looking man, well over six feet tall, with a massive Great Dane for a pet, Judge Comerford had one hellish torture invoked each summer on black men.

Hiring a voluptuous young blonde or redhead from a burlesque show and dressing her in a some flimsy, frilly frock, he had her follow him to one of the city parks bordering the Black Belt. Strolling until he saw some lone soul stud reposing on a bench in an isolated area, he would take a seat nearby, the Great Dane at his feet, open a daily paper, and signal his accomplice.

Looking as if she were taking an innocent walk alone, the girl would sit leisurely down on the grass some ten feet away from the dusky victim, facing him. Leaning back and relaxing on her elbows, taking a deep breath, her dress "accidentally" rose above her knees. Since she was not permitted to wear panties, immediately it became a moment of naked truth.

The unsuspecting man might have come to the park to get away from women following an argument with his sweetheart or wife. Or maybe he was jobless and craved peace and quiet as he tried to plot a course out of the economic jungle. Possibly he was planning something important and needed solitude to concentrate. Maybe he was a recent migrant from the South enjoying for the first time the comparative freedom of the North. Could be he simply loved nature and wanted trees and grass and open air.

But no matter what his reasons, they speedily faded. A normal man would stand a better chance of ignoring a stick of dynamite exploding beneath his bed than an alluring, sexy showgirl, dressed up, thighs parted, and enticingly bare where it counted. To make matters worse, this devastating distraction was little more than an arm's length away.

Naturally, the brother became violently aroused. His thoughts beamed like a powerful spotlight on the anatomy revealed before him. Automatically, he looked around. Sitting unsmiling on a bench some twenty or more feet away and off to one side was a huge, distinguished-looking white man with a giant dog. Whatever he might have intended on saying to the provocative broad died a-borning. After years of conditioning, a black man doesn't make advances to a strange white woman in a public park with a stern-looking white man and a mean-looking dog within earshot. So he looked back to the girl. By now she was smiling invitingly at him. Up jetted his temperature again. And when he stole another glance at the white man, Judge Comerford would have folded his paper and been staring coldly in his direction. By now the dusky victim's face would reveal the strain of his internal tug of war between desire and the gal who aroused him and fear of violence from the white man and his dog if he made a pass. He struggled within as long as he could stand it, then arose and doddered away, his nerves completely shot.

49

Despite the artistic stimulation, my relationship with fantastic Frances began to pale. I felt as if I were living in a glass cage. After Thelma returned to Atlanta, we began corresponding. With her connections, Frances repeated to me verbatim what I wrote in my letters to Thelma as well as what Thelma wrote to me. If I took a second look at some desirable darling, within two days Frances would reveal to me her entire history since conception to show this was nobody on whom I should waste one moment of my time. Should some babe indicate she might welcome more than a nodding acquaintance with me, Frances found an excuse to introduce herself and put down such a way-out spiel that the chick was scared into a six-inch thick shell.

In order to avoid complete dependence and get away from her all-seeing eye, I went back to the Gary *American* for a day and a half each week to do a fast editing job, staying overnight at Fritz Alexander's home. The Depression still roared around Chicago. However, Roosevelt's New Deal experiments made hard times more bearable among the jobless. With the end of Prohibition, bootlegging was no longer big business. Some of those who had operated speakeasies now ran taverns at the same locations and with the same customers. Competition was intense for loose cash. Beer drinkers never had it so good. Shouting window signs proclaimed, "32 oz. for Ten Cents." On certain days, bars offered free lunches; by watching schedules, beer lovers could keep full bellies and bladders at little cost by trotting from neighborhood to neighborhood.

On 47th near Indiana, a restaurant operated by an extrovert who called himself "Dreamy-Eyed Sweet Black" became one of the South Side's biggest money makers. Clean and classier looking than most of the area's cafes, its prices were ridiculously low even for then. Fifteen cents bought a well-cooked and tasty meal of soup, boiled turnips or beans with bacon, hot bread, and coffee. A two-bit meal gave you a choice of roast pork, roast beef, or meat loaf, plus salad and dessert. A juicy steak cooked to order and served with all the trimmings set you back only thirty-five cents. The shrewd owner obviously depended on volume for his profit, and he got it.

Sometimes with only a few customers present, he leaped on the counter, walked from one end to the other and beat Tarzan-like on his chest, shouting, "This is Dreamy-Eyed Sweet Black. I want you all to know me anywhere you see me." Nobody seemed to mind this or any of his other exhibitions. Good food at low prices plus several unusually attractive waitresses brought in the business. Sweet Black, unfortunately, had a weakness for flashy cars. This led to his undoing, for while traveling through Indiana at high speed, he was killed in a crash. Without his peculiar personality, the restaurant folded soon afterward.

50

My first book, *Black Man's Verse,* appeared in summer of 1935. Beautifully bound and printed, the price tag of three dollars was a lot of money during the Depression. I knew few novels sold well and poetry had an even smaller market. I hoped Norman Forgue would at least get back his investment. As for me, I wanted critical recognition. Luckily we got both, particularly after several influential critics, including Harriet Monroe of *Poetry* magazine and William Rose Benét of the *Saturday Review of Literature,* printed high praise.[1] I was now an Author with a certain prestige—but my wallet was as flat as ever.

A few months later I joined the staff of the Associated Negro Press (ANP) where I was to remain for thirteen years. Percival Prattis had just left ANP to become an editor of the Pittsburgh *Courier.* I was at last in a position to be completely independent of Frances, for the relationship had become too nerve-wracking. Jobs were still scarce; even the two wealthy and powerful Hearst dailies paid some reporters only fifteen dollars weekly and required them to use waste newsprint for paper towels. Even with my experience and reputation as a newspaperman, getting any kind of work in my field during these dark days of the Depression was a real achievement.

Irene Roland, a provocatively plumpish yellow gal from Mississippi, was secretary and office manager—a job she held at ANP when I first went to Chicago and maintained until the agency closed its doors in 1964. Except for occasional contributions from the director, Claude Barnett, most of the actual writing fell to Charles Stewart and myself, with the editing speedily becoming my exclusive province.

Stewart was an eternal bottle baby, ready to pounce on anything that gurgled. He was short and chunky with a cherubic face, but you could find something softer than Charlie in any rock pile. He was spoken of with awe in Atlanta. While an officer at Fort Benning, Georgia, during World War I he had once beaten up two honky cops on Auburn Avenue and had gotten away with it—a hell of a feat even for a Caucasian.

Nationally known leaders in various fields submitted regular columns to ANP, but most of our material came from correspondents all over America, the Caribbeans, Africa, and some parts of Europe, including London and Moscow. Usually small space rates were paid, although some, such as Nancy Cunard, maverick heiress to a steamship fortune, wrote because they had ideas that begged for exposure.[2] ANP prided itself on mirroring black activities everywhere. Occasionally, we missed a good story, but considering the lack of adequate funds, coming primarily from subscribing newspapers, many of them financially shaky, I still marvel at the comprehensiveness of our operations.

With all our members, except the Atlanta *Daily World* and a few of its twice-a-week Scott Newspaper Syndicate (SNS) affiliates publishing only once a week, we sent most of our news airmail special delivery to subscribing newspapers. The major release went out Friday afternoon, with a shorter deadline release following on Monday. We kept a record of each member's publication day and wired or telephoned important last-minute news to those requesting this special service. Irene Roland supervised extra workers who came in Friday and Monday for mimeographing and mailing. During WPA days, a special crew was assigned to help bring our library up to date.

I personally edited or rewrote every item released. In addition, each week I read virtually every black newspaper in the nation, from thirty-five to forty key dailies from every section of America, leading magazines, foreign publications printed in English, and the ambitious efforts of would-be journalists. It was essential that I know what was happening to black people everywhere as well as remember names and past events; I needed to be an ambling encyclopedia as well as a writer. Luck sat with me. In those instances when there was not time to check for accuracy, if an event occurred thousands of miles away, I had to rely on intuition and hope I was right or play it safe and lose a week or more while waiting to check it out. My judgment, frankly, was usually correct for I was able to avoid that bane of newspaperdom—the libel suit.

On joining ANP I began writing a theatrical column under the name of Franklyn Frank, enabling me again to chronicle the show world and bathe in hot jazz. A favorite haunt was the Club DeLisa at 55th and State where the house band was headed by Albert Ammons, one of the giants of boogie woogie piano. A perpetual star was an exotic dancer known simply as Valda who packed in both men and women to see her nearly nude dances under soft, deeply colored lights. I described her in print as a young woman whose hips "were so educated they must have earned a Ph.D." And yet, strangely enough for me, I could not become personally interested. Wearing little more than a promise when she danced, in her dressing room she was a model of coy decorum taking care to keep her skirt hem beneath her knees.

When Valda had become convinced I was not on the make, I became her confidante. She described many of her amorous adventures, including a session one night after work with a well-dressed, personable stranger in a Loop hotel. "I don't really know who he was," she told me, "but let's say he could pass for Clark Gable anywhere." Once, assuming I had white connections, she asked me to make dates for her away from the black compound at a goodly percentage of the contemplated large take.

A few blocks away from the DeLisa, on 55th near the El, was Dave's Cafe, a roaring brightery with a balcony for those who liked to look down upon the proletariat. Not a hot spot, but only a couple of streets south was a Chinese restaurant remembered for the proprietor's name painted in big, bold letters on the window, Tung Me Lo. Now if only some wag had placed nearby a sign advertising that new St. Louis beer whose name made eyebrows lift! It was the brew known as Griesedieck (pronounced Greasy Dick).

A transplanted New Orleans musician, François Mosely, headed the band at Dave's until replaced by a small combo led by Ray Nance. Later Ray joined Duke Ellington where he starred for many years on trumpet and violin. One November night, I went to Dave's to catch the debut of a new dancer. She was only seventeen, lithe, and lovely, and as catlike as any woman I ever saw. Born Bernice Bruce, she took the stage name of Tanya in order not to be identified with her sisters, then rulers of the terpsichorean roost. As soon as she began her opening performance, I knew she had what it took. A genuine contortionist, she could make a pretzel neurotic. I forthwith launched a publicity buildup, believing there was gold in them thar brownskin hills. Despite the fact that most scribes who saw her wanted to boost her career without fee, I was able to maintain a professional relationship throughout her career.

She toured for several years with stage shows headed by Ellington, Cab Calloway, and others, retiring when she tired of fighting off an army of all-nations admirers, including an Arabian who got his kicks from biting her big toe. Like many show people, she was a nut on astrology and numerology, finally changing her stage name to Sanya because Tanya "no longer vibrated correctly."

Another interesting haunt was the Cabin Inn at 33rd and State, a house of impersonators where all the "boys" were "girls" and vice versa. When I entered the large common female dressing room to interview some performer, the rest of the gals thought nothing of peeling to their skins, walking around completely naked or with bare breasts, and changing costumes as if I were not there. I held no interest for these assorted dykes. But when I went to the men's dressing room, the air filled with giggling and nervous laughter as the "girls" coyly covered themselves. Often I left the Cabin Inn so confused I walked two blocks north before realizing I should have headed south.

I also maintained my interest in sports. When Oze Simmons of Iowa flashed like a meteor into the Big Ten football constellation, I dug into my alliteration bag and came out with "the hula-hipped Hawkeye hoghide handler"—a name which took more time to pronounce than many of his sensational touchdown runs. The star gridder (he had a brother, Don, who was almost as good) had been a 9.8 century sprinter in high school down Texas way, was quite shifty, and had one special trick which often demoralized the opposition. When it seemed Oze was about to be cornered in the open field, he put on the brakes and thrust the football toward the would-be tackler, who almost invariably reached for it. In that split second, Simmons cut away before the opponent could recover his wits. I believe he would have been an all-time great in the National Football League. But the pros then had a rigid color bar, erected after Duke Slater and Smokey Joe Lillard of the Chicago Cardinals quit the game and maintained until World War II.[3]

Another moniker I gave out was for Joe Louis. When he began his fabulous career after creating a sensation in the 1934 Golden Gloves tournament, I called him "the heavyweight to end all heavyweights"—a description which retained accuracy for some ten years.

51

In March of 1936 Frances told me she, her husband, and son were moving to California. I felt no regrets; our relationship had now deteriorated to no more than occasional telephone calls. A month after Frances left, I heard from Thelma for the first time in more than a year. She was now working in Washington, D.C., and wrote she wanted to spend a week with me in Chicago. The timing was a little too pat for these twin developments to be a mere coincidence, but I could never prove otherwise.

We took a small apartment on South Parkway at 38th. One of our neighbors, named Leo, worked for a large Loop optical firm with suburban branches. Until then I had had no interest in photography, but shortly Leo started bringing me camera magazines and I was hooked. He then brought me an inexpensive folding camera and sold me roll after roll of film and basic darkroom equipment at only a fraction of retail cost. I learned how to develop and print. I could not afford an enlarger, but after I shot Tanya in costume she was so pleased with the results she ordered two hundred copies for her fans. When close figuring showed I could pay for an enlarger from this job, I bought the cheapest and spent every night for two weeks turning out her blowups.

As I gained confidence behind the lens, I turned to nudes. Obviously, the female body fascinates me, both aesthetically and emotionally. The steatopygian aspect (I use the word advisedly) of black women pleases me; lack of an adequately outstanding (another apt adjective) derriere is my chief complaint against the majority of Caucasian women. However, brown thighs are sometimes too heavy proportionately for my personal ideal of beauty. But other attributes being desirable, I never let that stop me. If breasts, waist, legs, and face were pleasing, I simply posed them to minimize bad features and accentuated the positive.

I was amazed at the number of gals eager to strip and stand unclothed before the all-seeing eye of the camera. Sometimes husbands brought their wives to pose nude—apparently so that in later years when mates developed middleaged spread they could look back with graphic nostalgia on what used to be. Thelma was helpful in getting models. She had no hesitancy about asking a shapely gal to have her picture taken with nothing on her but lights. Usually Thelma was present, but that would have made no difference anyway.

I forget personal sex when I photograph a nude woman. Before me is an object with contours and a wide range of tones. My problem is how best to use lights, shadows, backgrounds, etc., to mold all into an aestheti-cally pleasing picture. The model might as well be made of marble, leather, or hay. Until I realized my subjects were not as detached as the photographer, I thought nothing of using my hands to move a breast or a thigh to a position where it would best photograph. No matter how appealing the model under normal conditions, I become a robot in back of a camera. I have no male reaction until I develop negatives and make prints. I find many other serious photographers share this attitude.

A couple of days before the Joe Louis–King Levinsky fight, which I was to cover for ANP, Leo showed up with a 35 mm Leica and urged me to use it.[4] I looked at this beautiful and expensive camera, sighed, and handed it back. I was not ready then for anything so complicated. At that time I could not have operated the original Argus without a guide. He returned it to the store.

Leo was not the only employee "borrowing" from the optical firm. Actually, he was a piker compared with others. Some had fully equipped deluxe darkrooms at home with the finest still and cinema equipment on the market. The company liquidated its photographic department when an inventory showed some fifty thousand dollars in merchandise had unaccountably disappeared. Ironically enough, Leo lost his job sometime later but not for taking camera equipment. He sent away to New York to buy a revolver by mail and paid for it with postage stamps. To make matters worse, he used a company envelope. The quantity of stamps was so large the suspicious gun firm wrote back to confirm the order, which of course uncovered the pilferage.

As years passed I prided myself on my versatility as a newspaperman. I served not only as straight news reporter but as rewrite man, editor, editorial writer, political commentator, theatrical and jazz columnist, sports writer, and occasionally news photographer. I liked sports, particu-larly basketball, football, track, and boxing.

I covered the first annual National Professional Basketball Tourna-ment, promoted on a thin shoestring at the Chicago Coliseum in 1939. It proved so popular that the next year the Hearst afternoon daily took over and continued sponsorship until the growth of the National Basketball Association during World War II made the event impractical. In the mid-1930s, there was no league worthy of the name; most teams were indepen-dent, and what passed as a pro league operated with such queer playing rules that it was ignored in droves by the public.

The renowned New York Celtics still existed, but the two best teams in the nation were black, the New York Rens out of Harlem and the Harlem Globetrotters out of Chicago.[5] In Atlanta I had watched the Rens on their annual barnstorming tours and had sat openmouthed staring at the wizardry of Fats Jenkins, Tarzan Cooper, Zack Clayton, Wee Willie Smith, Bill Yancey, Casey Holt, and Bruiser Saitch. In that era a player standing six feet four was an oddity; today a college team without a couple of players at least six feet eight leaves a coach crying the blues.

The Rens' specialty was blinding speed and passing. When comfortably ahead of their opponents, they staged a dazzling passing exhibition. So swiftly did they whip the ball from one player to another that often competing athletes quit and, placing hands on hips, watched as if they were spectators. The Rens maneuvered into position for sure lay-ups, then passed the ball back out rather than take a shot. There was no twenty-four-second rule, and a team could control a ball an entire quarter without shooting. Minutes often went by with no attempt made to shoot a goal, yet no Ren would hold the ball longer than a second or two. Wee Willie Smith, tallest Ren and center, often placed such a fantastic spin on the sphere with his huge hands that it would curve when it bounced off the floor toward another Ren.

The Globetrotters, then as now, put on an entirely different kind of show. They clowned, mixing basketball with football, baseball, sleight of hand, juggling, and just plain monkey business—but within the rules. There were no stooge teams. All opponents were sincerely interested in beating the Globetrotters, who also waited until they had the game safely tucked away before reverting to their crowd-pleasing antics. The Globetrotters usually played white teams in the central western states; the Rens roamed primarily in the East and South meeting black teams exclusively in Dixie.

The Rens and Globetrotters met in the finals of this first National Professional Basketball tourney. Never before had they played each other and there was strong speculation as to which was better. Of course, both had put on their usual exhibitions in the early rounds, but from the semifinals on it was hard and straight basketball. Neither team had time to clown. And in the finals, before a packed house, the Rens won. For the first three years, the championship went to either the Rens or the Globetrotters. It was the fourth tournament before a white team turned the trick.

I think the initial success of the Rens and the Globetrotters in a national test of strength was the first step toward breaking the color barrier in this pro sport. Until then, teams were usually all-black or all-white. After the first few annual tournaments, they started showing up with mixed personnel. One of the black stars was Dolly King, who had been a shining light at Long Island University. The rest of his squad was white. The following year, wholesale raiding took place as competing fives presented the best talent money could buy in an effort to win the title and the prestige which went with it. A tournament team often bore little resemblance to the aggregation that had competed all year. The Rens surprised spectators by showing up with a couple of former Globetrotters; the Globetrotters took the floor with a brace of ex-Rens. An independent team from Cleveland appeared with Wee Willie Smith of the Rens and Babe Pressley of the Globetrotters, a truly great guard, plus three white stars. Meanwhile the interest aroused by the annual tournament revived the pro league and resulted in integrated teams and the spectacular kind of game familiar today. In the 1940s the Rens ran into serious financial problems. Finally Abe Saperstein bought them and combined their top players with his Globetrotters, thus bringing an end to the story of an almost legendary hardwood aggregation.[6]

52

In 1936 America got swing religion. The messiah who fed and then converted the multitudes was Benny Goodman.

Goodman became known as the "King of Swing" because he was white and therefore acceptable to the white public. Most jazz critics know there were several bands superior to Goodman's, among them those of Duke Ellington, Fletcher Henderson, Chick Webb, Jimmy Lunceford, and McKinney's Cotton Pickers. But these bands were black and therefore merely "quaint." The white public would accept and identify only with a white band that copied Afro-American music.

It had been that way when jazz began in the South. Early pioneers such as Buddy Bolden, Freddy Keppard, Bunk Johnson, and Jelly Roll Morton had no standing in the white world. They produced only "low nigger music." White America refused to accept it until the white Original Dixieland Jazz Band came north from New Orleans in the World War I era. That this group was sadly inferior to black New Orleans bands meant nothing. No matter how poor an imitation, whites had to learn how to play it before the nation would listen.

To say that whites would not accept jazz because of its red-light beginnings, as some writers would have you believe, is ridiculous. Fact is, whorehouse music came mainly from the piano; early jazz came from the streets and dance halls. Marching bands, parades, funeral processions, and horse-drawn advertising wagons all used these bands. They were a functioning, vital part of black life, especially in New Orleans.

Nobody knows where and when the first jazz was played. Why it came about is more easily explained. Jazz came into existence as a result of our unique status in America. African musical concepts, differing radically from the musical traditions of Europe, were the only ancestral art permitted to survive under slavery. With a distinctly different approach to rhythm, timing, and tonality, African music was basically functional, and this carried over into hymns, worksongs, and playsongs. Even when master and slave sang the same songs, observers in the eighteenth century detected a decided difference in their renditions. Spirituals, well-developed by emancipation, had a practical use as signals to leaders of the Underground Railroad. Because of their topical content and protest against untenable conditions, blues undoubtedly came into existence after the Civil War and nominal freedom; slaveowners would not have tolerated this type of music.

During the last quarter of the nineteenth century, the nation rapidly became industrialized. Railroads and new inventions accelerated the tempo of living. Black Americans, flocking to urban centers, for the first time had access to musical instruments denied them under bondage. But economically and socially, they were still low man on the totem pole—a condition which still exists. Even when able to buy Caucasian instruments (usually secondhand), most lacked the money for formal training. The early Afro-American bands therefore found self-taught musicians playing European instruments—and often European music—with African concepts that had survived under slavery.

Since traditional African music is functional, it was only logical that an oppressed minority blend what it valued of the music of the majority with its own concepts and extend the personal protest of the blues into the united protest of what came to be known as jazz music. Whites originally would not accept jazz because it was revolutionary, defying and rebelling against all the traditions built up in Western European music for several hundred years. Since it violated all their precious rules and originated among an "inferior" people, this new music itself had to be "inferior." But so strong and insistent was its assault against the boundaries of white culture, which tried to reject any values not established by itself, that shortly white musicians themselves turned to its radical new devices and began imitating black bands. Despite opposition from critics, schools, and musicians seeking to preserve the pale, narrow standards of traditional Western European music, the revolutionary concepts of jazz forced their way into the mainstream of American music.

Many of its best early white practitioners were members of minorities suffering, like us, from prejudice. It is no accident that Jews and Italians became excellent jazzicians. As for America generally, jazz signified the speedy tempo of life in big modern cities as contrasted with the slow pace of Old World existence. The democracy inherent in the jazz band and the equality of all its members became a national nosethumbing at the royalty and rigid class structure of Europe. Its new devices of tone, interval polyrhythms, and innovative use of various instruments along with the revival of improvisation (long a lost art in the music of Western Europe) shocked American traditionalists. At the same time it stimulated European composers who borrowed heavily from jazz and recognized it as the chief American contribution to the world artistic stream.

Although only grudgingly accepted even now by the die-hard champions of the musical status quo, the white American masses took jazz to their hearts when produced by whites who at best could render only a diluted product. The first "King of Jazz" was Paul Whiteman who played, in the main, popular music and produced jazz only when such sidemen as Bix Beiderbecke, Jack Teagarden, Frankie Trumbauer, Joe Venuti, and one or two others were showcased.

Nevertheless, jazz had been and still is one of our major weapons. In the beginning, New Orleans jazz (Dixieland is white jazz) said musically "Look, man, I may be black but I'll be damned if you'll keep me down because I'm as good as you any day." Jazz today is different from what it was at the turn of the century, but so is our overall position as a people. Today jazz generally blends far more with European music than it did in 1900, just as there is more blending or integration now with American life as a whole. Significantly, today there are growing numbers of angry black musicians who have turned to Africa and Asia for their musical inspiration. Their music has disturbed and upset many whites, just as have the angry black political activists with their complete rejection of the white world. Jazz is not only a weapon but a mirror of black thought.

Despite the improved position of the dusky musician in today's world and the acceptance of integrated bands, Afro-American jazzicians still suffer from discrimination, and racism continues to drive soul stars away from the land of their birth. But it was far worse in 1936 at the start of the swing era. And the irony is that, despite the restrictions imposed by the white world, jazz and entertainment were fields in which black Americans had the biggest opportunities.

Unfortunately there exists a tendency to put down what we haven't experienced. Many contemporaries acquainted only with Archie Shepp, John Coltrane, Ornette Coleman, and Pharoah Saunders look down their noses at such early giants as Buddy Bolden, Freddy Keppard, and King Oliver; yet the musical militancy of these pioneers shone as brightly within the framework of conditions that existed then, as do the breathtaking improvisations of the most inspired of today's jazzicians. The jazz of that period turned on the listeners of that period. That's where it was, man. As for me personally, nothing in all jazz has topped hearing Louis Armstrong challenge the whole world with his defiant horn back in the late 1920s and early 1930s, distilling the meaning of black in sharps and flats in a way he was incapable of telling it by words or actions. And there was Fats Waller, taking the pretty aural confections of Tin Pan Alley and shoving them back down the white world's throat, dipped in the sardonic salt and vitriol of black living.

Like most people, jazz musicians took a beating during the early years of the Depression. Even Sidney Bechet, the undisputed king of the soprano sax, was forced to make a living as a tailor. When white America finally found a white band playing the kind of music with which it could identify, the widespread acceptance proved a lifesaver for Afro-American stars such as Bechet and others. The increasing demand for more and more swing bands opened jobs in new areas. The success of the white imitator, Goodman, proved economically profitable to the originators.

Before long, Benny Goodman smashed the color barrier by hiring Teddy Wilson on piano. Never before had a white name leader attempted to front a mixed band. There had been integrated recording sessions in studios since Jelly Roll Morton cut sides with the white New Orleans Rhythm Kings some fifteen years earlier, but these were not public performances.

When Earl Hines went on tour, Fletcher Henderson brought a stupendous unit onto the Grand Terrace in Chicago. Such greats as Roy "Little Jazz" Eldridge, Buster Bailey, Chu Berry, John Kirby, Joe Thomas, and Big Sid Catlett were in the band. They had air time, sometimes immediately following Goodman who was playing in the Loop. Since

Benny used many Henderson arrangements, the listener could compare both groups, often on the same tune only minutes apart. The Goodman band had smoothness but lacked the subtlety, reserve, and controlled power of Big Smack's. I felt Benny's outfit constantly blew to capacity. As for individual soloists, Harry James and Gene Krupa were excellent but in all frankness neither was the equal of Eldridge or Catlett. Chu Berry was unchallenged on tenor sax, and the Goodman bassist was not the equal of Kirby. I concede Benny's superiority on blackstick, but that was all. Nevertheless, Goodman raked in heavy cash while Henderson had to be satisfied with peanuts. Meanwhile in Kansas City, Count Basie and Andy Kirk were attracting attention. Often at night I tuned in Hot Lips Page broadcasting from the Reno Club.

When Goodman reached California on his tour, his band was signed to appear in a movie with, among others, Martha Raye. After I learned the trio number with the comedienne had been canceled, I assumed it was due to prejudice on Miss Raye's part and so stated in my syndicated column. Shortly after I received a note from John Hammond setting me straight.[7] Miss Raye was far from prejudiced, he emphasized, and the trio sequence was cut not from racism but because their music was so overwhelming it outshone Martha's vocalizing. I was happy to send out a correction.

I knew of John Hammond by reputation. Born of wealthy parents, he was not only an apostle of good jazz but a tireless fighter against discrimination. More than any other person, he was responsible for launching the boogie-woogie craze which swept the nation in the mid-1930s. Discovering an obscure recording made by Meade "Lux" Lewis for a label which had since folded, he recognized the genius of the pianist and spent the next few years on an intensive search, finally locating him in Chicago where he was a cabdriver with his close friend, Albert Ammons.

Hammond straightway yanked him back into music. His new recordings caught the ear of Bob Crosby who had them arranged for full band featuring Bob Zurke on piano. The Crosby versions of "Yancey Special" and "Honky Tonk Train Blues" were immediate hits and started a fad for eight to the bar—still another instance of black music having to come down through whites before receiving general public acceptance.

Hammond was responsible for Benny Goodman breaking the color bar by first hiring Teddy Wilson and then Lionel Hampton. Slowly other bands followed down the interracial trail, sometimes with severe tribulations. Not only was integration fiercely opposed by many whites, but

highly vocal black nationalists also objected. Occasionally white bands-
men such as Harry James and Buddy Rich got into fistfights with white
racists over the presence of soul stars. However, integrated bands have
since then become commonplace. Hammond was also responsible for
bringing Basie out of Kansas City and for getting black musicians into
theater and network orchestras; because of his persistent championing of
our rights he was elected to the NAACP board of directors.

Shortly after our correspondence on the Martha Raye incident, Hammond came through Chicago and we talked for several hours. He told me
how black bands were being robbed by white managers, bookers, and
promoters. At that time, the only name leader with a thoroughly honest
adviser was Fletcher Henderson—and usually Big Smack ignored his
advice. I received some scornful looks from white managers when the
black bands they advised appeared.

Hammond also outlined his plans for history's first "Spirituals to
Swing" concert scheduled for Carnegie Hall late in 1938 and invited me
to be his guest in New York at this epoch-marking event. Unfortunately,
I could not accept. The Depression simply wouldn't let me.

53

Prior to the publication of *Black Man's Verse,* I had met few creative
writers, white or black. Afterward this changed. Harriet Monroe, who
seemed quite impressed with the volume, invited me to visit her at *Poetry,*
the most influential of such magazines, and I accepted. She was most
charming and gracious and asked me to submit material for possible use
in the monthly. With my usual time lag, she passed away before I got
around to sending in anything.

On one of his infrequent trips to Chicago, I met Langston Hughes.
Although he was only a few years older than I, he had been one of the
leaders in the Harlem Renaissance and already possessed a worldwide
reputation; I therefore considered him a writing generation ahead of me.
Small in stature, he was as warm and disarming in person as was his
writing. Although we never developed a really close friendship, we did
correspond, and Lang frequently went out of his way to see that I received
the honor that he felt was due me. But that was part of his character. Not
only did he help fellow writers but often contributed original work to
publications badly in need of a big name to attract attention.

In those days Lang was looked upon as Communist by the establishment. To those professing shock at some of his poetry, he once wrote, "my
work is not a pasture to feed all breeds of cattle." And while he was so
often highly controversial, his longtime friend and close associate, Arna
Bontemps, was not.

I first met Arna during this period, when he headed a WPA Writer's
Project. I knew he had won a coveted prize for poetry awarded by *Opportunity: A Journal of Negro Life* in the early 1920s. He was far more shy and
retiring than Langston, scrupulously avoiding personally anything tainted
with a touch of the radical. At the same time he was always able to work
well with those whose ideas were left of center, including Langston and
Jack Conroy.

During this period I became associated with Richard Wright. I first
heard of Dick when the National Negro Congress was organized at the
old Eighth Regiment Armory in 1936.[8] Enthusiastic leaders came from all
parts of America to launch what was intended as a mass civil rights
movement. The previous twelve months had witnessed the birth of the
CIO under John L. Lewis; at last black workers stood on the threshold of
recognition. The new National Negro Congress, with A. Philip Randolph, leader of the Pullman Porters, as its first president and guiding
genius, had the blessing of Lewis and the infant CIO.

The meeting was laced with leftists, and it was from them that I
heard the name of Richard Wright, a rising young poet whose work had
attracted attention in the *New Masses*. Ben Davis, Jr., was among those
active in the founding meeting, and for the first time I understood how it
feels to be a chameleon. Because we were both about the same size and
age, answered to the same last name and had been identified with Atlanta,
strangers walked up to me, shook my hand, and praised my handling of
the Angelo Herndon case. At the same time Ben was receiving compli-
ments for his first book of poems. And since both Richard Wright and I
lived in Chicago and wrote poetry, it was naturally assumed we knew
each other.

I did not meet him, however, until a few weeks after the congress
had adjourned. I was invited to join another of those writers' groups
which shoot up, burn brightly, then plummet back to earth. In addition
to Dick, the group had another member destined to achieve fame in
literature: Margaret Walker, later winner of a Yale award for her brilliant
book of poems, *For My People,* and more recently an outstanding novelist.
Another seemingly destined for greatness as a critic, Edward Bland, died

before reaching his goal. Both Miss Walker and Wright, incidentally, were members of the WPA Writers Project headed by Bontemps.[9]

Dick and I speedily developed a personal friendship that lasted until the publication of *Black Boy* in 1945. He was an extrovert, warm and outgoing with an often ribald sense of humor. He was also frank in his opinions, freely expressing what he liked and disliked of the work read before our group. By now he had already turned his attention almost exclusively to the short story. At one meeting he read "Big Boy Leaves Home," which was selected for *The New Caravan* and later appeared in his first volume of novellas, *Uncle Tom's Children*. I can still recall the impact of this magnificently vivid piece of writing. When he finished, nobody spoke for several minutes. We were too much moved by his power. Then there was a flood of praise. Frankly I was overwhelmed. We realized his was a major talent, but none of us dreamed how great he would become. I was also tremendously impressed by Margaret Walker—small, dark, and dynamic—who read us a chapter from a historical novel she had begun. It was obvious she also had an unusual gift for narration. I did not know at the time of her interest in poetry.

At another meeting I read "I Am The American Negro," the title poem for my next book. Wright's main criticism was what he called its "hopeless bitterness" and "lack of a positive resolution for the plight of black people." He said he would have had his giant crush all opposition. That was logical within his frame of reference as a Communist. He was sincere in his beliefs. Curious and fascinated, I asked many questions. Sometimes I noticed a furrowing of the brow when he carefully replied, as if some things disturbed him. Quite often I needled him about Communism, but he took it all good-naturedly. Later I learned why he often seemed unhappy when I talked about his activities. He felt his major contribution would be as a writer. He was temperamentally unfit for such tasks as handing out literature on street corners and organizing various kinds of action committees. It was a waste of his very special talents, and the growing resentment undoubtedly played no minor part in his open break with the party in 1944. After meeting Dick, I became acquainted with a number of other members gifted in the arts who flatly refused to accept assignments for which they considered themselves unfit; they stated frankly their value would be far greater to the party in the long run if they continued their uninterrupted development as artists rather than dissipating their energies in other fields. In several instances I know their position was completely correct.

A dozen or more South Siders regularly attended meetings of this writers' group until it broke up after rumors that some of the girl members were lesbians and had gotten into a dispute over still another chick. I mentioned the dissolution in a letter to Dr. Alain Locke of Howard University, the guru of the Harlem Renaissance of the early 1920s, who replied:

> I was looking forward to meeting the South Side Writers Group but have enough experience not to be surprised at the disintegration. It really is a morbid, almost psychopathic effect of prejudice; this suspicion, jealousy, and libidinous envy. I can only understand it as that, for I know the mask of the happy carefree Negro conceals deep hatred, cynical nihilism, etc. Its closest parallel perhaps was the Russians of the early Nihilist movement only they were intellectual; and that's what I can't forgive these Negro groups for; that their reactions are so lacking in rationalizations and are so snared in the purely emotional mire. The rumor about the Lesbian trap is priceless, if it weren't so sad from the point of view of action. I tried to integrate the first New Negro generation, and they just wouldn't; only Park Avenue teas and Harlem gin kept them from each other's throats.[10]

Despite the collapse of the South Side writers group, I met more and more persons vitally interested in creative literature, among them Fern Gayden, one of the most poised and gracious women I have ever seen, and Bill Attaway, a young novelist beginning to attract attention.[11] Earlier I had met his sister, Ruth, a talented actress, through Frances who once took me to a party in a thoroughly bohemian studio above a barn. Ruth left soon after for New York.

The most successful group on the South Side with which I was ever associated was the Allied Arts Guild, from 1938 to 1939. I think its success came largely from its assembling of people from various fields rather than from one, thus minimizing the possibility of jealousy. We held Sunday morning breakfast meetings at members' homes which were not only social but encouraged closer contact between writers, dancers, singers, pianists, and painters. Among those who regularly attended were Grace Tompkins and Enoc P. Waters, Jr., both of the *Defender,* Nelmatilda Ritchie, Gerald Cook, Fostoria Gaiter, Lorraine Williams, Anna Louise DeRamus, Leroy Gentry, Margaret Bond, and Talley Beaty. Some have since won wide acclaim in their fields. I remember especially Margaret Bond, plump but with the loveliest complexion I ever saw, who at the time was engaged to Andy Razaf, co-writer with Fats Waller of many hit songs of that day, and a natural comedian. Later Margaret herself attracted attention as a composer. The Allied Arts Guild was to suspend meetings in summer of 1939 when some of the key members planned to attend an annual musicians' convention; they went to New York and remained. The group was never reactivated.

Richard Wright left Chicago shortly after the South Side writers' group disbanded to take a job with the *Daily Worker* in Harlem. Not too long after reaching New York his book, *Uncle Tom's Children,* appeared and created a sensation. Although we did not correspond, we had developed what I looked upon as a warm friendship, and when he came to Chicago he usually found time to visit me at my small apartment. Being on welfare had never embarrassed him. Once at a dinner given in his honor after he had become famous, he publicly introduced one of the guests as "my welfare worker when I was on relief."

When his most noted book, *Native Son,* was completed and accepted, he sent back galley proofs which I read. Included was a graphic masturbation sequence at the Regal Theater when Bigger Thomas and some of his buddies watched the latest Jean Harlow movie. Meanwhile the Book-Of-The-Month-Club was considering *Native Son* as a possible selection. They decided on distribution, but this episode had to be eliminated. In 1940 this was considered pornographic, although today it would not raise an eyebrow. Incidentally, he told me the opening chapter was the last to be written.

On one of his trips to Chicago, Wright said it was the policy of major publishers to have not more than one black author on their lists. "It's like shoes," he explained. "Most well-dressed men will own one pair of white or tan shoes to be used, perhaps, on special occasions. But one pair is all a man needs. Anything over that would be considered superfluous. It's the same way with colored authors."

On another trip he introduced me to his first wife, Dhima, a dancer reputedly of White Russian parentage. She impressed me as very good-looking but somewhat aloof—but of course that may have been due to my own standoffishness. Later when they went to Mexico, word came back he was near death as the result of a bite by a poisonous insect. I learned soon afterward he had been nipped by a scorpion—a painful experience but not necessarily fatal.

The walls of my living room housed a changing exhibition of salon photographs. Dick had, of course, seen them but I do not believe they fully registered until he visited me while preparing *12,000,000 Black Voices.* I told him I wanted to make some portraits.

He looked intently at my display while I set up camera and lights. After I made a couple of shots he asked:

"How much did you pay for that camera?"

"It cost $29.50." It was a twin lens reflex taking 2 1/4 by 2 1/4 negatives. In those days you could buy a good instrument for that price.

"I'll give you thirty-five dollars for it now."

"Why? You can get one tomorrow."

"No, I want this one. I like the way it operates. And I want to learn how to take pictures now."

Well, why not? I had recently bought a thirty-five millimeter Welti with an F 2 Xenon lens and really didn't need two cameras.

"Okay," I said, "as soon as I finish the roll."

I removed the film after taking the last shot and handed the instrument to him. I also gave him brief instructions on loading and focusing and exposure.

A year passed before I saw him again, and I showed him eight-by-ten-inch enlargements of himself. He was so pleased he requested copies. When I asked him to autograph my copy of *12,000,000 Black Voices* he wrote: "To Frank Marshall Davis who opened my eyes to the joy of photography." Later he showed up with a brand new Leica hanging from his neck and was well on his way to proficiency with the lens. Richard also announced he was planning to use his favorite shot I had taken of him with full credit in the picture that would accompany the review in *Time* magazine of his autobiographical *Black Boy*. It appeared in March 1945, and is the only instance, to my knowledge, in which my name ever appeared in *Time*. But at that period in history my attitude toward Wright, the man, had undergone a major change, although I have never altered my opinion that, as a writer, he is by far the most powerful yet produced in black America.

From what I knew of his personality and his differences with the top leadership, I was not surprised when Wright quit the Communist Party. I thoroughly understood his antagonism. But I thought his resultant series of articles in widely read publications was an act of treason in the fight for our rights and aided only the racists who were constantly seeking any means to destroy cooperation between Reds and blacks. What Dick had done was throw the full weight of his worldwide prestige into a position which, while it gave him emotional release, damaged our battle. What's more, he had been paid for his attacks and at very nice rates. I recalled that Angelo Herndon, in incomparably worse financial straits, had turned down an opportunity to "tell all" to the Hearst press for substantial financial gain. He had refused as a matter of principle. In my review of *Black Boy* for ANP member papers I touched on these matters—and I never saw or heard from Wright again. And the irony of it all is that despite his continued Redbaiting during his final years, his writing showed that basically he was still a Marxist. When you get down to the nitty gritty, he had merely quit the organization and dumped his former comrades, not the ideology.

54

Indirectly, through Wright, I became acquainted for the first time in my life with a number of white writers, some of whom later became famous. Then they were struggling, many of them on the WPA Writers Project, and militantly leftist.

Our common denominator was the rise of fascism in Europe and Mussolini's rape of Ethiopia followed by the Spanish Civil War. By now I had learned considerable black history through the writings of Dr. W. E. B. Du Bois, Dr. Carter G. Woodson, and J. A. Rogers. This kind of education and sense of black identity I had to assimilate independently of the school system. Until the Ethiopian war, Afro-Americans generally had little feeling of closeness with their kinsmen in Africa— except for some followers of Marcus Garvey. Brainwashed by the racist propaganda system, by and large we were either indifferent or held ourselves superior to "those savages" inhabiting the big, dark continent. But *Il Duce* woke us up. When his son spoke in public print of the "joy" of seeing black bodies hurled skyward when he bombed them from his planes, as a group we suddenly realized these were our ethnic brothers being slaughtered and for the first time felt mass ties from thousands of miles away. Incidentally, I failed to find any report from the Vatican condemning this wanton war. But when the Fascists seized the government of Addis Ababa and sent young Ethiopians to Rome for training in a religion foreign to their Coptic faith, the Vatican shouted itself hoarse in praise.

With the sepia scalp of Ethiopia hanging from his belt, Mussolini joined with Hitler in helping Franco overthrow the democratic legal government of Spain. Emperor Haile Selassie, as first victim of the international Fascist grab, appeared before the impotent League of Nations at Geneva, Switzerland, to plead eloquently but fruitlessly for united action to stem this monster danger. He knew what was to come: World War II.

Meanwhile American writers grew increasingly alarmed at the rising power of Hitler and Mussolini. A national organization, the League of American Writers, was formed, and its first major action was publication of a booklet, *Writers Take Sides,* in which several hundred of us went on record condemning Fascism as a mushrooming threat to world peace.[12] Of course, we were all duly listed in Washington as "un-American" for opposing the Rome-Berlin Axis. We were "premature antifascists" for not waiting until the thief entered before trying to lock doors. Those who secretly mourned the defeat of the Axis were long powerful in Washington.

I did not know at the time I joined the league that it was created following a decision by the Communist Party to close down the John Reed Clubs and established a broad, united front organization among writers. And had I known, it would not have made one particle of difference. I was wholly in sympathy with the expressed league objectives. Fact is, membership and supporters read like a Who's Who among U.S. writers.

Wright, who had been active in the John Reed Clubs, was one of the founders of the league. It had been in existence a year or more before I joined, and I suspect I was asked to become a member through Dick's recommendation. Interestingly enough, neither Wright nor anyone I met through the league made any effort to recruit me into the Communist Party. Despite my obvious anger and alienation, I may have been considered too bourgeois. I was privately employed, had no direct ties with the proletariat, had never been on relief or with the Writers' Project.

I worked actively with the Chicago chapter. The league partially emancipated me from the ghetto, and I became personally acquainted with such writers as Nelson Algren, Stuart Engstrand, and Meyer Levin, who all later attained wide fame as novelists; Jack Conroy, already well known as author and editor; Theodore Ward, dramatist and author of the play, *Big White Fog;* Professor Guiseppe Borgese, a refugee from Italy then teaching at the University of Chicago; Harvey O'Connor, Socialist writer; and Paul Romaine, writer and critic.

These were all socially conscious "proletarian writers," painfully aware of economic inequalities which brought on the Depression and determined to help change the world. Roosevelt's New Deal policies had brought relief from starvation; his make-work program provided jobs at bare subsistence pay in their fields for the unemployed. Those on the WPA Writers Project got little more than enough for board and shelter.

Although I was privately employed, my finances were not too much better. In appearance most league members resembled forerunners of the beatniks, except that lack of material possessions came from necessity, not choice.

Meyer Levin was the only white writer I knew with a well-paying job. He worked for *Esquire* magazine and a short-lived weekly affiliate. But he rarely attended chapter meetings unless he had a beef involving *Esquire*. Serious-faced and intense, when he appeared we assumed automatically he wanted our help with a problem endangering his job. Once he was thoroughly upset because of a threatened Catholic boycott of *Esquire* over publication of those sexy cartoons which were that magazine's trademark.

Nelson Algren lived a block away from me, in an ancient arcade building on the Caucasian side of Cottage Grove Avenue. Although we were in frequent contact for several years and he visited my apartment, we were impersonal friends. I looked upon him as sort of standoffish. I presume I often gave the impression of living behind a wall, undoubtedly due to my early training of necessity in self-sufficiency and resultant development as a loner.

He had already authored one book, *Somebody In Boots,* which gave promise of greater things. At the time it brought little in royalties. In recent years, because of the well-established Algren reputation, it has been reissued in paperback. At this time, however, he was promising but penurious. Doleful in appearance, as if he couldn't quite make up his mind which of two evils was the lesser, and often looking as if he had just been caught with his hand in the cookie jar, he had a dry, crackling wit. I remember, too, he had an unruly cowlick seemingly determined to live an independent existence. He was married when I first met him and lived with his wife in one of the small, characterless, cubicle apartments in the Arcade Building. I visited his place a day before he and his wife split up. She was unusually busy packing things away. When I learned several days later that they had parted, he seemed completely unconcerned, although it appeared to sour him permanently on marriage.

Jack Conroy, his virtual sidekick, differed greatly in personality. Big and heavy, with a long facial scar giving the impression of physical toughness, Jack was a smiling extrovert. Thoroughly Irish, he could talk entertainingly for hours, cracking jokes and relating experiences in various parts of America. He already had a reputation in literary circles as editor of the proletarian magazine, *The Anvil.* [13] Later he worked with his longtime friend, Arna Bontemps, on the highly regarded sociological study of black migrants to Chicago, *They Seek a City,* which in the late 1960s was revised, brought up to date, and reissued.

Nelson and Jack did most of the work for league fund-raising affairs. Regular meetings were held at any available locale—sometimes my apartment—but parties were usually given in an old North Side two-story house inhabited by Stu Engstrand and his schoolteacher wife Sophia, who later made a name for herself as a novelist.[14] They were the only members with quarters big enough for a large party. Stu himself puffed regularly on a pipe and loved to walk around in his socks. Always calm, nothing seemed to upset him, not even Maxwell Bodenheim. And if Bodenheim didn't make you blow your cool, you were immune.

I met him only once, although I had read his poetry and knew he was one of the free-verse pioneers in the poetry revolution starting around 1914. I had also read his book in which he introduced each poem by announcing, "This failed in every contest where it was entered"; "This was rejected by the *Atlantic Monthly*"; "Nobody would pay me even $10 to publish this poem." In short, he was a character.

We built a fund-raising party around his appearance after learning when he would be in Chicago. Naturally, it was at the Engstrands'. I forget the purpose, but it was probably for the benefit of the Spanish Loyalists or the Chinese, then being well ravished by the Japanese militarists. During this period, politically conscious women wore cotton stockings (there were no nylons yet) in protest against Nipponese control of the silk industry.

Widely known as completely uninhibited and thoroughly unpredictable, as well as a lush and a woman chaser, these attributes were expected to pull in a crowd that night. But we wanted to be able to present a body reasonably in control of itself, particularly since this was also something of a homecoming event. Keeping him fairly sober was the special assignment of Jack Conroy, but it was a task beyond the capacity of any one man.

Jack did his best. He would have had an easier job trying to level Pike's Peak with a teaspoon. Max drank a half-pint of liquor the way most men polish off a single shot and permitted nobody to interfere with his consumption. He was still conducting a one-man mopping up campaign against all booze. Every iota of diplomacy and persuasion was needed to get Max to knock it off in late afternoon and retire to the Engstrand home where he could sleep it off upstairs for a few hours before the party. It might have worked, had not Jack discovered later that Bodenheim had smuggled in another pint to tide him over.

When guests began arriving around eight, Max was upstairs having cup after cup of black coffee poured down his gullet and his face washed with icy towels in a desperate effort to sober him enough to talk and read. But it was no dice. Each time he was patiently and gingerly placed upright and supporting hands moved gently away, he collapsed. This continued for several hours. Finally, after profuse apologies and a public admission that Max was his usual inebriated self, Jack and Nelson read some of his representative work to the gathering.

But it was not the original article people had paid to see. Somewhere around 11:00 P.M., Bodenheim was revived sufficiently to be led slowly and carefully downstairs, with firm support under each arm. He was placed on exhibit in the drawing room in a sitting position on a couch, like a rare and highly prized specimen. As everybody watched him closely, Max slowly looked around, his eyes bleary and glazed. He was one of the few people I've seen who could stagger sitting down. A couple of feet away sat an attractive young blonde. When Max, with great effort, eventually brought her in focus, he licked his lips, grinned, and lunged. Calmly, as if she knew what to expect, she arose and moved unconcernedly to another seat. Bodenheim's momentum carried him past where the target was, and he went over the edge of the couch to the floor. There he remained, seemingly at peace with the world.

Almost immediately the party began breaking up.

"I'm sorry about what happened," Stu Engstrand tried to apologize.

"Oh, we're all quite satisfied," somebody replied as others nodded agreement. "We got what we came here for: the sight of Maxwell Bodenheim drunk and making a pass at a pretty girl. You didn't think any of us believed he'd actually be in condition to read, did you?"

Not too long afterward the Chicago chapter dwindled and passed to that special heaven reserved for worthy efforts, but not without granting me special benefits. Never before had I worked closely and voluntarily in equality with a number of whites. At this period I had already rid myself of the worst elements of my teenage inferiority complex by studying black history. At last I had come to possess what is called race pride. Still, I doubt whether anybody reared under the constant hammering of white superiority can ever fully free himself of its personality-crippling effects.

But for all practical purposes I felt equal to my white peers. Around them I could not sniff the offensive odor of condescension. You see, I like people despite being basically a loner, but experience had taught me never to immediately trust anybody white. Even when mine was the only dark face in the group, which often happened unless Ted Ward was present, I found nothing identifiably chauvinistic. Harvey O'Connor, who with his wife occupied unique quarters atop Hull House, the settlement center, reached by an elevator and a trek across rooftops, often hosted fun parties of an all-nations flavor which included national dances of European countries as well as American jitterbugging; and in a determined effort to become cosmopolitan or bust, I participated in all.

I still have warm personal feelings for those with whom I worked. This is a big reason why I cannot support the black extremist postulate that all whites are our enemies. I know differently from personal experience. Unless you have allowed yourself to become completely dehumanized by American racism, you value and retain your proven friends, no matter what their color.

55

When Jack Conroy revised his old *Anvil* magazine under the name *New Anvil,* I was able to arrange the debut of a new young author who later appeared regularly on the bestseller lists. This was Frank Yerby, whose short stories had previously appeared only in his college publication. I might add that at the Atlanta *World* I had been able to grant exposure to Chester Himes, then in prison in Ohio, by printing a number of his short stories before he won his spurs as a novelist.

I met Frank Yerby through his relative, Barefield Gordon, who wrote sonnets and had been a member of the first writers' group I joined soon after coming to Chicago. Frank was still attending college in Georgia. Small, light-brown, goodlooking, and a very intense youth who became quite animated in any discussion that interested him, he was thoroughly sick of racism. At that time, he wrote grim and realistic short stories about discrimination. I selected one I thought was unusually vivid and gave it to Jack Conroy for publication.

For several summers I saw Yerby when he came to Chicago for a breath of comparatively fresh air after a school year in Dixie. He had a knack for attracting good-looking gals, several of whom he brought around for me to photograph. After earning his master's degree, he taught in another southern college. Meanwhile he had grown pessimistic about ever winning acclaim by writing about black-white relations. He told me there was no money in that field, and he was going to leave it alone. The last time I saw him he had gotten married and was enthused over research he was conducting for a historical novel. From this came *The Foxes of Harrow* and a highly lucrative career. Now affluent, he moved to Europe. Today many who have read his books or seen film versions do not know Frank Yerby is a black American. He is far removed from the day when he was an Afro-American writer.

56

From late summer 1936 until the November elections, I worked in the publicity section of the black division of the Republican National Committee, trying to sell Governor Alf Landon of Kansas to an unwilling electorate. Blind support of GOP candidates among us was dead. It was not that Afro-America had decided to reverse itself and go Democratic; it was due instead to the personal appeal of Franklin D. Roosevelt and his New Deal administration which had put bread into the mouths of starving people.

As usual, Claude Barnett of ANP was head of publicity. I went along because the price was right. Charlie Stewart had been replaced at ANP by Albert G. Barnett (no relation to Claude), dubbed "The Senator." Albert was at ANP part time, working regularly as a waiter at a Loop hotel. Resembling the classic picture of a balding Irishman, he ran into trouble during the 1919 Chicago riots because he looked as if he could belong to either side. When he came home at night, roving bands of soul brothers were ready to attack him thinking he was white; when he went downtown Whitey wanted to give him the works for venturing outside the ghetto.

Saturday ordinarily was a slack day at ANP. Each Saturday we whipped out GOP propaganda for all the weeklies. Heading the Negro Division were Dr. Redmond and Perry Howard, national committeemen from Mississippi. The positions of Perry Howard and Ben Davis, Sr., during this period were a paradox. In both states the scant Republican party membership was composed almost exclusively of those few Afro-Americans who voted in national elections. Nevertheless, a tiny segment of honky politicians tried to muscle in and elect their own lily white slate of delegates to the big convention, only to be regularly defeated in contests. Despite the white supremacist attitudes of Dixiecrat politicians, under

GOP administrations deals had to be made with Howard and Davis for appointments. The Senator Bilbos and the Howards put aside racism when dollars and cents were involved.

By 1936 FDR was in solid with the plain people, black and white. Under Hoover, they had seen big business get all the money that was poured in at the top to slow down the Depression. Very little found its way down to the needy. Roosevelt, on the other hand, was shelling out to those in want. Hungry and jobless citizens not only were sent welfare checks, but surplus food was given directly to them. It was no disgrace to be on the dole. It's difficult to look down on your neighbor for accepting the same aid you get.

As usual, we were hardest hit by the Depression. And, as usual, Dixie administrators brazenly discriminated against starving blacks. Those who could scrape enough together came to Northern urban centers where they wrote back that even relief recipients lived better than those breaking their necks for coolie pay in Birmingham, Jackson, and Little Rock. So they started saving until they got enough for bus tickets out of Dixie. Reaching New York, Detroit, and Chicago, they crowded in with friends and relatives in the already full compounds long enough to establish legal residence and qualify on their own for welfare. It is bitterly ironic that a black family on relief in Cleveland had a higher standard of living than when privately employed in Memphis with its racist wage differentials.

I recall releasing an ANP story about a New Jersey relief administrator called on the carpet to answer complaints by white welfare recipients who said they were victims of discrimination. They received dried beans and salt pork, while the souls received frying chicken, pork chops, and watermelon in season.

But the administrator had an ironclad defense.

"I'm merely following orders," he assured his superiors.

"What orders?"

"Right here," he said, pointing to mimeographed instructions. "This comes directly from the top. It plainly states those on relief are to be supplied food in keeping with their traditional dietary habits. And everybody knows niggers always eat fried chicken, pork chops, and watermelon."

This was one of the few instances in American history when we benefitted from rigid adherence to the stereotypes.

On a national basis, the black voter, who had been paying dues to Abraham Lincoln since emancipation by blindly supporting the GOP, backed Roosevelt. Refugees from southern starvation, now voting for the first time, were in his corner out of gratitude. Despite our reams of copy, I doubt if our publicity won any votes for Landon. We tried everything we could devise, including a national essay contest on "Why I Shall Vote For Alf Landon," in which we offered thousands of dollars in cash prizes. The top award was in four figures with others in lesser amounts on down to several hundred five-dollar prizes at the bottom. But when all entries were in, there were not enough from throughout the nation to equal the number of prizes.

Momentarily this posed a problem, since it is an unwritten rule never to return campaign funds to the party treasury. Overspend, if you like, and clamor for an additional allocation, but do not commit the gross faux pas of *under*spending, for this indicates that somehow you have fallen down on your job. Accordingly, it behooved "Senator" and me to see that all contest money was awarded. So after sending a winner's check to every person who sent in a contest letter, no matter how poorly written, we added the names of our friends to receive the leftover cash. Then we wrote or telephoned them they had "won" and would get checks in the mail to be turned over to us.

But we learned, to our sorrow, that many of our pals were downright dishonest and not worthy of trust. We got back less than twenty dollars of a couple of hundred given away.

After the fall elections, I applied for a Julius Rosenwald Fellowship at the suggestion of Claude Barnett.[15] Critical reaction to *Black Man's Verse* had been so uniformly excellent that we felt there would be little difficulty in getting an honorarium for a year. Further, Claude was closely allied with the Rosenwald group. Knowing the right people is always valuable no matter to what fund one applies. Rosenwald had made and given away millions to further the careers of promising Afro-Americans and white southerners and for rural black education, health, and libraries in Dixie. White schools got the official appropriations; black schools in backwoods areas were often conducted in buildings which would serve only as privies for whites.

In 1937 I received a grant of $1,500 for "creative writing, especially poetry," payable at $125 monthly. This was big money for that period. My pay at ANP was far less, yet I was able to rent a three-room furnished apartment and support myself and Thelma. By the time of the award, incidentally, I was awaiting publication of my second book, *I Am The American Negro,* also by the Black Cat Press. Most of the material had been written while I was still involved with Frances and after the manuscript for *Black Man's Verse* had gone to the publisher.

Of course I did not expect to make money from this venture. Writing poetry is hardly a bread and butter occupation. For many years, the only black who lived by the returns of creative writing was Langston Hughes. Even such widely acclaimed white bards as Vachel Lindsay died of malnutrition, and Edgar Lee Masters, of *Spoon River Anthology* fame (my major influence next to Sandburg), died in the charity ward of a hospital. I write poetry because there is something I feel I must say. Often I like to share it in a magazine or a book, hoping somebody will read it and get a moment of pleasure or a bright flash of truth. Maybe I can light up someone's mind. And if it's the right torch, it will burn as brilliantly a thousand years from now as when newly lit.

Again I received high praise from a number of critics, resulting in my first radio appearance. Arthur Trask, who conducted a book review hour over station WAAF each Sunday afternoon, invited me for an interview and to read some of my work over his program. This would be the first time he had ever reviewed poetry or chatted with a poet on his broadcast.

I went down on Saturday to rehearse. Studios were located on the top floor of the Palmer House, one of the big Loop hotels. Next day I arrived in the ground-floor lobby a half-hour before broadcast time, at Trask's request, and started to enter an elevator.

The operator, a white youth, barred the door.

"Sorry, but I can't carry you," he said.

"Why not?" I asked. Inside, I knew. The Palmer House had that kind of reputation.

"Colored have to use the freight elevator. Manager's orders."

"But I rode the passenger elevator yesterday."

"Can't help it," he said, closing the door and pressing up.

I turned to another directly opposite. The operator hurriedly shut the opening when he saw me start in his direction and zoomed skyward with an empty car.

By now I was boiling. I looked around for a phone to call Trask and tell him to come the hell down and get me if he wanted his scheduled program to go on, when another elevator stopped and the door opened. I decided to make one last try and strode belligerently over. The operator was apparently unnerved by the sight of a big, angry black man storming toward his car for his eyes grew large and his mouth hung open. I got in and bellowed out my floor. He visibly gulped, said nothing, and carried me express to my destination. I told Trask immediately. He was surprised. However, there was no trouble going down. Evidently they were glad to get me out of the hotel.

I once had a similar experience in a white residential hotel, the Windermere, near the University of Chicago where I had gone to a League of American Writers' meeting at Professor Borgese's apartment. I was alone, and the operator did not want to take me up on orders of the management because I was black. It was straightened out only after the manager called Borgese who raised hell by phone at this act of discrimination. As I left the lift on an upper floor, an elderly honky broad who happened to be passing paused, placed her hands on her hips, and intoned loudly, "What's HE doing on that elevator?" I did not change expression, walking past and ignoring her as I would any other pile of trash.

This policy of relegating us to freight or service elevators was fairly common. At the time, many whites were unaware of this kind of discrimination imposed by the racists and were shocked on learning it had happened to personal friends. In fact, many liberal and intelligent Caucasians didn't believe leading Loop cafes maintained rigid color lines. I learned the convincer was to ask them to count the black faces present when they frequented certain restaurants. They were aware of segregation in the South, but discrimination in Chicago was something they never thought existed. And, of course, the payoff is that after learning of its presence, few tried to help correct the injustice.

57

Afro-America was desperately in need of a hero when Joe Louis stepped into the spotlight. No black fighter had held that most prized of all titles, the heavyweight championship, since Jack Johnson, and the white media had done a thorough hatchet job on him. Under racist Tex Rickard, the boxing czar, the kingpins had been lily white, and he kept it that way until his death.

Such pro sports as football, baseball, and basketball were strictly segregated. There were several "quaint" musicians and vaudeville headliners but no stage, screen, or radio stars of wide acceptance. The political world was also empty; Rev. Martin Luther King, Jr., was twenty years away. Except for an occasional amateur athlete and several champs in boxing's lighter divisions, we were nowhere.

Our cupboard was bare.

Joe had the backing of the powerful Chicago *Tribune*, where he won recognition as a Golden Glover from Detroit. With the maneuvering of important whites who knew a good thing when they saw it and grabbed a piece of the action, he couldn't miss. Louis had the talent to take and wear the crown. Also he was not likely to defy the establishment by openly associating with white women, as Jack Johnson had done. Although he possessed tremendous race pride and overflowed with soul, he was "safe."

Praised by both the daily and weekly media, Joe Louis caught on in a hurry. As this young "heavyweight to end all heavyweights" blasted opponents while moving closer to a title shot, his prestige skyrocketed in the ghettoes. The financial returns, of course, went to Louis, his family, and entourage—including management—but the emotional gain went to most of black America. The Brown Bomber's ring victories made it easier for the slum dweller to live among his rats and roaches. It was easy to identify and point with pride to a soul brother who won success with his fists. His victories made life less miserable. As further proof of his hero status, three of our foremost artists produced "King Joe Blues" on the Okeh label. Richard Wright wrote the words, Count Basie played, and Paul Robeson sang.

In addition to my intense interest in boxing, I had a special reason for closely following the Louis career. His glory rubbed off on me. I didn't plan it that way; it just happened. Habitually I was mistaken for the Brown Bomber.

Personally I considered this ridiculous. I was nine years older, several shades darker, had a less prominent chin, and my physique was less impressive. But these were mere details. The casual observer judged by the total impression. Had the mistake been made only by whites, I could have blamed it on the standard excuse that "all coons look alike to me." But when soul people made this error, it assumed a more serious dimension. From my college description of the-poet-who-looks-like-a-prize-fighter, I had now progressed to the-poet-who-looks-like-Joe-Louis.

One summer afternoon as I walked down South Parkway, I suddenly became aware of a swarm of kids buzzing behind me. Looking around in surprise, I heard them commenting, "There goes Joe Louis. He's gonna be champ." When I told them I was not the Brown Bomber, they shouted, "Whoya think you're jivin'?" To get away from them I had to duck into a small store and out the back way into an alley.

Another day as I rode a street car I noticed a white passenger gaze in my direction, stiffen, and nudge his companion. He, too, looked sharply at me and elbowed the guy next to him. Soon the whole front section of the car was staring, and I wondered what the hell was wrong. Finally a brother, exercising the privilege that goes with ethnic kinship, grinned and yelled back, "Hi, Joe Louis!" I was now on the spot. I hated to let a brother down in front of Whitey, but at the same time I wondered why these people didn't have sense enough to realize the Brown Bomber would not be riding a street car for he was already in the chips. I rang the bell and hopped off at the next corner.

Once when the Chicago *Defender* carried a photo of Louis in street clothes in the general news pages, at least a dozen of Thelma's friends told her they thought it was me until they read the caption. And at the South Center Department Store one morning when I stopped to make a small purchase, a crowd formed looking in my direction. I knew why, even before somebody shouted, "Why don't you buy the whole damn store, Joe, an' gimme a job?" As I crossed South Parkway at 35th one day, an elderly, sand-brown woman fell in step beside me. I looked questioningly at her. She said, "You's Joe Louis, ain't you?" When I shook my head, she came back with, "Then you has got to be his brother. Ain't no use in you tellin' me nothin' different."

This saga of confused identities reached its climax when Joe fought James J. Braddock for the title at White Sox Ball Park in 1937. Ric Roberts, the Atlanta sports writer and cartoonist, wrote me he was coming to cover the bout for the *Daily World.* He also said he was bringing along his fiancée and intended to marry her while in Chicago. Knowing Ric and his jokes from vivid experience, I discounted this part of his letter. But I was mistaken. He arrived in Chicago with a very lovely and charming young woman who was introduced as his intended.

Ric and I sat together in the press section as Joe knocked out Braddock for the crown. Immediately afterward Ric met his fiancée and dashed to the dressing room to interview the new champ, of course leaving her outside. Next day the daily press printed human interest stories describing how Marva, Joe's wife, patiently waited outside the dressing quarters until the new king had finished holding court with reporters. This puzzled me because I knew Marva was in a South Side apartment with friends listening to the fight by radio.

Next day I took Ric and his near-bride to City Hall to buy a marriage license, then to the building next door where a number of dollar-hungry preachers maintained tiny offices. They hired young boys to hang around the license bureau and steer couples straight to their offices for an immediate ceremony. While awaiting the elevator, I observed a dozen or more whites staring silently and intently in my direction. I thought, "There goes that Joe Louis stuff again," but immediately dismissed it because I was with Ric and his girl. After long moments of silent stares (the elevator was delayed), I lit a cigarette. Right away one of the white men relaxed.

"I thought you were Joe and Marva," he said pleasantly, "until you took out that cigarette. Then I knew I was wrong. Joe doesn't smoke."

The small crowd silently dispersed. Then a light dawned. The "Marva" mentioned in the newspapers was Ric's fiancée.

This mistaken identity pattern followed me for years, even when the Brown Bomber dropped out of the headlines and photographs showed him becoming bald. I still have my hair.

Nevertheless, I covered each of Joe's Chicago fights. I learned that whenever he fought, Afro-America was quiet. From five-year-olds through octogenarians, they crowded around radios. When he won, wild celebrations followed. Since virtually all his opponents were white, it was a vicarious triumph over the countless dragons breathing fire on ghetto life, a symbolical group triumph over white superiority. The night he lost to Max Schmeling there was mourning in the compounds.[16] But the film of this defeat had big grosses, particularly at white theaters in Dixie.

Joe's triumphs stimulated young tan fighters. The bars were now lowered at last. And the Golden Gloves Tournament, with three rings in simultaneous action, became a proving ground. Boxing was one of the few fields in which we might earn a decent living. It looked easy. Win in the Golden Gloves and turn pro. With this goal, we were uniformly in the best possible physical condition and deadly serious. We knew also we had to kayo white opponents or prove outstandingly superior; if the match was at all close the white boy would nine times out of ten get the decision. Also we had to steel ourselves against white spectators shouting "Kill the nigger!" Without exception, we had a little something extra when we met honky foes from Dixie; the knowledge that these opponents came from this area turned us on full blast.

Sometimes from my working press seat I looked around and saw souls standing above prone pale fighters in all three rings. Year after year, bronze boxers dominated the Golden Gloves out of proportion to their numbers. There were so many black winners that rival editors began privately labeling the annual tournament "Uncle Arch's Cabin." But the *Tribune* sports editor, Arch Ward, merely laughed all the way to the bank.

I got a special kick out of trying to forecast which fighters had it and which couldn't make it. A number of fine young heavyweight prospects were catapulted into the limelight during the 1930s, among them Otis Thomas, the St. Louis southpaw who almost upset the applecart when Primo Carnera was being built up for the championship. There was Lorenzo Pack from Detroit, who roomed next door to me the year he won the title and who was impatient to take on Joe Louis. He did well as a pro until he fought Tony Galento. His career came to an end when he got into a fight with his father-in-law and lost an arm after being knifed. Afterward he wrote popular songs and wound up with several hits to his credit.

But the prospect who completely sold me was Lem Franklin from Cleveland. He could knock out an opponent with either hamlike hand. The night he kayoed Runge of Germany, for years the European amateur champion who never before had been knocked off his feet, he looked like the hottest property since the Brown Bomber. Smelling a potential gold mine, I arranged with his father to handle publicity. But I soon learned his hands were too brittle for his powerful punch and broke easily. He was also too slow-witted for the smart pros. He busted his hands again early in a fight with this same Tony Galento and received a savage beating. Instead of waiting until he had fully recovered, he took another match too soon and died from brain damage.

I was also impressed by a middleweight from Cincinnati named Ezzard Charles.[17] I noticed how smoothly he handled himself under pressure as an amateur and believed he had real potential. I followed his career as he grew into a light heavy and then a heavyweight and won the crown. I wonder how great he would have been had he not killed an opponent in the ring and suffered an emotional scar that hampered the rest of his career. I consider him a vastly underrated champion.

58

The U.S. Supreme Court in 1937 rendered its historic Gaines case decision, establishing the precedent that a state must provide equal educational opportunities for all citizens within its borders—a break in the dike of discrimination paving the way for the high court decision seventeen years later outlawing segregated schools. This primary right to equal education had been consistently denied in southern states. However, the 1937 edict was generally ignored by Dixie commonwealths.

Lloyd Gaines had sued for admission to the law school of the University of Missouri. Denied admittance because of color, he took the case up to the top tribunal and won. In Missouri, at least, the walls of Jericho started tumbling.

Most rigidly segregated states, in an attempt to delay the day of reckoning, pretended the decision applied only to Missouri. Jim Crow states customarily provided a few out-of-state scholarships to northern universities for black students seeking advanced education. The decision now made this practice unacceptable. In a desperate effort to circumvent the edict, some crackers proposed that their states pool resources and establish regional professional schools "for Nigras" although even this was a flagrant violation of the new decision.

However, other southerners, seeing the handwriting on the wall, spoke aloud of integration. Jim Crow schools, they said, were a waste of money. Those states determined to maintain the status quo were the poorest in the nation and least able to afford the luxurious folly of separate schools. For instance, Mississippi could not pay even for first-rate mixed schools; splitting these already inadequate funds two ways, no matter how inequitably, resulted in poor education for both white and black. Since this was so very obvious, a number of white students at the University of Mississippi stated frankly they would not object to mixed classes if it meant more money and higher educational standards for their institution. Remember, this was twenty-five years before the first Duskyamerican student was enrolled there under armed guard. But the state power structure was bitterly opposed then, just as later.

However, Missouri could not stall and was forced to take immediate action. State officials had the choice of admitting Gaines to the law school or establishing a completely equal separate law school within Missouri borders. They chose the latter and shelled out taxpayers' funds to start a law school at Lincoln University, the state's Jim Crow institution of higher learning.

Meanwhile Miss Lucile Bluford, now managing editor of the Kansas City *Call* and who had worked with me in Atlanta, sued to enter the journalism school at Missouri for postgraduate study. Immediately the high priests of racism rigged up a journalism school at Lincoln and told her, "You've got your own now. Enroll at Lincoln." But Miss Bluford refused to register because the state was still violating the edict specifically ordering "equal educational opportunity" within the borders of a state.

In their frantic effort to get the separate school off the ground, I had been indirectly approached about possibly organizing and heading it. I turned it down flatly. I am unalterably opposed to segregated education and believe only in complete integration of students, faculty, administration, and subject matter. Further, having worked with Miss Bluford I would not have dreamed of aiding any plot to block her entry to the state university. Finally, it was utterly ridiculous to think a little subterfuge school at Lincoln could be the scholastic equal of that at Missouri U. For years the Missouri School of Journalism had been widely recognized as the nation's finest; if such renowned universities as Columbia in New York and Medill at Northwestern had not become its equal after decades of operation and millions in expenditures, how could it be equalled overnight at Lincoln?

I often wondered what would happen if black students tried to register in every course offered at Missouri not in the Lincoln curriculum. Either the state would have spent untold millions expanding Lincoln into the most diversified university in black America or the white power structure would have had to eliminate many courses then offered at Missouri.

Today, of course, Missouri not only accepts black students but recruits promising prep athletes. And again I want to stress that this drastic change came about only through militancy on the part of Afro-Americans.

59

Edgar Brown would have made a fitting companion for Stokely Carmichael.[18] Unfortunately he died before the Supreme Court handed down its long list of historic rulings outlawing segregation. But in the 1930s and early 1940s the goateed one-time National Negro Tennis Champion with the hide of an elephant and the courage of a lion fought with all his might against racism. For a time he battled in the nation's capital as a high official of Roosevelt's Civilian Conservation Corps. In Chicago he roamed the South Side with a sound truck rallying all to active battle against discrimination. He also formed the National Negro Council to lobby for our rights in Washington, and, in 1942 at the annual East-West all-star baseball game before fifty thousand at Comiskey Park, brought out some of the prettiest brownskin gals in the city and collected several thousand dollars for his war chest.

Edgar would hardly have taken first prize in a popularity contest among those who knew him personally, but he did have unlimited guts and the ability to needle Mr. Charlie. He even dared to file as a congressional candidate in racist Rankin's home district in Mississippi and would have gone there to campaign personally (and face almost certain death) had he not been talked out of this then rash step.[19] Many who were not completely in accord with his tactics (his goal was not in dispute) welcomed an occasional bring-down for this Freedom Fighter. His tenacity was sometimes irritating (if I saw him enter the ANP office when I was trying to beat a deadline, I'd duck out the back way). Once when he was attacked and beaten by a white page from Texas inside the Senate Office Building, we viewed this happening with mixed emotions. But just the same, nobody wanted to see him go to his death in Rankin's bailiwick, for a black man of his militancy was extremely rare.

He was also involved, although in a minor way, with the threatened national March on Washington at the start of World War II which resulted in Roosevelt breaking all precedent by establishing a Fair Employment Practices Commission (FEPC). A. Phillip Randolph, an old-line labor leader, spearheaded this movement backed by a black America bitter at rampant discrimination in defense industries. On the eve of the scheduled mass demonstration, the White House issued a directive setting up FEPC, and the march was called off. And it was a good thing, too. The marchers would have fallen far short of the publicized figure of two hundred thousand. Unlike the 1963 March on Washington, the first had more spiritual than physical support. But FDR did not know this when he capitulated. Like a smart poker player, Randolph bluffed and won, although on democratic grounds the victory had long been overdue. The president realized our claims were justified.[20]

In fact, our drive for equality was accelerated in the years immediately before World War II. Aware of the super race theories of Adolf Hitler, so like the ideas of our own white supremacists, we felt a vital stake in not only fighting the Nazi ideology abroad but in moving with all-out strength to combat similar beliefs at home. We knew of Der Fuehrer's snub of Jesse Owens and our other athletes at the Berlin Olympics in 1936, but realized it could just as easily happen in America. As our nation became more deeply involved on the side of the "democracies," we gave our support but also pointed out that charity begins at home—a lesson still not learned by the establishment. In addition we had the active backing of the new CIO, then a militant labor organization.

In such a climate, the aptly named House Committee on Un-

American Activities came into being, headed by congressman Martin Dies of Texas and over the opposition of Roosevelt.[21] As a handmaiden of reaction, the committee became a leading weapon in the attempt to block Afro-American progress. Dies promptly cited two of the nations ablest black leaders as "Communists," Dr. Mary McLeod Bethune, president of Bethune-Cookman College in Florida and head of the black division of the National Youth Administration in Washington, D.C., and Dean William Pickens, field secretary of the NAACP.[22]

Pickens was a frequent visitor to ANP offices and a regular syndicated commentator. A former educator and a brilliant scholar, he had the knack of getting right down and endearing himself to the little people. They listened to what he had to say—not only because he made it plain but because he possessed one of the deepest, most dominating voices I have ever heard. When he spoke, you had to listen whether you wanted to or not. The irony is that, after being branded by Dies as a "dangerous Red," he was later fired by the NAACP for "lack of militancy."

Once, an FBI agent (white, naturally) came to ANP to make a security check on Pickens, who also held an advisory post with a federal agency. Of course, this was before the FBI began calling on others to make a check on me. Obviously, he was from the South, and I learned he was a native of Alabama.

I had a standard formula when the FBI checked with me regarding some Afro-American. If I considered the subject Uncle Tomish, I classified him as "dangerous" and a "rotten security risk." If the subject was militant, I painted his Americanism in my most glowing terms. I do not claim this technique was effective, but it gave me emotional satisfaction.

"What do you know about this fellow Pickens?" the agent began. "Do you consider him dangerous?"

"Definitely," I said, "to anybody who doesn't believe in the Constitution and who thinks a human with a white skin is superior to the rest of mankind."

He looked at me intently, his face reddening. But he had a job to do. "Would you call him a radical?" he went on.

"Yes, the same way I'd call Thomas Jefferson and Benjamin Franklin radicals. They didn't like being kicked around by the British rulers. Pickens doesn't like being kicked around by white overlords."

His face was now definitely crimson. He stiffened. But he had to continue.

"In your opinion, is Pickens a good American?"

"Absolutely! He takes the Declaration of Independence and the U.S. Constitution so seriously he is willing to lay down his life, if need be, to see that all Americans get the freedom and equality promised by these documents. So when he finds some people refusing to give freedom and equality to others, as in Alabama, he gets mad."

That shot got him. The agent mumbled a "thank you" and stalked out. No doubt about it; I had not won a friend.

Many of us utilized every opportunity to underline our dissatisfaction with the status quo. As it became increasingly clear that war with the Axis was inevitable, we knew we would be in there fighting and sacrificing and dying. We would be called upon to help preserve "the American way of life"—but if this American way of life would continue to consist of lynching, segregation, disfranchisement, and the master race theory of Hitler, it was not worth fighting for. Knowing Hitler had sent his lieutenants to these shores to learn our racist techniques, it made no sense to go abroad to fight the same kind of ideology millions faced daily in Dixie unless white supremacy were concurrently attacked on the home front. Frankly, many black men would have preferred shooting at Bilbo instead of Herr Hitler. We still had the festering memory of World War I, when we were called upon to battle the Kaiser and "make the world safe for democracy"—only to come home and find we had merely made America safe for continued racism. We had been promised the moon of equality for our all-out support and, after the armistice, had been showered with the same old mud of discrimination. Thus at the start of World War II we had wised up to where we demanded more democracy as we went along, instead of accepting promises to be broken when hostilities ended.

During World War I, most dark doughboys were in labor battalions or the quartermaster corps—all nicely segregated. The South, fearful of black revenge and suffering from a guilty conscience, bitterly opposed training soul troops in the use of guns. The minority assigned to duty in front-line trenches was staffed almost exclusively by white officers—and those officers who showed flagrant prejudice became early casualties in combat action without being felled by German guns.

After the armistice in 1918, tan Yanks were speedily demobilized, and those who returned home to Dixie dreaming of better treatment were rapidly awakened by the lyncher's rope and the sheriff's gun. Between the two world wars, Afro-Americans in the regular army were restricted to a handful of cavalry and infantry units staffed by honky officers. The smattering of black officers (including a few who had finished West Point) could hold a convention in a telephone booth without fear of overcrowding. The navy was even worse for our sole rating was that of messman.

One day with the war clouds looming ominously over Europe, a young man named Levi Pierce, recently discharged from the army at Fort Riley, Kansas, walked into our office. He was like manna from heaven. Intelligent and informed, he provided me with enough factual material on the prejudice against Afro-American soldiers to send out articles for several months. We kept a running expose in our press on the disgraceful treatment accorded black soldiers wearing Uncle Sam's uniform. There is no doubt in my mind that this series influenced the Pentagon and helped change official policy when Washington called for total mobilization.

60

The year of 1940 was historically significant for Afro-America, marking the 75th anniversary of the Emancipation Proclamation. In Illinois one James W. Washington wangled a seventy-five-thousand-dollar grant from the state legislature to set up a National Negro Exposition from 4 July through 9 September at the Chicago Coliseum, close to the southern boundary of the Loop.

But there was one serious flaw. The appropriation was earmarked only for Coliseum rental, traveling expenses, printing, construction of exhibition booths, preexposition rentals, and a basic staff expected to work from July 1939 through 9 September 1940. After the exposition ended, twenty-five thousand dollars had to be returned to the state despite thousands of dollars still owed in outstanding bills. The unused funds had not been spent for their designated purpose because Governor Horner did not get around to appointing a State Exposition Commission until six months late, in December 1939.

Strangely enough, the forthcoming exposition, expected to attract attendance from all over America, was a closely guarded secret until 1940 was two months old. Then, as soon as the Exposition Commission began functioning, it became painfully clear that money—and lots of it—had to come from somewhere other than the original appropriation to prepare adequate exhibits showing the progress of black America. The Roosevelt agencies bridged this great gap. Both the WPA and NYA (National Youth Administration) turned out posters, charts, and dioramas—the latter graphic enough to present a condensed course in black history. Meanwhile, with the exposition desperately in need of cash, the federal government came through with a grant of seventy-five thousand dollars a few weeks before opening date.

To Truman Gibson, Jr., went the post of executive director and the lion's share of official headaches which multiplied faster than rabbits. I headed the publicity section, shooting out bales of articles, cartoons, and photos, working closely with the cartoonist Jay Jackson. Exhibits were generally excellent and on a dignified level. One of the major features was a national art exhibit for which we borrowed from abroad several highly valuable canvases by Henry O. Tanner, first Afro-American painter to win international acclaim. We also conducted a national photography contest won by a camera artist from Kansas City who never received his cash prize. A national poetry contest brought many entries. Langston Hughes, Arna Bontemps, and I judged the manuscripts and awarded first prize to Melvin B. Tolson, who went on to win wide acclaim until his death a few years ago. The nationwide competition for a mural depicting the history of the black press was won by Charles White, who became one of America's foremost contemporary artists. He died in 1979.

But culture and displays of group achievement were not enough. People remained away in overwhelming numbers. Special days for different states were inaugurated. Cash registers still rang only spasmodically. Even as with white expositions, we learned we needed to provide eye and ear entertainment in the flesh for the masses.

After intense rehearsals, we nightly presented a jazz version of the operetta *The Chimes of Normandy,* taking a tip from the New York success of *The Hot Mikado* starring the great dancer Bill "Bojangles" Robinson. A portion of the upstairs section of the coliseum was converted into a bar and nightclub with leading cafe entertainers brought in for regular performances. We also conducted a Miss Bronze America national beauty contest, with winners from various states brought to Chicago for the finals. With these added attractions, the exposition finally caught on. But it was now late August; the packed closing days could not compensate for the initial weeks of sparse attendance. During the final days we contracted for Duke Ellington's band. This was the period when Jimmy Blanton was revolutionizing string bass and Johnny Hodges was drawing raves for his alto sax etching of "Warm Valley." Paul Robeson also appeared in concert before a crowded house.

Shortly before the scheduled closing of the exposition, I received word that a Kansas poet named Mrs. Irma Wassall, of Wichita, would be in Chicago on Labor Day and wanted to meet me. Immediately envisioning a stout, mousey, middle-aged white woman with a clock-stopping face who escaped from gray boredom in a rainbow world of words, I did not relish the meeting. But in view of developments over the previous two years, I felt obliged to at least go through the motions.

Three or four years earlier the first *Anthology of Kansas Verse* published at Kansas State College had included a number of poems by Langston Hughes, who grew up in Lawrence and Topeka, and myself, bringing immediate protests from several racist readers that "Negroes were over-represented" in the collection. Some white supremacists would even like to restrict words to the ghetto.

Evidently these racists were influential, for the Kansas Authors Club announced that the 1938 club contest would be open only to white writers. Immediately there arose a tornado in a teapot. Some of the leading members resigned in protest, among them Dr. Karl Menninger of the world famous Menninger Clinic, Senator Arthur Capper, ex-Senator Henry J. Allen, Kirke Mechem, and Nelson Antrim Crawford, a former president of the organization who issued a statement saying: "At least three Negro writers in Kansas have produced much more significant poetry than most of us white authors will ever produce. I refer specifically to Langston Hughes, Claude McKay, and Frank Marshall Davis."

Although a native of the West Indies, Claude McKay had attended Kansas State for a brief time, long enough to be pointed to with pride when literature was discussed. In another ten years, incidentally, Crawford would have been able to add the name of Gwendolyn Brooks, first to win the Pulitzer prize for poetry.

Meanwhile at Winfield, Kansas, some fifteen miles from my hometown, was a fiery young Cuban named Ruben Menendez who wrote a regular column headed "Among Kansas Poets" for the weekly Winfield *Record.* Menendez, who I had never met, became so incensed at the announcement by the Kansas Authors Club, I later learned, that he challenged the president to a duel. It never transpired, but Menendez went out of his way to print favorable comment about me, including a special article by Dr. Kenneth Porter, a Kansas poet then teaching history at Vassar College.

And in 1941, when the *Tourist Guide to Kansas* was published by the Kansas Coronado Cuarto Centennial Commission, I was amazed and gratified to find listed among historical facts about my native Cowley County: "Frank Marshall Davis, Negro poet, born at Arkansas City." I have not yet been able to decide if this recognition was from genuine appreciation or whether that section of the state was such an intellectual desert that the Kansas State Historical Society in desperation grabbed at any straw.

Realizing from such incidents as these that I had a pretty fair image among Kansas writers, I knew it would be best for me to meet Irma Wassall. I'd be polite but get rid of her as soon as possible.

I screwed around in my office upstairs at the Coliseum, went to the bar and downed a couple of Cuba Libres, and at last reluctantly, a half hour late, started slowly for the information desk where I was to meet my guest. Around 150 feet away I spotted a young woman who even at that distance was positively stunning. Immediately I bemoaned my fate in not having a gorgeous doll like that waiting instead of the grizzly bear I would meet. Then the dazzler turned her head in my direction, saw me, and smiled.

It was Irma Wassall, of course. She knew me from the description given her.

I tried for that old poker face from high school but don't think I quite made it. I must have looked like a hound dog that had treed something nice but didn't know what it was. Irma was in her late twenties and exquisitely lovely with an exotic, continental look that came from Hungarian gypsy ancestors. She wore clothes so well that she modeled newly designed dresses, created by a close personal friend, for buyers at Kansas City department stores and for Marshall Field's in Chicago. In addition to her unusual appearance, she wrote sensitive poetry, played guitar, and was so well informed on jazz she was a correspondent for *Down Beat* magazine.

Inwardly, I berated myself for throwing away that half hour through fear of boredom. But I did my best to compensate. With the aid of innumerable daiquiris, I occupied her time for some six hours straight until she had to return to her hotel. Since then I have taken no chances on another goof when somebody wants to meet me; I have learned to be on time.

As soon as the exposition closed its doors, I again joined the publicity staff of the Republican National Committee, this time to help put over Wendell Willkie for president. Unlike in 1936, I could give this candidate wholehearted support for I had confidence in his ability. During this campaign I spent a couple of hours daily at GOP headquarters in the Loop where I was assigned a private office.

This led to my first meeting with Mrs. Charlotta Bass, militant and courageous editor of the *California Eagle,* on leave from Los Angeles to work at party headquarters. Unfortunately, there was obvious dissention among dusky leaders. The nominal head of the division was so determined to impress the white national leadership that he vetoed a number of programs and expenditures proposed by the veteran and experienced old guard and after the election proudly returned several thousand dollars in unspent funds. Veteran leaders shook their heads in disgust. Deficit, yes; surplus, no!

61

In 1941 registration day came for all adult males up to the age of thirty-five. We knew we would soon fight the Axis. Hitler had gobbled up most of Europe west of Russia and had laid siege to the British Isles. Obviously only the armed intervention of the United States could halt his conquest of the world.

I did not doubt I would be deferred because of my job at ANP. My problem was whether to take the time to register. For many years, since I was in high school and college when I was occasionally mistaken for my mother's husband or her brother, I had looked from five to fifteen years older than I was. At the Atlanta *World* I had at first found it impossible to convince them I was only twenty-five, instead of the thirty or thirty-five they insisted I had to be. Thus it occurred to me I should be able to make it without registering.

But suddenly the pendulum began swinging in the opposite direction. For no ascertainable reason, instead of overestimating my age people began asking if I was "still under thirty." So when the day came I registered. The young white woman who filled out my draft card was determined not to offend. Under the heading "complexion" she hesitated, then slowly wrote "light brownskin." This I carried on my identification card for the duration of the draft. Luckily I did not need to use it or I might have been charged with forgery.

With the nation daily expecting to be sucked into the vortex of global conflict, General George Marshall, chief of staff, scheduled a conference in Washington with black editors from all over America to rally support.[23] The administration realized discrimination had produced strong dissatisfaction among darker citizens, yet at this same time some semblance of national unity was essential for victory.

Of course both Claude Barnett and I could not attend. Claude usually took care of such conferences anyway.

"I want to get your ideas on what might be presented to the chief of staff," he told me. "If you have any kind of program in mind, let me know and I'll see that it gets aired."

Here, virtually handed to me on the proverbial platter, was the chance of a lifetime to attack, before witnesses and at the very top, a disgraceful policy of long standing. That was our entrenched system of two armies, one white and one black. It was as economically wasteful and spiritually divisive as Jim Crow schools. Further, I had studied the history of the armed forces. I knew that in the Revolutionary War many units were completely integrated and that in the War of 1812, black and white seamen served together as equals on our ships. But instead of progressing, our official policy was now separatist and reactionary.

Friction between black and white military units then in training frequently broke into the open. Although the Pentagon tried to keep it secret, race riots had exploded in a number of camps, and more would occur. Greater effort was put forth by some Caucasians in fighting Afro-Americans than in preparing to battle Nazis and Fascists.

"Tell General Marshall," I said to Claude, "that the time has come to field only one American army. It is ridiculous to talk of destroying fascism abroad while maintaining rigid master race policies within our own ranks. Ask him to use his power and influence to smash our own ethnic barriers in the armed services. Tell him we want an integrated, unified army instead of two separate and distinct armies who, by the very nature of American racial practices, are going to waste time, energy, and blood fighting each other.

"Of course I know what his answer will be. He's going to reply that the army is not the place to engage in 'sociological experiments,' that it must 'follow the traditions of the nation at large.' When he springs that line, here is an alternative. Ask him to lend his power and prestige to volunteer mixed units. In other words, try to get his cooperation in permitting those white and black soldiers willing to serve together to form new integrated units. In this way nobody will be forced into a relationship he is not willing to accept. Nor can the Pentagon be accused of shoving a sociological experiment down the resisting throats of its soldiers."

This historic meeting between General Marshall and Afro-American editors was scheduled for 8 December 1941. One day before came the attack on Pearl Harbor which led to the declaration of war against Japan, Germany, and Italy. Nevertheless, since the editors had already reached or were enroute to Washington, the conference went ahead as scheduled.

Barnett presented the proposal to Marshall substantially as I had outlined, and the general vetoed it in the same way I had anticipated. But the issue had been raised and the chief of staff put on the spot in front of the widest possible coterie of our leaders. The question of an integrated army was officially on the record before many witnesses.

Immediately after the close of the conference, the NAACP launched a nationwide petition campaign, creating strong sentiment for the proposal and obtaining thousands of signatures demanding mixed army units. Many newspapers wrote strong editorials in favor. Liberal white college groups joined the action, obtaining still more signatures on petitions which were sent to the Pentagon.

I asked ANP correspondents everywhere to interview white and colored soldiers at random and write of their reactions to the proposal. From the resultant stories, widely printed in our publications, I learned that many white youths even from deepest Dixie did not object to serving in the same units with black Americans if it meant a speedier victory over the Axis.

With the pressure mounting from many areas, the big brass in the Pentagon finally had to take action. During the Battle of the Bulge, the American army at last broke with custom and inaugurated the radical innovation of an experimental voluntary fighting unit, just as I had proposed through Claude Barnett. Although those who signed for this special outfit knew they had to give up their ratings and be reduced to private, there were more than enough men of good will who chose to make this sacrifice on behalf of practical democracy to fill the initial quota. This was the beginning of the end for two separate and distinct armies. At last jim crow as the official Pentagon policy was crumbling.

Undoubtedly, had I not been able to have the concept of voluntary integration brought up before General Marshall in front of reputable and influential witnesses, the change to mixed units would have taken place as a fact of evolution. Nevertheless, it was presented to the highest soldier in the armed forces the day following Pearl Harbor, and under circumstances where it could not be shunted aside or ignored. I cannot think of a more strategic moment this century.

62

I received my anticipated occupational deferment. Selective Service headquarters assumed I would be far more valuable for maintaining morale by working as an editor than as a draftee. Yet as the war progressed, I came to believe certain forces in Washington may have thought they had made a serious mistake, for I kept up a running battle with the Office of Censorship throughout the duration.

Of course, the war and our inferior status brought into being many topical and realistic blues songs. In keeping with the bitter beauty of "Strange Fruit," first recorded by Billie Holiday, Josh White sang six stirring songs of angry protest in an album produced by Keynote Records called *Southern Exposure, An Album of Jim Crow Blues.* Liner notes were written by Richard Wright. Under such titles as "Jim Crow Train," "Hard Times Blues," "Defense Factory Blues," "Uncle Sam Says," "Bad Housing Blues," and "Southern Exposure," an accurate picture of the status of Afro-Americans was tellingly rendered. More than thirty-five years later, many of the complaints are still valid.

With the white masses seemingly determined to enforce the disgraceful conditions pinpointed in these and similar works and our soldiers split into two armies, riots occurred with disgusting frequency. For the most part, our shooting interracial civil war was ignored by the Caucasian press unless battles were of such magnitude they could not be sloughed over. As for me, I duly recorded and released to our newspapers a report on these as well as other overt acts of raw prejudice. I felt Afro-America was entitled to know the truth. Many of these reports came to me laboriously written in longhand by some of the servicemen involved, often signed jointly by several. Fort Huachuca in Arizona was a key training post with a hospital staffed by dusky doctors headed by Dr. M. O. Bousfield, on leave from the Julius Rosenwald Fund. Some of the soldiers, formerly of a National Guard unit from Chicago, were personal friends of both Claude and myself. We were also personally acquainted with others sent to training camps all over America.

The Office of Censorship at Washington dutifully monitored every black paper in the nation. Most appeared toward the end of the week with copies reaching the capitol on Saturday or Monday. Shortly afterward, I would receive a long-distance call from Washington. Every conversation was so similar, I sometimes had the feeling we were both reading from the same previously rehearsed script:

O.C.: I'm calling concerning that story released by ANP and appearing in Negro papers about that little trouble in ————.

Me: What about it?

O.C.: You should not have released it.

Me: Why not? Didn't it happen?

O.C.: That's not the point. Such stories hamper national unity.

Me: So did the trouble. ANP doesn't create the news. We merely report what happens.

O.C.: Yes, but you should not have sent it out.

Me: Tell you what. If the federal government will eliminate racism and get away from the two-army system, one white and one black which so often fight each other, then we won't have these riots and clashes, and I won't be able to send out such news stories, will I?

O.C.: You know the army can't engage in any sociological experiments. We've got a job to do without spending time trying to change community attitudes.

Me: If Uncle Sam can't do it, who can?

O.C.: You know we got a war to fight.

Me: Then why doesn't the army fight it, instead of black troops?

O.C.: You're getting away from the point. You should stop sending out news releases which give aid and comfort to our national enemies.

Me: Stop the prejudice, and the stories will stop themselves.

At this point, our conversation usually ended. My caller had dutifully performed his assigned task, and I had said what I believed was right. This dialogue continued throughout much of World War II and after a number of conversations, my assorted callers and I developed a pretty fair long-distance relationship.

Then, after V-day, I learned that despite the number of stories sent out by ANP, we had come nowhere near covering the violence between troops of the two armies.

Nevertheless, by giving the widest possible publicity to the many instances of racism and the dissatisfaction of Afro-America with the status quo, we forced significant changes in Pentagon policy. Unlike during World War I, we now had a vocal and widely read national press. Our support was essential to victory. Barriers crumbled. At the beginning of the war, we could rise no higher than messman in the navy (despite this, Dorie Miller was a hero at Pearl Harbor[24]); and we were completely barred from the marine corps and from flying war planes, so strongly condemned in Josh White's *Southern Exposure* album. Other ratings were opened in the navy; black marines came into being; a pilot training school was established at Tuskegee, Alabama; and for the first time in history we could point to a general.

Of course the Pentagon patted its own back, detailing the great strides forward in its treatment of darker citizens. And of course I, and others like me, pointed out that certain of these innovations were not progress but served instead to bring us back up to the level of the early 1800s. When the WACs came into being, I took great relish in pointing out that a black woman, Deborah Gannett, fought the entire Revolutionary War with a New England outfit which, of course, saw her color but did not know her sex until she was mustered out.[25] Then, in gratitude, she was granted a pension for the rest of her life. She deserved the rating of first WAC in American history.

During the Battle of the Bulge, when the army finally gave in to insistent pressure and Eisenhower authorized the formation of the volunteer integrated unit, this was in certain ways the salvation of our image in many areas abroad. As the victorious white army liberated various parts of Europe from the Axis, they had begun to replace European fascism with "the American way of life" and its tradition of racism, actually infecting some sections of Europe which never before had known the virus of color prejudice. Integrated liberators provided an antidote before the disease had a chance to permanently cripple its new European victims.

Currently the armed forces are officially integrated. I have felt keen delight in seeing black and white personnel not only serving together but buddying around on leave. Nevertheless, racism still exists, particularly in promotions, ratings, and treatment. Despite gains, white supremacy is still part of the American way of life. The armed forces may be desegregated, but discrimination still lives.

63

Close to ANP headquarters on the second floor of the Supreme Liberty Life Insurance Co. building at 35th and South Parkway was a small office occasionally used by a serious, good-looking dark brownskin youth who was a kind of glorified handyman for Attorney Earl B. Dickerson. A top official at the insurance firm, Dickerson was also a politician. He had served as alderman of the second ward in the city council and had his eye on Dawson's seat in congress. He lost. But the feud between Dawson and

Dickerson remained bitter. However, when FDR appointed Dickerson to the FEPC, the two rivals temporarily buried the hatchet—and for the first time not in each other.

The serious youth was named John Johnson. For some time now, he had a dream of starting a magazine patterned after the *Readers Digest.* Often he came to our office and discussed the possibility with me. And in one of the glaring mistakes made in my ample history of errors, I discouraged him. There had not yet appeared a successful Afro-American magazine. I knew of only two being published at that time: *Opportunity,* by the National Urban League, and *Crisis,* by the NAACP. These were, of course, subsidized. In the past there had been two grandiose attempts: *Reflexus,* in the early 1920s, and *Abbott's Monthly,* which the Chicago *Defender,* despite its resources, found unprofitable. The mortality rate among magazines had been almost 100 percent. I told him I could see no future in such a venture.

Nevertheless, Johnny said he was going to try. Meanwhile, since I read scores of white publications every week, he asked me to save for him any articles which I thought might merit condensing. I agreed. If I could not encourage him, the least I could do was aid in this way.

One day he announced the first issue would soon appear. I looked incredulous, wondering where he had obtained financing since those South Siders with money that I knew saw this proposed venture as a harebrained scheme. Then I learned from other sources that, during the Dawson-Dickerson truce, Johnson had been given a political job requiring little time away from his regular duties. A year or so earlier, he had married a social worker who remained on her job. Johnny and his wife lived on his regular salary and saved her paycheck along with the income from the political job to finance the magazine.

Not only I, but virtually everybody in the South Side newspaper field was dumbfounded when the first issue of *Negro Digest* appeared, crammed with articles culled and condensed from a variety of publications. In looks and format, it was thoroughly professional.

"Here it is," Johnny said. "And now that it's actually out, some of those I begged to invest in it months ago have been calling me and saying they've changed their minds and want to put in some money. But I've turned them all down. They weren't available when I really wanted them, and now I don't need them. There's nobody's cash involved but that of my wife and me. We have enough to bring out a few issues, and we're going to sink or swim on nobody's money but our own."

Negro Digest was an almost instant money maker. Each month circulation took a great leap upward. Originally published from the little office down the hall, Johnny soon had to take bigger quarters, hire a larger and larger staff, and quit his job with the insurance company. This was 1941. Because of widespread unrest and demands for a share of the democracy we were asked to defend, white publications devoted considerable space to "the Negro problem," thus automatically providing a rich source of material for *Digest* condensation. But that was not all. Original articles and reviews were bought for the new magazine. As for Johnny, he not only had a surprisingly sound business head but, what was equally important, the knack of hiring talented people, white and black. Among them was Ben Burns, a brilliant young white editor of strong leftist leanings who had worked wonders with the *Defender* but was now fed up with the trials of that job. For considerable time, I was listed as a contributing editor and wrote several original articles. But when the war drew to a close and the flood of articles for condensation dwindled, Johnny turned to a picture magazine. Thus was *Ebony* born, the most successful publishing project in Afro-American history. For over thirty years now, the money has Niagaraed in.

Undoubtedly, a major cause for the surprising, instant success of *Negro Digest* was its birth at the time when black America hungered emotionally for a magazine of this type. Even two years earlier, it might have failed. But the timing was right. Even more right has been the Johnson judgment which has catapulted him into the millionaire class and made him one of the most influential men in America.

64

During the opening years of the war, away from the office, I did little more than vegetate. I wrote little poetry. My creative energies were channeled almost exclusively toward photography. As head of the Lens Camera Club, I became bitten by the salon bug and was successful in having some of my prints accepted and hung in international exhibitions. Otherwise I did nothing but put on weight, ballooning up to 250 pounds.

Then came two developments within a short space of time that shocked me out of my mental stupor. They were a lynching at Sikeston, Missouri, and the race riot in Detroit. Despite our noble objectives neon-lighted in Washington and the attitude of collective righteous indignation aimed at the Axis, our own great nation, that champion of democracy and freedom, had permitted the same kind of atrocities found in Hitler's Germany. Not even a global war would make our racists curb their color hate. The mob victim in Missouri and those slaughtered in the Detroit ghetto were just as dead as any Jew slain in Warsaw or Berlin and for the same reason—the master race ideology. With millions of my black brothers fighting these beliefs abroad, I felt compelled to battle this ideology actively right here at home.

But there would be this one important difference for me. For the first time in my life I would quit being a loner.

No matter how consuming my wrath, I could get nowhere by myself. My poetry was primarily a one-man protest. Until now I had been a solitary rebel, a lonely anarchist. Only once had I joined formally with others, and that was during the days of the Chicago chapter of the League of American Writers. From this time on I resolved to join hands with others seriously interested in curing the disease of American racism. I simply could not make it as a one-man gang.

I knew, of course, that the establishment tolerates the solitary protester. It smiles and points to him as proof that free speech *does* exist in America. The unwritten rule is that you can yell as loudly as you please—by yourself. But when two or more of you get together you become a threat even though you speak only in whispers. Two or more automatically become a conspiracy which endangers "Our Way of Life"; and those agencies, such as the FBI or House Committee on Un-American Activities, which ignore the injustices triggering your protests, now begin hounding you as dangerous radicals. I had seen this happen over and over again.

From now on I knew I would be described as a Communist, but frankly I had reached the stage where I didn't give a damn. Too many people I respected as Freedom Fighters were listed as Red for me to fear name calling. Actually I knew personally only a handful of genuine Communists, among them Angelo Herndon and Ben Davis, Jr., in Atlanta, plus, in Chicago, Richard Wright and William L. Patterson, an attorney by profession. I was fully aware of Patterson's efforts on behalf of the Scottsboro boys long before I first met him in Chicago, where he was actively engaged as an editor in addition to his many other endeavors. As for me, in the past I had once contributed an article to *New Masses* as part of a special symposium of Afro-American editors. The genuine Communists I knew as well as others so labeled had one principle in common: to use any and every means to abolish racism. From now on, I would join hands with anybody going my way. Knowing that labor unions had become strong since the birth of the CIO and were battling racism, I contacted several including that headed by my old friend, Willard Townsend, and volunteered my services. Also I immediately started writing a weekly column of editorial comment for ANP members.

Since those smeared with the Red brush were accused of "taking orders from Moscow," I should explain my attitude toward Russia. It had shifted as time passed. Like most readers of the general press, I had been brainwashed for years after the Bolshevik revolution. These pathological screams of hate continued without letup, led by the Hearst press. But at some point, I began hearing about the official policies of the Soviet Union and its determination to stamp out discrimination. Knowing also that Russia had no colonies and was strongly opposed to the imperialism under which my black kinsmen lived in Africa, and that those American forces which most staunchly resisted our own demands for equality were the most rabid foes of Russia, I concluded the Soviet Union held the same position internationally that blacks were in domestically. Russians were looked upon as the niggers of the globe. Moscow also bitterly opposed the Italian conquest of Ethiopia and alone of the major powers supported Haile Selassie when he pleaded for League of Nations help. Like the vast majority of Afro-Americans who thought about the issue, I considered Red Russia our friend.

This feeling had grown at ANP. One of our most active correspondents was a former Minneapolis postal clerk now living in Moscow and writing under the name of Chatwood Hall. I also interviewed Afro-Americans who had gone to Russia to get employment in keeping with their specialized abilities. What they told me differed drastically from propaganda in the general press. America was as intentionally misinformed about the Soviet Union as were Caucasians about Afro-America.

And I had felt betrayed when Stalin signed that nonaggression pact with Hitler. So the Russians were as hypocritical as the rest of the white world! I, and other souls I knew, felt we had been deserted by our only potential champion. But after all, since the Russians were white, what else could you really expect?

Frankly, I was happy when Hitler attacked the Soviets. Now order had been restored, and again I could feel kinship with the sprawling Red nation. Of course, Hearst and other ultra-violent critics said that Russia was an empty shell and its army would collapse under the first gentle zephyr. When this did not happen, we black editors generally took this as added misinformation disseminated by the general press. Reactionaries had fallen victims to their own propaganda. With the United States and the U.S.S.R. joining hands in total war against the Axis, none but our own ultra-conservatives held enmity toward that nation. This merely underlined my determination to pay no attention to Red-baiting by those forces who had never been my friends.

Thus I worked with all kinds of groups. I made no distinction between those labeled Communist, Socialist, or merely liberal. My sole criterion was this: Are you with me in my determination to wipe out white supremacy? Because I had some smattering of prestige as a writer and wielded some influence as an opinion maker in the black press at large, my active participation was welcomed.

The interracial American Youth for Democracy was being organized.[26] I became a national sponsor and frequently addressed young people, mainly those of college age. I helped organize and chair conferences on black-white unity, white collar workers, and legislation for servicemen; addressed mixed audiences on black history; accepted membership on the board of directors and became vice chairman of the Chicago Civil Liberties Committee headed by Ira Latimer; worked with the Boy Scout movement; became a member of the board of directors of the Abraham Lincoln School in the Loop, where I conducted courses in the history of jazz music; helped organize the Hot Club of Chicago and emceed a number of the monthly jam sessions; spoke before meetings of various CIO unions in Chicago and Indiana; became an active board member of the National Committee to Combat Anti-Semitism; and began an annual series of lectures at Northwestern University. With all this rash of activity, I took off some fifty pounds of flab.

Naturally I had to cut down on photography, just after my salon acceptances had finally gotten me a national listing among exhibitors. But there was compensation. My multiple interests had brought me into contact with Margaret Taylor Goss, whom I first met at the American Negro Exposition. Margaret had as many things going as I. By profession a schoolteacher, she was also a talented artist, writer, poet, and public speaker. She has since authored several children's books, and her drawings and paintings have hung in international exhibits. In recent years she has also served as director of the DuSable Museum of African-American History in Chicago. But her special value to me was her ability to turn me on poetically, making her one of a small number of people to have that strange power. Thus after a long, fallow period, I began writing poetry again.

I was positive that by now I had attracted the special attention of the House Committee on Un-American Activities. If so, I would accept any resultant citation as an honor, for it would indicate I was beginning to upset the white power structure. But what I had not anticipated was equal success in upsetting associates who were dedicated Communists. This was during what was known as the Earl Browder period, when the party's official position was to soft-pedal harsh criticism of American racism for the sake of "national unity"—an attitude similar in effect to that of conservatives who tried to shoosh anybody who might rock the boat. But I did not listen to that kind of stay-back song from either the left or the right.

Continuing to voice opposition to fascism at home as well as abroad, I wrote a long poem that took up several pages in the April 1944 issue of *Crisis* magazine. Entitled "War Quiz For America" and intended to be read aloud by a leader and a chorus of eight voices, the poem was an effort to paint a realistic portrait in verse of our goal in the war and at home.

Here is the part that made them tear their hair!

Leader: Are these the Four Freedoms for which we fight? Freedom from want

Voice: ("So sorry but we don't hire Negroes. Our white employees won't work with them. The union, you know")

Leader: Freedom from fear

Voice: ("Nigger, take off yo' hat and say 'sir' when you speak to a white man in Arkansas. A smart darky down here's a curiosity—and sometimes we embalm curiosities")

Leader: Freedom of religion

Voice: ("Of course you can't come in here! This is a white church")

Leader: Freedom of speech

Voice: ("We gits along with ouah niggers, so unless you want to leave here feet first don't be puttin' none of them Red social equality ideas in their minds")

       *   *   *

Leader: Have you heard about regimentation in Washington?
           Ten men to run the war
           A hundred to ration black participation

       *   *   *

1st Voice: Uncle Sam, Uncle Sam
Why send me against Axis foes
In the death kissed foxholes
Of New Guinea and Europe
Without shielding my back
From the sniping Dixie lynchers
In the jungles of Texas and Florida?

*   *   *

Leader: Down in Georgia a soldier said:

2nd Voice: "Me? I'm from Paine County, Alabama
"Born black and I'm gonna die the same way
"Went t' school three yeahs befo' it rotted down. By
the time the white folks got around t' fixing it my first
wife had done died.
"But you oughta see my brothah. Finished State
Teachuh's College an' now he's makin' forty dollah uh
month back home. That's ovah half uh what they pays
white teachuhs.
"Been helpin' Pappy work the same fifty acres fo'
Mistuh Jim his own pappy had. Pappy bought a
single barrel shotgun from Mistuh Jim five yeahs ago.
Paid ten dollahs down an' a dolluh a week an' he still
owes twenty mo'
"Sheriff came 'round an' told me they wanted me in the
Army. Came heah to Fort Benning an' they give me
a gun and a uniform an' three good meals a day.
Fust time I evah knowed a white man to give me
anything
"This mawnin' I heard somebody on a radio say we was
all fightin fo' democracy
"Democracy? What's democracy?"

Leader: Nothing is so final as a bullet through heart or head
And a correctly thrust bayonet is an unanswerable
     argument
For democracy against fascism
For Four Freedoms against oppression.
This you taught me in camps from Miami to Seattle
To use against Nazi, Jap
And it works;
It works in the Pacific Islands

In Africa, In Europe
Everywhere it works
You have convinced me completely
Even as I have become expert
In killing the mad dogs
Leaping high to tear
Democracy's soft throat—
And if that's the technique
If it works in lands I never saw before
Against strangers with faces new to me
Then it must be the right thing to use
Against all foes of freedom
Against all apostles of fascism
Against some people I know
Right here in America.

* * *

So if I'm going to clean up the Rhine
I might as well include the Mississippi
With the understanding
Of course
That it will be only
For democracy against fascism
For Four Freedoms against oppression—
Say, Uncle Sam,
Are you sure you want me to have a gun?

The irony of the situation is that this was far too militant for many leading Communists who belonged to what was generally labeled a subversive, radical movement, thus making Roy Wilkins and his associates at *Crisis* far more belligerent than the avowed Reds of that era.

I never uncritically accepted party positions anyway. Considering myself a freethinker, I openly disagreed with what I thought was wrong. I was skeptical after the Nazi attack on Russia caught the U.S. party with its ideological pants down. One day, what with Hitler and Stalin having signed a nonaggression pact, the American comrades were using every resource at their command to resist American entry into the conflict; in their eyes Roosevelt was a warmonger. While their antiwar propaganda was still flowing, they awoke and found themselves in the embarrassing position of having to eat their words. Unable to get out of their own way, they tripped and fell flat on the ground as they reversed and ran into themselves, now dashing in the opposite direction. I could not place confidence in a leadership that one day condemned FDR to hell and the next painted him as Saint George.

Of course, I could not accept the idea that the struggle against racism must be sacrificed on the altar of national unity. I was eager to aid in any program aimed at increasing intergroup cooperation and respect, but I held tenaciously to my basic belief that the war against fascism must run concurrently at home and abroad. I was called a "black nationalist." Later, at the end of the Browder period, many openly confessed their mistakes. But I could never understand why grown men and women, who considered themselves the leaders of the masses, would blindly follow a program which even a moron could find faulty.

Still another area of basic disagreement was the issue of "self-determination for the black belt." And as to whether those Southern counties with an Afro-American majority "constituted a nation" under Stalin's definition of nationhood, my frankly expressed reaction was that Stalin's criteria in the Soviet Union had no practical relevancy among us souls who couldn't care less about Stalin's views, and that at that time the prevailing goal was complete integration, not separation into a black nation.

After FDR's death and the rapidly widening split in those forces which brought victory in the shooting war, I wrote a note to Ben Davis, Jr., suggesting that the party make a strong effort to maintain the huge reservoir of good will stored in the black press. Our editors were warmly inclined toward the Soviet Union which was looked upon as a staunch foe of racism; and the U.S. party had regained prestige lost during the Browder period through its militant action since then for civil rights, equal opportunities, antilynching legislation, and abolition of the poll tax. I felt it would be detrimental to the interests of black citizens to allow the white power structure to bust this alliance. I suggested therefore that the national headquarters assign a capable liaison man whose exclusive duty would be traveling around the nation and becoming friends with all our editors. Ben wrote back enthusiastically endorsing the proposal and asked me to spell it out in detail for submission to the top echelon. This I did. But nothing happened. And before long, Afro-American newspapers became almost as violently anti-Communist as the general press.

However, despite these and other differences, I worked with known and suspected Communists when I believed our goals were similar. I have never felt it worthwhile to burn down the house merely to get rid of the cockroaches.

Despite my vacillating association with the left, I looked upon Claude Barnett's and my activities as complementing each other. Each of us was working in his own way for an end to white supremacy. Claude sincerely felt he could get farther by joining with those men of means willing to spend money to better our conditions without really drastic changes in the establishment. I felt that together we covered both sides of the street.

However, my activities once got Claude into temporary difficulties. He was special assistant to Henry Wallace, then Secretary of Agriculture, and when the time came for reappointment he received a routine check by the FBI. Imagine his surprise when the FBI produced a dossier showing he had spoken at public meetings and sponsored groups along with known Communists! I laughed. The FBI had goofed again. Apparently lending substance to the belief that all niggers look alike to white men, the agents had confused Claude with me. The mistake was easily rectified—but this did nothing to change my low opinion of the ineptitude of this key agency on matters involving blacks.

Two months or so after another particularly brutal double lynching in Florida during the war years, witnessed by a mob of several hundred jeering whites, an FBI agent called on Joe Johnson, a South Side postal employee, to question him about rumored Communist affiliations. When the agent revealed the reason for his visit, Joe looked at him with wonder straddling his face.

"I am truly amazed," he told the agent. "Here the federal government has been able to track me down and go to all the expense of sending a special man to investigate my actions and associations, yet I am a virtual nobody, unknown to all but a few people, not in the public eye, and completely inconspicuous.

"Yet a whole group of agents was sent to Florida after that lynching and although several hundred whites were present and took part in this atrocity, with photographs freely taken, after two months the FBI has been unable to arrest or even identify any one of the culprits. From your own proven ability to track down nonentities like me, don't you think *you* might be able to get results if you were assigned to the Florida case?"

65

Shortly after becoming a member of the board of directors of Abraham Lincoln School located on a top floor of a building in the heart of the Loop, I initiated possibly the first regular courses ever given in the History of Jazz at a school. It was instigated primarily by Art Stern, a young Jewish intellectual, who realized the significance of this music in our continuing struggle for equality. This was 1944.

Since 1937 I had been collecting jazz records. Two years later I started writing reviews for ANP, regularly receiving news releases directly from the manufacturers. John Hammond had been helpful in establishing contacts. At that time Columbia, Victor, and Decca had the field virtually to themselves. There were a few small independents, such as Commodore; Blue Note came later, and gradually hundreds of others sprang up, many in the infant days of bop.

I considered myself more of a historian and reporter than critic, although I did try to rate each platter passing through my hands. Virtually all jazz records were ten-inch spinning at 78 rpm, although now and then on very rare occasions a twelve-incher would come through. By saving what I considered the best of the current production and searching through secondhand stores and junk shops, plus calling on persons whom I learned had collections, I had been able to accumulate a historically representative library. It now rests at the Moorland-Spingarn Research Center of Howard University.

The course was planned not only to present the effects resulting from this revolutionary music but to explore the socio-economic factors which caused its creation. My continually growing knowledge of our history here and in Africa enabled me to isolate those strong and persistent elements of African culture which survived slavery and were the heart and soul of jazz. An album made in the bush by an expedition from the Field Museum of Natural History and a number of private recordings from the files of Dr. Melville Herskovits of Northwestern University, world-renowned anthropologist who had specialized in African peoples, were specially valuable.[27] In this way I was able not only to underline the growing global importance of jazz but impart considerable facts about black history here and in Africa.

Although this new course received wide publicity in South Side publications, only two or three souls enrolled during the several years I taught at this thoroughly integrated adult evening school. One reason was a reluctance to leave the ghetto at night and journey several miles to downtown Chicago; another was the tendency on our part, born of experience, to feel uncomfortable around whites no matter how liberal their attitude. Equally important was a lack of interest in the anatomy of jazz. As a group, we were too close to the music. Jazz was an emotional part of our daily lives. We made it happen and were not too interested in why. I knew of only two prominent nonmusician collectors and serious students of jazz in Afro-America: Sterling Brown, noted poet of Howard University, and E. Simms Campbell, the cartoonist who won his fame at *Esquire* magazine.

On the other hand, when I had discussed jazz and the blues with representative recordings on the home grounds of the South Side, say at the Hall Branch Library, South Side Community Center, or at special events in private homes before virtually all black audiences, interest was uniformly high with many listeners confessing afterward they had never realized how fascinating and significant was the story of jazz.

My Lincoln classes thus consisted almost exclusively of young Caucasians, most of them collectors and serious students of jazz, who were far more concerned about its past and developers than were we, its creators. Some of the city's leading critics and apostles dropped by periodically, among them the late George Hoefer, Paul Edward Miller, and Dr. John Steiner. Among the enrollees was a young white drummer, Bill Page, originally from Georgia, who amazed me by telling how in his home state he had fronted a small mixed band specializing in college gigs. Still another enrollee for a brief period was Martha Glaser, who flipped particularly over Illinois Jacquet's tenor sax meanderings when Norman Granz's Jazz at the Philharmonic played Chicago for the first time. Shortly afterward she became personal manager for Errol Garner, a post she held until his death. I established good rapport with most members of the class, especially Helen Canfield, a tall, longhaired, young blonde of obvious Scandinavian ancestry whom I later married.

This class also became the nucleus of the far broader Hot Club of Chicago, a city-wide group of musicians and fans formed mainly to present jazz artists in monthly jam sessions under far more favorable playing and listening conditions than were possible in bars and nightclubs. We featured not only local musicians but visiting stars filling engagements elsewhere in Chicagoland. We brought back into the spotlight such former stars as Chippie Hill, the blues singer, who had dropped out of sight and was found working as a dishwasher. On the strength of our rediscovery, she sang again at clubs and in concerts until her death in New York several years later. Some of the combinations we assembled clicked so well together they made recordings for Victor. I personally emceed a number of the sessions; Dave Garroway, then a disc jockey, but later a TV personality, took charge of several. However, few South Siders attended the concerts, held at Moose Hall on the near North Side, unless they were personal friends of some of the musicians, despite my constant publicity aired on my radio program.

I had added the job of disc jockey to my other activities late in 1945 with a short show called Bronzeville Brevities, Monday through Friday over WJJD, the Marshall Field radio station. This fifteen-minute broadcast was sponsored by a wine company romancing more Black Belt sales. I had arranged my schedule to take time off from ANP. No stranger to radio, I had appeared numerous times on jazz and discussion programs. But I was virtually shaking with fright at my own inaugural broadcast. I was now alone and completely responsible for what went over the ether. When I was on somebody else's show, any fluffs could be covered up or glossed over, but by myself there was no hiding place. Luckily I was sitting down; if it had been necessary to stand I think I might have keeled over from sheer terror on that maiden show.

But in a couple of days I lost my nervousness. Since the program was only fifteen minutes long (I was paid as much for this job, incidentally, as I made at ANP), I had to make each moment count. Because I wanted Bronzeville Brevities to differ musically from the rhythm and blues fare aired over other wavelengths beamed to the South Side, I played three or four genuine jazz recordings, giving current news of the musicians between platters. Each disc was a collector's item from my own library, and I named the personnel as well as pointed out what especially to listen for. I selected at least one recording daily with a mixed personnel, thus enabling me to propagandize on the democracy of jazz and suggest increased integration in other fields. I also played upcoming jazz jam sessions of the Hot Club.

One day I received a note from a white youth named Harold Marks who wrote he was one of my regular listeners and a lover of good jazz. He said he would like to attend the next session but wanted to know if Moose Hall would be difficult to get to with crutches. I thought it over a couple of days, then asked Helen to call and say we would pick him up at his residence for the following Sunday performance.

It was December, with its unpredictable weather. By Sunday there was snow and ice on the ground. When Helen and I drove up and we saw the flight of steps leading up to his first-floor apartment, I knew that using crutches would be impossible. I picked him up bodily, carried him to the car and then into the hall. When the concert was over I reversed the process. Afterward I thought no more about it until a couple of weeks later when I opened the Chicago *Daily News* to the radio section and found a three-column headline, "Swing Fan Gets a Helping Hand to a Concert—Not On The Radio." Harold Marks had written a letter to the radio editor detailing the entire episode and concluding: "You are probably wondering how come all the flag waving and all the good words and everything else. There are a number of reasons. One is that Mr. Davis is colored and I am otherwise white. Then we are perfect strangers. Then you're wondering what the trouble is. It's some pretty strange illness called multiple sclerosis, but with fine people like Mr. Davis things go a lot easier."

This story in the city's largest afternoon paper, plus a similar story in the *Defender,* did not hurt my radio show. Unfortunately, my audience was overwhelmingly white. Although I seemed to get across my ideas to them, I did not materially increase wine sales on the South Side, and the sponsor declined to renew the initial contract. When it was announced Bronzeville Brevities would be discontinued, so many telephone calls and letters came in from white listeners that WJJD kept me on for several additional weeks. They expected to sell the spot to an independent auto manufacturer in Michigan who was preparing to publicize a new postwar car. The auto firm then ran into production problems complicated by a strike. Since it was now impossible to set a definite target date, WJJD discontinued the sustaining show but asked me to stand by. Meanwhile I accepted the executive editorship of the Chicago *Star,* a citywide labor weekly; and between these added duties and my job at ANP I had no time for a radio show.

My course on jazz came near the end of the swing era and when the big bands were declining. A new kind of sound, that of bop, was rising. On recordings by Jay McShann and his Kansas City band, I had heard an alto sax with a unique but moving solo style. That was Charlie Parker, later to become one of the gods of bop along with Dizzy Gillespie, Thelonious Monk, and a few others. The Hot Club had little interest in this new music. John Lucas, chairman, was hung up on New Orleans and Chicago style; Catherine Jacobson, co-chairman, was the wife of Bud Jacobson, well-known Chicago-style clarinetist; George Hoefer, treasurer, was an authority on collector's items and recording personnel; and John T. Schenck, secretary, was impatiently awaiting a legacy which he was to spend promoting a recently resurrected Bunk Johnson, legendary New Orleans cornetist who was a teacher of Louis Armstrong. Schenck, incidentally, ran rapidly through his inheritance but died happy.

As for me, at the beginning I resented bop, not so much because of the radical sound but because some of its practitioners admitted they were trying to curve jazz into a form acceptable to traditional white standards. They wanted to make it "respectable" for use on the concert stage. Personally I felt jazz was strong and dynamic enough to rise or fall on its own terms. Of course, change was inevitable; the music could not remain static. I enthused over the innovations of Duke Ellington's band, believing this amazing group stayed years ahead of its peers; and I could never fault the leader's experiments. But at all times his music remained strongly rooted in the blues and its characteristic tonal scale, as well as in African rhythmic complexity. And as time passed, I accepted this brand new bag of Parker and Gillespie because of its anchor in the blues, just as I accepted vigorous Latin American music because of its pulse emanating from Africa, only slightly adulterated through its sojourn in Spain and Portugal before being rejuvenated by Africans in the Caribbean and South America.

I was strongly motivated by black pride. Although jazz came from the integration of European melodic concepts with African musical traditions, it was black in emotional content and could have been created only by a people suffering from the socio-economic pressures of living black in a white world. I have no objections to blending, but I oppose any attempt to absorb and neutralize jazz, the only original artistic contribution to the world coming from the United States. Let jazz alter the work of Bartok and Stravinsky and the other leading composers, but I do not want classic European traditions to sap the vitality of jazz. For that reason, I later had little patience with the West Coast groups who came out with watered down contrivances, as well as most of the Third Stream experiments. In this music, the black soul of jazz had been emaciated. Conversely, I have praise for such artists as Art Blakey, Coltrane, Rollins, Redd, Mingus, Saunders, Shepp, and the rest who have not only returned to Africa for renewed inspiration but have tuned their ears to the sounds of Asia in developing a broader, more encompassing music of dynamic protest derived from non-European sources.

I also have unlimited praise for those white artists who are genuine first-class jazzicians—but they attain this ranking by growing roots in the blues, by moving around in its very guts. Jazz is no longer an exclusive black preserve as it was near the turn of the century; today it has absorbed and reveals the relevant experiences of other ethnic groups. The skin and flesh of American culture has changed and with it the skin and flesh of jazz. But basics remain, even if in new raiment. The spiritual descendants of those horrified by the revolutionary protest of jazz in the early part of this century are those today upset by the blazing anger of an Archie Shepp or an Albert Ayler.

Not only Lincoln School but other groups with which I worked closely found jazz and the blues immeasurably valuable in helping put across a point of view. Big Bill Broonzy, the topical troubadour from Arkansas, found ready audiences for his realistic blues commenting on the contemporary scene, as did Leadbelly, the legendary blues and folk singer who made many appearances. Folk music and the blues blended together anyway in the many hootenannies which included such folk singers as Pete Seeger, Woody Guthrie, and occasionally Burl Ives. As for myself, one of my most interesting evenings was when I shared the spotlight on stage with Paul Draper, renowned dancer, and Larry Adler, harmonic virtuoso.

With the number of noted Broadway performers whom Lincoln School presented when they came to Chicago, it was inevitable that the Chicago *Tribune,* then the bulwark of reaction, would turn its battery our way. They laid down an editorial barrage in a series of articles lambasting Lincoln School as the "little Red school house." But in a way, it backfired.

Marshall Field III, heir to the vast fortune left by Chicago's foremost merchant prince, received several hundred million dollars and almost as huge a guilt complex. After going to a psychiatrist, he was told, so the story goes, to get rid of some of his money and his guilt by helping mankind. In New York, he had backed that experimental afternoon daily, *P.M.* Then he came to Chicago where he founded a morning newspaper, the Chicago *Sun,* in direct opposition to the *Tribune.* The *Sun* strongly supported Franklin D. Roosevelt and his policies; the *Tribune* was an uncompromising foe. Thus when the *Tribune* launched its attack on Lincoln School, Field sent over a personal representative and quietly contributed fifty thousand dollars to the institution. Field followed the policy of liberals and progressives; they supported whatever the *Tribune* attacked. As one young woman active in her union told me: "If the *Trib* ever comes out editorially against syphilis, I'll do my damndest to get infected tomorrow."

People generally were not frightened by Red baiting during the war years. Russia was our "noble ally," and the unyielding defense of Stalingrad had warmed most of our hearts. FDR had conferred with Stalin and parted on friendly terms. Thus the "united front" brought together nations and individuals who soon, under a different President, would be at each other's throats. I can't even begin to remember all the meetings I chaired or the book reviews I gave or the speeches I made. Once when the great historian Dr. Herbert Aptheker came to Chicago for a series of lectures, I chaired his appearances on three consecutive nights in as many sections of Chicago.

66

I was a Herskovits fan long before I ever met the famous anthropologist. His volume *Myth of the Negro past* (1941), part of the series which produced Myrdal's *An American Dilemma* (1944), had been like a Bible, providing facts to refute confused blacks who believed we were merely carbon copies of Whitey. I had long felt Afro-Americans are a distinct new people, unlike any others on the face of the globe. Both culturally and biologically, we are a goulash of Europeans, Africans, and American Indians—with African dominant. This varies from individual to individual, from section to section. But it exists. Through personal investigation, the noted scientist had uncovered and documented a long list of surviving Africanisms, showing that despite slavery and its crushing repression, we retained strong cultural and behavioral patterns traceable directly to the land of our dark ancestors.

We became personally acquainted following a lecture he gave at the Hall Branch Library on the South Side when he played private recordings made of "Sankies" in Trinidad and Jamaica. This music vividly illustrated how these Baptist hymns originating in England had been completely transformed by African musical patterns retained in this section of the Caribbean. I was so fascinated he gave me duplicates to be used in my study of jazz music. A warm friendship developed, culminating in an invitation to address a special class at Northwestern where he was a professor.

This was a unique class in social studies, all members remaining together through four years of college. I was to address the sophomores. As Dr. Herskovits phrased it, textbooks and professors could provide only part of the instruction. Since I was a working black newspaperman with practical knowledge of conflicting forces, he was certain I could give what he called "a realistic, hardboiled approach" to race relations.

My first lecture was in 1944. Evidently I made a highly acceptable presentation, for at a luncheon immediately afterward attended by the professor and others in the department, Dr. Herskovits asked that I return next year for the same kind of lecture. In 1945 every member of the staff who could get there was present, and the anthropologist had planted liberal students to ask leading questions in the discussion period following my talk.

"Most members of this class come from fairly wealthy to rich white North Shore families," he explained. "Many of them cannot see how racism ever directly touches their lives. I want you to shake them up."

After I finished my discussion and had answered a couple of polite but innocuous questions, a plant asked:

"Why is it most Negroes are crowded mainly into one section on the South Side with so many of the buildings decrepit and rundown?"

"Because it means more profits for the landlords," I replied.

"Why is that? Who are the landlords?"

"The landlords are mainly wealthy whites who live elsewhere, quite often in spacious estates on the North Shore."

I was watching my audience closely, and for the first time I saw some of the students stiffen.

"But how does that mean extra profits for those white absentee landlords?" the plant continued.

This was my cue to explain how the system worked. White realty agencies, on order from these absentee landlords, arbitrarily set the boundaries of the ghetto, enforced by restrictive residential covenants. Black Chicagoans were thus herded into a compound denser than any other part of the city. Housing was therefore insufficient, creating artificial shortages and forcing higher rents through intense competition for living quarters. Absentee landlords chopped large apartments into small flats, with each unit sometimes renting for more than the entire apartment before partition. Since the owners did not live here, they usually did not care how badly the buildings deteriorated so long as the income remained high. They knew that even when these old buildings became rank slums, rat-infested, windows broken, and plumbing busted, they would still be snapped up at good rentals. Landlords who owned property in the ghetto usually made three or four times as much profit as those who owned comparable property in white neighborhoods. This glutted income assured gracious living in North Shore suburbs.

By this time, some students had become red-faced, and others squirmed uncomfortably in their seats.

"But not everybody who signs a restrictive residential covenant is a large landowner. Some don't own any ghetto property at all, yet they sign. Why is that?" another plant asked.

"Because the real estate agencies feed them a smooth line of racist propaganda, and they swallow it all, hook, line, and sinker," I answered.

Since it would never do to let the small white property owner know the real reason for restrictive covenants was to produce whopping profits for the giant absentee landlords, he had to be sold from another angle. He was frightened therefore into believing that without the protection afforded by covenants, he would wake up one morning and find a black family moving next door. Niggers were not only his inferiors and socially unacceptable, he was reminded, but merely by living in a neighborhood they automatically lowered property values. A home owner who had struggled to buy his property could find its value reduced from 20 to even 50 percent. To protect his investment, he should join with other whites and sign an agreement banning blacks from the area. This technique seldom failed.

When it was impossible to get a covenant, still another scheme, known as "block busting," was worked by white realtors. An agent himself bought a building in a white area and resold it at a handsome profit to some soul with good bread anxious to quit the ghetto. Then the agent sat back until the new tenant moved in. As soon as neighbors got a good look, the agent called on them, pointed to the intruders, and offered to buy their property immediately before it decreased too greatly in value. Even a month from now, the deterioration in market price might be 50 percent. The gullible, white, small home owner, virtually quaking in his boots over the fear of great financial loss, often sold immediately. Whereupon the real estate agent promptly resold to black buyers at a huge profit or divided the building into many rental units which soon returned his investment.

As luck would have it, the week prior to my talk a white realtor had bought a three-flat building bordering the eastern edge of the ghetto renting at seventy-five dollars per apartment. Immediately, he divided each floor into three small units and had already signed up nine families willing to pay him sixty dollars each. Instead of the $225 former income, this building would now bring the owner $540 monthly. Racism was again paying off in hard cash.

At lunch afterward, Herskovits and his staff virtually glowed with pleasure. One assistant told me, "For the first time in their lives, some of these kids who lead sheltered lives have learned how directly involved they and their immediate associates are. I actually saw some of them look shocked when you showed how their family affluence resulted from prejudice. You did a hell of a swell job."

"I'd like for you to come out here around this date each year," Herskovits said, "and talk the same way each time to each class. They need it."

I appeared for five consecutive years, up until I left Chicago for Hawaii. In 1948 the political atmosphere had become quite cloudy. The House Committee on Un-American Activities was having a field day and reaction was in general control. I asked the anthropologist whether I should continue addressing his class.

"Of course!" he exploded. "Fact is, I'm likely to be branded a danger-ous Communist any day by the House Un-Americans. And if so, I shall expect the university to take care of my defense. As a matter of fact, Northwestern faces a dilemma anyway. This is basically a conservative church school. But in the social sciences the administration has the choice of a conservative staff—and losing its high rating in this field—or having the best instructors available—and getting the label of radical. Frankly, the best social scientists are looked upon as dangerous Reds in some quarters. But as long as I am here I do not intend to kowtow to the reactionaries. I want you to talk out here next year, and the next, and the next after that. I want you to come back just as long as you can spare the time."

Meanwhile the U.S. Supreme Court had rendered its Hansberry decision outlawing restrictive residential covenants. But that had little effect on the ghetto where most of the population rents. This benefitted mainly Afro-Americans with money to buy outside the ghetto—and too often the black landlord, incidentally, was as much of a rent gouger as a white landlord. However, white owners frequently still would not sell to blacks, especially in suburbia. This was knocked out by the U.S. Supreme Court in June of 1968. Like most civil rights victories, this was of direct benefit mainly to middle-class Afro-Americans. Those mired down in the ghettoes were not likely to find immediate relief.

67

The meeting room at the large Loop hotel housing the sessions of the Democratic Platform Committee was about three-quarters full this sum-mer evening in 1944 on the eve of the national convention. Congressman

McCormack of Massachusetts, chairman, sat patiently listening as speakers told why the party should have a plank specifically outlawing anti-Semitism. As Rabbi Wise finished speaking, the announcer intoned over the loudspeaker:

"Speaking next on behalf of a plank to outlaw anti-Semitism will be Frank Marshall Davis, executive editor of the Associated Negro Press."

What had been a comparatively routine session immediately perked up. My cohorts on the daily press and wire services (I knew none of them) straightened and looked up in disbelief as I arose and walked to the microphone. Even Representative McCormack registered surprise. Jews plunking for such a plank were one thing, but a black man making such a presentation was unprecedented.

Completely extemporaneously (I was in good form through constant practice), I made my plea. Both blacks and Jews were targets of Hitler's Nazi ideology on a world front and were under fire at home from the Father Coughlins, Gerald L. K. Smiths, and other domestic fascists. Jews were lynched in Germany and Nazi-dominated Europe; America had its own pogroms in Detroit and Dixie. Since both minorities suffered from discrimination and prejudice, I felt our cause was joined and anti-Semitism and white supremacy were twins, therefore, by the scurrilous hate sheets circulated throughout the land. There were no mass murders of blacks under Hitler only because there were no sizeable black populations where he held power; should the Axis conquer America we would be decimated, for we were hated as much as Jews. It was time, therefore, that the Democratic Party let the nation know it was opposed to bigotry by adopting a strong plank in its national platform outlawing anti-Semitism and condemning our homegrown crop of Hitlers. Such a strong stand, I added, would simultaneously blast the white supremacists.

When I resumed my seat, reporters from two wire services came up and asked for copies of my address. I told them I had no prepared speech. They then asked that I try to write out exactly what I had said so there would be no possibility of misquoting. I accompanied them to the press room where I had the strange experience of typing out a speech after I had delivered it. However, it was worthwhile. The uniqueness of the facts around the presentation received wide publicity all over the nation.

Leonard Golditch, of New York, executive secretary of the National Committee to Combat Anti-Semitism had asked me to make the presentation on behalf of this group after several of us appeared before the Republican Platform Committee headed by Senator Taft of Ohio; both conventions were held in Chicago in 1944. The talk before the Republican committee was made by a Jewish leader. When members of our committee were introduced, many of those in the room turned and gawked in amazement when my name was called and they saw me. On the strength of this reaction, we decided my speaking before the Democrats would be a real bombshell. The National Committee to Combat Anti-Semitism was sponsored by an impressive array of distinguished Americans, among them Tallulah Bankhead, Elmer Benson, Van Wyck Brooks, Rep. Emanuel Celler, Bishop Cushman, Lion Feuchtwanger, Fannie Hurst, Lillian Hellman, Harold Ickes, Thomas Mann, Rep. Vito Marcantonio, Rev. A. Clayton Powell, Jr., Edward G. Robinson, Carl Van Doren, and a host of others.

For several months I had been actively working with Jewish leaders to combat bigotry among both large minority groups; I am opposed to color prejudice among Jews and to anti-Semitism among Afro-Americans. I was and still am painfully aware of rent gouging and cheating among some Hebrew businessmen just as I was and still am conscious of Jew-baiting and physical attacks on the persons and places of business of this cultural—not racial—group. Nevertheless, the chief oppressor of both remains the white gentile who profits when his victims attack each other instead of joining forces to fight the common foe. We do not strengthen our fight when we become cats-paws of the racists by mouthing anti-Semitic propaganda and libeling an entire people, nor do Jews help their own fight for full acceptance by ridiculing and oppressing black Americans. And so I worked closely with liberal and progressive Jews, speaking before youth groups and occasionally attending banquets in which mine would be the lone black face. In many ways it was as much of an education for me as it was for them. For years our leaders had exhorted us to "unite and work together like Jews." But at their meetings, I heard their leaders plead with their listeners to "unite and work together like Negroes" to attain their ends. We were both living in a dream world for neither group was monolithic. Yiddish people were as disorganized and simultaneously galloping off in as many different directions as were black Americans.

I began this close association soon after joining the board of directors of the Chicago Civil Liberties Union when the Chicago group was accused of spending too much time on black civil rights cases. The Chicago committee not only fought against civil rights violations but pressed for legislation, inaugurated a campaign to fight bigotry in Chicago's public schools, and held mass meetings and large fund-raising dinners. I was elected vice-chairman of the committee, whose board included liberals from all sections of the city, and headed the special committee to combat religious and racial intolerance in the school system.

At one fund-raising annual banquet, attended by some fifteen hundred guests at the old Stevens Hotel, the main speakers were Marshall Field, publisher of the Chicago *Sun,* and Paul Robeson, then starring in his premier stage hit, *Othello.* Virtually the entire afternoon prior to the dinner, the actor talked alone with the multi-millionaire and that night Field gave a fire-breathing speech on civil liberties. At still another mass meeting conducted at a crowded Orchestra Hall, Rev. A. Clayton Powell unleashed his powerful oratory along with Mike Quill, head of the Transport Workers Union and then a fighting progressive.

For those who think violence in the cities is a new thing, we at the committee annually planned a course of action should hot weather bring riots in the ghetto. Thirty-five years ago we realized the compound could ignite anytime. We were especially concerned also about the violence frequently occurring when a black family moved into a previously lily white neighborhood. Racist agitators materialized from under damp stones to lead rock-throwing, dynamiting, and gunplay which often followed. Police were required to stand guard day and night—although at times protection was also needed from police. Many of the worst white supremacist acts took place in strong Catholic neighborhoods populated by first-generation descendants of Italian and Polish immigrants who obviously were themselves struggling for acceptance and were out to prove how solidly American they had become by adopting our national pattern of prejudice. Our efforts to enlist the aid of area priests in fighting racism usually met with complete indifference; Chicago had no Father Groppi, the Milwaukee priest who won national acclaim for his uncompromising fight against racism.

When the national Civil Rights Congress was formed, the committee joined the new group of which I happened to be a board member. I remained active until I left Chicago.

68

In 1944 I turned down my third opportunity to fatten my purse at the Republican trough and worked at no pay for the reelection of Roosevelt with a special Midwest committee, writing the keynote speech for Ferdinand Smith of the National Maritime Union who came to Chicago for a black convention. I was sold on FDR. And although skeptical of his choice of running mate for vice president, Harry Truman, I had faith in the president. I had seen tremendous gains made by my people in the previous four years, starting with FEPC. Our men and women now served in all branches of the armed forces; employment opportunities were at their peak; many colleges and universities, such as Notre Dame, had lowered the colored bar, and others, such as my old Kansas State, had demolished athletic barriers; the American Football League had been formed using black players in contrast with the old National Football League which would soon be forced to abolish lily white teams.

Nevertheless, we still had a long way to go. Henry Wallace had set a goal of full employment in peacetime. But we were optimistic as we planned for the future. We believed continued pressure on congress would bring passage of federal antilynching legislation and repeal of the poll tax. To attain these goals, we depended on the dynamic leadership of the White House and support of the CIO unions who had been a major source of Roosevelt's power. We believed that the impending defeat of the Axis nations would sound the death knell of meaningful reaction at home, and we further expected the cooperation of the Soviet Union and the United States in winning the war would establish a precedent for cooperation between these great powers in building a new, peaceful world. The United Nations, we knew, would see to that.

Then Roosevelt died.

With his passing, the progressive coalition floundered at home and abroad. Under Truman and following victory over Japan, antagonisms previously imprisoned or at least muzzled under FDR burst into the open. There had always been powerful partners in the Pentagon-Industrial complex who would have preferred fighting Stalin's Russia instead of Hitler's Germany. Now that we had the dreaded atom bomb, they were impatient to drop it immediately on Moscow. But the friendship between the two peoples could not be turned into bitter enmity overnight; by the time the American public had been brainwashed into accepting a shooting war with the Soviets they, too, had the A-Bomb and our advantage had been lost. I do not say that the excellent relationship between Moscow and Washington would have continued had Roosevelt lived, but I firmly believe it would not have deteriorated so rapidly as occurred under Truman, beginning with the Marshall Plan aimed directly at the Soviets. From Roosevelt's wartime record, I am convinced he would have devised a way of helping needy nations without aiming a gun at Russia.

While conservative forces regained control of national policies, the united front of liberals, leftists, and Afro-Americans split up for want of a strong father figure. Labor unions which had backed Roosevelt were torn between supporting the Truman doctrines and trying to adhere to the old Roosevelt policies. Civil war raged within the CIO, sapping its strength. Support given Afro-America in its continuing fight for civil rights dwindled, although many powerful labor leaders still rendered it lip service.

Organized labor, looking back to the period after World War I, knew management would launch a campaign to bust the unions. But things were different now. Before, at the end of the first great war, unions were lily white and management could use the huge reservoir of unorganized black labor as a tool to break strikes. The CIO had busted this wide open. For instance, unlike at the end of World War I, the strikes in the giant meat-packing industry in Chicago now found even the black middle class supporting strikers by providing funds and food. Some picket lines were so predominantly black that union leaders rushed white strikers into them to avoid any possibility of the demonstration being turned into a racial confrontation. Despite the worsening political atmosphere, black workers had now become a solid, militant force in organized labor.

This was the atmosphere into which the Chicago *Star* was born in 1946. A cooperative weekly newspaper financed by a number of CIO and some AFL unions, progressives, liberals, and ghetto dwellers, I was named executive editor and, as usual, wrote a regular column. Carl Hirsch and Len Lewin were the key full-time newsmen. Roughly a third of its subscribers were black, for South Siders independent of the dictates of the white power structure paid little attention to Red baiting. I personally knew of a sizeable number of lawyers, doctors, and schoolteachers who made cash contributions to the ghetto headquarters of the Communist party with the admonition, "keep my name out of it—but give 'em hell!" On a national basis, the black membership of the party in its heyday was estimated as over 25 percent of the total.

The Chicago *Star* fought desperately to heal the growing rifts in organized labor and steer the administration back into Roosevelt's path of cooperation between the two strongest nations to emerge from the global conflict. One of our regular contributors, incidentally, was Senator Claude Pepper of Florida until the conservatives aimed their big guns at him.

The *Star* wholeheartedly backed Henry Wallace when he ran as an independent candidate for President. The new Progressive party in Illinois hitched its wagon to the *Star,* and in the summer of 1948 the Progressive party apparatus became actual owners of the newspaper. When it seemed thousands of black Democrat voters would desert Truman for the more appealing Wallace program, the Missourian astutely came out in support of bold new civil rights legislation. Like a magnet, this political move drew back enough Afro-American voters to win Truman an upset victory at the polls that November.

69

In May 1946, I crossed the color line to marry Helen, the blonde student from my jazz class at Lincoln School.[28] She was eighteen years my junior and looked like a model. One of my associates told me immediately afterward, "When you say you believe in complete integration you ain't just whistlin' Dixie."

The small, quiet ceremony took place on a Saturday afternoon. Next day we were to attend a tea opening an exhibit at the South Side Art Center. As we left our apartment Charles Henry Manney, then a concert singer, drove up and stopped. Very dark and chubby, Manney himself had been married to a white woman. When he learned our union was less than a day old, he insisted on driving us to the art center. He bounced out of the car, and as we followed, strode over to two ladies I already knew as leaders of ghetto society who were chatting together on the sidewalk. Grinning broadly and with a devilish gleam in his eye, he introduced us as "The newlyweds, Mr. and Mrs Davis." Even today I chuckle inwardly when I recall the looks of utter consternation on their faces as they stammered out an acknowledgement. Inside the center, Manney continued diabolically to drop his little bombshell so he could gloat as ordinarily sophisticated South Siders momentarily blew their cool. And I must confess I enjoyed their confusion while being thankful I could still put on the poker face I learned to wear in high school.

Helen, herself quite talented as a writer and artist, knew that marrying me would mean a break with her wealthy and conservative family, but that did not stop her. She, too, had taken a long, agonizing look at racism following the 1943 Detroit riots and was impatient to do all she could to help change conditions. She joined and worked in American Youth for Democracy and after our marriage helped organize tenant groups to fight rent gouging and the neglect by absentee landlords. Following an antilynching rally held near the monument at 35th and South

Parkway at which Tallulah Bankhead, actress daughter of the Alabama senator, was a principal speaker and Kenneth Spencer, after Paul Robeson the leading progressive baritone of that period, sang, Helen accompanied a delegation to Washington to call on congressmen and ask passage of federal legislation outlawing this traditional American pastime.

There were, as I anticipated, some objections to our union by members of both groups. An attorney whom I knew came up to me shortly after our nuptials and asked, "Hey, how come you married outside your race?"

"But I didn't," I replied. "I married another human."

"You know what I mean. Why didn't you marry your own kind?"

"I couldn't. Being a lawyer, you know as well as I that homosexual marriages are illegal."

"Don't be ridiculous. What made you marry into the white race?"

"I didn't marry a race. I married a woman."

He looked at me in exasperation, then turned and walked away.

I expected strong objections from some of our women, and I knew this had a logical base. Black women have long been at the very bottom of the totem pole. When an Afro-American male with a steady income marries into an out group, it further reduces the number of brothers potentially able to provide for their economic needs. Nevertheless I do not believe color should be the determining factor in such a personal, close association as marriage. So when one asked me why did I marry a white woman, I answered I did not marry a *white* woman. I married a woman who happened to be white.

As a matter of fact, on occasion Helen was catalogued as "a light-complexioned Negro girl, maybe a creole." Bunk Johnson, the trumpet player, had told us we could appear together all over New Orleans and nobody would give us a second glance. However, Chicago was somewhat different. I had given Helen an ANP press pass which she sometimes used to cover jazz concerts.

One night on the South Side she hailed a Yellow Cab. The driver, a middle-aged white man, took one look at her blonde hair and blue eyes and in a fatherly tone asked:

"What's a good-looking young white girl like you doing in a neighborhood like this?"

"What's wrong with it?" she replied.

"Why, you could get dragged into an alley and raped. You know how niggers are about white women. They're just like beasts."

Instead of a heated reply, Helen pulled out her press pass and handed it to the cabbie. He looked, gulped, turned red, and stammered with embarrassment:

"I'm sorry, lady, but I didn't know you was colored." He drove to her destination without another word.

When she went to Omaha in 1948 with Tillie Pearson, a very light complexioned young woman, to visit the Pearson family, neighbors automatically assumed Helen was Afro-American since it was unthinkable that a soul sister would bring home a white woman as a house guest. And on the train to Omaha, some dining car waiters assumed Tillie was white and Helen was Afro-American.

In Chicago away from the ghetto, undoubtedly many honkies who saw us together were strongly upset. Several times on elevated trains I turned quickly around and surprised male Caucasians beaming daggers at me, but they changed expressions and turned their faces away. I have no doubt some would have attacked me had they dared, but again my size and resemblance to Joe Louis doused any overt act. I could imagine some thinking, "What if he really *is* Joe Louis!" Resentment against our being together would manifest itself only if we awaited a bus on a corner. On several occasions a group of young honkies drove by in a car, spotted us, hurled insults from the safety of their vehicle, then circled the block to come back and repeat their diatribes. We simply ignored them.

Only once was there a threat of violence. That occurred one Sunday afternoon at a white tavern near the University of Chicago where we had gone to hear one of our favorite small jazz combos. In the past we had attended with a number of other couples, white jazz enthusiasts; but this day we went alone. We were sitting at the bar when my wife nudged me. Standing directly in back of me were two honkies in their twenties. One said to the other, "He must be a real sweet nigger. But why don't they stay on 47th Street with the rest of the niggers where he belongs?"

I jumped up from my stool. "What was that again?" I asked.

"I wasn't talking to you. I was talking to my buddy," the speaker said, thrusting his hand into his pocket as if he had a gun.

The bartender, immediately sizing up the situation, leaped over the counter and grabbed the man as he called for the bouncer. The two buddies were rushed to the street and told to stay out. To my gratification—particularly since I was the only Afro-American in the tavern—others at the bar who saw the disturbance agreed with the banishment.

One man commented loudly to his date: "They fought for us in the war, so why aren't they good enough to associate with anybody they please? Besides, he was minding his own business, not bothering anybody."

Helen grew to know emotionally the meaning of living in the ghetto. All around her she saw daily the bitter fruits of white oppression and the frustration it created. And it was good she absorbed this lesson, for it was her salvation after a traumatic experience one night.

She was on her way home alone from a tenant's meeting a block or so away from where we lived. At this moment the street was virtually deserted. But she did notice a small, elderly black man, obviously intoxicated, weaving down the sidewalk toward her. She regarded him with no more than normal curiosity until they were about to pass. Then he stopped in his tracks. As she walked by, he spit directly into her face.

She opened the door of our apartment a few minutes later, still wiping her cheeks and visibly shaken. Then she related the incident and told how she felt.

"I was outraged," Helen said. "But instead of blowing up, I realized immediately why he had done this and felt sorry for him instead of anger. I've lived on the South Side long enough now to understand how people feel. Undoubtedly all his life that little old man has had to suffer all kinds of indignities from white people. When he saw me, I embodied all the whites who had made his life a living hell since birth. All his hate boiled over, and his liquor gave him the strength to vent his years of anger. When he spit on me he was revenging himself on every white person who had made him feel less than a man. Because I'm white, to him I was automatically as guilty as any of the others."

Her analysis, as I saw it, was quite correct; and I was proud of her understanding and compassion—particularly since she had just left a meeting where she had been doing her utmost to help improve the living conditions of the spitter's ethnic kin. And this is one reason why I cannot condone those who look upon all whites as devils and who would indiscriminately smash every Caucasian as a mortal enemy. There are now and have been many whites who have worked harder than most Afro-Americans to end racism.

70

In early summer of 1948 my third volume of poetry, *47th Street,* came off the press. The long title poem was written as a word picture of the main thoroughfare of "Chicago's Congo" during wartime. I had started it many years earlier. The opening pages had been shown to Richard Wright and Margaret Walker when they visited me on one of Dick's trips back from New York. Both were enthusiastic. Then for a long time it lay dormant, during my fallow period, until I again got the urge to write through association with Margaret Taylor Goss.

A number of us drew close together in 1943. The brilliant Gwendolyn Brooks, later to win a Pulitzer prize for poetry, was attracting high praise in literary circles. Her husband, Henry Blakely, was also a promising writer. We met often, usually socially and informally, at their second-floor apartment above a store on 63rd Street. Gwendolyn Cunningham, also on the threshold of fame as a poet, Fern Gayden, Mavis Mixon, and a number of others were in this group.

For the benefit of the Flower Children of twenty-five years later, we held a Mushaira one Sunday afternoon at the South Side Art Center without a Shamiama. In India the Shamiama is a type of tent and a Mushaira is a gathering for the reading of poems on national themes. Our theme was "The Writer's Role In Wartime," and following a discussion by Jack Conroy, Ted Ward, and myself, the meeting was turned over to poets reading their own creations. Despite the general lack of interest in verse, the attendance was excellent. Undoubtedly the novelty of a Shamiama and Mushaira captured the imagination. Jack Conroy, incidentally, was one of the few white writers who could be depended upon to participate in South Side activities.

The art center was a focal point for all the arts. Gordon Rogers Parks, the photographer, author, and motion picture director, made the center his headquarters. The Lens Camera Club maintained darkroom facilities in the basement and met and held meetings on upper floors. Virtually all painters and sculptors in the ghetto often came around, including the late Marion Perkins. When in Chicago, Eldzior Cortor, Charles White, and Hughey Lee-Smith, among others, could usually be found at the center. South Siders of all political persuasions actively supported it and served on the board of directors; the annual fund-raising Artists and Models Ball held at the Savoy was one of the social highlights each year.

I wrote virtually all the material in *47th Street* during this period of contact with various artists of all kinds, most of us quite conscious of the special problems of creative persons during the war and after victory. I contributed a long poem, "For All Common People," which led off the February 1944 issue of *Free World,* an ambitious international magazine. For my new book, I changed the title and some wording in the *Crisis* magazine poem which had upset the comrades and called it "Peace Quiz For America."

Because I felt my writing showed much greater maturity, I was especially pleased to get a note from Langston Hughes who told me, "I read *47th Street* with excitement and pleasure. You are one poet who has 'grown' and each of your books seems to me a step forward in poetic effectiveness."

With the rapidly deteriorating political situation and the growth of the witch hunts during the Joe McCarthy period, a number of libraries removed my books from their shelves and stored them in the basement along with other controversial literature until the nation began returning to sanity. And while this was occurring at home, a number of European editors began translating some of my poems for use in foreign anthologies. I was "safe" abroad but "dangerous" at home. More recently, in 1967, some thirty-two years after the publication of my first volume, *Black Man's Verse,* editors of literature textbooks for general school and college use started including some of my poems. Of course, financial returns have been nominal, but the spiritual satisfaction is not measurable in dollars and cents.

And in the area of spiritual satisfaction, my experience at the Fifth Annual Writers Conference held at Northwestern University in July 1944 is hard to top. I appeared in an afternoon session to read a number of poems of America.

As I sat waiting on the rostrum, looking out at the audience, I felt an overwhelming urge to shock them. I saw a sea of well-fed, white, comfortable, conservative, upper middle class women, most of them bored to distraction and taking up poetry for lack of anything else to occupy their time. I simply had to shake them out of their smugness.

I began by reading the poems I had previously selected, then for my last number switched to "Coincidence," which I had not planned to use. This poem describes two boys, one white and one black, born the same day in Birmingham to a white woman and her maid, one in a private room at the city's most exclusive hospital, the other in a small jim crow ward. Both boys grow up, virtually in the same house, catch similar diseases, and have similar experiences, although the black boy's life of course is only a minor reflection of the white lad's. As grown men, both die accidentally the same day. At the end of the poem is the question whether it would help explain the similarity of their lives if it were known that the same day he sired the white boy, the husband of her mistress also sired the son of her maid.

As I finished and turned toward my seat, there was momentary silence and a loud collective gasp as it sank in. The applause met only the bare minimum of politeness; then the women arose, gathered themselves in bunches, and drifted toward the exits.

Two young ofay women in their mid-twenties came up to me, huge grins on their faces and eyes gleaming with enthusiasm.

"God, am I glad you read THAT," one said. "Did those old biddies need it!"

"Yes," her companion said, "just seeing the scandalized looks on their faces is worth ten years of my life. You've really made my day."

Although I kept a straight face, inwardly I was elated. I also knew I would not be invited back again. And I wasn't.

Davis (*at left*) listening to a jazz broadcast with friends (ca. 1935)

Davis signing copies of his poetry collection. Photograph used with the permission of the Frank Marshall Davis estate.

Davis with writers Stu Engstrand (*left*) and Jack Conroy (*right*) in Chicago (1936)

Davis (*standing, far left*) at a planning session for the National Negro Exposition in Chicago (1939)

Frank Marshall Davis (1946)

1949-1980

71

During the summer of 1948, Helen read an article in a woman's magazine describing how it was to live in Hawaii. She put it down, turned to me, and wondered wistfully if Hawaii was as wonderful as it seemed. I suggested we investigate. We decided to go there in December and stay two or three months, long enough to miss the worst of another Chicago winter; if we liked it, we would live there permanently. Meanwhile in the next few months I tried to learn all I could about Paradise through the Hawaii Visitors Bureau, Hawaiian magazines, Honolulu newspapers, and the *National Geographic*. When I learned the islands were free of snakes, I was automatically sold. Carefully, we packed our most prized possessions, our record collection, in cartons and stored them.

When some of our fellow freedom fighters learned we were going to Hawaii with the possibility of remaining, they accused me of "deserting the battle." This I ignored, for I was already aware that Paradise had serious problems of its own. I had also talked with Paul Robeson who the previous year had appeared there in a series of concerts sponsored by the International Longshoremen's and Warehousemen's Union (ILWU), the most powerful labor organization in the territory. Paul enthusiastically supported our pending trip and told me how much he wanted to return to that delightful place. I also wrote to Harry Bridges, head of the ILWU, whom I had met at Lincoln School. He suggested I get in touch with Koji Ariyoshi, editor of the Honolulu *Record,* a newspaper that was generally similar to the Chicago *Star*.

Japan's attack on Pearl Harbor took place 7 December 1941. We launched our invasion of Hawaii by leaving Chicago on 7 December 1948. Some cynics say that in certain ways, the second was worse than the first.

I fell in love with Paradise as Howard K. Morris, our travel agent, drove us from the airport to our hotel, the old Willard Inn in Waikiki. I was also prepared emotionally to identify with the shifting kaleidoscope of peoples living on these shores. I knew, of course, that Japanese predominated, and after their appalling treatment on the West Coast when they were placed in concentration camps during World War II, I felt deep kinship. I had known very few. Prior to World War II, the entire Japanese population in Chicago numbered around two hundred. One of these was Shigeta, a world-renowned commercial photographer I had met. Despite many years of residence, his equipment was confiscated during the conflict, merely another in a long chronicle of governmental stupidities. But because his ability was so great, other studios invited him to supervise their operations at a fat fee. When we left Chicago, the Japanese population had soared to twenty thousand, virtually all of them refugees from the West Coast; and they were generally quiet and subdued as a result of their racist wartime treatment. I had also attended a sumo match staged by World War II veterans.

Almost immediately I learned that the Japanese of Hawaii, who were then around 40 percent of the total population, seemed completely self-assured, totally unlike those in Chicago. After Japanese, whites were the largest ethnic group. But the Chinese, Koreans, Filipinos, Puerto Ricans, Hawaiians, Samoans, Tongans, several hundred Afro-Americans, and smatterings of other Pacific peoples gave Honolulu away from Waikiki an overwhelmingly light brown to black look which my eyes hungrily devoured.

Our ANP correspondent in Hawaii, Hubert White, who also wrote for the daily press, had arranged for interviews. I knew of no area on the mainland where the white press would have printed our pictures and comments. This smoked out an old friend, Carl Beckwith, a linotypist with whom I had worked in Chicago and Atlanta. It also brought experiences with the aloha spirit I'd heard about. Strangers called and invited us to yachting parties. As we once stood on a corner waiting for a bus, a lone motorist drove by, recognized us, and insisted on chauffeuring us to our destination. He was Ed Toner, active in Democratic politics. We were invited to a number of dinners and house parties. And for as long as five or six years afterward, local men and women came up to us on the street or in stores and spoke, telling us they remembered seeing our pictures in the papers when we first arrived.

Virtually from the start I had a sense of human dignity. I felt that somehow I had been suddenly freed from the chains of white oppression. On the mainland, whites acted as if dignity were their exclusive possession, something to be awarded only as they saw fit. Yet dignity is a human right, earned by being born. In Hawaii I had at last come into ownership of this birthright, stolen by the white power structure as a penalty of being black. Even on the Chicago South Side, where I was but another drop in a black pool, I was painfully conscious we had been baled, like cotton, into this area because whitey so decreed. It was a relief to soar at last with no wings clipped by the scissors of color.

Nevertheless, I sensed that under the placid surface of aloha was an undertow of racism, but this I was not supposed to see. In my interviews with the daily press, I had stated I planned a vacation of several months and meanwhile would write a weekly syndicated column for ANP subscribers. Since Hawaii wanted to maintain its image of aloha for all, it was hoped I would see little evidence of prejudice. Accordingly, our travel agent, Howard K. Morris, took us to at least one well-known restaurant which I later learned barred souls. The territorial legislature also refused to pass a civil rights law—on the quaint reasoning that such a statute would be an indirect admission that discrimination *did* exist in Paradise. Many bars therefore posted signs near the entrance stating "we reserve the right to refuse entrance to anyone." This meant we could be barred without recourse. Some well-known cafes also barred Orientals.

In fact, the vast nonwhite majority was banned from living in certain exclusive and highly desirable residential areas. Despite the Hansberry case decision outlawing restrictive covenants, some of the gigantic estates rigidly enforced residential bars. A huge portion of Hawaii's livable land is leasehold, owned by a few estates. A purchaser may buy a home from one source and pay land rental to still another. The owner of the land might insist that the perspective tenant appear in person with his family for the transfer of the lease. If the landowner wished to restrict an area, a lease was not tendered for a number of "legitimate" reasons, although all concerned knew the basic one was color. Later, this practice began disappearing—especially when next door there might be fee simple property which the tenant bought outright along with the house and which would be sold to anybody with the purchase price.[1] There is still occasional discrimination against Afro-Americans in rental property, but this is a matter of individual policy on the part of the landlord. Duskyamericans live all over Honolulu and its suburbs, rarely side by side except in military housing. Black tourists, however, get equal and courteous treatment at the best hotels in Waikiki, and those affluent enough to pay premium rentals of several thousand can occupy dream vacation houses right on the beach.

When we arrived in 1948, the Big Five (several wealthy white firms) had an iron grip on island economy. Organized labor led by the ILWU with Jack Hall at the helm was still struggling to break its hold. Groups of oriental businessmen were forming cooperatives and attacking from another angle. Today the Big Five are no longer the economic despots of earlier days. Business in general has realistically accepted the ILWU (its top leaders are now "respectable"), and other unions have made tremendous gains. Oriental millionaires are numerous. For several years, the largest per capita income of any group, including white, was among Chinese.

Accustomed to mainland patterns of prejudice in which native white gentile reaction toward blacks, Jews, Hispanics, and Orientals could be predicted with reasonable accuracy, I soon found I had to adjust to different and often more subtle techniques. There was little on the surface, but underneath ran complex crosscurrents. The reconciliation of many group antagonisms had been a prime goal of the ILWU. To further complicate matters, there was great division between Okinawan Japanese and Japan Japanese. The former were considered inferior by the latter. Parental suicide had resulted on occasion when a son or daughter married an Okinawan, so strong was this prejudice.

I addressed an Okinawan club, the Hui Makaala, soon after reaching Hawaii. In the question period which followed, I could have closed my eyes and imagined I was back at a meeting in the Parkway Community Center in Chicago, so similar were questions and Okinawan reactions to prejudice shown by Japan Japanese and whites. Thankfully, this intragroup tension has now diminished.

Despite propaganda spread by southern whites imported to work for Uncle Sam during World War II and the unofficial attitude of the territorial administration then headed by Governor Stainback, a native of Tennessee, local people generally were ready to accept Afro-Americans at face value. Of course many had strongly warped ideas, drawn from traditional stereotypes perpetuated by press, movies, and radio. But in the final analysis, they based attitudes on personal relationships. I soon learned many Japanese went through a sizing-up period when blacks moved into a predominantly Japanese neighborhood or they came in contact with them at work; but when they decided to accept you, it was on a permanent basis, not as a fair-weather friend. Dark Hawaiians tended to dislike Afro-Americans as a group (many lived in mortal fear white tourists would mistake them for Negroes) but developed strong friendships with individuals; Hawaiians are traditionally warm and outgoing. Black preachers from the mainland have developed fiercely loyal followers in their Pentecostal Church (roughly similar to Holy Rollers) congregations that are composed mainly of Hawaiians, Puerto Ricans, and Filipinos.

Portuguese are a kind of in-between group. They, too, were brought to Hawaii in large numbers as plantation workers. Generally they resent being called "haole," the local word for white, and many accept without embarrassment African ancestors whose photos often appear in family albums. Actually they range from blonde to black. At the same time a considerable number resent Japanese and Filipinos while accepting Chinese, Hawaiians, and Afro-Americans. And a large percentage of the nonwhite population could be transplanted to mainland ghettoes and accepted without question as black. I have seen kinky-haired Chinese and Japanese. There was then a good market here for Fuller's hair products. On the mainland I never thought of myself as anything but black. In Paradise I have been mistaken frequently for Hawaiian, Tongan, and Samoan; once it was assumed I was a native of India. On another occasion, a haole jeweler, on being questioned the day after I saw him, thought for a few minutes then said I was Caucasian, so unconscious of color do many become after a while. Usually, however, local people are extremely aware of mixtures. A glance reveals that most souls are not "pure Africans"; instead they are considered "part colored," and the curious like to know what other strains are involved. Many point with pride to their own amalgam of, say, German, English, Portuguese, and Chinese. Some of the most beautiful people you ever saw may have as many as eight identifiable ethnic strains in their ancestry.

Over the years the epithet "nigger" has lost much of its sting, except when applied by a mainland white. Hawaiians frequently call each other nigger. One of my close Chinese friends, criticizing a state official of roughly three-fourths Caucasian and a quarter Hawaiian ancestry, told me "he ain't nothing but a nigger like the rest of us." Some white tourists, taking their first look around, occasionally say with disgust that the islands are "lousy with niggers." There have been white prostitutes who, in restricting their trade, announced they would "service no niggers: Chinks, Japs, kanakas (Hawaiians), or any other kind." And for the benefit of the militant black activists, many island people considered the word "Negro" insulting and preferred using "colored"—although this became nonsensical when a Hawaiian several shades darker than me told me his best friend during World War II was "a colored man." Trummy Young, the well-known black trombonist, for several years led a band in Honolulu in which he was by far the lightest member.

There are, of course, individual members of all groups who have strong prejudice against us, some of which is retaliatory. During the Korean War, more than once I heard cars of black and white servicemen pull in at drive-in restaurants and loudly and insultingly discuss "gooks," "slant-eyed bastards," and "goddam Japs" while parked beside cars containing Japanese families. "Jap" is as offensive to Japanese as "nigger" is to us. Sometimes we are as insensitive as whitey.

For seven years Helen and I lived at Hauula, a predominantly Hawaiian village on the ocean some thirty-one miles from Honolulu. When I began driving daily to town and back, local boys who knew my schedule often waited beside the highway, sometimes for as long as three hours, to flag me down and ask me questions about their personal lives, explaining "You're not haole so I know I can trust you." In Hauula I joined the Democratic precinct club, virtually ran the organization, and was sent to the state convention by the predominantly Hawaiian membership who told me that since I was educated and articulate, I could speak for them. Once I upset a white woman and her husband who came to my house, brought by a Hawaiian, because the wife wanted to be postmistress of the tiny local postal station. My endorsement was needed. When I left the room briefly, she asked my wife, "Your husband is Hawaiian, isn't he?" "No, Negro," came the discomforting reply. The Hawaiian who accompanied them, and who knew the score on mainland patterns, sat unobtrusively to one side during the entire interview, hands in front of his face to hide his laughter.

Across the highway from where we lived was a Pentecostal church. Meetings usually began at around nine or ten o'clock at night and continued until daybreak. Around two o'clock in the morning, a kind of picnic lunch was served. Since we were friendly with many of the members, almost solely Hawaiians, Helen once went over to help them prepare their feed. Members were amazed, commenting to each other, "Imagine! A haole waiting on *us!*" Believing my recorded spirituals would move them, one day I played several for the church sisters—but they were not particularly impressed. Then I slipped in an old rhythm and blues number by Blue Lou Barker, "Don't You Feel My Leg," which had been banned on the radio in Chicago. They liked it so well I had to play it three more times before they left. Then they departed singing the erotic lyrics to each other. Many Hawaiians like blues and boogie-woogie anyway.

In the years since moving into town in 1956, I often run into people from Hauula. At times it's like a reunion. If they're with friends, they proudly introduce me as "a Hauula boy." I also learned they would be hurt should I pass them in a car and not wave. Usually it was a loss of prestige should I not see them for they had told their companions, "I know him. He's a friend of mine." Hawaii is basically a warm, friendly place. Give friendship, and it will be returned. As time passed I learned that not only Hawaiians but members of other groups liked me because I was not white.

At the same time, I developed strong friendships with many haoles because I am not Oriental. I was somebody who came from the same general environment and overall background. At first it was shocking to hear Caucasians tell me what "we" must do when, on the mainland, they would likely say "you people." Many whites of considerable residence here are as bitter about racism as any of us and are glad to live in a place where overt prejudice is not customary. I have known haoles to go back home for a long visit but return ahead of schedule because they couldn't stand the attitudes of their old friends. To complete the picture, some of my best friends are whites from Mississippi, Alabama, Texas, and Georgia who say they could no longer live in those areas. One especially good friend has been Grover Godfrey, a wealthy cemetery executive who flabbergasted me in the late 1960s by recalling that we met some thirty years earlier when I edited the Atlanta *Daily World*. I am personally acquainted with one white man from Mississippi, now retired, who fifty years ago helped a Duskyamerican escape from a mob in his home state.

Because of the long established patterns of miscegenation, a mixed couple attracts no special attention except, possibly, from tourists. Beach boys, who hang around Waikiki making their living teaching swimming and surfing, vary from tan to black. White female tourists have a yen for these "boys" (some past fifty), and it is a common sight for beach boys clad only in swimming trunks to parade down the main thoroughfare with bikinied blonde and brunette beauties, arms around each other. Summer sessions at the university bring thousands of co-eds intent on having a ball. However, there have been near rhubarbs between local beach boys and black musicians making plays for the same haole girls. Although there have been a few battles between soul brothers and local males, by far the biggest beefs are between Island lads and haole youths. On occasion, gangs of local toughs hunt out haole males to beat up. In some instances, Island boys have jumped into fights between white and black servicemen on the side of the blacks. I have known a few Orientals who are so belligerent they will go to a bar hoping to pick fights with haoles.

Goodly numbers of Caucasian females shed their inhibitions in

Hawaii and go on a strong soul kick. At the same time many haole youths flip over the local dolls of various strains and combinations, for Paradise has some of the most lushly beautiful women on earth. Many local studs are frantic to bed a soul sister who is not a pro; propaganda painting their passion and horizontal ability has fallen on receptive ears. Afro-American brothers make out with all kinds of dolls. One pure black African student from Ghana wreaked havoc among co-eds at the university, and the wife of a prominent white local politician considered shucking her husband for him; another student from Kenya split leaving two pregnant blondes. Since armed forces integration, I have often seen a group of two or three white servicemen and one black serviceman strolling arm in arm in Waikiki with white girls. Haole service wives think nothing of taking two or three brownskin kids along with their own on picnics, and black wives return the favor by overseeing towheaded tots in public along with theirs.

In other words, the fiftieth state has much of the good and bad of the rest of America along with characteristics distinctly its own. Honolulu has tall buildings, air pollution, a serious traffic problem, mansions, and slums—but thus far no serious racial conflict. It is thoroughly complex. In 1948 Herman Burrell came here to work on his Ph.D. in sociology from the University of Wisconsin, expecting to gather all relevant information in a couple of years. But the more he delved, the greater became his conviction that no thesis could adequately paint a clear picture. He is still here. At the same time, there are so many purely and distinctly local patterns resulting from the blend of different cultures that some astute observers believe Hawaii is developing a new civilization of its own.

72

Hawaii is the only area in the United States which has successfully shown the possibility of integration with integrity. Here various ethnic groups have been able not only to maintain group identity and pride but work together with other peoples of vastly different traditions and live side by side without noticeable tension. And while it far surpasses the harmony found in the rest of the nation, it is not yet full integration for in some ways white America still lays a restraining hand.

In Hawaii, for example, Japanese-Americans generally are proud of their national background and history and observe holidays and customs deeply rooted in their traditional culture. There are various strong Chinese societies and a Chinese Chamber of Commerce. Filipinos and Koreans have active organizations limited only to people of those ancestries. Part and full Hawaiians have numerous clubs. Instead of hindering, this has helped promote integration in Hawaii. They are better able to exert Japanese power or Hawaiian power or whatever in order to obtain their goals. This determination to maintain group identity and respect undoubtedly is largely responsible for the deepening of equality existing in Hawaii today. As such it sets an example for the rest of America.

Yet at the same time there are efforts by some forces to "Americanize" them all—which is another way of trying to eliminate those customs not a part of Anglo-Saxon traditions. I oppose this attempt to turn everybody under the Stars and Stripes into a copy of whitey—especially when whitey shows little inclination to banish his pet prejudices based on color. I firmly believe each group must cherish, reinstate, and reinforce its cultural patterns which deepen and enrich the entire kaleidoscope of America. There is no sound reason why other peoples ought to renounce worthwhile customs only because they did not originate in Western Europe.

Unfortunately, this white idea of belittling unfamiliar patterns has hurt Hawaiians in particular. In Hawaii, for generations the "good Kahunas" had many remedies for ailments that the most accomplished graduates of leading medical schools did not begin to approach. I became a close personal friend of Dr. Alexander Kaonohi, a fantastic naturopath whose work was frowned upon by the saints of the American Medical Association (AMA). Many times while visiting socially at his office, I heard patients voluntarily tell each other of cures he had brought about when renowned specialists here and on the mainland had produced no relief even with miracle drugs. Had these testimonials been taped for commercial use on the air, the Federal Communication Commission (FCC) would have kicked them off as false advertising, so improbable did they sound. Dr. Kaonohi was my family physician for some ten years until his death, remedying every ailment and providing the best care we ever had, often without cost. Some of Hawaii's foremost families secretly called him in when AMA doctors were ineffective, and were never disappointed.

Dr. Kaonohi subscribed to *Ebony* and *Our World* magazines, telling me he "wanted to see what other black people are doing"; he hosted Afro-American friends visiting from the mainland and turned down membership in otherwise white organizations on the ground he did not want to be an "exception" and would join only when the bars were lowered for all nonwhites. He was about my color, dark brown. When he died, most of his vast knowledge of old Hawaiian herbal remedies was buried with him, for younger Hawaiians had been brainwashed by whites who followed the AMA line of ridiculing "herb doctors" and did not care to learn his skills. Haoles have been more successful with Hawaiians than with any other group here in creating a low self-image. The stereotyped Hawaiian is "lazy, carefree, loud, happy, superstitious and childlike"—which sounds painfully close to the old stereotypes of Afro-Americans.

Around the turn of the century, Booker T. Washington visited Hawaii to evaluate the possibility of plantation labor for black workers then in Dixie. I became friends with a Puerto Rican of French extraction, A. E. Minvielle, Sr., who had been a labor contractor for the Big Five plantations and who was assigned to conduct the Tuskegee educator on tours of the islands. (Incidentally, Minvielle surprised me one day by presenting a Bessie Smith recording, in virtually new condition, of "Don't Cry Baby" and "You Don't Understand," from his private collection.) After studying the picture, Washington left convinced that island working and living conditions on plantations in that period were even worse than in the South. Nevertheless, a shipload came here anyway but after a year all but a few were glad to return to Dixie.

Currently the numbers of workers on sugar and pineapple plantations have been greatly reduced due to mechanization, but there are many job opportunities for black skilled workers. I have seen vast changes since 1948. When I first arrived, jobs in private industry were scarce with all but a few souls working for Uncle Sam. Today the largest department stores hire us as clerks, both men and women. There are teachers in the public schools and at the university. There are policemen (those in the past posed as members of other ethnic groups). For over thirty years Lucius Jenkins was a foreman over two departments at Dole Pineapple, often the only Afro-American in the entire cannery and with haoles under him. Bill Winston, a drummer from Chicago's ghetto, was head of street lighting for the city of Honolulu and virtually ran the Musicians' Union. The key man in traffic safety education for Honolulu is Herman Burrell, who came here originally to work on his Ph.D. Mrs. Helene Hale, elected as mayor of the entire island of Hawaii, is a niece of the late Dr. Ralph Bunche. The leading Republican politician and a judge on the island of Maui was Wendell Crockett, Jr., whose father came from Michigan and was a member of the territorial senate. Nolle Smith and his offspring are top people in their varied chosen professions. There is at least one home building contractor and many small businesses of many kinds. Recently, the head of the state mental health hospital was a black doctor. There are nurses and a few doctors. Al Stacey, the leading bridge instructor, and Alonzo De Mello, the state's foremost hypnotist, are black. Charles Campbell, former chairman of the county Democratic party and city councilman, more recently a member of the state legislature, is a high school teacher.

These and similar jobs and elective positions were obtained solely on merit. There are not enough souls here to wield political or economic power. There is no ghetto, hence no potential Black Power. Hawaii is therefore unique, and this departure from the American norm often confused black militants temporarily in Hawaii. The white-black confrontation doesn't exist here. I speak, of course, of the few thousand black civilians who call these islands home. Those in the armed forces, on the other hand, may take a different view of Hawaii for the various military installations show the same prejudice found back on the mainland, including occasional riots between black and white personnel.

I do not pretend to know what would happen should Hawaii find itself with a large Afro-American population; but unless there was also a big white population with hardened mainland racist attitudes, there would be no necessity for the sharp confrontation often found from San Diego to Boston. I firmly believe the large number of nonwhites in policy-making positions—plus the many key Caucasians who left the bulk of their prejudice back on the mainland—would assure us a fair deal. Generally speaking, the darker peoples of Hawaii are sympathetic toward the black revolution. I have discussed these matters many times with Orientals, many of them concerned about the increasing migration of whites to Hawaii. After living here thirty-two years, I am now looked upon by some Orientals as a "local boy," one now thoroughly familiar with island life-styles and concerned over the future of Hawaii. And, of course, there is a lunatic fringe including a branch of the John Birch Society and a radio station which daily airs the opinions of outspoken reactionaries, mainly white but including a few well-heeled and ultra-conservative Orientals, primarily medical doctors.

But despite its far greater freedom from racism, I do not recommend any black settling in the fiftieth State unless he has special skills, a sizeable bank account, or an assured monthly income from outside sources. Living costs are higher here than in any other section of the nation except Anchorage, Alaska. Rental housing is currently so scarce as to be virtually nonexistent for anybody, no matter what his color, unable to pay four hundred dollars or more per month. Obviously this eliminates the common laborer. The lowest paid, unskilled jobs are held down mainly by Hawaiians, Samoans, and Tongans, along with some Filipinos, who by necessity are forced to live in crowded slum conditions like those of mainland ghettoes. Public housing developments here are as mismanaged and as certain breeders of crime and juvenile delinquency as their counterparts in Chicago and New York. Yet they have waiting lists of thousands of applicants because of low rents. There are black common laborers, but like those of other groups they are forced to live together or share crowded quarters with impoverished islanders with whom they have established rapport.

Food takes a big bite out of the budget unless one is ready to switch to local eating habits, such as catching fish and squid and gathering watercress and some types of fruit growing wild in rural areas. Beef and pork are high, although watermelon may be available in small quantities even for Christmas dinner.

Although there is much barbecue sold here, it is mainly oriental in type. I had to learn to make my own sauce as well as sweet potato pie which is an unknown dish to most islanders. Generally speaking, oriental cooking is not hot and spicy except for certain Korean viands; their Kim Chee can blow your head right off. Incidentally, many native Hawaiians go for chitlins and tripe stew. They also dig roasted sweet potatoes.

I once spent an entire afternoon teaching a Chinese minister how to cook candied yams. He had attended school in New York and acquired this taste through trips to Harlem. After returning to Honolulu, he had almost gone wild with frustration trying fruitlessly to cook his own. Shortly after arriving, I introduced a number of Japanese friends to red beans and rice with cornbread. I now add spicy Portuguese sausage to my red beans and either ham hocks or salt pork. The Portuguese themselves combine red beans with white potatoes for a thick soup.

All five of my children were born and reared in Hawaii. They like cornbread and biscuits; but they care equally for such local foods as saimin and sushi, pick and eat mangoes, and have the taste for the salty preserved fruits and cracker seeds which I have never learned to dig. An ordinary meal may consist of foods originating in many countries. And many Hawaiians, living mainly on fish and poi, look upon hamburgers and hot dogs as I view filet mignon: a luxury dish.

Hawaii is not for those who can be happy only in Soul City. This is no place for those who can identify only with Afro-America. "Little Harlem" is only a couple of blocks of bars, barbershops, and a soul food restaurant or two. When I arrived, the local establishment was trying to shunt black servicemen, gamblers, pimps, dope peddlers, and prostitutes into this area to better localize the racism by police and others imported from the mainland, but this disappeared after a confrontation between a group of us and the police chief.

Unfortunately, many settling in Hawaii want to lose their black identity. To them the black revolution had little meaning. They consider themselves as achieving, on a personal level, what others want as a group, and they are satisfied. As for me, I identify automatically with other souls on sight—although later, on acquaintance, I may wish I had not. Being black grants no special right to be loud and wrong. But I have not renounced my black heritage.

73

Not long after arriving in Hawaii, I began writing a regular weekly column for the Honolulu *Record,* a newspaper supported mainly by the ILWU membership, and was openly friendly with its leadership. Within a week I had decided to settle here permanently, although I knew it would mean giving up what prestige I had acquired back in Chicago where I was now appearing each year in *Who's Who In the Midwest* and had been told by the editors that in 1949 my biography would be included in *Who's Who In America.* But the peace and dignity of living in Paradise would compensate for finding a way other than as a newspaperman to make a living. The *Record,* of course, did not have the financial resources to add me to its payroll. Koji Ariyoshi and Ed Rohrbough, son of a West Virginia congressman, were its editorial mainstays.

The local establishment, which evidently had been given a file on me by the FBI, flipped. I was a Communist and a subversive and a threat to Hawaii. Not too long before my arrival, all Democrats were tarred with this same brush by the ruling Republican clique.

In my column I tried to spell out the similarities between local leaders who thought my fight against white supremacy meant I was antiwhite. I opposed any and all white imperialism and backed the nations seeking independence following World War II. I so incensed members of the white power structure that I became the constant radio target of an anti-

labor organization known as IMUA, formed to combat the long water-
front strike in 1949, and whose membership was overwhelmingly haole.[2]
Even the two dailies were not above taking occasional potshots at me.

This confirmed my belief that my columns were having some effect.
Even more telling was the relationship I developed with a number of
oriental businessmen. Many privately confided I voiced what was in their
hearts but they did not know how to express. I think also that for the first
time I caused many islanders to realize their stake in our battle for equal
rights.

I believe Honolulu, because of its hash of cultures, has more indivi-
dualists per thousand population than any other place in America. As
McCarthyism settled like a pall over the nation, many haoles thumbed
their noses at the establishment by openly defying the witch hunt atmosphere. Some were glad I had shaken up the power structure. I was then
operating a small wholesale paper business. These businessmen not only
traded with me in preference to Big Five concerns but after placing orders
would complain that "you must be slipping" when several days passed
without an attack on me by IMUA. A number of oriental businessmen,
recognizing me on sight from my photo in my column, supported me
because I openly defied "the big haoles." I soon learned also that personal
rapport outweighed unpopular labels. Those who liked you simply ignored all smear attempts.

This was brought home strikingly during Hawaii's Smith Act trials.
As in other cities, several Honoluluans were arrested and indicted as
Communists dedicated to "overthrowing the government by force and
violence." Interpreted by many here as instigated by the Big Five in
another attempt to bust the ILWU and including not only Jack Hall but
Koji Ariyoshi as editor of the *Record* and Charlie Fujimoto, chairman of
the party, the arrests and trial attracted little attention except among the
rabid supporters of the status quo, mainly reactionary whites. Ordinary
citizens dismissed it as "haole humbug" and went on about their business.
Since those indicted were either born here or were longtime residents,
islanders were not impressed. Those who had attended school with the
defendants and had known them all their lives considered it impossible
that their friends and acquaintances wanted to overthrow the government. As some expressed it, "Maybe Mainland Communists want to but
not our own. I know them personally." The whole episode was completely
ridiculous in the first place. The tiny local Communist group was quite
ineffectual, with running feuds between leaders. I doubt that it could have

overthrown itself. Nevertheless, the trials went on with all solemnity. But a solid section of the local government was opposed.

Proving the individuality of Hawaii, Mayor John Wilson of Honolulu appeared as a character witness for the defense. His special assistant, W. K. Bassett, had long been belligerently anti-Big Five and was a *Record* columnist who became one of my best friends. Federal Judge Delbert Metager, who single-handedly shackled army dictatorship during World War II, had reduced bonds of the defendants to the bare minimum and had dismissed contempt charges against ten persons who took the Fifth Amendment when the House Committee on Un-American Activities held local hearings. I know of no other place in our nation where this could have happened.

74

To many black Americans, the FBI was the J. Edgar Hoover gestapo, a powerful federal police force dedicated to maintaining the oppressive white power structure. Only in the recent past have Afro-Americans been given courtesy cards by the establishment and allowed to join as regular agents. The FBI is noted for spending more time on neutralizing or intimidating those who want a change in the racist status quo than in exposing persons or groups guilty of violence in support of white supremacy.

Immediately after the end of World War II, the FBI began its harassment of those demanding democracy at home. Agents questioned neighbors of whites actively fighting for equality, asking if the suspect "ever entertained Negroes in his home," and used this information as a standard for determining if a person was a Communist. Even Catholics, white and black, lost their jobs because of FBI probing.

I first drew FBI attention when I joined with others in speaking my mind back in 1937 when the League of American Writers published the booklet, *Writers Take Sides.* Undoubtedly, a huge dossier was compiled on me because of my activities during World War II. When I left Chicago for Hawaii in 1948, I am confident this dossier arrived as soon as I did. Undoubtedly Honolulu agents were told to watch my every move. Usually those wanting telephones installed waited months for service and then could get only party lines. Invariably I received a private line a day or two after application, which permitted the FBI to monitor all my calls more easily. When they could find no evidence I was plotting to overthrow the government by force and violence, the Hoover gestapo turned to other tactics. Friends told me FBI agents had approached them asking if they knew whether I was "peddling dope" and if I were a brother of Ben Davis, Jr. To underline the absurdity of it all, some of those later accused as Communists suspected I was "an FBI plant" trying to get the goods on them.

It is only during the past twenty years that the FBI seems to have given up on me.

One day, as I was leaving a customer's shop in a neighborhood away from downtown, I was approached by a white man who had parked and waited behind my station wagon. Showing his FBI credentials, he said he wanted to talk with me. My first reaction was to tell him to go to hell. But on second thought I agreed to meet him in a public park one day at noon.

He showed up accompanied by another agent who closely clutched a briefcase during the entire conversation. I am reasonably certain it must have contained a small, transistorized tape recorder.

"I want to see you," the first agent began, "to talk about your Communist activities. I know you're not a member of the party now, and I wondered how you ever got mixed up with those guys in the first place."

"I don't consider myself being mixed up with anybody," I said. "However, I admit having been close friends with many persons who said they were Communists. I have always been happy to work with anybody who was willing to help me get the equal treatment promised me—and never given."

"Yes, but why did you work with Communists?"

"I believe as did the late Nannie Burroughs, one of our foremost educators, church leaders, and fighters for justice. She once said, 'I'll work with the devil himself if he will stand beside me and help me overcome white supremacy.'"

"Where are you from?" asked the other agent.

"He was born in Arkansas City, Kansas, December 31, 1905, finished high school there, then went to Friends University in Wichita, and then Kansas State College," the other cut in before I could answer.

I looked at him, then turned to the agent who had asked the question. "Anything you want to know about me, ask him instead. He probably has a record of happenings over the years I have completely forgotten."

Ignoring this, the first asked, "What made you feel like you do?"

"It goes back to high school when I first became aware of the meaning of raw, naked prejudice. I expect to feel this way until racism stops or I die. And from the way things look, I'll be dead a hell of a long time before racism ends." I detailed some of my experiences with white supremacy not only in school but out in the world. They nodded without comment. After all there wasn't much they could say.

"Do you know," the first said when I finished, "that I've been assigned to you ever since I was transferred to Hawaii? As I said, I know you're not a member of the Communist Party now. Would you mind telling us why you decided to quit?"

"Listen," I replied, "I've never told you I ever was a member. How, then, can I tell you I quit? Really now, that doesn't make sense."

We parted without visible rancor. But I can't help feeling guilty over taking up FBI time for so many years when apparently the Hoover gestapo needed agents to find the murderers of the black and white civil rights leaders in Mississippi, and the killers who threw the bomb in that Birmingham church and murdered those little children. I owe the FBI an apology for causing them a needless waste of so much energy on me.

75

In June 1969, I began living in a section of Waikiki known as the Jungle. Surrounded by big, pretentious tourist trap hotels, this area consisted of one- and two-story studio cottages, small hotels, and old homes converted into rooming houses and apartments. My quarters were a little studio facing a narrow, one-way street. My tiny porch with three stone steps was only two feet from the sidewalk, thus permitting me to hold conversations with pedestrians—and occasionally motorists—on both sides of the thoroughfare.

My neighbors were young men and women mainly from the mainland between eighteen and twenty-five years old, here on vacation or to attend the University of Hawaii. For the most part, they were from California, with a few from as far away as Maine and Florida. In addition there were others from South America, Europe, Asia, Africa, Australia, Canada, the Caribbeans, Samoa, Tonga, and the other islands of the South Pacific. Hippies were still numerous, but the majority I thought of as members of the Now Generation. My relationships and experiences were so interesting and fantastic I detailed them, along with my three trips to the mainland in 1973 and 1974 to read my poetry, in a separate tome entitled "That Incredible Waikiki Jungle."

What immediately impressed me about these young Americans, by far the numerical majority and most of them meeting for the first time in Hawaii, was their warm camaraderie and my ability to communicate on their own terms with no hint of a generation gap. Virtually all the young brothers consorted with ofay chicks (at least 80 percent of them longhaired blondes), and the sisters were affiliated with white boys. Occasionally a brother, a honky lad, and two white girls rented quarters together. Young blacks in bountiful Afros and wearing dashikis crashed in pads rented by ofays they never knew before; occasionally I permitted young white girls to sleep overnight on my floor. I saw no signs of racial hangups; these were all members of the Now Generation associating with whom they liked and color be damned.

Young whites of both sexes frequently called to me from across the street, "Hey, brother, what's happening?" meanwhile giving me a victory sign and the upraised clenched fist. And as I talked to them, I found many far more aware than most older blacks of the dynamics of the black revolution and the urgent need for fundamental socio-economic change. Amazed and pleased by the lack here of interracial polarization then prevalent on the mainland, they were especially appreciative of coming to a land where they could talk and move freely without fear of trouble.

I looked upon these young white rebels—along with Indians, Latin Americans, and the dispossessed poor—as natural allies of the black revolution. (I have virtually given up on most of organized labor's leadership.) Although I did not doubt that as time passed many of these rebellious white young would drop back into the mainstream of society, I believed enough would retain their anger with the status quo to continue their fight. I consider it a matter of necessity now for their own survival.

The present young generation is the first in the history of the globe to face the prospect of annihilation from five sources. The solution of none of these problems can be long delayed:

1. *Nuclear War.* Both the Soviet Union and the United States already have enough nuclear bombs to kill at least five times as many people as now live on this planet. This is apart from the fallout which would make this entire globe uninhabitable anyway. Nor does it include the atomic and hydrogen weaponry of Great Britain, France, China, India, and probably Israel and South Africa. And yet we continue this senseless race of building and stockpiling new, devastating weapons which impoverish nations. Any power-drunk madman could start the third—and final—world war.

2. *Bloody Revolution.* The black-white powder keg could be ignited on both a national and international basis. The vocal diehard racists and the silent white majority who do not oppose their attitudes are faced with increasing resistance from black patriots who would rather die than live under dehumanizing oppression. The spirit and legacy of Hitler still lives in many areas. Many of the rising young nations of the world will willingly fight for their right to freedom and self-determination against colonial control. We have seen this in Vietnam, Rhodesia, and South Africa.

3. *Population Explosion.* Within thirty years the world population is expected to at least double its current total of over four billion. Our nation, the richest and most powerful in existence, has not yet solved the problem of adequately feeding, clothing, housing, and caring for the basic needs of 220,000,000; what will we do with the 300,000,000 to 400,000,000 or more that is expected in thirty years?

4. *Pollution and Disappearing Natural Resources.* Water, air, and soil are being rendered unfit for use through pollution as our population and industry expands and needs more and more of these essentials. Many forms of animal life have disappeared and others are on the verge of extinction. The earth has finite quantities of coal, oil, metals, and similar necessities beneath its surface. When they are gone, there will be no more. Meanwhile, we are poisoning air, water, and land while at the same time we need greater quantities than ever for the mushrooming world population.

5. *Gas and Germ Warfare.* Scientists have produced huge quantities of these weapons designed for mass murder which could not only decimate hundreds of millions of people but make huge areas of the world unable to sustain any form of life for generations. The accidental detonation of these lethal devices would wipe out an entire nation overnight.

Faced with these horrible potentials brought into existence by their elders, is it any wonder that many of the young are concerned about their future and rebel against parents who have permitted all mankind to be pushed to the brink of total disaster?

And unless the young of all colors can turn back this senseless march to oblivion, we deserve to die. And we ought to halt it before we branch solidly into outer space and pollute another planet. The hope of humanity lies in the young who have not yet become plastic victims of perpetual brainwashing by the mass media and their skilled shills who program us for acceptance of mass jackassery.

Afro-Americans are, of course, concerned primarily with the possibility of death through white violence or neglect (the jobless rate of our young who finish school is triple that of whites). Yet should we win our black revolution today and defuse this national powder keg, we would still face annihilation from the other four potentials for instant death. Black victory will be meaningless if we all die through nuclear holocaust, an over-populated planet unable to support its inhabitants, a globe with air unfit to breathe, polluted water which poisons our systems, and depleted soil on which nothing will grow. Lethal gases and disease germs from the world's arsenals can not be programmed to spare soul sisters and brothers.

Racism, the cornerstone of our sick society before our nation began two hundred years ago, must be destroyed along with the other threats to world suicide. For survival, people of all colors must begin working together to formulate long-range goals. This requires international planning on a scale never hitherto possible. Obviously this would herald the end of the suicidal arms race and initiate the use of the billions saved to end the starvation and bad housing of the poor people of the world. Instead we continue racing down the path leading to the end of the human species.

Spiritually, I travel with the young. As a black writer I like to think my activities have helped advance Afro-America from the, say, 40 percent black acceptance of my youth to the perhaps 75 percent acceptance of today. However I will not be satisfied until we reach 100 percent parity with all other Americans while retaining black integrity.

We as a group are learning our identity. Our young know who they are. We are through producing carbon copy Caucasians, and we are learning to do our own thing, man, without shame. At last we have learned to take pride in our hair, clothing, coloring, food, music, and history as well as our other traits setting us apart as a people. We are saying at last, "America, this is how we really are. This is what we have given this nation and the world, and we glory in our history and achievements. Whitey, we have had enough of your bullshit. From now on, treat us like equals, or the whole goddamn mess called America will go up in flames."

And for the first time the white power structure is finding difficulty in locating "different Negroes" to save itself from niggers, for today many of the formerly different Negroes have blossomed into blacks. The old ploy was to locate a talented Afro-American basically white under his skin, accept him into the club as a courtesy Caucasian with limited membership privileges because he was "different from the rest of your people," and prop him up as a puppet leader in the ghetto. He would receive a comfortable salary and promises of a few crumbs to be flung to the masses in return for keeping them from grumbling too loudly. But that no longer works. Today black is not only beautiful but far wiser.

Some concessions have been made in a bow to the militancy now eating away the foundations of the white power structure.

Looking back upon my existence between 1905 and 1980, I have seen radical changes. I saw my first airplane in 1911, a biplane which landed in a pasture a few miles outside Arkansas City. Dad and mother walked out with me for a close look at this newfangled flying machine. But many years were to pass before blacks took to the sky. There were few even when World War II began, probably the most noted being Hubert Julian, the Black Eagle, and Col. John C. Robinson, both of whom flew for Emperor Haile Selassie of Ethiopia; but also Bessie Coleman, Willa Brown, and a handful more. But after formation of the 99th Pursuit Squadron at Tuskegee Institute, black aviation literally took off. Today there are not only black military flyers but black commercial pilots and black air force generals.

When I was a kid, there was Morse code but no voice broadcasts for the general public existed until my high school days. Talking pictures did not appear until after I went to Chicago in 1927. Television was not widely known until after I came to Honolulu in 1948. For years these media were barred to blacks—and many barriers still remain.

Fortunately for me, I have lived on the periphery of jazz and the blues since I was eight. I watched and listened as this revolutionary new music developed through New Orleans, Dixieland, swing, bop, progressive, and the avant garde of today. I felt with them the frustration of black musicians and bands, who originated the art, as they received only a fraction of the adulation they deserved while honky musicians received the lion's share of the glory and money. I recall that when Mamie Smith recorded "Crazy Blues" in 1921, she was the first sister on wax, although several white women had received acclaim for vastly inferior platters.

Except for prizefighters and some track and field stars, there were hardly any black athletes in the sports mainstream during my youth. For many years Duke Slater of Iowa, later a judge in Chicago, and Joe Lillard, a former star from Oregon—both of the Old Chicago Cardinals—were the only black players in the top pro football league. Notre Dame was lily white until World War II. Only a handful of blacks were on big college basketball teams, and the two major baseball leagues barred us until after 1945. Now all that has changed, but even today some college coaches look upon black players primarily as trained baboons.

Except for a few places like Boley, Oklahoma, and Mound Bayou, Mississippi, there were no black mayors in my youth. From the Reconstruction era until 1928, when Oscar Depriest was elected in Chicago, there was not a black congressman anywhere and pitifully few judges. That, too, has changed for the better. Until the election of Franklin D. Roosevelt, we could aim our hope no higher than selection for what was termed the president's "Kitchen Cabinet." Since then we have been inching our way slowly toward the Oval Room.

What Afro-America accepts today as normal did not exist in my youth. But Jim Crow is not yet down for the count—although I like to think it is staggering in all areas except employment. Legal miscegenation is more common and accepted now than in 1946 when I took a white wife. And although we have made tremendous gains in education and human rights, we still have a long way to go.

As for me personally, along with my profession, I have never claimed to be a great editor. But I was careful and conscientious. I have never been sued for libel. Threatened, yes, by some belligerent persons over the telephone who had never seen me. But when they walked into my office with mayhem in mind and I stood up from my desk, somehow they suddenly smothered their hostile intentions. And I have watched approvingly as black journalists joined the staffs of major newspapers and magazines, radio stations, and television networks. This was not possible in my youth—but there has been compensation. I have been able to watch close up as much black history was being made.

My health has been good throughout my life except for the past few years. So rarely did I need medical attention I had no regular physician. In 1942 I stayed overnight at Provident Hospital in Chicago for a tonsillectomy; my next trip was thirty-one years later in Honolulu in 1973 when I found I had damaged discs, a pinched nerve in my left hip, and high blood pressure—that scourge of black life. Fortunately for me and my poor wallet, my body waited until I began collecting social security, and I was on Medicare before my parts began wearing out. Since then I have been hospitalized for phlebitis, bleeding ulcers, thrombosis, and stassis dermatitis. But this has not been severe enough to curb my consumption of tobacco and alcohol.

In Hawaii I accumulated five offspring—all by my second wife from whom I was divorced in 1970. They are four daughters and one son. Strange as it may seem, I have impregnated only three women, all white. One had a miscarriage and the second an abortion. For years I assumed I was infertile and went about blithely behaving as if I could not become a father. Then after I was forty-three along came five including a pair of twins. Crazy, huh?

When I was a kid in Kansas I received a lifelong inferiority complex which I have learned to control. Nevertheless I know it resides deep in my psyche. And that is why I still consider myself as livin' the blues.

Frank and Helen Canfield Davis (1947)

Frank and Helen Davis with their first child, Lynn, in Honolulu (1949)

Davis at his Paradise Paper Company (1952)

From his front porch, Davis, at age sixty-nine or seventy, observes life in the Waikiki "Jungle."

APPENDIX
NOTES
INDEX

Appendix

From "That Incredible Waikiki Jungle"

In Livin' the Blues, Davis spoke excitedly about a manuscript that was intended to detail his life experiences in the Waikiki ghetto called "the Jungle." Unfortunately, little of this manuscript survives. However, one portion we have, section 28, describes one of the three trips he took to the mainland in 1973 and 1974 to read his poetry.

28

In October of 1973 I returned to the mainland for a series of poetry concerts. This was the first time I had left Hawaii since coming here in 1948, some twenty-five years before. Two of my three volumes of poetry were out of print: *Black Man's Verse* (1935) and *47th Street* (1948). Only *I Am The American Negro* (1937) was currently available. Although I had received a Julius Rosenwald Fellowship in poetry in 1937, nothing much had happened until 1967 when the black revolution brought wider interest in black history and literature. Ethnic study courses came into being at schools and colleges all over the nation. The nation's leading book publishers contacted me asking permission to reprint my poetry in anthologies, collections, and textbooks on the high school and college levels. By the time I began this trip, I was appearing in some sixty collections and had received more in reprint fees than came to me from the three original volumes.

The groundwork was laid in March of 1972 when an old friend, Dr. Margaret Goss Burroughs, curator of the DuSable Museum of African American History in Chicago and herself a talented writer and artist, visited Honolulu with her husband, Charles, and sister, Marion. I had known Margaret since 1940 when I was director of public relations for the first National Negro Exposition at the Chicago Coliseum. She asked if I would consider appearing in Chicago to read my poetry. This thought had never crossed my mind.

"What makes you think anybody would want to hear me read, let alone pay enough to make such a trip worthwhile?" I asked.

"There's a whole new generation of black writers now," she said. "Many have read your poetry and are quite anxious to meet you in person. Being out here in the Pacific Ocean, I doubt you fully realize the changes since you left Chicago in 1948. Chicago—in fact, the whole mainland—has changed. I can guarantee you will be well received."

I pondered this several days, then tentatively agreed to venture from my voluntary hibernation come October after Margaret returned from her annual summer trip to Africa and settled down to teaching school. A couple of months after she went home, I received a letter from Dr. Stephen Henderson, head of the department of Arts and Humanities at Howard University, Washington, D.C., wanting to know if I would appear there and in several other cities for poetry recitals. I suggested he contact Dr. Burroughs and the two of them arrange an itinerary.

They could not click for that year. Margaret asked me to come to Chicago in February. I shuddered. Me come from Paradise to Chicago in February? One of the reasons I remained in Hawaii was to avoid winter in the Windy City. I wrote her that even if a contract were put out to return me as a corpse in February, I would find some way of protecting my cadaver from such a horrible scene as Chicago that time of the year. As a consequence, we decided on my appearing in autumn of 1973. Margaret assured me I would be well received, "earring and all." (In the spring of 1972 I had had my right ear pierced, not unusual in the Jungle. In other parts of town I was occasionally asked, "Why d'you wear one white gold earring?" My stock reply: "Because I am a confirmed nonconformist." In the Jungle it attracted no special attention except to further indicate I was not a working member of the conservative older generation.)

Before leaving I did the usual thing for a man going to the mainland in cooler weather: I borrowed a topcoat. In Honolulu they are rarely used except by those who frequently travel in other climes. I borrowed it through Sally, an expert in oriental art and a member of one of Honolulu's leading families whose father was roughly my size. When I reached Dulles Airport near the nation's capital I had immediate need for it. The thermometer registered thirty-five degrees. I hadn't experienced weather like this in twenty-five years. In Honolulu it's considered a cold wave when it drops to fifty-five degrees in the dead of winter. I felt like taking the next plane home. I began to cough and sneeze. My throat grew hoarse. But I had been sent a round-trip air ticket and was committed to a number of personal appearances. Nothing I could honorably do but stick it out.

Yet I knew my respiratory discomfiture was no sound way to begin my tour. Thankfully I brought with me a large supply of vitamin C; they work for me. I have used them religiously since 1970 when Dr. Linus Pauling first preached their virtues and have not had a bad cold since, once getting rid of my only siege of pleurisy after two days of gigantic dosages. As soon as I reached my hotel I took three thousand units, another three thousand six hours later, and a final three thousand before I went to bed. When I awoke next morning I was my usual self. Ascorbic acid had done it again.

After an absence of two and a half decades, coming back to the mainland was almost like entering a new world. I was aware of major changes, but seeing them was far more impressive. In August, Dudley Randall of Detroit, himself a fine poet, editor, and book publisher, had visited Honolulu and taped an interview with the "mystery poet" who had "vanished a quarter of a century earlier," as he described me. This special article appeared in the January 1974 issue of *Black World*, after I had returned to Paradise.

At Howard I was amazed to find I was looked upon as "a long lost folk hero of black poetry." I was introduced before each appearance as the "daddy" and a "forerunner of modern black poetry." I learned my out-of-print books brought big prices at auctions, when found. A London auctioneer had just sold a copy of *Black Man's Verse* for over one hundred dollars. A Howard professor told me President Senghor of Senegal, himself one of the world's foremost poets, had wanted to contact me to ask permission to translate some of my poems into French because of what he called the fine examples of Negritude running through my work. I also renewed my acquaintance with Sterling Brown, one of the few major poets produced by black America, and for the first time I met Nick Aaron Ford of Morgan State, a poet and editor whose volume, *Black Insights,* was one of the best anthologies yet produced.

In question and answer periods following my concerts, not only at Howard but elsewhere, I was invariably asked about living in Hawaii and especially about the Jungle. I did not detail any of my factual experiences for I did not believe my listeners would be likely to believe me; I hardly believed some of them myself even though I had seen them unfold. I said only that the Jungle was noted for sex and drugs, whereupon one professor shot back, "just like Howard University."

I was indelibly impressed by the alertness of young college brothers and sisters. Many now wrote, and a lot of good material was being produced and published, often in paperback. This was several light-years of advancement over my early days at Kansas State and in Chicago, where black poets were as scarce as the Loch Ness monster or the Abominable Snow Man. However, there was also some stuff being palmed off as poetry which I dumped under the general heading of Annotated Washroom Graffiti.

I spent three days in Washington with its overwhelming black population, then flew to Atlanta. I had not been there since 1934 when I edited the Atlanta *Daily World,* oldest black daily in America. At that time Atlanta was so openly prejudiced I vowed never to enter the city again. If anybody had seriously dared suggest that Atlanta would ever have a black mayor, he would have been placed in a straitjacket and rushed to the funny farm. Now Maynard Jackson was in office, and many city officials were black, and miscegenation was open. When my plane set down at the airport, I recalled that a number of us risked going to the Georgia chaingang by putting up worthless checks to allow Colonel Hubert Fauntleroy Julian, the original Black Eagle, to stage an exhibition flight at the municipal airport. He was given a decrepit craft about to be junked but handled it so beautifully even the air terminal manager gave him a grudging word of admiration. Now there were black stewardesses and other personnel working integrated with whites. What a marvelous change!

I read at Spelman, Morehouse, and Clark colleges. I was steadily called "living history" through having personally known many noted black figures that were names only to most of my audiences. As a working newspaperman, I had met or become friendly, after arriving in Chicago in 1927, with such as Jack Johnson, Jelly Roll Morton, W. C. Handy, Louis Armstrong, Paul Robeson, Duke Ellington, Langston Hughes, Richard Wright, and many others. Enough questions were asked me in rap sessions about such people to have kept me talking the rest of the year.

But the most frequent query was that of some young writer, usually with wonderment, "How could you have written poetry in the 1920s and 1930s which sounds like it could have been written this morning?" My stock reply was that I am a realist. Although many critics considered me thirty or forty years ahead of my time, we still suffered from the same basic disease that had crippled us for centuries: racism. Although Atlanta had dramatically improved, the evil had not been stamped out here or in the rest of America, and I wrote what I saw and felt. I settled in Hawaii, I told them, because I found less prejudice there than any place I had ever been. But not even there had it completely disappeared, and I am disturbed by racism now in the same way I was in the 1920s and 1930s.

I flew to Chicago after two busy days in Atlanta, arriving at the DuSable Museum before my telegram, sent the day before, was delivered to Margaret. This was my old stamping ground; I had lived here longer than any place except Honolulu. And if ever I needed a topcoat, it was here in late October. I did not see the sun during my short stay there.

My audience at DuSable Museum included many friends I had neither seen nor heard from since 1948, among them Gwendolyn Brooks; Pat, the virtual twin of Jacque, who had visited Honolulu the year before, was also there. I received a black hand-carved cane from Kenya and a necklace from Tanganyika, both of which I have since worn on public occasions to underline my blackness—if ever there was any doubt. I was also guest of honor at a reception given by Etta Moten Barnett, former star of stage and screen and widow of Claude Barnett; the passing years had not faded her charm or loveliness.

While at the DuSable Museum I was handed several xeroxed pages of a book entitled *47th Street and Other Poems by Frank Marshall Davis* and asked if it was an authorized reprint of my third volume, *47th Street*. The frontispiece read, "Type for this book set up in 1941." Below, on the same page, was another line, "Type destroyed by fire in 1943." This I considered a real miracle because *47th Street* was not written until 1946 nor published prior to 1948. I have never been able to learn who pirated this unauthorized book.

I left Chicago one day earlier than originally intended because of a mix-up in my scheduled appearance at the University of California in Berkeley. I appeared in the afternoon at the university and that night appeared before the Afro-American Historical Society in San Francisco. In between, I was a luncheon guest at the Rainbow Sign in Berkeley, a community center headed by Mary Ann Pollar, a saintly sister of vision I had once met in Chicago. Unable to find a copy of *Black Man's Verse,* she had borrowed a copy from the university library and painstakingly typed each poem. She was also using some of my verses on the back of her Expresso coffee bar menus.

At my Afro-American Society appearance I ran into a situation I had not expected. A brother who had operated a bookstore in San Francisco told me had read all three of my volumes of poetry as well as another book of prose I wrote. I looked at him curiously. He said, "I mean *Sex Rebel: Black*. Although it did not list your name as author, I wracked my brain trying to figure out what other black writer might be in Hawaii. I could think of nobody but you. Then I reread your poetry. I saw the similarities in style and phraseology. I hit it right on the head, didn't I?" I could not then truthfully deny that this book, which came out in 1968 as a Greenleaf Classic, was mine. Incidentally, I stayed in the Bay City for two extra days to be with Jacque who had completely floored me in the Jungle. It was then I discovered the magic had evaporated.

I returned to Honolulu with my ego, which nobody had ever mistaken for a molehill, looking down on Mount Everest. In no way was I prepared for the enthusiastic receptions I received in both Chicago and northern California. I began hitting my stride in Atlanta, and when I reached the Windy City I had a confidence and a sureness I had lacked at Howard. As a result, my audiences reacted so warmly, so supportively with their spontaneous shouts of "Right on, brother" and "Tell it like it is" that I had to summon all my willpower to keep from losing my cool and bawling like a baby from joy on the stage. I simply was not accustomed to anything like this. I received unexpected standing ovations. And yet, despite this, I was glad when I touched Hawaiian soil again in Honolulu.

Whoever said events travel in threes must have had me in mind. As I returned from my concert tour, I had a letter from Frances Norton Manning in Southern California wanting to know if I would appear at several colleges there. A white woman, she had been responsible for finding a publisher for my first book in 1935. I had not heard from her in twenty-seven years. She now operated a publicity agency in Orange County at Santa Ana. Under her aegis, I made two trips to Southern California and also met Mae West, the ageless glamour gal with whom I spent an afternoon and from whom I received an invitation to come back next time I was in the Hollywood area.

I also walked down Central Avenue in Los Angeles and left depressed, the same reaction I had had in Chicago. Empty, broken buildings squatting in tired, crippled dejection with poorly scrawled "For Rent" signs and busted windows made me feel the city was rotting on the vine. Is this today the inner city image of our giant metropolises? I did not sense this kind of hopelessness in Washington or Atlanta or San Francisco, but they are far smaller. I would surely strangle were I to try living in Chicago or Los Angeles of the 1970s.

But I did see many beautiful sisters in all these places. Fine young foxes were everywhere. I knew I would have no problem relating to them. And in my whirlwind tour I learned some would undoubtedly match my interest.

Notes

Introduction

1. Alain Locke, "Propaganda or Poetry?" *Race* 1 (1936): 73; Sterling A. Brown, *Negro Poetry and Drama* (1937; rpt., New York: Atheneum, 1972), 78; Harriet Monroe, "A New Negro Poet," *Poetry: A Magazine of Verse*, 48.5 (1936): 295.

2. Robeson's comment was quoted in "Robeson in Honolulu Backs Wallace, Denies Communist Peril," Honolulu *Star-Bulletin*, 22 March 1948, rpt. in *Paul Robeson Speaks*, ed. Philip S. Foner (New York: Brunner/Mazel Publishers, 1978), 182.

3. See, for example, Davis's stirring defense of W. E. B. Du Bois, who, with other members of the Peace Information Center, had been indicted on charges of subversion: "When you get right down to it, the deciding factor is whether we will meekly allow the ring of silence to be placed in our noses, or whether we will fight every effort to take away our liberties. That's a problem that will be solved only by you and people like you" (Davis, "Frank-ly Speaking," Honolulu *Record*, 6 December 1951, 8). Another representative instance of Davis's militance can be found in a three-part series of "Frank-ly Speaking" on the subject of "Fighting Racism," Honolulu *Record*, 27 December 1951, 3 January 1952, and 10 January 1952. Writing during the era of anti-Communist hysteria, Davis revealed how the same irrational impulse used to silence American communists was being used to deny equal opportunity to blacks. As he wrote: "Many of us will not accept the false words that the high court decision hits only the Communists. Quite a few of us have believed from the start that the laws and actions supposedly aimed at Communists were merely a disguise under which any of us who objected to the status quo could be silenced or jailed. That obviously would mean any of us who objected to the status quo of white supremacy or to the status quo of stratospheric profits for the giant corporations and low wages for laboring people." He concludes that eventually, even the Supreme Court would have to relent and support fundamental rights of free speech. But at this time, ". . . no thoughtful person can deny that at the moment, the clock has been turned backward in the struggle for equality and against white supremacy" (Honolulu *Record*, 10 January 1952, 6, 8).

4.   James M. Cox, "Recovering Literature's Lost Ground," *Autobiography: Essays Theoretical and Critical,* ed. James Olney (Princeton: Princeton University Press, 1980), 143.

5.   Roy Pascal, *Design and Truth in Autobiography* (Cambridge: Harvard University Press, 1960), 183.

6.   Although Davis never specified, he undoubtedly read Du Bois's *The Souls of Black Folk* (1903), Woodson's *The Miseducation of the Negro* (1933), and Rogers's *World's Great Men of Color* (1946–47).

7.   Letter, Helen Davis to John Edgar Tidwell, 15 August 1991; also *Livin' the Blues,* section 65.

8.   John Edgar Tidwell, "An Interview With Frank Marshall Davis," *Black American Literature Forum* 19 (1985): 107.

9.   Sterling A. Brown, *Negro Poetry and Drama* (1937; rpt., New York: Atheneum Press, 1972), 27.

10.   "Modern Jazz is a Folk Music That Started With the Blues," *The Worker,* 25 December 1955; rpt. *The Negro in Music and Art,* ed. Lindsay Patterson (New York: Publishing Company, 1969), 108.

11.   For instance, under the name Marshall Davis, he published "Booga Red: Part 1" in *The Light: America's News Magazine* (4 February 1928): 5–6; "Booga Red: Part 2" in *The Light* (11 February 1928): 7–8, 19; and "Wreckage: A Faithless Wife Shattered Ferdol Jackson's Ideals," in *The Light* (24 March 1928): 5–6, 19.

12.   The potboilers don't stop here. Discovered among his papers were several other unpublished manuscripts. Using the pseudonym Floyd Marshall, Davis wrote "Mixed Sex Salad"; again using Bob Green (without the "e"), he wrote "Penguins in Paradise"; and finally, "In Reverse," a fiction bearing no identification, except for the title. There are no extant data to confirm whether *Sex Rebel: Black* was commercially successful. Greenleaf Classics, Inc., the publisher of the novel, apparently still exists in some form, although efforts to contact them have been fruitless.

13.   In the foreword to "That Incredible Waikiki Jungle," Davis writes: "In popular use a Jungle is a place where people struggle fiercely to survive. That describes the Waikiki Jungle and most of its residents. What with the dominance of sex, drugs[,] and violence, survival was no easy task. Being addicted to neither drugs nor violence, I specialized in sex. I have not attempted to detail all my experiences in this unbelievable area. . . . But I think I have presented a true picture of what it was like to live in the Waikiki Jungle between 1969 and 1976. . . . Let me assure you this account is entirely factual."

Note on the Text

1.   *Cottonwood Magazine* 38/39 (Summer/Fall 1986), guest edited by Ger-

ald R. Early. The special issue was part of the celebration of Kansas's 125 years of statehood.

2.   Unpublished interview. E. Ethelbert Miller with Frank Marshall Davis, 24 October 1973, at Howard University.

3.   Letter, Davis to John Edgar Tidwell, 14 January 1982. In response to his reply, I then sent him a copy of the *retyped* manuscript. But five months before his death, he wrote again: "Do you have a *complete* copy of LIVIN' THE BLUES? . . . My original has disappeared and xeroxed copies are so mixed up as to be confusing. Should you have a good copy, will you send it to me?" Letter, Davis to John Edgar Tidwell, 19 February 1987.

4.   Telephone interview with Marion Taylor Hummons, 27 November 1991.

5.   In a 27 May 1983 letter to me, Davis indicated that Howard University had finally returned the manuscript.

1905–1923

1.   In 1963, Floyd McKissick was elected national chairman of the Congress of Racial Equality, and, in 1966, became its national director. The quote paraphrases McKissick's assessment in his *Three-Fifths of a Man* (New York: Macmillan, 1969): "The Emancipation Proclamation attempted to free the slaves, but no substantial changes have occurred in the system since that historic document was written. Since the end of the Civil War, America has made serious mistakes, miscalculations that are having grave consequences. One of the most serious mistakes was the failure to provide forty acres and a mule to every freed slave, as was promised by the military when Black troops were needed by the Union to win the Civil War. . . . By not providing economic opportunity for the former slaves, America missed the one chance to absorb Black people into the economic system" (36).

2.   Asafetida is the name for the resin of various plants in the carrot family and is used in folk remedies for warding off illnesses. It is usually worn in a bag, suspended from the neck by a string, and gives off a strong, garlic-like odor.

3.   "Emancipation Day" is an unofficial holiday celebrated by African Americans, in commemoration of President Abraham Lincoln's issuing of the Emancipation Proclamation on 22 September 1862 and its going into effect on 1 January 1863.

4.   Pearl White (1889–1938) was one of the most successful of the early American film stars who gained international fame for her work in "chapter stories"—long-running melodramatic series such as *The Perils of Pauline*. The most successful example of its genre, *Perils* typified the short-episode serial that emphasized suspense, danger, and the cliff-hanger ending that aimed at bringing

the audience back for the next sequel. Eddie Polo was the star of the first purely Western serial *Liberty,* which ran twenty episodes.

5.   A British-born American actor and director, Charlie Chaplin (1889– 1977) won international fame with his portrayal of a pathetic yet humorous little tramp in American-made silent films. Fatty Arbuckle was born Roscoe Conkling Arbuckle (1887–1933). He rose from vaudeville and carnivals to become a star in silent comedy motion pictures. He was quite agile, despite weighing 320 pounds. The Keystone Cops, an insanely incompetent police force, dressed in ill-fitting and unkempt uniforms, appeared regularly in Mack Sennett's silent slapstick farces from 1914 to the early 1920s. They became enshrined in U.S. film history as genuine folk art creations, whose comic appeal was based on a native irreverence for authority. Originally named Michael Sinnott (1880–1960), Mack Sennett created the Keystone Cops and became the "father of slapstick comedy" in motion pictures. A master of comic timing and effective editing, Sennett was a dominant figure in the silent era of Hollywood film production, becoming one of the first directors of comedy to develop a distinctive style. His name is generally associated with the bathing beauties who adorned his comedies with the Keystone Cops.

6.   Named for Tomas de Torquemada, the Spanish Dominican monk and first inquisitor general for all Spanish possessions in 1498. His name has become synonymous with persecution.

7.   The Knights of Pythias is a fraternal organization established to promote friendship, charity, and benevolence. Its founder, Justus H. Rathbone, hoped to facilitate healing the wounds caused by the Civil War. The organization, started 19 February 1864, was incorporated by Congress on 5 August 1870. Its principles are based on the Roman story of Damon and Pythias, whose friendship in ancient Syracuse was so strong they were willing to die for each other.

8.   Mahalia Jackson (1911–72) enjoyed the distinction of being one of the greatest gospel singers ever to perform.

9.   "Signified" is a term meaning a verbal contest, especially among young blacks, involving antifamily insults; this is sometimes also called "sounding."

10.   In her *The Music of Black Americans: A History* (New York: W. W. Norton and Company, 1971), Eileen Southern locates the origins of Storyville in a 1897 New Orleans city resolution that instituted vice segregation by establishing a "tenderloin district" (or a part of the city where vice and police corruption operated freely, as in the district in New York City that gave this form of districting its name). Alderman Sidney Story, for whom the New Orleans district was named, could hardly have imagined the cultural exchange that would take place between the best creole and black musicians. Ragtime, blues, and jazz flourished in the district before 1917, when the U.S. Navy exerted pressure to close down the district and thereby initiated the migration of the musicians and their music up the Mississippi River, to Memphis and Chicago.

11.   James Reese Europe (1881–1919), a classically trained violinist and student of music theory and instrumentation, found employment in a variety of

positions, including musical director of *The Shoofly Regiment* (1906), a successful musical play produced by Bob Cole and J. Rosamond Johnson. He later organized the Clef Club, a union comprising many of the best Negro musicians in New York City. His fame was increased by the successful band he organized to perform in Europe during World War I.

12.   Davis explains that the expression "gotta cut a hog" means "to commit a social error."

13.   Davis provides this gloss for "woofin' " : "barking instead of biting; spouting off."

14.   *Shuffle Along* was an all-black musical revue written and produced in 1921 by Noble Sissle and Eubie Blake, who were also highly regarded for their singing and piano wizardry, respectively. At the time, such shows were the main way out for black performers seeking to escape the vaudeville circuit.

15.   Davis was forever the punster, trying new ways of expressing commonly held ideas. The coinage "Duskyamerican," as a reference to black Americans, might have originated with him, although we can't be sure. Clearly, he follows in the tradition of such writers as George S. Schuyler and even Gwendolyn Brooks. Schuyler often referred to blacks as "smokes" and "blackamoors." But his purpose was probably more parodic since he took these pejorative terms and inverted them to reveal the folly of distinctions made according to race. Brooks, though, was not acerbic when she referred to the black community in Chicago as "Bronzeville."

16.   Jamestown was the site of the first permanent British settlement in North America, founded 14 May 1607. In 1619, the first group of Africans were landed here, as indentured servants, which subsequently gave way to regular slave trading between Africa, America, and Europe.

17.   During the 1870s, the immigration of Chinese into the United States coincided with an economic depression, and the Chinese were made the scapegoats. Americans accused them of unfair competition in business, of lowering wages, and of immoral and unsanitary habits. Congress attempted to restrict their entry into the country when it passed the Chinese Exclusion Act of 1882 and extended this law with another one in 1892. Both were intended to be temporary, but Congress made exclusion permanent in 1902.

18.   Sax Rohmer was the pseudonym of Arthur Sarsfield Ward (1883?–1959), an internationally popular British writer who created the sinister Chinese criminal genius, Fu Manchu. The character, made popular in fiction, later appeared in motion pictures, radio, and television.

19.   Born George Lewis Rickard (1870/71?–1929), Tex Rickard was an American gambler and fight promoter who made boxing fashionable and profitable. His promotion feature Jack Dempsey, world heavyweight from 1919 to 1926, attracted the first five-million-dollar gate. He promoted Jack Johnson's successful defense of the heavyweight championship against former title holder James J. Jeffries at Reno, Nevada, on 4 July 1910.

1923–1926

1.   Robert Green Ingersoll (1833–99) enjoyed a successful career as an attorney and politician. His reputation was greatest, however, for what were called "his numerous witty attacks on certain popular forms of Christian teaching, as well as on the divine authority of the Bible." When his complete lectures were published in 1883, they included such titles as "The Gods," "Some Mistakes of Moses," and "Skulls." His life is succinctly described in *The National Cyclopedia of American Biography* (New York: James T. White and Co., 1907), the source for this information.

2.   Washington's notorious concession to the rising tide of racial separation in the 1890s is expressed in his speech given at the Atlanta Cotton States and International Exposition on 18 September 1895. His speech anticipated the U.S. Supreme Court case *Plessy v. Ferguson* in 1896, which conferred legal sanction on segregation by race when it introduced the principle of ":separate but equal."

3.   Monroe Nathan Work (1866–1945), who had become aware of the importance of accurate documentation in Negro studies while at the University of Chicago, accepted Booker T. Washington's invitation in 1908 to become director of records and research at Tuskegee Institute. In 1912, he edited and published *The Negro Yearbook and Annual Encyclopedia of the Negro,* which, with some exaggeration, "summarized all the information available in regard to existing conditions." Nine editions were published by Work.

4.   Sam McVey (1885–1921), a black heavyweight fighter from California, fought one of the most grueling contests ever fought with Joe Jeanette, in Paris in April 1909. The fight went forty-nine rounds, after which McVey collapsed and was counted out. He died penniless in New York in 1921 at the age of thirty-six.

5.   Davis's treatment of his experiences from 1923 to 1924 at Friends' University are not clear in the *retyped* version of the manuscript. Either a portion of the original manuscript was omitted when it was first typed, or it was omitted from the *retyped* version. Whatever the explanation, the *retyped* version of the manuscript experiences a break in continuity here. In order to ensure a more readable text, I have changed the order of several incidents, thereby guaranteeing textual continuity and preserving chronological sense. One paragraph that had to be omitted reads as follows:

> Friends University, on the west side of Wichita, was located in a huge old building. Total enrollment was under five hundred. Only recently had it accepted black students, and there were seven of us registered, five men and two women.

6.   Ernest H. Lindley was elected chancellor of Kansas University in 1920. The reference alludes to prevailing prejudicial and racist attitudes on the KU campus during the 1920s and "the reluctance of Chancellor Lindley . . . to fight them head on," writes Clifford Griffin in his *The University of Kansas: A History.*

In a section that has been omitted from the final copy, Davis offers further insight for his decision not to attend Kansas University when he observes that Lindley

> was eloquent and, as the head of an important university, supposedly intelligent. But whenever he made a telling point, he pounded the table and shouted: "And the Anglo-Saxon is the greatest race in the annals of civilization." . . . In the Germany of a decade and a half later, Lindley might have become one of Hitler's chief lieutenants. I learned also that some of the departments at Kansas U. were strongly prejudiced; no black student did well in mathematics because the head of this division had said "no nigger is capable of learning calculus" and, to prove his point, automatically flunked any rash enough to take advanced courses.

7.   Fletcher Henderson (1897–1952), band leader, arranger, and pianist, led the most important of the pioneering big bands and helped set the pattern for most later big jazz bands playing arranged music. A tenor saxophonist, Coleman Hawkins (1904–69) was a brilliant musical thinker who was remarkably open to new developments in jazz as well as classical music. This was reflected in both the personnel and the repertory of his groups. In February 1944, he led a band that featured Dizzy Gillespie, Max Roach, and others in what are now generally considered to be the first bop recordings. Another session later the same year was the earliest to include Thelonious Monk.

8.   The curse of Ham, from Gen. 9:20–27, refers to the curse laid upon Ham by his father, Noah, after Ham observes his father's nakedness and tells his brothers Seth and Japheth about it. Noah upon awakening places the curse of bondage upon Ham and his descendants—the Canaanites: "Cursed be Canaan, slave of slaves shall he be to his brothers." During slavery, the curse was widely believed to have been placed on black Africans, thus providing a convenient justification for slavery in the United States.

1927–1929

1.   Louis Armstrong (1898–1971) had a musical presence, technical mastery, and imaginative genius that so overwhelmed jazz musicians of his day that he became their principal model. Throughout his life, Armstrong habitually put himself under the wing of a tough, aggressive older man. One of these was King Oliver (1885–1938), then considered to be the best jazz cornetist in New Orleans. When Oliver left New Orleans for Chicago in 1918, during the general migration of blacks to the North, Armstrong took his place in a band led by Kid Ory. In 1922, Oliver invited Armstrong to Chicago to play second cornet in his band, which was then working at a black dance hall called Lincoln Gardens. This Creole Jazz Band had an extraordinary impact on musicians in the Chicago area, and through it Armstrong began to draw their attention. At this time, he also

made his first recordings with Oliver's group. Armstrong's greatest significance, in the minds of many experts, lies in his music up to about 1936, after which he became primarily a popular entertainer.

2. *The Light: America's News Magazine* was a weekly African American magazine published in Chicago beginning in 1925.

3. According to the Online Computerized Library Catalog (OCLC), the *Broad Ax* (with no "e") was published in Chicago by Julius F. Taylor.

4. Davis distinguishes "policy" from "numbers" in section 43.

5. Davis appears to err here. Joe Gans held the lightweight title from 1902 to 1908, but Gans, who was born 25 October 1874, died 10 August 1910.

6. In *Poetry: A Magazine of Verse* (vol. 30, no. 5 [1927]), Harriet Monroe includes a fairly extensive introduction of Santie Sabalala. She writes:

> The life-story of Mr. Santie Sabalala should have a volume. Born about 1895 into a Kaffir tribe in South Africa, he went "through the usual native-boy life of dew-drier, mat boy, stomach-ripper-of-the-dead-and-dying in battle"; was confirmed by the witch-doctor, fang-marked by his father, and "took part in the Ukulu battle and five other smashing raids." In 1902 his mother sent him through the British and Boer war lines, whence he was forwarded by parcel post to England, and trained in the Kaffir Boy Choir, which later toured England and America. . . . Since then Mr. Sabalala has been a chemical engineer, an art student, a magazine employe [sic], a poet, and most of all, a confirmed traveller. (297)

As an example of the kind of poetry Sabalala wrote, Monroe published his "The Raid" in what she describes as a "cosmopolitan" issue of *Poetry:*

The Raid

> See—the red sun sets in the gloom!
> The heaven clouds of scudding plume!
> Grease up your bodies for the coming fight—
> We shall cut our foeman down this night,
> And blood will flow where the corn-stalks bloom.
>
> > *Boom—Boom—Boom!*
>
> Oh, listen to the wind shouting through the trees—
> > *Zoom—Zoom—Zoom!*
> Listen to the drums roaring down the breeze—
> > *Boom—Boom—Boom!*
> Down on your bellies creep—creep—creep—
> Down on the enemy asleep—sleep—sleep,
> And wait for the drums' call of doom!
> > *Boom—Boom—Boom!*
>
> Spread out, warriors, there is plenty of room,
> And hearken to my voice on this night of doom.

Not a word or a sound, for the man dies
Who wakes the kraal with the cattle prize,
Be he single, old, or new bridegroom—

Boom—Boom—Boom!

7.   Black Patti Records, part of Paramount's "race record" series, was a record label named for the opera singer Sissieretta ("Black Patti") Jones. The first twenty of the label's fifty-five issues were advertised in May 1927; trading appears to have ceased around four months later.

8.   Decca Records was an American off-shoot of an English recording company formed in 1929. The trade name dated back to World War I, when it denoted a portable phonograph much favored by British soldiers. The American company was formed in 1934 by Jack Kapp and E. R. Lewis, and their *raison d'être* lay in the conviction that good phonograph records did not need to be expensive. Jack Kapp's gambit was to offer the biggest personalities in popular music at thirty-five cents a record.

9.   An advocate of international shipping, Captain Harry Foster Dean (1864–1935) was a black sea captain who attempted to control land in South Africa for the ultimate reestablishment of a black nation. The name of the shipping vessel he purchased, *Pedro Gorino,* also provided the title for his autobiography, which he wrote with the assistance of Sterling North.

10.   Davis refers to *The Pedro Gorino,* published in 1929 by the Houghton Mifflin Company. In his preface to the book, Sterling North acknowledges his collaboration with Captain Dean in this way:

I had been called in [by the Director of Activities at the University of Chicago] to help Captain Dean with his life's story, and although it was tremendously exciting I thought how incapable I was of such a task. I had published a few poems and stories in various magazines, and I had had three years of college work—there was little else to recommend me. But what a glorious adventure! It was his first book and mine, he a poet of sixty-three, I one of twenty. (vii)

The title page credits Captain Harry Dean as author, but also says "written with the assistance of Sterling North." North, however, provides no corroborative statements that Houghton-Mifflin stipulated that he assist Captain Dean.

11.   John Arthur Johnson (1878–1946), sometimes called "Little Arthur," was the first black to hold the world heavyweight boxing championship title, which he won by knocking out Tommy Burns in Sydney on 26 December 1908. His victory gave impetus to the search for a "Great White Hope" to dethrone him.

12.   In *Big Bill of Chicago* (Indianapolis: Bobbs-Merrill Co., 1953), their

political biography of "Big Bill" Thompson, Lloyd Wendt and Herman Kogan describe the Chicago mayoral campaign of 1926, during which Thompson deflected criticism from himself onto his opponents. During one campaign appearance, after making several choice comments about his rivals, Thompson then switched gears:

> "I wanta make the King of England keep his snoot out of America. . . . I don't want the League of Nations! I don't want the World Court! America first, and last, and always! That's the issue of this campaign. That's what Big Bill Thompson wants! . . . What was good enough for George Washington is good enough for Bill Thompson! . . . If you want to keep that old American flag from bowing down before King George of England, I'm your man. If you want to invite King George and help his friends, I'm not." (248–49)

13. The Black Dragon Society, also called Kokuryukai, was an ultra nationalist secret society given the Chinese name for the Amur River in Manchuria. The name indicated an emphasis on Manchuria, and one of the society's avowed objectives was to incite trouble among the Chinese so that the Japanese army would have an excuse to enter Manchuria to restore law and order.

14. Gertrude Stein (1874–1946) enjoyed a reputation for being unconventional in both living and writing. Her home in France was a *salon* attracting such prominent writers and painters as Ernest Hemingway and Pablo Picasso. Such early fiction as her *Three Lives* (1909) shows a breakdown of traditional plot structure and discursive writing, and the dependence upon intuitive means of expressing actual present. By the use of partly repetitive statements, each making a limited advance in the theme, Stein presents an uninterrupted series of instantaneous visions, so that one grasps a living moment in precise, ordered forms.

15. The woman Davis refers to is Frances Norton Manning. He comments more fully on his relationship with her in section 47.

16. No extant reference to *The National Magazine* has been located, which means the magazine probably did not materialize.

17. Claude Barnett (1889–1967) founded the Associated Negro Press in 1919. It began by exchanging national news releases for advertising space; soon publishers began to subscribe for the ANP service. For a minimum weekly fee, ANP would mail out to subscribers a packet of original stories two or three times per week. At the height of Barnett's popularity, ANP supplied copy to nearly two hundred newspapers or 95 percent of the Negro press.

18. "Tin Pan Alleyism" is a nickname for the popular songwriting and sheet music publishing district centered in New York from the 1890s until the 1940s. It came to be applied to the general type of song purveyed by the industry. Suggesting the tinny sound of the overworked upright pianos used by songwriters, the term evolved into a pejorative description of commercialized and thus cheaply made music.

19. Octavus Roy Cohen (1891–1959) was a North Carolina–born writer and humorist. His less than flattering depictions of small-town Southern blacks appeared in such collections as *Assorted Chocolates* (1922) and *Florian Slappey Goes Abroad* (1928), and in such magazines as the *Saturday Evening Post.*

20. From 1876 to 1978, the Chicago *Daily News* established a reputation as one of the nation's finest newspapers, winning fifteen Pulitzer Prizes. Its foreign service was outstanding for many years, and it numbered Carl Sandburg and Ben Hecht among its staff.

21. A businessman and politician, Oscar DePriest (1871–1951) accumulated considerable wealth as a real estate agent who took advantage of the rising property values that accompanied Negro population growth in Chicago. As part of Mayor William ("Big Bill") Thompson's political machine, he got elected to a series of positions and ultimately became the first Negro elected to United States Congress in the twentieth century, serving three terms from 1929 to 1935.

22. The Gary *American,* a black newspaper, was established in 1927 in Gary, Indiana, by A. B. Whitlock. It still exists and has a current circulation of around twelve thousand copies.

23. "Frogskins" is a slang term of unknown origins for one dollar bills.

1929–1930

1. Davis's description here of his discovery of Bix Beiderbecke may appear to contradict his earlier account of hearing "loudspeakers blaring the new Bix Beiderbecke–Frankie Trumbauer recording, 'Singin' the Blues'" when he first arrived in Chicago in 1927 (see sec. 20). However, Davis probably did not know who Beiderbecke was at that time since the loudspeakers were connected to record players, not to radios, and so the artists were not identified.

1931–1934

1. The Pittsburgh *Courier* was founded in 1910 by four people affiliated with a Pittsburgh Methodist church. Unable to operate the paper successfully, they brought in Vann, a lawyer with journalism experience. At one time, the circulation of the paper was close to three hundred thousand, making it the largest circulating black newspaper in the country. The reason for its success was not only Vann's managerial skill but also his staff of some of the major black journalists in the first five decades of this century, including George S. Schuyler, P. L. Prattis, and William G. Nunn.

2. One of the oldest and most powerful black newspapers, the Baltimore *Afro-American* is now published in five editions (four regional and one national). The son of John H. Murphy, Carl Murphy (1889–1967), took over running the paper after his father's death and was one of the most vigorous editorial managers.

In the 1930s, next to the Pittsburgh *Courier,* the *Afro-American*—with its city and regional editions—was a very powerful black newspaper.

3. The Kansas City *Call* is another historically important black newspaper. It was established in 1919 by Chester Arthur Franklin, and although a weekly, still has a circulation of about thirty-five thousand.

4. In a general way, Davis's assessment of black newspapers is correct. Recently, however, their role has been the subject of closer scrutiny. For instance, and most notably, Taylor Branch, in his *Parting the Waters: America in the King Years, 1954–63,* makes the point that the Atlanta *World,* under the ownership of W. A. Scott's brother C. A. Scott, offered little support to King. Indeed, the *World* systematically opposed King.

5. On 25 March 1931, nine black youths, ages twelve to twenty years, were arrested near Scottsboro, Alabama, and charged with criminal assault. They were hoboes on a freight train. A fight had broken out between them and a group of white boys, also hoboes, who subsequently were thrown or jumped from the train in Stevenson, Alabama, where they reported the fight to the stationmaster. Two towns down the line, in Paint Rock, authorities stopped the train and took the boys into custody. Two white women were also on the train; twenty minutes after the train had stopped, one of them accused all nine black youths of rape. (Later, Ruby Bates repudiated her testimony and took part in efforts to free the boys.) Within three weeks, all nine were convicted, and all but the youngest had been sentenced to death. The NAACP and ILD intervened. On 7 November 1932, the U.S. Supreme Court reversed the decision of the Alabama courts. Eventually, beginning in 1937, the men were either pardoned or paroled, the last one in 1950, nineteen years after his arrest.

6. Born in Wyoming, Ohio, in 1913, Eugene Angelo Braxton Herndon latched onto Communism as a young adult. In 1930, he was arrested under Georgia's insurrection law for trying to organize workers at a mine. At this time, he formally joined the party and became the chief organizer for an Unemployed Council's demonstration in Atlanta on 30 June 1932. His arrest eleven days later "on suspicion" merely provided a smoke screen for his "real" crime—that he was a Communist. The Party's International Labor Defense (ILD) made his case nationally known; five years later, after two appeals to the U.S. Supreme Court, the conviction was overturned on the grounds that the Georgia insurrection law violated the fourteenth amendment to the Constitution.

7. Except for two facts, Davis's recollection of the incident is accurate. Hayes was beaten because his wife had taken a seat too far forward in the shoe store and had demanded that she be served or she would take her business elsewhere. The incident occurred in Rome, but Hayes *was born* in Curryville, Georgia.

8. An ultraconservative writer and often sardonic satirist, George S. Schuyler (1895–1977) wrote for the Pittsburgh *Courier* from 1944 to 1964. In

addition to his newspaper work, he distinguished himself by writing *Black No More* (1931), *Slaves Today: A Study of Liberia* (1931), and an autobiography, *Black and Conservative* (1966).

9.   As a student at the University of Minnesota, Roy Wilkins (1901–81) edited the Minnesota *Daily,* the campus's student newspaper, and the St. Paul *Appeal,* a black weekly. After graduating, he went to work for the Kansas City *Call* and eventually became managing editor. He left in 1931 to become assistant NAACP secretary; in 1934, he added the editorship of *Crisis* to his duties and kept it for fifteen years. In 1955, Wilkins became executive director of the NAACP.

10.   See note 2 above regarding Carl Murphy.

11.   Between 1931 and 1968, the Mills Brothers had seventy hit records. Originally, the group was composed of four brothers—Herbert, Harry, Donald, and John. When John died in 1935, he was replaced by their father, John, Sr. In the early days, they imitated instrumental sounds with their voices and were most often accompanied only by a guitar. "Paper Doll," their biggest hit, was number one for twelve weeks in 1943.

12.   After Cab Calloway and his band left the Cotton Club in 1934 and began a series of theatre tours, Jimmie Lunceford's band replaced them at the Cotton Club. Born in Mississippi (1902–47), Lunceford received his bachelor's degree in music at Fisk University, did graduate work at Fisk and at New York City College, and then took a job teaching music at the Manassa High School in Memphis. The Lunceford Band was organized with students in his music class. When they graduated from high school and went on to Fisk, he resigned his position and went to Fisk as assistant professor of music. After the students graduated, the pattern continued, only this time the collective move was to New York.

13.   The story is told that Colonel Hubert Fauntleroy Julian or "the Black Eagle" announced in 1924 that he would fly solo across the Atlantic to Africa. Donations were not forthcoming, so he approached the NAACP for funding. James Weldon Johnson turned him down, saying their policy was to assist Negroes in court battles. Julian, however, persisted. He launched a subscription campaign in papers like the Pittsburgh *Courier;* not long after, a postal agent visited Julian to tell him he had to make the flight or he would be prosecuted for collecting funds through the mail with intent to defraud. After many other setbacks and the eventual purchase of "Ethiopia I," a WW I third-hand hydroplane, he took off to much fanfare from a launch site in Harlem on the Fourth of July, 1924. Two thousand feet up, Julian's plane started tilting heavily and refused to turn. The right pontoon then broke off. He couldn't bail out, and the plane crash-landed in Flushing Bay. He had been in the air for fewer than five minutes. He escaped the fraud charges, but could not prevent two dislocated shoulders and a lot of bruises.

14.   Davis's reference to a "Silver ticket" specifically points to a political struggle between proponents of silver or gold as the nation's monetary standard. One of its earliest divisive moments occurred in February 1873, when Congress passed the Coinage Act of 1873, in effect demonitizing silver. In response, a movement was begun among states located primarily in the West and the South to restore a silver standard, in the ratio of sixteen to one (gold). A temporary victory was won in 1878, with the passage of the Bland-Allison Act. It called for the monthly purchase of two to four million dollars of silver, which, when minted, would be "as good as gold." Although the debate over the issue would extend through the end of the century, two events essentially foreclosed the discussion and restored the gold standard. First, new gold deposits were discovered in South Africa, Australia, and the Klondike, thus making gold abundantly available. Second, the discovery of the cyanide process more efficiently and quickly extracted gold from ore. While Davis alludes to Mrs. Manning's father as a presidential candidate on a Silver ticket, history remembers most often the efforts in this area of William Jennings Bryan, the gifted orator from Nebraska.

15.   Born in Metropolis, Illinois, in 1870, Annie M. Turnbo Mallone was a pioneer in beauty culture and hair care. She was the founder and owner of Poro College, what today would be called a "beauty school." In addition to the study of beauty culture, or the skills and occupation of a beautician or cosmetologist, Poro's founder invented several hair and toilet preparations. As a result, at the peak of her career around 1925, she was considered the richest African American women in the United States—even richer than Madame C. J. Walker, who became a millionaire in old age. Although the title "Madame" often had a seedy connotation, many African American businesswomen of the time took the title to gain respect.

1935–1948

1.   See Harriet Monroe, "A New Negro Poet," rev. of *Black Man's Verse,* by Frank Marshall Davis, in *Poetry* 48 (1936): 293–94; and William Rose Benét, "The Phoenix Nest," *Saturday Review of Literature,* 18 January 1936:19.

2.   Born in Leicestershire, England, to an English baronet and a young American woman, Nancy Cunard (1896–1965) can be best described as a rebel. She married at an early age in order to escape her mother's clutches, only to divorce in less than two years. She broke with her past completely, living an unusual and unconventional life, often surrounded by artists of one sort or another. One of her ultimate gestures of rebellion was the relationship she developed with an African American pianist named Henry Crowder. Crowder, older and more conservative, and a member of the musical group Eddie South and Alabamians, had sworn not to get involved with a white woman while in Europe. He eventually gave in to Cunard's relentless pursuit, and even accompanied her on a

tour of New York and Harlem in 1931. During this visit, she crusaded for the Scottsboro boys and even wrote an article for *Crisis* with the title "Does Anyone Know any Negroes?" based on a comment made by her mother. One of her major achievements remains the publication of *Negro: An Anthology* (1934). Its 855 pages, containing 250 contributions made by 150 authors, was no small accomplishment. As editor and publisher, she financed the project herself, thus providing herself the opportunity to let her communist bias be known.

3. Slater and Lillard, both of whom were black, played for the Chicago Cardinals, Slater from 1926 to 1931, and Lillard from 1932 to 1933. (The first known African American player in the NFL was Henry McDonald of the Rochester Jeffersons; he began in 1910.) Although in its own historical accounts of its growth the NFL has been amazingly silent about the issue of enforcing a code barring all African American players from the game, anecdotal evidence suggests this was a commonly accepted, although informally expressed, rule. Historians suspect the excellent play of African Americans not only stole the show but proved volatile, causing opposing white players to fight. The bar was lifted in 1946, probably because the NFL encountered competition from the All-American Football Conference, which had no such ban.

4. The Joe Louis–Kingfish Levinsky bout occurred on 7 August 1935 at Comiskey Park before fifty thousand fans. Louis knocked the fifth-ranked heavyweight down three times in the first two minutes of the first round, earning a TKO.

5. Davis refers here to the legendary New York Renaissance basketball team, founded by Robert L. "Bob" Douglas in 1922. The Rens compiled 2,318 victories over the next twenty-two years, averaging 105 triumphs annually.

6. Abraham Michael "Abe" Saperstein (1902–66), professional basketball player, coach, and executive, formed the Harlem Globetrotters in 1926. The squad, whose name was chosen to indicate a Negro (Harlem) and barnstorming ("Globetrotters") team, played its first game on 7 January 1927. Saperstein's main contribution came not as a basketball coach or strategist, but as a promoter and entertainer. Ultimately, the team became almost pure entertainment, combining basketball skills and comedy in classic, designed rehearsed routines.

7. John Hammond was a jazz record producer and critic whose contribution to the development of American jazz has yet to be fully determined. As a record producer, he supervised the likes of Fletcher Henderson, Benny Carter, Benny Goodman, and Teddy Wilson, among many other jazz notables. In 1938 and 1939, he organized the two historic "Spirituals to Swing" concerts in Carnegie Hall.

8. Organized in 1936, the National Negro Congress elected A. Philip Randolph as president and John P. Davis as executive secretary. The founding convention was held in Chicago from 14 to 16 February 1936. The original executive board included Ralph Bunche, Mande White, and James W. Ford—all

of whom were either members or fellow-travelers of the Communist Party. The NNC, however, was independent of the Communist Party but not unfriendly to it.

9. The Federal Writers' Project was one of Roosevelt's Works Progress Administration (WPA) programs designed to provide useful work for thousands of writers displaced by the Depression. A primary goal of the FWP was to write and publish a series of local, state, and federal guidebooks, combining the features of a tour book with historical facts and data. Arna Bontemps (1902–73) enjoyed a distinguished career as poet, novelist, and children's story writer. His relationships with writers were quite varied, from Langston Hughes, with whom he corresponded for over forty years, to Jack Conroy, another staff member of the Federal Writers' Project with whom he cowrote *They Seek a City* (1945), a history of the migration of rural black Americans to urban centers.

10. Locke's letter to Davis was undated; however, internal evidence suggests it was written in 1937 or 1938. Specific recognition is given to Sterling A. Brown's Guggenheim Fellowship, which he won in 1937, and to Locke's Bronze Booklet series, which appeared in 1938.

11. William Attaway, from Mississippi, wrote two novels: *Let Me Breathe Thunder* (1939) and *Blood on the Forge* (1941). The second one was quite important for opening up the wealth of materials to be found in industrial communities where there was a problem of racial competition.

12. In January 1935, a call for an American writers' congress went out from the pages of *New Masses,* in an effort to mobilize writers into a revolutionary cultural movement aimed at accelerating "the destruction of capitalism and the establishment of a workers' government." The call, signed and answered by some of America's most prominent literary figures, led to the creation of the League of American Writers, an organization affiliated with the International Union of Revolutionary Writers. Edited by Donald Ogden Stewart (New York: Harcourt Brace and Co., 1940), *Writers Take Sides* published material from the Third Congress of the League of American Writers, held in New York, 2–5 June 1939. Members of the League found outlets for their creative efforts in a variety of radical magazines and newspapers, including *The Anvil, New Masses,* and the *Partisan Review.*

13. *The Anvil* (1932–35) and *The New Anvil* (1939–40) were the two most successful and vigorous of the magazines devoted to proletarian writing in the 1930s. They exclusively published creative work—fiction and poetry—but no criticism. Editor Jack Conroy has written that his magazines were "tough-hewn and awkward, but bitter and alive from the furnace of experience—and from participants, not observers, in most instances." Contributors included Richard Wright, Langston Hughes, William Carlos Williams, and Erskine Caldwell.

14. As Davis observes, Engstrand's wife was a schoolteacher who also wrote fiction. Sophia Engstrand wrote *Miss Munday* (Dial, 1940), a novel about a

schoolteacher who gives her students an education as well as instruction in the conduct of life. Set in River Port, Wisconsin, the novel depicts how the teacher's professionalism gets in the way of romance. A second novel, *Wilma Rogers* (Dial, 1941), is set in Milo, Illinois, and portrays the life of a librarian. Donald W. Maxwell describes these novels in his *Literature of the Great Lakes Region: An Annotated Bibliography* (New York: Garland Publishing, 1991), 116.

15. The Julius Rosenwald Fund was created by Rosenwald in 1917 to further educational and social advances for blacks, among other philanthropic benefactions. Founder and president of Sears, Roebuck & Co. (1895), Julius Rosenwald (1862–1932) turned to a wide range of philanthropies which transcended race, creed, and nationality.

16. Louis lost this fight on 19 June 1936, in New York. A rematch was held two years later, on 22 June 1938, and Louis knocked Schmeling out in the first round.

17. Ezzard Charles (1921–75) rose up through the boxing ranks to win the heavyweight championship, after Joe Louis's retirement. He wrested the title from an overage "Jersey Joe" Walcott on 22 June 1949.

18. In her *Richard Wright: Daemonic Genius* (1988), Margaret Walker describes Brown as a radical black man nicknamed "Billy Goat" because of his goatee.

19. John Elliott Rankin (1882–1960), from Mississippi, served in the U.S. House of Representatives from 1921 to 1953. A committed segregationist and states' rights advocate, he was consistently vituperative in denouncing efforts to accord blacks the constitutional guarantees of life, liberty, and the pursuit of happiness. During the mid-1940s, he often found conspiracy theory to be an effective means for attacking racial integration. For instance, he vilified the Fair Employment Practices Commission (FEPC) for subverting democracy and threatened to lynch "communistic Jews and Negroes" who attempted to integrate the House of Representatives cafeteria. He posed a similar xenophobic argument in a diatribe against the American Red Cross, whose efforts to collect blood from blacks he characterized as a communist plot to mongrelize America.

20. On 25 June 1941 Roosevelt issued an executive order establishing the Fair Employment Practices Commission; its charge was to promote Negro equality in defense industries and government employment. It was issued in response to a threatened mass march by blacks on Washington, organized by A. Phillip Randolph (1889–1979). Randolph's career as a labor and civil rights leader led to several important milestones, including the publication of *The Messenger* (1917–28) and the organization of the Brotherhood of Sleeping Car Porters (1925), which later became affiliated with the American Federation of Labor.

21. Dies was notorious during the 1930s and 1940s for his persecution and "Red-baiting" of socialists and prolabor radicals. Under his leadership, the House

Committee on Un-American Activities became the prototype of the inquisitorial committees that infested the legislative branches of national and state governments during the McCarthy era. When the United States became a participant in World War II, as an ally of the Soviet Union against the Axis powers of Germany, Italy, and Japan, Dies's strident anticommunism and divisive attacks on the Roosevelt administration were out of step with the times.

22.   A graduate of Yale in 1904, William Pickens was the second black to receive a Phi Beta Kappa key from the institution. For the next sixteen years, he taught classics and sociology at Negro colleges. At Morgan College in Baltimore, he became the college's first Negro dean, thereafter the constant reference to him as "Dean" Pickens. In 1920, he moved to New York and became field secretary of the NAACP. A dynamic speaker, he also served as contributing editor to the Associated Negro Press (1919–40). Taking leave from the NAACP in 1941, he assumed the directorship of the Interracial Section of the U.S. Treasury Department's Savings (later War) Bonds Division. His autobiography, *Bursting Bonds* (1923; rpt. Bloomington: Indiana University Press, 1991), has recently been reissued, with an important introduction by William L. Andrews.

23.   As chairman of the combined chiefs of staff, General George Marshall was the principal Allied strategist in World War II. He served as secretary of state (1947–49) under President Harry Truman and was responsible for the Marshall Plan, which assisted European countries devastated by the war. In 1953, he was awarded the Nobel Prize for Peace.

24.   Under the discriminatory policies of the United States Navy, the only training available to blacks was that of messman. But Dorie Miller (1919–43) was awarded the Navy Cross for heroism, when, during the Japanese invasion of Pearl Harbor on 7 December 1941, he moved the mortally wounded captain of the battleship *Arizona* to a safe place and then shot down four enemy aircraft, even though he had never received training in the use of the guns. He was killed in 1943 when the *Liscome Bay,* the small carrier on which he was stationed, was sunk by a Japanese submarine. His bravery was celebrated in several ways, but none more important than in Gwendolyn Brooks's poem "Negro Hero."

25.   The story of Deborah Gannett is well-known. She enlisted as a man, serving seventeen months undetected as a regular soldier under the name of Robert Shurtleff, and at the close of the war received a grant of thirty-four pounds sterling from the Massachusetts legislature in appreciation of her "female heroism" and a pension from Congress. But whether she was a *black* woman is under question, since available evidence indicates that she was a white indentured servant, who decided to serve her country when her indenture ended.

26.   In 1943 the American Youth for Democracy organization succeeded the Young Communist League, which had operated as the youth wing of the Communist Party. After the succession of American Youth for Democracy, party youth sections grew but did not especially flourish; what youth activity took place

in the immediate postwar years centered around the revival of fraternal movements such as the Jewish People's Fraternal Order, friendship work with the Soviet Union, coalitions joined to the broader liberal movement, and Henry Wallace's Progressive Party campaign for the presidency.

27. Melville J. Herskovits (1895–1963) was a well-known and controversial anthropologist. Early in his career, he argued that if any cultural differences existed between Harlem blacks and the white culture surrounding them, it was "merely a remnant from the peasant days in the South. *Of the African culture, not a trace.*" But the work for which he is most noted, *The Myth of the Negro Past* (1941), radically revised these conclusions.

28. In a 14 August 1991 letter to me, Helen Davis writes: " . . . the two of us had just acquired our divorces, his from his wife of 13 years, Thelma Boyd Davis, I from Donald Henry Kline, married for two years . . ."

1949–1980

1. A "leasehold" is a legal term describing a right to occupy premises. It does not mean ownership of the premises. A "fee simple" designates full and absolute ownership of the property in question. In Davis's example, then, the land and the house on the land could be owned by different persons. The possessor of the "leasehold" merely has a right to occupy the property, as in a landlord-tenant relationship. The holder of a "fee simple" actually owns the property and has the right to sell, mortgage, or rent it. The point of Davis's distinction is that the property owner, in offering a leasehold estate, often flouted the prohibition against restrictive covenants by selling or renting to anyone of his choice.

2. From early May to late October 1949, the International Longshoremen's and Warehousemen's Union (ILWU) conducted a 178 day strike for increased wages and benefits in Hawaii. Management countered with an interesting strategy. The wives of the employers and company executives organized themselves into a collective anti-labor group, and chose the Hawaiian word *imua,* meaning "to move forward," as its name. The anti-strike effort of IMUA often consisted of counter-picketing the striking workers. But IMUA also made direct appeals to the wives of striking workers, inviting them to join a presumably better life by siding with management. The ILWU attempted to expose these subversive tactics and used the editorial pages of the Honolulu *Record* to voice their opposition. In a typical example, from the 9 June 1949 issue, an editor wrote:

The Million-Dollar Picket Line in front of Pier 11 is something to behold. The prime movers there are the wives of the bosses who are trying awfully hard to make the picket line look like a bona fide [sic] housewives' protest against striking longshoremen, that is representative of the community.

Representatives of these women have approached certain housewives and have offered money for the latters' services to go on the picket line or to rally others to "hit the bricks" with them. We were happy to learn that "money" did not talk" to these laborers' wives who rejected the offer. (8)

Other issues of the *Record* attempted to expose, for example, the pretext of visits made by IMUA members to the homes of strikers's wives in order to deliver cans of milk to families deprived of income by the labor strike. The "Million Dollar Broom Brigade," as the IMUA members were often called, provided a perfect complement to the harder-hitting legal, and possibly illegal, tactics of their husbands, who headed up the so-called "Big Five" companies.

Index

Marian Anderson
My Lord, What a Morning
Introduction by Nellie Y. McKay

American Women's Autobiography: Fea(s)ts of Memory
Edited by Margo Culley

Frank Marshall Davis
Livin' the Blues: Memoirs of a Black Journalist and Poet
Edited, with an introduction, by John Edgar Tidwell

Joanne Jacobson
Authority and Alliance in the Letters of Henry Adams